TRANSLATION AS A COGNITIVE ACTIVITY

Translation as a Cognitive Activity provides an overarching account of translation as a cognitive activity, from the pioneering use of think-aloud protocols as a sole technique used to investigate the translation process in the mid-1980s to the latest developments in the field.

This book focuses on the main aspects of translation as a cognitive activity, including detailed descriptions of translation process research as well as research on translation competence and its acquisition. Providing thorough information into ways of studying translation as a cognitive activity by means of systematic references to empirical-experimental investigations, this innovative textbook promotes knowledge about the cognitive study of translation to related fields.

With detailed explanations about models related to the functioning of the translation process and translation competence as well as an updated account of methods and instruments used in empirical-experimental research in translation, this is the ideal resource for students and translator trainers as well as novice and experienced translators.

Fabio Alves is Full Professor of Translation Studies at Universidade Federal de Minas Gerais (UFMG) and a Senior Research Fellow of the Brazilian National Research Council (CNPq).

Amparo Hurtado Albir is Chair Professor of Translation and Interpreting at Universitat Autònoma de Barcelona.

TRANSLATION AS A COGNITIVE ACTIVITY

Theories, Models and Methods for Empirical Research

Fabio Alves and Amparo Hurtado Albir

LONDON AND NEW YORK

Designed cover image: Jacob Wackerhausen

First published 2025
by Routledge
4 Park Square, Milton Park, Abingdon, Oxon OX14 4RN

and by Routledge
605 Third Avenue, New York, NY 10158

Routledge is an imprint of the Taylor & Francis Group, an informa business

British Library Cataloguing-in-Publication Data
A catalogue record for this book is available from the British Library

ISBN: 9780367439989 (hbk)
ISBN: 9780367439972 (pbk)
ISBN: 9781003006978 (ebk)

DOI: 10.4324/9781003006978

Typeset in Sabon
by Deanta Global Publishing Services, Chennai, India

CONTENTS

FIGURES

TABLES

ABBREVIATIONS

CBT	Competence-Based Training
CTS	Cognitive Translation Studies
GTC	General Translator's Competence
ITT	Interpretive Theory of Translation
L1	Native/First Language
L2	Foreign/Second Language
L1/L2 translation	From Native/First into Foreign/Second Language (Inverse Translation)
L2/L1 translation	From Foreign/Second into Native/First Language (Direct Translation)
STC	Specific Translator's Competence
TAP	Think-aloud Protocol
TC	Translation Competence
TCA	Translation Competence Acquisition
TICQ	Translation and Interpreting Competence Questionnaire
TPR	Translation Process Research

INTRODUCTION

For many years, we have investigated cognitive-related aspects of translation and carried out comprehensive empirical-experimental research on the translation process and on translation competence, its acquisition and levelling. Together, we have also written substantially about problems and challenges concerning the study of translation as a cognitive activity (Hurtado Albir & Alves, 2009; Alves & Hurtado Albir, 2010, 2017). These publications have provided us with a starting point for the current work which addresses the cognitive-oriented study of translation from an interdisciplinary perspective.

We thought the time was right for a book that would offer a comprehensive account of how translation functions cognitively by addressing the main aspects related to the study of translation and cognition, including detailed descriptions of research on the translation process, on translation competence, its acquisition and levelling, and a thorough review of empirical-experimental research in translation as a cognitive activity. Our focus is on written translation and, deliberately, we have only marginally addressed the issue of post-editing. We have decided not to address issues related to interpreting (in all its forms), audio-visual translation and other varieties of translation.

Starting in the late 1960s, the study of translation as a cognitive activity has given rise to a series of pioneering studies and theoretical proposals. Throughout the past six decades, we have seen the development of a type of research that has become more and more prominent in the field of translation studies. Over this period, researchers have attempted to tackle the study of translation and cognition by drawing on different theories, thus providing several models of the translation process as well as models of translation competence and its acquisition.

DOI: 10.4324/9781003006978-1

Cognitive research on translation has been the subarea in translation studies in which empirical-experimental research has been most productive. Such empirical developments have led scholars to propose the name of *Translation Process Research* (Alves, 2003; Jakobsen, 2011), *Cognitive Translatology* (Muñoz, 2010) or *Cognitive Translation Studies* (Halverson, 2010) for this emerging field. More recently, Alves and Jakobsen (2021) have discussed in depth the name and nature of the study of translation as a cognitive activity and have subscribed to Halverson's proposal, insisting that cognitive translation studies (CTS) should be the umbrella term to accommodate the several aspects that underlie the study of translation and cognition. In this book, we follow Alves and Jakobsen (2021) in our terminological choice for the study of translation as a cognitive activity.

By revisiting cognitive research in translation since its infancy, this book aims to bring together the development of empirical-experimental research in written translation. In order to do so, we present a chronological overview, starting from the pioneering use of think-aloud protocols as a sole technique used to investigate the translation process in the mid-1980s to the latest developments in the field, which incorporate a multi-methods approach, combining the use of (retrospective) verbal protocols, keylogging, screen recording, eye tracking, and more recently, neuroimaging techniques, to tap into translation task execution in real time and provide an overarching account of translation as a cognitive activity.

The approach used in the book focuses on the chronological development of the triangulation approach (i.e. multi-methodological perspectives) in empirical-experimental research on translation as a cognitive activity. We have divided the development of empirical research into five chronological phases (1960–1990, 1990–2000, 2000–2010, 2010–2020 and 2020–present) to describe the results and developments as well as the shortcomings observed in each phase.

The book also argues in favour of standardizing procedures for data collection and data analysis so that replication of studies can be carried out. This, we believe, will increase the power of generalization of the results achieved by the empirical-experimental approach in CTS.

In a nutshell, the aim of this book is to provide a unified account of CTS by means of developing the following specific goals:

- To embed the cognitive study of translation within the broader interdisciplinary field at the interface with neighbouring disciplines.
- To enhance knowledge about theories and methods pertaining to the field of CTS.
- To describe the main traits of the translation process and present the models which have been proposed to date.

- To describe the main characteristics of translation competence and its acquisition and present the models which have been proposed to date as well as describe the studies about translation competence levels and the establishment of scales of descriptor levels in translation.
- To assess and describe the state of the art of empirical-experimental research in translation as a cognitive activity.
- To ground CTS as a consolidated subdiscipline within translation studies.

The book consists of this Introduction and five main chapters. Chapter 1 situates the study of translation as a cognitive activity at the interface with neighbouring disciplines and offers an interdisciplinary account of the development of CTS. It examines interdisciplinary boundaries which are directly or indirectly related to the study of translation and cognition and highlights relevant aspects for the cognitive-oriented study of translation in neuroscience, cognitive science, psycholinguistics, reading and writing research and expertise studies. In short, Chapter 1 aims to offer an interdisciplinary framework to ground the study of translation as a cognitive activity.

Chapter 2 focuses on the historical development of translation process research and presents a descriptive analysis of the most representative models conceived from the 1960s to the present date. Starting from Seleskovitch's (1968) interpretive theory of translation, it introduces models of the translation process in chronological order, highlighting the models proposed by Krings (1986), Königs (1987), Wilss (1988, 1996), Hönig (1988, 1991), Bell (1991), Lörscher (1991), Gutt (1991/2000), Alves (1995), Kiraly (1995), Halverson (2003, 2010), Tirkkonen-Condit (2005), Jakobsen (2011), Schaeffer and Carl (2013) and Carl and Schaeffer (2017, 2019), and offering graphic displays of some of these models. Chapter 2 also discusses the main features and phases of translation process research and concludes with a summary of the main traits of the translation process.

Chapter 3 addresses the study of translation competence, its acquisition and levelling. It presents the models conceived by Cao (1996), Campbell (1998), PACTE (1998, 2000, 2003, 2005a, 2005b, 2017, 2020, etc.), Kelly (2002, 2005, 2007), Alves and Gonçalves (2007), Shreve (1997, 2006) and Göpferich (2009), among others, including graphic displays of the most relevant models. Chapter 3 also discusses the fundamental aspects of translation competence, its acquisition and levelling, corroborated by results of empirical-experimental investigations, and brings it in line with studies about expert knowledge and expert performance.

Chapter 4 presents a chronological overview of the development of empirical-experimental investigation in translation as a cognitive activity, the methods and techniques used, the success and shortcomings of the empirical-experimental approach and the tendencies and challenges for its further development. Chapter 4 also offers methodological guidance and addresses the impact of research on different objects of study (translation units, segmentation patterns, subject profiling, translation competence and its acquisition, etc.).

Finally, Chapter 5 brings together the main points presented in the previous four chapters into a coherent whole. It also looks into the future and discusses the main challenges ahead for the study of translation as a cognitive activity.

All chapters are structured and integrated around a coherent central theme. They situate the topic of each chapter within the field of CTS in particular, but also make references to neighbouring disciplines when necessary. All five chapters provide an introduction, a discussion, and a conclusion.

In order to enhance readability, the book also includes tables and figures summarizing the main points in each chapter, complementing detailed explanations about models related to the functioning of the translation process and translation competence as well as an updated account of methods and instruments used in empirical-experimental research in translation.

We have chosen to use abbreviations for selected terms and these are presented in a list of abbreviations.

We have tried to be consistent with our terminology but opted to use interchangeably terms like cognitive-oriented studies of translation and the study of translation as a cognitive activity when we account for specificities in CTS. Finally, we refer interchangeably to translation into the foreign/second language as inverse or L1/L2 translation, and to translation into the native/first language as direct or L2/L1 translation.

We would like to thank all the authors mentioned throughout the book for their invaluable contributions to the study of translation as a cognitive activity and for the input they provided us with to write this book. In particular, we are deeply grateful to Willy Neunzig (*in memoriam*), an esteemed colleague and dear friend, who was instrumental in inspiring us in the development of our work.

It is our hope that this book will provide a relevant contribution to the development of cognitive translation studies and the dissemination and consolidation of the study of translation as a cognitive activity.

Fabio Alves and Amparo Hurtado Albir
Belo Horizonte and Barcelona, February 2024

References

Alves, F. (1995). *Zwischen Schweigen und Sprechen: Wie bildet sich eine transkulturelle Brücke? Eine psycholinguistisch orientierte Untersuchung von Übersetzungsvorgängen zwischen portugiesischen und brasilianischen Übersetzern.* Hamburg: Dr. Kovac.

Alves, F. (Ed.). (2003). *Triangulating translation. Perspectives in process oriented research.* Amsterdam: John Benjamins.

Alves, F., & Gonçalves, J.L. (2007). Modelling translator's competence: Relevance and expertise under scrutiny. In Y. Gambier, M. Shlesinger, & R. Stolze (Eds.), *Translation studies: Doubts and directions* (pp. 41–55). Amsterdam: John Benjamins.
Alves, A., & Hurtado Albir, A. (2010). Cognitive approaches to translation. In Y. Gambier & L. van Doorslaer (Eds.), *The John Benjamins handbook of translation studies*(pp. 28–35). Amsterdam: John Benjamins.
Alves, F., & Hurtado Albir, A. (2017). Evolution, challenges, and perspectives for research on cognitive aspects of translation. In J.W. Schwieter & A. Ferreira (Eds.), *The handbook of translation and cognition* (pp. 535–554). Hoboken, NJ: John Wiley & Sons, Inc.
Alves, F., & Jakobsen, A.L. (2021). Grounding cognitive translation studies. Goals, commitments and challenges. In F. Alves & A.L. Jakobsen (Eds.), *The Routledge handbook of translation and cognition*(pp. 545–554). London: Routledge.
Bell, R.T. (1991). *Translation and translating*. London: Longman.
Campbell, S. (1998). *Translation into the second language*. London: Longman.
Cao, D. (1996). Towards a model of translation proficiency. *Target*, *8*(2), 325–340.
Carl, M., & Schaeffer, M. (2017). Sketch of a noisy channel model for the translation process. In S. Hansen-Schirra, O. Czulo, & S. Hofmann (Eds.), *Empirical modelling of translation and interpreting* (pp. 71–116). Berlin: Language Science Press.
Carl, M., & Schaeffer, M. (2019). Outline for a relevance theoretical model of machine translation post-editing. In D. Li, V. Lei, & Y. He (Eds.), *Researching cognitive processes of translation*(pp. 49–67). Singapore: Springer.
Göpferich, S. (2009). Towards a model of translation competence and its acquisition: The longitudinal study 'TransComp. In S. Göpferich, A. L. Jakobsen, & I.M. Mees (Eds.), *Behind the mind: Methods, models and results in translation process research* (pp. 11–37). Copenhagen: Samfundslitteratur.
Gutt, E.-A. (1991). *Translation and relevance: Cognition and context*. Oxford: Basil Blackwell. Second revised edition (2010). Manchester: St Jerome.
Halverson, S.L. (2003). The cognitive basis of translation universals. *Target*, *15*(2), 197–241.
Halverson, S.L. (2010). Cognitive translation studies: Developments in theory and methods. In G. Shreve & E. Angelone (Eds.), *Translation and cognition* (pp. 349–370). Amsterdam: John Benjamins.
Hönig, H.G. (1988). Wissen Übersetzer eigentlich, was sie tun? *Lebende Sprachen*, 33/1, 10–14.
Hönig, H.G. (1991). Holmes' 'Mapping Theory' and the landscape of mental translation processes. In K. van Leuven-Zwart & T. Naajkens (Eds), *Translation studies: The state of the art. Proceedings from the first James S. Holmes Symposium on Translation Studies* (pp. 77–89). Amsterdam: Rodopi.
Hurtado Albir, A., & Alves, F. (2009). Translation as a cognitive activity. In J. Munday (Ed.), *The Routledge companion to translation studies* (pp. 210–234). London: Routledge.
Jakobsen, A.L. (2011). Tracking translators' keystrokes and eye movements with Translog. In C. Alvstad, A. Hild, & E. Tiselius (Eds.), *Methods and strategies of process research* (pp. 37–55). Amsterdam: John Benjamins.
Kelly, D. (2002). Un modelo de competencia traductora: bases para el diseño curricular. *Puentes*, *1*, 9–20.
Kelly, D. (2005). *A handbook for translator trainers*. Manchester: St. Jerome.
Kelly, D. (2007). Translator competence contextualized. Translator training in the framework of higher education reform: In search of alignment in curricular design. In D. Kenny & K. Ryou (Eds.), *Across boundaries: International perspectives on translation studies* (pp. 128–142). Cambridge: Cambridge Scholars Publishing.

Kiraly, D. (1995). *Pathways to translation.Pedagogy and process*. Kent: The Kent State University Press.
Königs, F.G. (1987). Was beim Übersetzen passiert. Theoretische Aspekte, empirische Befunde und praktische Konsequenzen. *Die Neueren Sprachen*, *86*, 162–185.
Krings, H.P. (1986). *Was in den Köpfen von Übersetzern vorgeht. Eine empirische Untersuchung der Struktur des Übersetzungsprozesses an fortgeschrittener französischer Lernenden*. Tübingen: Gunter Narr.
Lörscher, W. (1991). *Translation performance, translation process, and translation strategies. A psycholinguistic investigation*. Tübingen: Narr.
Muñoz Martín, R. (2010). Leave no stone unturned. On the development of cognitive translatology. *Journal of Translation and Interpreting Studies*, *5*(2), 145–162.
PACTE. (1998). *La competencia traductora y su aprendizaje: Objetivos, hipótesis y metodología de un proyecto de investigación*. Poster, IV Congrés Internacional sobre Traducció. Barcelona: Universitat Autònoma de Barcelona.
PACTE. (2000). Acquiring translation competence: Hypotheses and methodological problems in a research project. In A. Beeby, D. Ensinger, & M. Presas (Eds.), *Investigating translation* (pp. 99–106). Amsterdam: John Benjamins.
PACTE. (2003). Building a translation competence model. In F. Alves (Ed.), *Triangulating translation: Perspectives in process oriented research* (pp. 43–66). Amsterdam: John Benjamins.
PACTE. (2005a). Investigating translation competence: Conceptual and methodological issues. *Meta, Journal des Traducteurs*, *50*(2), 609–619.
PACTE. (2005b). Primeros resultados de un experimento sobre la Competencia Traductora. In *Actas del II Congreso Internacional de la AIETI (Asociación Ibérica de Estudios de Traducción e Interpretación)* (pp. 573–587). Madrid: Publicaciones de la Universidad Pontificia Comillas.
PACTE. (2017). Defining features of translation competence. In A. Hurtado Albir (Ed.), *Researching translation competence by PACTE Group*(pp. 281–302). Amsterdam: John Benjamins.
PACTE. (2020). Translation competence acquisition. Design and results of the PACTE Group's experimental research. *The Interpreter and Translator Trainer*, *14*(2), 95–233.
Schaeffer, M., & Carl, M. (2013). Shared representations and the translation process: A recursive model. *Translation and Interpreting Studies*, *8*(2), 169–190. Reprinted in M. Ehrensberger-Dow, B. Englund Dimitrova, S, Hubscher-Davidson, & U. Norberg (Eds.) (2015), *Describing cognitive processes in translation: Acts and events* (pp. 21–42). Amsterdam: John Benjamins.
Seleskovitch, D. (1968). *L'interprète dans les conférences internationales. Problèmes de langage et de communication*, Paris: Minard. [Translation into English. Seleskovitch, D. (1978). *Interpreting for international conferences: problems of language and communication*, Washington: Pen and Booth].
Shreve, G. (1997). Cognition and the evolution of translation competence. In J.H. Danks, G., Shreve, S.B. Fountain, & M. McBeath (Eds.), *Cognitive processes in translation and interpreting* (pp. 120–136). Thousand Oaks: Sage.
Shreve, G. (2006). The deliberate practice: Translation and expertise. *Journal of Translation Studies*, *9*(1), 27–42.
Tirkkonen-Condit, S. (2005). The monitor model revisited: Evidence from process research. *Translators' Journal*, *50*(2), 405–414.
Wilss, W. (1988). *Kognition und Übersetzen: Zu Theorie und Praxis der menschlichen und der maschinellen Übersetzung*. Tübingen: Niemeyer.
Wilss, W. (1996). *Knowledge and skills in translator behavior*. Amsterdam: John Benjamins.

1

TRANSLATION AND COGNITION

This chapter addresses the study of translation as a cognitive activity at the interface with neighbouring disciplines and offers an interdisciplinary framework for the development of cognitive translation studies. It examines interdisciplinary boundaries which are directly or indirectly related to the study of translation and cognition and highlights relevant aspects in neuroscience, cognitive science, psycholinguistics, reading and writing research, and expertise studies for the cognitive oriented study of translation. In short, it aims to offer an interdisciplinary framework to ground the study of translation as a cognitive activity.

Introduction

Translation is a complex human activity which entails a set of knowledge and abilities, requiring a lot more than simply handling the transfer of linguistic structures between two languages. Therefore, one cannot translate isolated and decontextualized units but only texts (and respective text units) whose operating mechanisms (coherence and cohesion, registerial features, genre conventions of various kinds, etc.) differ across languages and cultures. Translation is also an act of complex intercultural communication that always takes place in a context in which various elements are involved (initiator, audience, brief, etc.). Further, translation is also a particular type of behaviour that comprises the various tasks that translators carry out in the course of their work, which may vary according to market needs and different professional profiles. Last but not least, translation is the resulting cognitive activity of an individual (the translator) who requires a complex mental process to which specific knowledge and abilities (translation competence) must be applied so that the task is performed satisfactorily. Therefore, the study of translation as a cognitive activity entails a great deal of complexity.

In addition to this inherent complex difficulty of translation, the study of any cognitive activity involves phenomena which are not directly observable. Such traits, thus, increase the complexity of the study since many different types of knowledge and abilities must be taken into consideration as translation task execution unfolds.

DOI: 10.4324/9781003006978-2

Since the late 1960s and particularly from the mid-1980s onwards, the discipline of translation studies has seen a great deal of interest in the study of cognitive aspects of translation, resulting in different denominations for such endeavours. Initially, research carried out from the mid-1980s to the early 2000s built on the information-processing paradigm to make a case for the study of translation as a cognitive activity focusing on the specificities of the translation process. Aiming at a paradigmatic change, Muñoz Martín (2010a, 2010b) coined the term *cognitive translatology* to cover research on cognitive aspects of translation that are not directly associated to aspects of information processing but rather approach the study of translation as a cognitive activity on the basis of embodied, embedded, enacted, extended and affective factors in what is known as 4EA cognition. Jakobsen (2011), on the other hand, coined the term *translation process research* (TPR) to advocate a special status to empirical research carried out to investigate behavioural patterns related to the act of translating. Without neglecting to account for situated factors, TPR is primarily concerned with the empirical investigation of cognitive processing and its impact on cognitive mechanisms related to translation task execution. We assume that both *cognitive translatology* and TPR have their rightful place in the study of translation as a cognitive activity. In view of the overarching goals of our object of study in this book, we also refer to the term *cognitive translation studies* (Halverson, 2010) since we consider that this term encompasses not only aspects of research on the nature and specificities of the translation process but also, and equally important, on several other relevant aspects such as the study of expert knowledge in translation, translation competence and its acquisition as well as situated, distributed and extended aspects of human cognition during translation task execution. To that extent, we are in line with Alves and Jakobsen (2021a), who have also adopted *cognitive translation studies* (CTS) as an umbrella term for the study of translation as a cognitive activity. Throughout this book, we may occasionally also refer to cognitive-oriented studies of translation as an alternative rendering for CTS.

In this chapter, we draw on Alves (2015)[1] to claim that the study of translation as a cognitive activity should be part of the broader study of human cognitive activity and we propose a framework to accomplish that goal within cognitive translation studies.

1.1 Interdisciplinarity in the research of translation as a cognitive activity

In recent years, several authors have approached the issue of interdisciplinarity in CTS from different angles (Ehrensberger-Dow, Göpferich, & O'Brien, 2013). Regardless of the approach adopted, they all agree that interdisciplinarity is an inherent characteristic of the study of translation as a cognitive activity.

O'Brien (2013), for instance, gives an overview of the disciplines and subdisciplines from which research on cognitive aspects of translation has borrowed. Using analogies related to borrowing and lending across interdisciplinary fields to provide an account of past and recent exchanges, O'Brien considers the interdisciplinary interaction of CTS with linguistics, psychology, neuroscience, cognitive science, reading and writing research and language technology and points out that the breadth of borrowing in cognitive approaches to translation is made apparent, but there is minimal influence of CTS on these disciplines. Arguing that there has been much more borrowing than lending in academic interactions concerning research on translation as a cognitive activity, O'Brien pleads that CTS should strive to exert greater influence on other disciplines so that lending becomes as equally important as borrowing.

Alves (2015) also examines the intricacies of interdisciplinary exchanges related to research on translation as a cognitive activity and proposes a set of core disciplines that should be adopted to ground a theoretical and methodological framework for CTS. Alves (2015) scrutinizes translation process research at the interface with cognitive science, expertise studies and psycholinguistics and reflects on paradigmatic, theoretical and methodological issues in dialogue with these disciplines as he revisits the main assumptions of cognitive science, expertise studies and psycholinguistics to reflect on how they interface diachronically and synchronically with CTS. Building on O'Brien's (2013) borrowing argument, Alves (2015) considers what CTS has gained from interfacing with cognitive science, expertise studies and psycholinguistics, how much from these three disciplines it has incorporated into its own research agenda and how it is now able to contribute to the development of other related disciplines, not only by borrowing from them but also lending to them.

Additionally, special issues of journals and book series with an interest in this issue have tried to bridge the gap between works within CTS and related works in neighbouring disciplines. O'Brien, Ehrensberger-Dow and Göpferich (2013/2015) and Ferreira and Schwieter (2015) have put together edited volumes to discuss such exchanges. Alves, Hurtado Albir and Lacruz (2015), Ehrensberger-Dow and Englund-Dimitrova (2016), Jakobsen and Mesa-Lao (2017) and Schwieter and Ferreira (2017) have also edited a volume in which discussions concerning interdisciplinarity are at stake and so have Lacruz and Jääskeläinen (2018), Li, Lei and He (2019), Muñoz Martín and Halverson (2021) and Halverson and Marín García (2022).

Finally, Alves and Jakobsen (2021a) deserve a special reference for their edited volume, which looks at interdisciplinary in CTS from four different angles. First, they inquire into the epistemological and theoretical nature of such interdisciplinarity and then move on to address the relationship between translation, cognition and ten other disciplines. This relationship is then scrutinized across 12 different aspects that have an impact on translation as a cognitive activity. The volume closes with a look at interdisciplinarity across four emerging trends that are prone to push cognitive-oriented studies of translation further into the future. This joint endeavour, comprising contributions authored or co-authored by 40 scholars, has put together an interdisciplinary account to anchor CTS as a subdiscipline in its own right, proposing goals, commitments and challenges to ground it. In this book, we subscribe to the account put forward by Alves and Jakobsen (2021a), adding to it a differentiation between direct and indirect related disciplines that together contribute to the interdisciplinary consolidation of CTS.

1.2 Direct and indirect related disciplines

The works of O'Brien (2013), O'Brien, Ehrensberger-Dow and Göpferich (2013/2017), Alves (2015), Alves, Hurtado Albir and Lacruz (2015), Ehrensberger-Dow and Englund-Dimitrova (2016/2018), Jakobsen and Mesa-Lao (2017), Schwieter and Ferreira (2017), Lacruz and Jääskeläinen (2018), Li, Lei and He (2019), Muñoz Martín and Halverson (2021), Alves and Jakobsen (2021a) and Halverson and Marín García (2022), among others, have led us to make a distinction between direct and indirect disciplines that could make significant contributions to an interdisciplinary framework in CTS.

Direct disciplines, we would like to claim, would be those disciplines that provide an epistemological and paradigmatic basis for the study of translation as a cognitive activity. In our view, these disciplines are neuroscience, cognitive science, psycholinguistics, reading and writing research and expertise studies.

Indirect disciplines, on the other hand, would be those disciplines which provide contributions to the analysis of particular problems and highlight specific aspects pertaining to the issues under scrutiny. This is the case of applied linguistics and the related notion of communicative competence, which, to a certain extent, is implicated in some studies of *translation competence* (see Chapter 3). Among others, indirect disciplines would include anthropology, contact linguistics, corpus linguistics, ergonomics, human-computer interaction and linguistics – with a special emphasis on pragmatics, pedagogy and psychology of work.

In quite a few cases, the cognitive-oriented study of translation has incorporated a product-oriented approach to supplement the analysis of mental processes involved in the act of translating and relate the characteristics of the product (the translated text) to the traits of the translation process. Thus, for example, low-quality translations would not be representative of the translation process of expert translators. In this sense, other disciplines within linguistics, especially corpus linguistics, contact linguistics, pragmatics and discourse analysis, have served as reference for the study of translation as a cognitive activity and have provided a starting point for the selection and comparison of original and translated texts. Indirectly, these disciplines have also been useful for cognitive research in translation involving information and communication technologies (ICTs), mostly in relation to issues involving language technology and human-computer interaction. Such indirect disciplines have provided meaningful input for the design of technological tools as well as for developing tools for data collection and data analysis in CTS. However, since these disciplines are only indirectly involved in researching translation as a cognitive activity, we have decided not to include them more thoroughly in our descriptions. For a thorough account of the role of linguistics as an indirect discipline, we refer interested readers to Alves and Jakobsen (2021a) with special chapters dedicated to this interface, particularly to Halverson (2021) with her plea for a linguistic commitment to CTS.

In the next sections, we introduce the tenets of five disciplines which, in our view, contribute to building the foundations of a theoretical and methodological framework for CTS, namely neuroscience, cognitive science, psycholinguistics, reading and writing studies and expertise studies. An overview of each of these five disciplines is presented in the next section. Our point of departure is chronological. We aim to describe the tenets, tendencies, influences and impact of these five disciplines on research in translation as a cognitive activity. For this reason, we only mention those tendencies that are of interest to CTS.

1.3 Interdisciplinary approaches to human cognition

As we shall see, the study of translation as a cognitive activity has been carried out from disparate theoretical and methodological perspectives. A myriad of different models has been proposed to explain the translation process and to try to account for the underlying capabilities inherent to that type of process (translation competence). These models are related, sometimes implicitly and sometimes explicitly, to studies that have been carried out in other disciplines that also focus on human cognitive activities and investigate general and particular characteristics of human cognition.

Without being exhaustive, we present below a series of five disciplines which, in our view, have most directly influenced research on translation as a cognitive activity: neuroscience, cognitive science, psycholinguistics, reading and writing studies and expertise studies. Some of these disciplines, such as cognitive science and psycholinguistics, provide an epistemological, paradigmatic and experimental basis for the study of translation as a cognitive activity while others, such as reading and writing studies and expertise studies, focus on more specific aspects of our object of study and provide a conceptual paradigm for the study of certain aspects of translators' cognitive activity.

1.3.1 Neuroscience

Neuroscience is the scientific study of the nervous system. Traditionally, neuroscience has been seen as a branch of biology. However, it is currently an interdisciplinary discipline that collaborates with other fields such as chemistry, computer science, engineering, linguistics, mathematics, medicine and other related disciplines, such as philosophy, physics and psychology. Ultimately, neuroscientists aim to understand every aspect of the nervous system, including how it works, how it develops, how it malfunctions and how it can be altered or repaired. For the purposes of this book, special interest falls on the study of cognitive, developmental and behavioural neuroscience.

1.3.1.1 Tendencies in neuroscience

The scope of neuroscience includes several different approaches used to study the molecular, cellular, developmental, structural, functional, evolutionary, computational and medical aspects of the nervous system. The techniques used by neuroscientists have also been expanded from molecular and cellular studies of individual nerve cells to sensory and motor tasks in the brain. Recent theoretical advances in neuroscience have also stemmed from the study of neural networks.

As Bernston and Cacioppo (2009) put it, elucidating the neural bases of complex behaviours requires sophisticated approaches and methods. Only recently have such methods developed to include the ability to record electrical brain activity with neuroimaging techniques that can non-invasively monitor brain activity. Research in neuroscience focuses, among other relevant topics for CTS, on attention, motivation and emotion, as well as on the basis of functional neuroimaging, the neuronal basis of learning and thinking and implications for the study of inferential processes. Neuroscience can also be approached from a social perspective (Decety & Cacioppo, 2011) to investigate, among other topics, the evolution of social cognition, the neurobiology of social bonding and attachment and the interrelationships between emotions, consciousness and social behaviour. At present, neuroscience has evolved to distance itself from the beginnings of the discipline as we shall see in the following subsections.

Phrenology

One of the predecessors to cognitive neuroscience was phrenology, a pseudoscientific approach from the early 19th century that claimed that behaviour could be determined by the shape of the scalp. The most influential author was perhaps Gall whose book, *The anatomy and physiology of the nervous system in general, and of the brain in particular*, opened an avenue to what would be known as a localizationist view of the human brain (see Gall, 1835). The localizationist view was concerned with mental abilities being localized to specific areas of the brain rather than on what the characteristics of the abilities were and how to measure them.

Localization

The first serious attempts to localize mental functions to specific locations in the brain were the works of Broca and Wernicke. Broca (1861) discovered that damage to an area of the left frontal lobe, now known as Broca's area (Dronkers, Plaisant, Iba-Zizen & Cabanis, 2007), would result in language impairment. Wernicke (1874) discovered that a lesion in the area where the left parietal and temporal lobes meet, now known as Wernicke's area (Bogen & Bogen, 1976), would also result in language impairment. Broca's and Wernicke's discoveries strongly supported the localizationist view and influenced the development of neuroscience into the 20th century.

Behaviourism

At the start of the 20th century, a strong pragmatism characterized research in the northern hemisphere, particularly in North America, and this led to a preference for behaviourism as the primary approach in psychology. Watson (1917) was an early key figure in behaviourism with his stimulus-response approach. By conducting experiments on animals, Watson hoped to be able to predict and control behaviour. Some decades later, Skinner (1957) also became a leading figure in the stimulus-response approach. His work was quite influential in linguistics until it was challenged by Chomsky (1959) in his seminal paper criticizing behaviourism and opening the way for a paradigmatic change not only in neuroscience but also in linguistics and further along in cognitive science. Challenged by the Chomskyan innateness approach, behaviourism lost its impact since it could not provide a realistic psychology of human action and cognition, failing to explain phenomena like memory and thought. As a result, the Chomskyan approach led to what is often termed the *cognitive revolution* and to the rise of current-day neuroscience.

Cognitive neuroscience

Cognitive neuroscience is an academic discipline concerned with the scientific study of biological substrates underlying cognition, with a specific focus on the neural substrates of mental processes. Cognitive neuroscience relies upon theories in cognitive science coupled with evidence from neuropsychology and computational modelling. Ultimately, it is an interdisciplinary area of study that has emerged from many other fields, perhaps most significantly neuroscience, psychology and computer science.

There were several stages in the discipline that changed the way researchers approached their investigations and that led to the field becoming fully established. Although the task of cognitive neuroscience is to describe how the brain functions and creates the mind, historically, it has progressed by investigating how a certain area of the brain supports a given mental faculty. However, early efforts to subdivide the brain proved problematic. The phrenologist movement failed to supply a scientific basis for its theories and has since been rejected. The aggregate field view was also rejected as a result of brain mapping and eventually was replaced by methods such as *positron emission tomography* (PET) and *functional magnetic resonance imaging* (fMRI). More recently, advances in non-invasive functional neuroimaging and associated data analysis methods have also made it possible to use highly naturalistic stimuli and tasks such as feature films depicting social interactions in cognitive neuroscience studies. Such developments may open up the possibility of a closer interaction between neuroscience and research on translation as a cognitive activity.

1.3.1.2 Neuroscience and research on translation as a cognitive activity

Research on translation as a cognitive activity is necessarily concerned with ecological validity, engaging in making the experimental tasks as natural and as close as possible to the unfolding of translation task execution under normal conditions. The need for ecological validity has created difficulties for a closer dialogue between neuroscience and cognitive-oriented studies of translation.[2] It is an obvious fact that a neuroscience approach to research on translation as a cognitive activity must be constrained by the limitations imposed by the use of tools such as electroencephalography (EEG), PET scans, functional near-infrared spectroscopy (fNIRS) and particularly by fMRI.

Buchweitz (2006) was perhaps the first empirical study to use fMRI to investigate the cognitive processes of bilinguals and translators. The main conclusion of Buchweitz's work points to bilingual processing being amodal when located in the brain.

Tymoczko (2012) examined contemporary issues related to discoveries in neuroscience pertaining to memory, perception and brain plasticity and argued that these discoveries should be considered by researchers interested in cognitive aspects of translation. However, Tymoczko cautions about the inherent difficulties of carrying out such studies, which she deems as the "known unknown" in translation studies.

House (2013) also makes a plea for a new linguistic-cognitive orientation in translation studies. After a review of studies employing verbal methods and behavioural experiments, House assessed the value of neurolinguistic studies for translation and, on this basis, suggested a combination of a translation theory and a neuro-functional theory of bilingualism as a starting point for gaining further insights into the cognitive reality of translation.

Due to the difficulties inherent in using brain data in empirical research, it took some time before other studies were carried out. Those difficulties notwithstanding, some recent studies have attempted to bridge the gap between neuroscience and research on translation as a cognitive activity by focusing on translation-related activity using neuroimaging techniques. Sturm (2016), Szpak (2017) and Szpak, Alves and Buchweitz (2021) have all investigated translation in the brain with fMRI data using the framework of Theory of Mind and looking at perspective taking to account for what happens in the human brain during translation task execution. These studies were carried out in the form of auditory or reading stimuli related to brain activation since no writing activity can yet be recorded by means of fMRI equipment. Altogether, the results of these studies contribute effectively to the understanding of bilingual comprehension and the effects of input modality on brain activation. However, they can only contribute indirectly to the study of written translation.

The work of García (2012, 2013, 2019) and García and Muñoz (2021), as well as García et al. (2014) and García, Mikulan and Ibáñez (2016), have also been influential in the elucidation of what happens in the brain during translation task execution. García and Muñoz (2021) review the most important findings in the neuroscience of translation and claim that "despite an arguable dominance of the left-sided regions for interlingual reformulation (IR), relevant neurocognitive mechanisms seem to be widely distributed across both hemispheres" (García & Muñoz, 2021, p. 244). They add that this wide distribution across hemispheres may be more prominent in the case of subjects with considerable interpreting expertise. However, García and Muñoz warn that these results must be approached carefully as the impact of right-hemisphere lesions on translation skills remains poorly studied (García, 2015) and the neuroimaging results available are not entirely consistent (García, 2013).

Instead of adhering to Tymoczko's (2012) view of a "known unknown", García and Muñoz believe that "the neuroscience of translation and interpreting might be better described as an 'unknown known' within Translation Studies" and add that "as research continues to expand, a number of challenges and opportunities should be prioritized in the field's agenda" (García & Muñoz, 2021, p. 252) and "the integration of neuroscience into the central agenda of Translation Studies could foster similar advancements for the teaching and practice of translation and interpreting" (García & Muñoz, 2021, p. 253).

Regardless of the limitations with respect to approaching translation as a source of input for the experimental design, the advent of friendlier neuroimaging techniques may pave the way for other studies to emerge in a not-so-distant future and allow for a stronger interconnectedness between neuroscience and research on translation as a cognitive activity. The works of García (2012, 2013, 2015, 2019), García and Muñoz (2021), Sturm (2016), Szpak (2017) and Szpak, Alves and Buchweitz (2021), among others, have shown that there is an untapped potential in the exploration of neuroimaging techniques to investigate translation as a cognitive activity in the brain.

1.3.2 Cognitive science

Cognitive science is a relatively young discipline. It fosters the interdisciplinary scientific study of the mind and its processes, drawing, among other disciplines, on anthropology, artificial intelligence, linguistics, neuroscience, philosophy and psychology (Mandler, 2002; Miller, 2003). Within psychology, an important subdiscipline for the study of human cognition is cognitive psychology. In line with Posner (1989), we consider that cognitive psychology is an integral part of cognitive science.

1.3.2.1 Tendencies in cognitive science

One could trace the origins of cognitive science to a large-scale meeting of cognitivists held at the Massachusetts Institute of Technology (MIT) on 11th September 1956. In that meeting, Miller presented his seminal paper entitled "The Magical Number Seven, Plus or Minus Two". Dissatisfied with the term *psychology* that had been waning in the 1950s and 1960s, scientists, such as Miller, began to focus on the representation of language rather than on general behaviour and preferred to refer to this new field of research as cognitive science, and more specifically to the paradigmatic approach known as cognitivism.

Cognitivism

Departing from Miller's (1956) seminal paper, one could say that cognitivism grew out of cognitive psychology in the late 1950s as a reaction against behaviourism (Mandler, 2002). It presupposes that human mental activity can best be understood in terms of representational structures in the mind and computational procedures that operate on those structures. For cognitivists, human cognition is viewed mainly as a modular activity that is heavily specialized and operationally encapsulated in order to enable information processing to occur efficiently (Fodor, 1983). Theoretically, cognitivism postulates that cognition entails discrete, internal mental states, i.e. representations, which can be described in terms of rules and/or algorithms. Representation is, therefore, a crucial tenet for cognitivists.

Epistemologically, cognitivism is affiliated with positivism and insists on the use of experimentation and rigorous measurements to validate robust evidence only. Cognitivists tend to assume that cognitive processes are symbolic and linear in nature and controlled from a central cognitive processor. Research along this paradigmatic line sees cognition as a specialized form of information processing and has focused on studies of inner mechanisms of human thought and the processes of knowing, including the role of attention, memory, problem solving and decision making.

Nevertheless, with the advent of more powerful forms of computation, some researchers preferred to work under a different paradigm which would favour a distributional view of cognition with most processes running in parallel rather than being controlled by a central mechanism. Thus, a new approach, known as connectionism, emerged within cognitive science in the mid-1980s.

Connectionism

Connectionism arises from dissatisfaction with the assumption that cognition is basically symbolic and serial and defends a view of human cognition from the perspective of parallel distributed processing (PDP) (Rummelhart & McClelland, 1986). For connectionists, human cognition is viewed from the perspective of neural networks that operate in a distributed fashion with no need whatsoever for central symbolic processing to be implemented. To test assumptions about human cognitive processing, connectionism uses an architecture distributed in nodes throughout an artificial neural network which emulates the synaptic chains of the human brain. To account for this type of parallel processing, connectionists built on Hebb (1949) and applied *Hebbian learning* as an algorithm to trigger node activations and regulate the configuration of emergent computational processes.

In a way, connectionism presupposes some form of weak representations for the models to work and, therefore, does not exclude altogether the concept of mental representations. However, representations acquire a dynamic status in connectionist networks and are, therefore, considered as the results of cognitive processing and no longer as the prerequisite for cognition. In fact, Elman et al. (1996) have come closer to proposing an amalgam of cognitivism and connectionism by arguing that perhaps the right question to ask is not whether cognitive processes are intrinsically modular but rather whether these processes start or become modular.

Connectionism, in its latest form, favours plastic, flexible configurations which operate in parallel on the basis of recurrent networks that evolve as processing occurs. To that extent, processing tends to become highly specialized, i.e. modular, as learning is consolidated by experience.

However, as had happened in the paradigmatic dispute between cognitivists and connectionists, another paradigmatic alternative emerged within cognitive science in the late 1980s, favouring what is called situated or embodied cognition.

Situated or embodied cognition

An emerging trend within cognitive science is that of dynamical systems based on ecologically oriented models of the mind. This new approach has become increasingly influential, suggesting that a full understanding of the mind requires the systematic study of the dynamics of interaction among mind, body and the world. This approach is sometimes referred to as 4EA cognition, namely embodied, embedded, enacted, extended and affective cognition, i.e. a combination of approaches that reject the conception of mind and cognition seen as resulting from internal brain processes and argue that cognition should be grounded in human experience. Robbins and Aydede (2009) argue that this new orientation calls for a revolutionary new understanding of mind, according to which mental states and processes, and even persons, literally extend into the environment.

The origins of the embodied, situated approach within cognitive science can be linked to Maturana and Varela's (1987) *theory of autopoiesis*, a name which designates the dynamics of a network of transformations and molecular productions which constitute a living being. Maturana and Varela (1987) consider cognition to be a biological phenomenon and characterize the mind as a metaphor for thought processing. For them, the brain, as a vast network of cells which are interconnected with the rest of the nervous system, operates according to its own interconnected internal dynamics and its structure, in what is known as structural coupling.

In short, Maturana and Varela (1987) depart from a position that refutes the mind-body dichotomy and insist on viewing cognition as a biological adaptation of the species. In their perspective, the focus is on the organism's interactions with the environment. Therefore, for Maturana and Varela (1987), context plays a fundamental role in the process of acquiring knowledge. Maturana and Varela build on the notion of circularity and autonomy of living beings and compare cognition to a network closed in itself. Such network interactions are called structural coupling. They suggest that this results in a viable alternative to the notion of representation implied in the assumptions of both cognitivism and connectionism. Because of structural coupling and the system's own dynamics, a theory of embodied cognition can do without the notion of representation as an explanatory abstraction for cognition.

Further on, some researchers associated embodied cognition with phenomenology (Varela, Thompson & Rosch, 1991, second edition 2017) arguing that embodiment encompasses both the body as a living structure as well as the context or the environment of cognitive mechanisms. For Varela, Thompson and Rosch, in its more encompassing sense, cognition consists of enaction, in bringing something forth through structural coupling.

From the perspective of embodied cognition, the construction of meaning refers to a specific identity structurally coupled with the environment in its interactions. The core of the theory is the molecular system which constitutes a first-order system. Human beings are seen as aggregates of cells and, as such, constitute second-order autopoietic systems. Finally, social and linguistic interactions are derivatives of the second-order structural coupling and should be seen as third-order autopoietic systems.

The intricate relationship between neuroscience and the study of situated cognition has come to the fore in recent years. This can be linked to the emergence of social cognitive neuroscience. Ochsner and Lieberman (2001) have introduced social cognitive neuroscience as an emerging interdisciplinary field of research that seeks to understand phenomena in terms of interactions between three levels of analysis: the social level (concerned with the motivational and social factors that influence behaviour and experience), the cognitive level (concerned with the information-processing mechanisms that give rise to social-level phenomena) and the neural level (concerned with the brain mechanisms that instantiate cognitive-level processes).

1.3.2.2 Cognitive science and research on translation as a cognitive activity

When scrutinizing the epistemological and paradigmatic tenets of cognitive science from the point of view of research on translation as a cognitive activity, we observe that there has been a close relationship between tendencies in cognitive science and approaches in cognitive-oriented studies of translation.

Risku and Windhager (2013) take account of the extended and situated nature of human cognition. With the aim of investigating translation processes at a macro-level, they combine developments in cognitive science with a sociological perspective based on actor-network theory and activity theory. For Risku and Windhager (2013), consideration of developments in cognitive science is indispensable when defining research agendas addressing cognitive aspects of translation. One such development is the recognition of the extended nature of human cognition. Risku and Windhager argue that cognition is not just an information manipulation process in the brain. It is contextualized action embedded in a body and increasingly mediated by technologies and situated in its socio-cultural environment with strong implications for a situated cognition approach needed to describe cognitive aspects of translation.

Risku (2014) considers translation process research as a type of interaction research which goes from mental to socio-cognitive processes. For Risku, the main methodological approaches used in translation process research have been inspired by methods originally developed in the behavioural sciences, especially psychology. She contends that mainstream experimental research in laboratory settings needs to be complemented with other methodological approaches such as qualitative, ethnographic research in order to be able to account for the situated, embedded and extended aspects of cognition. Building on results of an ethnographic field study into the socio-cognitive aspects of translation, Risku (2014) shows the complexity of the social network involved in the observed case of freelance translation, the tendency of the translator to externalize parts of the process and thus transform the internal processing into an interaction with self-produced outer stimuli– thereby reconfiguring the cognitive space– and the existence of distinct, iterative interaction patterns that stand out as behavioural and cognitive routines in the way the translator works.

More recently, Risku and Rogl (2021) provide an account of situated approaches to cognitive science – namely situated, embodied, distributed, embedded and extended cognition – and address their historical roots and motivations to point out their consequences for the study of translation as a cognitive activity. They present a historical overview of first-generation (computational information processing) and second-generation (connectionist) cognitive science theories of the human mind to move on to a third-generation account within cognitive science which sees cognition as extending beyond the human mind and brain into the whole body, into social interaction and even into the environment and human artefacts. Risku and Rogl consider that this situated perspective in cognitive science presupposes that meaning always emerges in a specific context. Similarly, they add, translation always takes place in a specific physical and social environment within which translators interact and which impacts their cognition.

In a similar vein, Muñoz Martín (2017) has argued that research on translation as a cognitive activity has witnessed the emergence of an alternative to the information-processing paradigm and the analogy of mind-as-computer. Drawing on Wheeler (2005), Muñoz Martín defends an embodied, embedded, extended, enactive, affective approach to the study of mind and insists that, although not all authors carrying out research on cognitive aspects of translation necessarily agree with ascribing themselves to cognitive translatology, almost all of them question one point or another of the traditional cognitive approach from the 1950s, and they do so in line with assumptions and tenets of contemporary cognitive science.

Muñoz Martín and Martín de León (2021) also provide an overview of the main developments within cognitive science since its emergence in the middle 1950s. They point to the distinction between micro- and macro-cognition to discuss some models used to understand cognition and the locus where it is approached, the situatedness and distributedness of cognitive processes, their relationship with emotions and the compatibility of ethnographic studies and laboratory research. Muñoz Martín and Martín de León argue that studies of translation as a cognitive activity should not only focus on translators (and interpreters) but also consider other agents who participate in multilectal-mediated communication. Research should also include audiences, interlocutors and addressees into the picture in order not to leave part of the picture out.

On the interface with cognitive science and its evolution

As we will see further into this book, there have been five main phases in the research of cognitive aspects of translation, both in terms of research on the translation process as well as on translation competence and its acquisition. We shall refer to these phases as first, second, third, fourth and fifth-generation studies and will discuss them more extensively in Chapter 4. For now, we would like to point out that studies carried out in each of these phases seem to draw respectively on contemporary tendencies in the cognitive science paradigms of their time. Thus, first-generation studies, until the mid-1990s, tend to be very broad in their nature and indirectly affiliate themselves with cognitivism while second-generation studies, up to the mid-2000s, focus on more narrowly defined questions and hypotheses, indirectly affiliating themselves with connectionism. On the other hand, third, fourth and fifth-generation studies, up to the present day, tend to embrace a vision of cognition as embodied and situated action, yet preserving a view of translation as a dynamic, cyclic and recursive all-encompassing process, a view which one could associate with the notion of distributed parallel processing postulated by connectionism.

Overall, most cognitive-oriented studies of translation do not claim a direct affiliation to a particular cognitive science paradigm. However, as Alves (2015) points out, this does not imply that such an affiliation does not exist or cannot be ascribed to them. In fact, a clearer affiliation between such studies and a particular branch of cognitive science would be important in order to strengthen links between these two related fields of research and, indirectly, assert research on translation as a cognitive activity as an area of research in its own right. We shall discuss that in more detail in our concluding remarks in Chapter 5.

1.3.3 Psycholinguistics

Psycholinguistics can be understood as the study of human language processing concerning investigations of the psychological foundations of language (Garman, 1990). It deals with written and spoken language, their comprehension and production, and the nature of linguistic systems and models of processing.

1.3.3.1 Tendencies in psycholinguistics

Theoretically, psycholinguistic models of language processing focus on the nature of the language signal, the biological foundations of language, including auditory and visual systems, the organization of language in the brain and articulatory and manual systems to account for the perception and production of speech and writing, lexical storage and retrieval and the comprehension and production of multiword utterances (Garman, 1990). Methodologically, psycholinguistics has a strong focus on experimentation, precise measurements and statistical analysis of data.

Psycholinguistic modelling

At first, psycholinguistics studies consisted of behavioural tasks with subjects being presented with linguistic stimuli and asked to perform an action under controlled settings. Rigorous experimental design has, therefore, been considered extremely important to allow significant results and generate robust evidence. In a second stage, psycholinguistics research also used behavioural data such as *eye tracking* to study online language processing (Rayner, 1978), encompassing reading and writing processes. Just and Carpenter (1980) eye-mind assumption strengthens this line of research by suggesting a correlation between eye movements, and particularly eye fixations, with instances of effortful cognitive processing.

Psycholinguistics has also shown an interest in studying bilingualism. Studies tend to focus on how bilinguals manage to produce relatively pure monolingual language output when the communicative setting requires them to do so (de Groot & Christoffels, 2007). Models of bilingualism usually assume the existence of control processes that activate and/or inhibit language output so that speakers can alternate successfully between languages and concentrate on production without interference. Incidentally, this view of language processing has fostered research in interpreting within translation studies (Moser-Mercer, 1997; Shlesinger, 1995, 2000).

Recent developments

More recently, neuroimaging has offered psycholinguistics non-invasive techniques such as PET, fMRI and fNIRS. Complementarily, computational modelling has become a useful and promising way to allow insights into hypotheses and predictions made by researchers in psycholinguistics. One could, thus, expect that the interrelationships between neuroscience and psycholinguistics will increase. And as it happens, it is likely to assume that the impact of psycholinguistics on research in translation as a cognitive activity will also be observed.

1.3.3.2 Psycholinguistics and research on translation as a cognitive activity

As we have seen, psycholinguistics is concerned with how people, children and adults alike, acquire, learn, understand and produce language in the context of first and second language acquisition and learning as well as with respect to multilingual issues. It is also concerned with studies of reading and writing processes among children and adults in different situations. Therefore, as a field of inquiry, psycholinguistics shares closely related aspects with the study of translation as a cognitive activity, namely how understanding/reading relates to production/writing in cases of oral and/or written translation and their implications for translation competence and translation competence acquisition. Thus, models and methods stemming from psycholinguistics have been used by researchers interested in translation as a cognitive activity. However, as we shall see in Chapter 2, processes in translation are quite different from standard reading/writing processes and demand a more particular kind of approach.

From a standard psycholinguistic point of view, there are several conditions that may interfere with the results of studies which focus on translation as an object of scrutiny. For instance, pauses which are of interest to psycholinguistics are usually very short and necessarily refer to tasks being performed by subjects. On the other hand, pauses which are of interest to the study of translation as a cognitive activity are quite often longer and may not necessarily relate only to the cognitive processes occurring during translation task execution (see Section 4.3 in Chapter 4). Thus, keyboard and mouse activity or eye movements and eye fixations concerning translation task execution may not necessarily relate to patterns observed only on source or target texts and can also be motivated by external sources which would not be relevant for a standard psycholinguistics experiment. Additionally, certain processes emerging during translation task execution may be the result of fatigue, distraction or the need to interrupt translation task execution due to external circumstances and may not relate directly to the task being performed. From a strict psycholinguistics perspective, these factors would interfere with standard observations as the task under scrutiny unfolds and one might attempt to control all sources of interference in a laboratory setting. However, doing this would reduce the level of naturalness under which a translation task is carried out. This could have negative implications in terms of ecological validity and could render the task unnatural. Assuring a reasonable level of ecological validity for the translation task under investigation is a major problem in terms of developing a rigorous experimental design with controlled variables, which could also be considered a valid experiment in standard psycholinguistics. In Chapter 4, when we discuss the different types of research designs in the four phases of research in cognitive-oriented studies of translation (see Sections 4.3.1.1, 4.3.2.1, 4.3.3.1 and 4.3.4.1), we will elaborate further into this issue, trying to plea for a psycholinguistics approach to the study of translation which considers the specificities of our object of study. We shall argue that, in view of these disciplinary differences, a closer dialogue between psycholinguistics and cognitive-oriented studies of translation is needed to bridge the gap between the two disciplines and enhance the possibility of borrowing and lending between psycholinguistics and cognitive translation studies.

More recently, Chmiel (2021) provides an overview of historical developments showing the most relevant interactions between psycholinguistics and CTS since the 1980s. After presenting psycholinguistically motivated studies of lexical and syntactic processing in translation, temporal aspects of processing, memory and executive functions, directionality and reading patterns, Chmiel focuses on recent developments, such as attempts to integrate translation and interpreting models with psycholinguistic models of language processing and the use of psycholinguistic methodology and study designs in CTS. Chmiel also deals with how to design relevant tasks using authentic or manipulated materials; how to find a proper balance between control of variables and an ecologically valid simulation of experienced reality; what data to elicit and what measures to make; and how to triangulate findings based on analysis of qualitative and quantitative data, making a strong plea for the use of mixed-method approaches applied to well-powered experiments and use of strong statistics which report on effect sizes. Chmiel (2021) also points to future directions, highlighting a synergy effect that can be created to shed light on the relationship between cognition and translation from a psycholinguistics perspective.

1.3.4 Reading and writing research

Although we present the fields of reading and writing research here in the same section, we should stress that both areas of study have developed separately. We bring them together in this section because reading and writing processes occur in parallel in written translation. The fact that at least two languages are involved in translation task execution increases the complexity of relating reading and writing studies to research on translation as a cognitive activity.

1.3.4.1 Reading research

Empirical research on reading can be traced back to the beginning of the 20th century with seminal articles by Gray (1917) and Gray (1925). In the *Handbook of Writing Research*, MacArthur, Graham and Fitzgerald (2008) emphasize that Gray's pioneer effort not only provided direction to curriculum builders, teachers, administrators and researchers but it has also established a systematic practice of analysis of reading research. Dole, Duffy, Roehler and Pearson (1991) have also attempted to assess findings stemming from research about comprehension processes, comprehension strategies and teaching strategies in order to present an account of instructional practice in reading comprehension. Altogether, research on reading can be carried out from disparate yet complementary perspectives including methodological issues in reading studies related to the design and analysis of experiments and ethnographic approaches to reading research as well as research on basic processes related to building and testing models of reading processes, modalities of reading, the study of individual differences and underlying cognitive processes in reading as well as metacognitive skills and social and motivational influences on reading.

As far as the study of reading is concerned, the concept of readability (Dale & Chall, 1949; Harris & Hodges, 1995, among others) has been instrumental in determining the type and scope of research. Overall, readability can be broadly based on the combination of three textual variables, namely text structure, text texture and informational density of text (Amiran & Jones, 1982). One of the main research interests in reading research has focused on the development of a readability formula to measure the effects of reading-related activities (Spache, 1953; Fry, 1968; Mosenthal & Kirsch, 1998; Wang and Eccles, 2013, among others). Researchers have used various factors to measure readability, such as reading speed and reading accuracy, speed of perception (at a distance and in peripheral vision), fatigue in reading and so on. For most experimental studies, eye movements have been a source of primary input for data analyses. In the case of cognitive-oriented research of translation, the study of eye movements has allowed researchers to tap into what had always remained inside the black box, namely how reading processes unfold in the course of translation task execution.

Over the past years, reading research drawing on eye-tracking data has been quite influential in the cognitive-oriented study of translation. Therefore, one needs to consider the studies of reading processes carried out by Just and Carpenter (1980), Rayner and Pollatsek (1989), Rayner (1978, 1998), Hyona, Lorch and Rinck (2003) and Radach and Kennedy (2004), among others. Several basic facts about eye movements in reading have been convincingly documented. Research has established the typical duration and length of saccades and the typical duration of fixations. Reading research has also shown that factors such as word familiarity (Williams & Morris 2004), word predictability (Frisson and Pickering, 1999), word length and complexity (Kliegl, Grabner, Rolfs & Engbert, 2004, Bertram & Hyona, 2003, Rayner & Duffy, 1986) and lexical and/or syntactic ambiguity (Juhasz & Rayner, 2003) all affect fixation duration. The main focus in reading research has been on lexical processing and reading short strings of words, while less attention has been paid to eye movement behaviour during continuous reading, reading with different aims or reading under different circumstances.

1.3.4.2 Writing research

Empirical research on writing goes back a long way but gained momentum in the 1970s and 1980s with the application of theories and methods stemming from cognitive psychology to account for the nature and development of writing skills. Emig's (1971) seminal study of the writing processes of high-school students in the United States is considered as one of the first attempts of cognitive-oriented research in writing. Shanahan, MacArthur, Graham and Fitzgerald (2006) state that from a cognitive perspective, attempts to study writing have revolved around building more detailed models of writing processes and relating these processes to more general cognitive processes such as working memory and self-regulation as well as studies on how writing develops through social interaction in discourse communities building on a socio-cultural perspective. Altogether, research on writing can be carried out from disparate yet complementary perspectives including theories and models of writing, research methodology and analytic tools, the study of writing development as well as instructional models and approaches to writing.

Researchers' first attempts to understand cognitive processes in writing began in the early 1970s. They stem from studies about the teaching of writing and research in composition studies. For many years, it was assumed that the writing process generally operated in some variation of three to five stages, including prewriting, drafting, revising and editing. However, more recent research demonstrates that it is seldom accurate to describe these stages as fixed steps in a straightforward process. Rather, they are more accurately conceptualized as overlapping parts of a complex whole or parts of a recursive process that are repeated multiple times throughout the writing process.

Flower and Hayes (1981) are considered to be seminal authors in cognitive-oriented research on writing processes. The authors set out to discover the differences between good and bad writers and came to three results from their study, which suggests that good writers envelop the three following characteristics when solving their rhetorical problems: (1) good writers respond to all of the rhetorical problems; (2) good writers build their problem representation by creating a particularly rich network of goals for affecting a reader; and (3) good writers represent the problem not only in more breadth but also in depth. Flower and Hayes (1981) suggest that composition instructors need to consider showing students how to explore and define their own problems, even within the constraints of an assignment. The authors believe that writers discover what they want to do by insistently, energetically exploring the entire problem before them and building for themselves a unique image of the problem they want to solve.

Schilperoord (1996) has built on Flower and Hayes (1981) to study writing processes in terms of cognitive rhythm, namely rhythmical movements in the course of text production that include pauses, deletions and regressions. Schilperoord's results point to hierarchical phases in the course of text production that create a particular type of cognitive pattern.

1.3.4.3 Reading/writing studies and research on translation as a cognitive activity

Although the interface between reading and translation had been the object of concern of some authors for quite some time (Delisle 1980; Hurtado Albir 1990; Dancette 1995, etc.), it was only around 2007 that cognitive-oriented research of translation started using eye-tracking data in an attempt to tap into the *black box* concerning the role of reading in translation task execution (see Section 1.3.4.1). Most studies have drawn primarily on the works of Just and Carpenter (1980) and Rayner (1998) and rested on the overall assumption that eye-tracking data can be interpreted as correlates of ongoing cognitive processing and, thus, offer a window into human information processing. Building on Just and Carpenter's (1980) eye-mind assumption, authors in translation process research assume that eye fixations can be used to map instances of processing effort in source and/or target texts and account for cognitive traits that reveal features of human translation processes.

As far as the interface between writing research and translation is concerned, researchers have been using keylogging to investigate the recursive nature of the translation process, building on the work of Flower and Hayes (1981) and on the notion of cognitive rhythm (Schilperoord, 1996), first applied to translation process research by Jakobsen (2002) (see Section 4.3.2.1 in Chapter 4).

In a publication dedicated to the interface between writing studies and translation, Dam-Jensen and Heine (2013) state that, from a cognitive perspective, writing and translation are addressed as two different objects of study. The authors argue that, in general, cognitive-oriented studies of writing and translation have a lot in common. Cognitive studies of writing and translation traditionally employ the same sets of methods, which range from verbalizations, retrospective interviews and observation to electronic tools such as keystroke logging, eye-tracking and screen capture. Studies of writing and of translation also share many other characteristics, as revealed by the kinds of research carried out in the two fields. However, they differ in the way they approach their respective objects of study. The authors suggest that both writing and translation can be studied as types of text production. Different dimensions of text production are sketched as examples of research topics at the interface between writing and translation. Both writers and translators make use of strategies, a set of actions, as a steering force for handling challenges and problems, in order to meet goals effectively. Dam-Jensen and Heine (2013) also state that in order to bring the research in the two fields together, the research methods themselves need to be discussed further.

Along these lines, Ehrensberger-Dow and Perrin (2013) illustrate how a mixed-method approach that combines keystroke logging, screen recording and cue-based retrospective verbalization, which was originally developed to study the newswriting processes of journalists, can be applied in translation process research to gain insights into cognitive aspects of translation as a cognitive activity. For them, translation is a situated activity that involves more than simply producing target texts from source texts. In order to understand what translators actually do when they translate, their psychobiographies as well as the social setting of the workplace and the contextual resources must be considered.

Both cognitive research on reading and writing share methodological approaches with cognitive-oriented research on translation. Translation as a combined reading/writing task offers reading and writing research the possibility of extending the range of their interests well beyond their chartered territories and exploring unchartered spaces in which reading and writing converge. However, one still knows very little about how reading varies according to reading purpose, or according to the way reading is sometimes combined concurrently with other activities as in the case of sight translation and written translation. The same applies to our knowledge of writing for translation. The translator's visual attention is constantly shifted between two texts, a source text and the translator's emerging target text, amalgamating reading and writing into a single macro cognitive process. The possibility of tracking the translator's gaze pattern across the source and target text and matching these observations with the online recording of keystrokes has opened up new avenues for exploring and furthering research on reading and writing processes in the course of translation task execution (see Jakobsen, 2011). As we will show in Chapter 4 (see Section 4.3), Hvelplund (2011), Carl and Dragsted (2012), Dragsted and Carl (2013) and Alves, Pagano and Da Silva (2011, 2014), among others, have attempted to bridge the gap between studies of reading and writing and offer a broader, complementary perspective to account for the synergy of reading and writing in the scope of cognitive processes in translation.

1.3.5 Expertise studies

Expertise studies investigate the characteristics (knowledge and abilities) that distinguish domain experts from less experienced people in a given domain (Ericsson, Anders, Charness, Feltovich & Hoffman, 2006, second edition 2018). The discipline is concerned with those particular traits that allow individuals to achieve consistently superior performance on a specified set of representative tasks for a given domain that can be administered to any subject (Ericsson & Charness, 1997). Expertise studies can also be carried out from an interactional perspective (Collins & Evans, 2007) with a focus on distinguishing between contributory and interactional factors in the context of expert performance.

1.3.5.1 Tendencies in expertise studies

Overall, tendencies in expertise studies can be summarized in the debate between a view of expertise as an innate talent or as an acquired skill. According to Ericsson (2002), this debate can be traced back to Galton's (1869/1979) seminal book on "Hereditary Genius", which argues in favour of innate talent. This issue has been taken up by Ericsson and Charness (1994) and Ericsson, Krampe, and Tesch-Römer (1993), arguing that Galton's view is still present in contemporary theories of human ability, such as in Gardner's (1983, 1993) theory of multiple intelligences. Authors defending a common-sense view of expertise presuppose the need for a basic endowment, such as abilities, mental capacities and innate talent, as a condition for expert performance (Gardner, 1993). Ericsson (2002, p. 188) insists that the debate "validates the relevance and controversies over the role of limits set by innate abilities". Drawing on the works of Ericsson (1998), Ericsson and Lehmann (1996) and Ericsson Krampe, and Tesch-Römer (1993), Ericsson (2002, p. 188) insists further that "the firm empirical evidence backing the common-sense view of professional development is surprisingly limited and the available evidence is sometimes even inconsistent with the assumptions of this view of expert performance".

The discipline of expertise studies is relatively young and authors affiliated with it have engaged vigorously in defending a view of expert performance as the end result of an acquisition process. As stated by Ericsson et al. (2006/2018), a significant milestone is reached when a field of scientific research matures to a point that warrants the publication of its first handbook. The publication of the *Cambridge Handbook of Expertise and Expert Performance* in 2006 can be seen as an indicator of the consolidation of expertise studies as an autonomous discipline and a defence of the role of deliberate practice on the road to expertise. The second edition of the handbook, published in 2018, consolidates the study of expertise and expert performance in an even broader context.

Expertise as a result of deliberate practice

Similar to what happened in cognitive science, research on expertise and expert performance originates from cognitive psychology (Ericsson & Crutcher, 1990; Glaser, 1992; Scardamalia & Bereiter, 1991). It aims at defining general traits of behaviour that account for expert performance. By differentiating between performance traits of domain experts and traits of experienced non-experts, authors defending a view of expertise as an acquired skill hope to show what traits account for expert performance in a specific domain and across domains in general. This assumption explicitly differentiates between experience, measured mostly in numbers of years of practice, and expertise, a concept that relates unequivocally to consistently superior performance in a given domain. In that light, experience and expertise do not necessarily equate to one another.

Ericsson et al. (2006) claim that expertise is an acquired skill and the only innate genetic factors critical to successful expert performance are body size and height (Ericsson, 2002, p. 190). The author argues, for instance, that "above average height provides an advantage in basketball and below average height facilitates elite performance in gymnastics" (Ericsson, 2002, p. 190). Ericsson et al. (2006/2018) also argue that a set of characteristics distinguishes experts from non-experts. The authors focus on a series of concepts that we will introduce as follows.

1) Consistently superior performance. According to Ericsson and Charness (1997), a high level of consistently superior performance can be considered as a result of *deliberate practice*, a concept that presupposes the engagement of apprentices in training activities specifically designed for the purpose of developing high-performance levels in a given domain and keeping it consistent within that domain.
2) Metacognitive and self-regulatory behaviour. Ericsson (2002) argues that the key challenge for individuals aspiring to become experts is to avoid the arrested development associated with automaticity and acquire metacognitive skills to support their continued learning and improvement. Ericsson insists that expertise studies have demonstrated that expert knowledge and expert performance are acquired skills and that empirical studies show that there is no necessary relationship between domain expertise and general cognitive capacities such as intelligence or memory. Further, Ericsson et al. (2006) insist that the single biggest factor in the evolution of expertise is *deliberate practice* and that a particular type of trajectory is necessary in order to lead novices on the path to expertise.
3) Deliberate practice. Deliberate practice can be more narrowly defined as regular engagement in specific activities directed at performance enhancement in a particular domain, where the domain is some sort

of skilled activity. This is rather different from simply accumulating experience at performing a regular activity. Expertise studies insist that cumulative experience in a given domain is a necessary condition for expert performance. However, that does not suffice per se. According to expertise studies, deliberate practice only occurs under the following conditions, when (a) there is a well-defined task, (b) the task is of appropriate difficulty for the individual, (c) there is informative feedback and (d) there are opportunities for repetition and the correction of errors (Ericsson, 1996). Engaging in an activity with the primary goal of improving some aspect of performance is a prerequisite of deliberate practice.

4) Expertise trajectory. The notion of expertise trajectory was introduced by Lajoie (2003) to explain the path, through experience and practice, that leads to a type of behaviour that is characteristic of consistently superior performance found among experts. Shreve (2006) builds on Lajoie to account for a proposal of how expertise in translation is acquired (see Section 3.3.1.1 in Chapter 3).

From the perspective of the expert performance approach, one can identify two major tendencies, namely an absolute approach and a relative approach (Chi, 2006). The absolute approach builds on studying truly exceptional individuals to understand "how they perform in their domain of expertise" (Chi, 2006, p. 21). The relative approach draws on comparisons between experts and novices. Expertise in this sense can be either grossly assessed through such measures as academic qualifications, consensus among peers, seniority or years performing a task, or more thoroughly assessed through domain-specific knowledge or performance tests.

Expertise from an interactional perspective

Building on a sociological perspective, Collins and Evans (2007) posit several different types of expertise, two of which seem to be of relevance to studies of translation (and interpreting). The authors suggest that specialized tacit knowledge can be associated with two different types of specialized expertise, namely, contributory expertise and interactional expertise. In general terms, contributory expertise is what allows individuals to perform their activities in their domains (e.g. a surgeon operating on a patient), while interactional expertise is what allows journalists, reviewers, sociologists and translators/interpreters, among other professionals, to perform many of their tasks on conversations and interactions with those who have contributory expertise. As such, interactional expertise is co-created together with individuals who share the two types of expertise. In other words, contributory expertise allows individuals to perform directly in their own domain, whereas interactional expertise implies encyclopaedic knowledge and mastery of the language of another domain without knowledge of actual practice in that domain.

Collins and Evans (2007, p. 2) conceive of "expertise as real and substantive", rather than "relational". In other words, the authors are not interested in expert relations with others or in expertise as an attribution (i.e. the assignment of a label). They claim, however, that they adopt a realist approach that starts "from the view that expertise is the real and substantive possession of groups of experts and that individuals acquire real and substantive expertise through their membership of those groups" (Collins & Evans, 2007, p. 3). As such, expertise can only be acquired through a social process, that is, "socialization into the practices of an expert group". Such socialization takes time and effort on the part of the expert.

Collins and Evans's model is graphically represented in what they refer to as a "Periodic Table of Expertises", a table containing the type of expertise an individual has when they are able to achieve higher levels of performance. For our current purposes in this book, we single out the concept of specialist expertise which requires specialist tacit knowledge: contributory expertise and interactional expertise. Contributory expertise is the highest level of specialized expertise and is found among those individuals who effectively produce or work within a given domain. In general terms, contributory expertise is the kind of tacit knowledge that enables an individual to perform within a domain (e.g. surgeons who operate on a patient, civil engineers who project buildings). Meanwhile, interactional expertise, which is located next to contributory expertise in the periodic table, implies encyclopaedic knowledge and language fluency in a given domain without the practice counterpart. This is the kind of knowledge used by journalists, reviewers, sociologists and translators/interpreters, among other professionals, to perform most of their tasks after conversations and interactions with those with contributory expertise in the domain they are interested in. In other words, translators have contributory expertise in translation (i.e. they perform translation tasks and can contribute directly to practices in the domain), but most often only have interactional expertise in other domains (e.g. medicine, physics, law).

Interactional expertise is also relevant for contributory experts when they need to understand or review the work of colleagues in their own field, as no expert can master all knowledge in their domain. Collins and Evans (2007) propose a number of imitation game-based experiments to test the notion of interactional expertise. Such experiments, aimed to compare "the domain-specific linguistic abilities of interactional experts with that of contributory experts and that of nonexperts" (Collins & Evans, 2007, p. 93), have provided evidence that interactional expertise is a relevant notion to identify the abilities of individuals with different types of expertise.

1.3.5.2 Expertise studies and research on translation as a cognitive activity

Ericsson (2002) is perhaps the first author to address the question of expertise in relation to the domain of translation and interpreting. He applied the concept of deliberate practice to study the performance of conference interpreters who perform complex simultaneous interpretation. Although his research focuses primarily on interpreting, it paves the way for a discussion within the discipline of translation studies and, consequently in research on translation as a cognitive activity, about the role of expert knowledge in translation from the perspective of expertise studies. Over time, these multiple cognitive resources relevant to translation can evolve and become what Ericsson and Charness (1997) define as being consistently superior performance, i.e. a type of specialized behaviour able to successfully cope with adverse conditions and yet maintain a high standard of quality. As far as research on translation as a cognitive activity is concerned, Shreve (2006) and Göpferich (2008), among others, have drawn on expertise studies to account for the complexities entailed in the behaviour of translators (see Section 3.2.2.3 in Chapter 3).

As we have seen with respect to cognitive science (see Section 1.3.2), researchers working on cognitive-oriented studies of translation, which build on cognitive science, usually do not seek an explicit affiliation to a cognitive science paradigm. However, the situation changes when research on translation as a cognitive activity meets expertise studies. Some studies focusing on the translation process, and particularly those studies related to translation competence, show a clear tendency to seek an affiliation with a view of expertise and expert performance which consider it as an acquired skill that can be enhanced by means of deliberate practice developed along a trajectory towards expertise in translation (see Tiselius, 2013a, 2013b).

Shreve, Angelone and Lacruz (2018) have inquired into the nature of expertise vis-a-vis the concept of translation competence. They have argued that the concept of expertise could be a more robust and enlightening substitute for translation competence in CTS and that it is possible to subsume the most important aspects of competence models within expertise theory. We shall refer to this discussion in Chapter 3 when we discuss translation competence and translation competence acquisition.

It is worth mentioning that Jääskeläinen (2011) reminds us of the fact that evidence of features of expertise in translation (Jakobsen, 2005; Shreve, 2006) is similar to those identified in other domains (Ericsson et al., 2006). Therefore, we would like to argue in favour of a closer dialogue with expertise studies and insist on its paramount importance to identify common and different cognitive patterns observed between expert translators and experts in other domains. Such an attempt would represent a significant breakthrough in defining traits of expertise in translation. More robust findings could help to establish what characterizes translation task execution as a particular type of expert performance. After all, as Jääskeläinen (2011, p. 135) rightly puts it, "expertise in translation is substance in its own right".

More recently, the concept of expertise has been approached within CTS in a new light (see Da Silva, 2019, 2021). Alves and Da Silva (2021) point out that CTS has drawn on the expert performance approach (EPA) to investigate expertise for approximately two decades (Ericsson, 2002; Shreve, 2002). Nevertheless, they argue, current debates about translation as an embodied, embedded, enacted, extended and affective activity have challenged the status quo of the EPA, especially because of its primary focus on accounting for expertise solely under laboratory conditions (see Muñoz Martín, 2014, 2017). Additionally, calls for epistemological revisitations have led scholars to challenge the clarity, adequacy, consistency and effectiveness of some constructs and research traditions in the discipline, including the notion of expertise (see Marín García, 2017, 2019). Building on this background, Alves and Da Silva (2021) attempt to provide a novel framework aiming at potentially reconciling the expert performance approach (EPA) with the sociologically oriented approach proposed by Collins and Evans (2007), namely the interactional expertise approach (IEA), highlighting the notions of language and socialization as important aspects of expertise.

Along these lines, Da Silva and Silveira (2017) point out that, through an interactional expertise approach, translators can interact with domain specialists to pinpoint and solve problems before producing an adequate translation, improving confidence in their own work. The focus of such an approach is, therefore, not exclusively on the individual performer but rather on their interactions with others.

Alves and Da Silva (2022) build on the proposals made by Alves and Da Silva (2021) to suggest a framework which could provide CTS with the necessary basis to investigate expertise in translation under laboratory conditions and real-life situations. Alves and Da Silva (2022) propose to approach translation as a skill and focus on absolute expertise, i.e. on the behaviours and processes of individuals who do show consistently superior performance. This would require longitudinal studies or at least multiple task applications to the same individual. For Alves and Da Silva (2022), this approach allows the integration of a sociological perspective (Collins & Evans, 2007) into the expert performance approach developed by Ericsson and associates (Ericsson, 2002, 2006, Ericsson, Krampe, & Tesch-Römer, 1993; Ericsson & Smith, 1991), enabling the investigation of expertise both in natural settings and under laboratory conditions. Alves and Da Silva also posit that the sociological approach developed by Collins and Evans (2007) provides a framework to investigate cognition as situated, distributed and extended action, as their approach places emphasis on (a) language, especially the one used in spoken discourse, as an important component of expertise (in fact, language has been considerably overlooked in standard expertise studies), (b) socialization as an indispensable condition for acquiring, sustaining and expressing expertise and (c) the possibility of experimentation, as in the imitation game, which has been used by the latter authors as a proof of concept in relatively controlled conditions. For Alves and Da Silva (2022), the combination of EPA and IEA is in line with the proposal made by Alves and Jakobsen (2021b) in favour of a situated, distributed and extender (SDE) approach to ground cognitive translation studies.

The SDE approach to CTS aims at bringing together the several labels used to describe 4EA cognition under a common umbrella. For Alves and Jakobsen (2021b), the situated approach brings specific context and social factors into focus, the distributed approach can add a systemic view of interconnectedness at different levels and the extended approach, embracing information theory, artificial intelligence, cognitive ergonomics and human-computer interaction, among other relevant factors, accounts for intricate and complex affordances in the relationship of human beings with physical, virtual or digital artefacts. In line with Alves and Jakobsen (2021b), we consider that situated, distributed and extended aspects of cognition pertain to translational action and constitute fundamentally important pillars for CTS. We also subscribe to Alves and Jakobsen's (2021b) proposal that an SDE approach can ground CTS both epistemologically and theoretically and offer the field an opportunity to improve its internal coherence. It is also expected to advance our understanding of expertise in translation by grounding it on an epistemological basis, which is both consistent with CTS and embedded in inter/transdisciplinarity, being capable of working with and providing feedback to other disciplines which are also concerned with expertise.

Table 1.1 summarizes the main traits of disciplines related to the study of translation as a cognitive activity.

1.4 Towards an interdisciplinary framework for the study of translation as a cognitive activity

The disciplines we have approached in this chapter have a much longer-standing tradition of empirical-experimental investigation than investigations concerning the study of translation as a cognitive activity. This fact has enabled them to reach a stronger internal consensus in terms of how to approach their object of scrutiny. As Hurtado Albir and Alves (2009), Alves and Hurtado Albir (2010) and Alves and Hurtado Albir (2017) have insisted, the study of translation as a cognitive activity still lacks such a tradition and, therefore, needs to devote efforts to strengthen results both in terms of reliability and ecological validity.

TABLE 1.1 Main traits of disciplines related to the study of translation as a cognitive activity

Discipline	*Focus*	*Tendencies relevant to the study of translation as a cognitive activity*	*Key concepts relevant to the study of translation as a cognitive activity*	*Methods, techniques, instruments and tools more relevant for the study of translation as a cognitive activity*
Neuroscience	Study of neurophysiological aspects of the human brain	Cognitive neuroscience	Developmental, functional and computational aspects of the human brain	Use of tools: • Positron emission tomography • Functional magnetic resonance imaging • Functional near-infrared spectroscopy • Eletroencelography
Cognitive science	Study of the human mind and its related (cognitive) processes	• Cognitivism • Connectionism • Situated, embodied cognition	Processes of knowing: role of attention, memory, problem-solving and decision-making	Experimental studies related to memory, attention, problem-solving and decision-making
Psycholinguistics	Study of language processing	Psycholinguistic modelling	• Biological foundations of language • Auditory and visual systems • Lexical storage and retrieval • Bilingualism • General processes of comprehension and production	Experimental studies related to language processing, word recognition, reaction times and segmentation patterns

(*Continued*)

TABLE 1.1 (Continued) Main traits of disciplines related to the study of translation as a cognitive activity

Discipline	*Focus*	*Tendencies relevant to the study of translation as a cognitive activity*	*Key concepts relevant to the study of translation as a cognitive activity*	*Methods, techniques, instruments and tools more relevant for the study of translation as a cognitive activity*
Reading/writing research	Study of reading and writing processes	Cognitive (experimental) approaches to reading and writing processes	• Metacognitive activity • Attention units • Segmentation • Visual recognition • Eye fixations	• Surveys and questionnaires • Direct observation • Retrospection Use of tools: • Eye tracking • Keystroke logging
Expertise studies	Study of expert knowledge and expert performance	Expertise as an acquired skill Expert-performance approach Contributory expertise Interactional expertise	• Metacognitive activity • Deliberate practice • Consistent superior performance • Self-regulatory behaviour	• Surveys and questionnaires • Direct observation

Our current standpoint in this book is that complementarity and reciprocity should be pursued between studies of translation as a cognitive activity involving directly related disciplines such as neuroscience, cognitive science, psycholinguistics, writing and reading studies and expertise studies, as well as other indirectly related disciplines (anthropology, contact linguistics, corpus linguistics, ergonomics, human-computer interaction and linguistics – with a particular emphasis on pragmatics, pedagogy and psychology of work) so that borrowing becomes bi- or multi-directional. With the current advances in research on translation as a cognitive activity, these related areas have much to gain with closer affiliation links and probably nothing to lose in the process.

Notes

1 Some of the ideas proposed in this chapter were originally published in Alves (2015). They are expanded here to provide an updated framework for interdisciplinarity in CTS.
2 Since this book is concerned with written translation only, we refrain from commenting on the impact of neuroscience on research in interpreting. However, it is worth mentioning that there have been attempts to link neuroscience and cognitive-oriented studies of interpreting from the late 1960s to the present date.

References

Alves, F. (2015). Translation process research at the interface. Paradigmatic, theoretical, and methodological issues in dialogue with cognitive science, expertise studies, and psycholinguistics. In A. Ferreira & J.W. Schwieter (Eds.),*Psycholinguistic and cognitive inquiries into translation and interpreting* (pp. 17–40). Amsterdam: John Benjamins.
Alves, F., & Da Silva, I.A.L. (2021). Bridging paradigms to approach expertise in cognitive translation studies. In R. Muñoz Martín, S. San, & D. Li (Eds.), *Advances in cognitive translation studies* (pp. 89–108). Singapore: Springer Nature.
Alves, F., & Da Silva, I.A.L. (2022). Looking back to move forward: Towards a situated, distributed, and extended account of expertise. In S.L. Halverson & A. Marín García (Eds.), *Contesting epistemologies in cognitive translation and interpreting studies* (pp. 153–175). London: Routledge.
Alves, F., & Hurtado Albir, A. (2010). Cognitive approaches to translation. In Y. Gambier & L. van Doorslaer (Eds.), *The John Benjamins handbook of translation studies*(pp. 28–35). Amsterdam and Philadelphia: John Benjamins.
Alves, F., & Hurtado Albir, A. (2017). Evolution, challenges, and perspectives for research on cognitive aspects of translation. In J.W. Schwieter & A. Ferreira (Eds.), *The handbook of translation and cognition* (pp. 535–554). New Jersey: John Wiley & Sons, Inc.
Alves, F., Hurtado Albir, A., & Lacruz, I. (Eds.). (2015). *Translation Spaces, 4.* Special issue.
Alves, F., & Jakobsen, A.L. (Eds.). (2021a). *The Routledge handbook of translation and cognition.* London: Routledge.

Alves, F., & Jakobsen, A.L. (2021b). Grounding cognitive translation studies: Goals, commitments and challenges. In F. Alves & A.L. Jakobsen (Eds.), *The Routledge handbook of translation and cognition*(pp. 454–554). London: Routledge.
Alves, F., Pagano, A., & Da Silva, I.A.L. (2011). Modeling (un)packing of meaning in translation: Insights from effortful text production. In B. Sharb, M. Zock, M. Carl, & A.L. Jakobsen (Eds.), *Proceedings of the 8th international NLPCS workshop*(pp. 153–162). Copenhagen: Samfundslitteratur.
Alves, F., Pagano, A., & Da Silva, I.A.L. (2014). Effortful text production in translation. *Translation and Interpreting Studies*, *9*(1), 25–51.
Amiran, M.R., & Jones, B.F. (1982). Toward a new definition of readability. *Educational Psychologist*, *17*(1), 13–30.
Anderson, J.R. (1983). *The architecture of cognition*. Cambridge: Harvard University Press.
Bernston, G., & Cacioppo, J. (Eds.). (2009). *The handbook of neuroscience for the behavioral sciences* (Vol. 2). Hoboken, NJ: John Wiley & Sons, Inc.
Bertram, R., & Hyona, J. (2003). The length of a complex word modifies the role of morphological structure: Evidence from eye movements when reading short and long Finnish compounds. *Journal of Memory and Language*, *48*(3), 615–634.
Bogen, J. E., & Bogen, G. M. (1976). Wernicke's region – Where is it. *Annals of the New York Academy of Sciences*, *280*, 834–843.
Broca, P. (1861). Remarques sur le siège de la faculté de la parole articulée, suivies d'une observation d'aphémie (perte de parole). *Bulletin de la Société d'Anatomie*, *36*, 330–357.
Buchweitz, A. (2006). *Two languages, two input modalities, one brain*. Unpublished PhD Dissertation. Federal University of Santa Catarina. Florianópolis, Brazil.
Cacioppo, J.T., & Decety, J. (2011). Social neuroscience: Challenges and opportunities in the study of complex behavior. *Annals of the New York Academy of Sciences*, *1224*(1), 162–173.
Carl, M., & Dragsted, B. (2012). Inside the monitor model: Processes of default and challenged translation production. *Translation: Computation, Corpora, Cognition*, *2*(1), 127–143.
Chi, M.T.H. (2006). Two approaches to the study of experts' characteristics. In K.A. Ericsson, N. Charness, P.J. Feltovich, & R.R. Hoffman (Eds.), *The Cambridge handbook of expertise and expert performance* (pp. 21–30). Cambridge: Cambridge University Press.
Chmiel, A. (2021). Translation, psycholinguistics and cognition. In F. Alves & A.L. Jakobsen (Eds.), *The Routledge handbook of translation and cognition*(pp. 219–238). London: Routledge.
Chomsky, N. (1959). Review of Skinner's *Verbal behavior*. *Language*,*35*, 26–58.
Collins, H., & Evans, R. (2007). *Rethinking expertise*. Chicago and London: University of Chicago Press.
Da Silva, I.A.L. (2019). An interactional expertise-based approach to specialized inverse translation. *Tradução em Revista*,*26*(1), 86–98.
Da Silva, I.A.L. (2021). Translation, expert performance and cognition. In F. Alves & A.L. Jakobsen (Eds.), *The Routledge handbook of translation and cognition*(pp. 461–477). London: Routledge.
Da Silva, I.A.L., & Silveira, F.A. (2017). A expertise por interação como condicionante da competência do tradutor de textos técnicos e científicos. *Domínios de Lingu@gem*,*11*(5), 1746–1763.
Dale, E., & Chall, J.S. (1949). The concept of readability. *Elementary English*, *26*(1), 19–26.

Dam-Jensen, H., & Heine, C. (2013). Writing and translation process research: Bridging the gap (Introduction). *Journal of Writing Research*, *5*(1), 89–101.
Dancette, J. (1995). Organisation conceptuelle du domaine et structure de dictionnaire—L'exemple du commerce de détail. *TTR: traduction, terminologie, rédaction*, *8*(2), 151–174.
De Groot, A., & Christoffels, I.K. (2007). Processes and mechanisms of bilingual control: Insights from monolingual task performance extended to simultaneous interpretation. *Journal of Translation Studies*, *10*(1), 17–41.
Delisle, J. (1980). *L'analyse du discours comme méthode de traduction*. Ottawa: University of Ottawa Press. Translated into English as *Translation: An interpretive approach*. (1988). Ottawa: University of Ottawa Press.
Dole, J.A., Duffy, G.G., Roehler, L.R., & Pearson, P.D. (1991). Moving from the old to the new: Research on reading comprehension instruction. *Review of Educational Research*, *61*(2), 239–264.
Dragsted, B., & Carl, M. (2013). Towards a classification of translation styles based on eye-tracking and keylogging data. *Journal of the Writing Research*, *5*(1), 133–158.
Dronkers, N.F., Plaisant, O., Iba-Zizen, M.T., & Cabanis, E.A. (2007). Paul Broca's historic cases: High resolution MR imaging of the brains of Leborgne and Lelong. *Brain*, *130*(5), 1432–1441.
Ehrensberger-Dow, M., & Englund Dimitrova, B. (Eds.). (2016). Cognitive space: Exploring the situational interface [Special issue]. *Translation Spaces*, *5*(1). Republished in *Benjamins Current Topics*, 72(2015).
Ehrensberger-Dow, M., Göpferich, S., & O'Brien. (Eds.). (2013). Inter-disciplinarity in translation and interpreting process research. Special Issue. *Target*, *25*(1).
Ehrensberger-Dow, M., & Perrin, D. (2013). Applying a newswriting research approach to translation. *Target. International Journal of Translation Studies*, 25(1), 77–92.
Elman, J., Bates, E., Johnson, M.H., Karmiloff-Smith, A., Parisi, D., & Plunkett, K. (1996). *Rethinking innateness: A connectionist perspective on development*. Cambridge, MA: MIT Press.
Emig, J. (1971). *The composing processes of twelfth graders*. Urbana: The National Council of Teachers of English.
Ericsson, K.A. (1996). The Acquisition of expert performance: An introduction to some of the issues. In K.A. Ericsson (Ed.), *The road to excellence: The acquisition of expert performance in the arts and sciences, sports and games* (pp. 1–50). Mahwah, NJ: Lawrence Erlbaum Associates.
Ericsson, K.A. (1998). The scientific study of expert levels of performance: General implications for optimal learning and creativity. *High Ability Studies*, *9*(1), 75–100.
Ericsson, K.A. (2002). Expertise in interpreting: An expert-performance perspective. *Interpreting*, *5*(2), 187–220.
Ericsson, K.A., & Charness, N. (1994). Expert performance: Its structure and acquisition. *American Psychologist*, *49*(8), 725.
Ericsson, K.A., & Charness, N. (1997). Cognitive and developmental factors in expert performance. In P.J. Feltovich, K.M. Ford, and R. Hoffman (Eds.), *Expertise in context: Human and machine* (pp. 3–41). Cambridge: MIT Press.
Ericsson, K.A., Charness, N., Feltovich, P., & Hoffman, R.R. (Eds). (2006). *The Cambridge handbook of expertise and expert performance*. Cambridge: Cambridge University Press, second edition 2018.
Ericsson, K.A., & Crutcher, R.J. (1990). The nature of exceptional performance. In P.B. Baltes, D.L. Featherman, & R.M. Lerner (Eds.),*Lifespan development and behavior* (pp. 188–218). Hillsdale: Lawrence Erlbaum Associates.

Ericsson, K.A., Krampe, R.T., & Tesch-Römer, C. (1993). The role of deliberate practice in the acquisition of expert performance. *Psychological Review*, *100*(3), 363.

Ericsson, K.A., & Lehmann, A. (1996). Expert and exceptional performance: Evidence on maximal adaptations on task constraints. *Annual Review of Psychology*,*47*, 273–305. doi: 10.1146/annurev.psych.47.1.273

Ericsson, K.-A., & Smith, J. (1991). Prospects and limits of the empirical study of expertise: An introduction. In K.-A. Ericsson & J. Smith (Eds.), *Toward a general theory of expertise: Prospects and limits* (pp. 1–38). Cambridge: Cambridge University Press.

Ferreira, A., & Schwieter, J.W. (Eds.). (2015). *Psycholinguistic and cognitive inquiries into translation and interpreting.* Amsterdam: John Benjamins.

Flower, L., & Hayes, J. (1981). A cognitive process theory of writing. *College Composition and Communication*,*32*(4), 365–387.

Fodor, J.A. (1983). *The modularity of mind.* Cambridge, MA: MIT Press.

Frisson, S., & Pickering, M.J. (1999). The processing of metonymy: Evidence from eye movements. *Journal of Experimental Psychology: Learning, Memory, and Cognition*,*25*(6), 1366–1383.

Fry, E. (1968). A readability formula that saves time. *Journal of Reading*, *11*(7), 513–516, 575–578.

Gall, F.J. (1835). *On the functions of the brain and of each of its parts: With observations on the possibility of determining the instincts, propensities, and talents, or the moral and intellectual dispositions of men and animals, by the configuration of the brain and head* (Vol. 1). Marsh: Capen & Lyon.

Galton, F. (1869/1979). *Hereditary genius: An inquiry into its laws and consequences.* London: Julian Friedman Publishers.

Gardner, H. (1993). *Multiple intelligences. The theory in practice.* New York: Basic Books.

García, A.M. (2012). *Traductología y neurocognición: Cómo se organiza el sistema lingüístico del traductor* [Traductology and neurocognition: How the linguistic system of the translator is organized]. Córdoba: Facultad de Lenguas de la UNC.

García, A.M. (2013). Brain activity during translation: A review of the neuroimaging evidence as a testing ground for clinically based hypotheses. *Journal of Neurolinguistics*,*26*(3), 370–383.

García, A.M. (2015). Translating with an injured brain: Neurolinguistic aspects of translation as revealed by bilinguals with cerebral lesions. *Meta: Translators' Journal*,*60*(1), 112–134.

García, A.M. (2019). *The neurocognition of translation and interpreting.* Amsterdam: John Benjamins.

García, A.M., Ibáñez, A., Huepe, D., Houck, A., Michon, M., Gelormini Lezama, C., & Rivera-Rei, Á. (2014). Word reading and translation in bilinguals: The impact of formal and informal translation expertise. *Frontiers in Psychology*,*5*, 1302.

García, A.M., Mikulan, E., & Ibáñez, A. (2016). A neuroscientific toolkit for translation studies. In R. Muñoz Martín (Ed.), *Reembedding translation process research*(pp. 21–46). Amsterdam: John Benjamins.

García, A.M., & Muñoz, E. (2021). Translation, neuroscience and cognition. In F. Alves & A.L. Jakobsen (Eds.), *The Routledge handbook of translation and cognition* (pp. 239–259). London: Routledge.

Gardner, H. (1983). *Frames of mind: The theory of multiple intelligences.* New York: Basic Books.

Gardner, H. (1993). *Multiple intelligences: The theory in practice.* New York: Basic Books

Garman, M. (1990). *Psycholinguistics*. Cambridge: Cambridge University Press.
Glaser, R. (1992). Expert knowledge and processes of thinking. In D. Halpern (Ed.), *Enhancing thinking skills in the sciences and mathematics* (pp. 63–75). Hillsdale, NJ: Erlbaum.
Gray, C.T. (1917). Types of reading ability as exhibited through tests and laboratory experiments. *Supplementary Educational Monographs*, *1*(5).
Gray, W.S. (1925). Summary of reading investigations. *The Elementary School Journal*, *27*(6).
Göpferich, S. (2008). *Translationsprozessforschung: Stand – Methoden – Perspektiven*. (Translationswissenschaft 4). Tübingen: Narr.
Halverson, S.L. (2010). Cognitive translation studies: Developments in theory and methods. In G. Shreve & E. Angelone (Eds.), *Translation and cognition* (pp. 349–370). Amsterdam: John Benjamins.
Halverson, S.L. (2021). Translation, linguistic committment and cognition. In F. Alves & A.L. Jakobsen (Eds.), *The Routledge handbook of translation and cognition* (pp. 37–51). London: Routledge.
Halverson, S.L., & Marín García, A. (Eds.). (2022). *Contesting epistemologies in cognitive translation and interpreting studies*. London: Routledge.
Harris, T., & Hodges, R. (Eds.). (1995). *The literacy dictionary: The vocabulary of reading and writing*. Newark: International Reading Association.
Hebb, D.O. (1949).*The organization of behavior: A neuropsychological theory*. New York: Wiley and Sons.
House, J. (2013). Towards a new linguistic-cognitive orientation in translation studies. *Target. International Journal of Translation Studies*, *25*(1), 46–60.
Hurtado Albir, A. (1990). *La notion de fidélité en traduction*, Col. Traductologie 5. Paris: Didier Érudition.
Hurtado Albir, A., & Alves, F. (2009). Translation as a cognitive activity. In J. Munday (Ed.), *The Routledge companion to translation studies* (pp. 210–234). London: Routledge.
Hvelplund, K.T. (2011). *Allocation of cognitive resources in translation: An eye-tracking and key-logging study*. Unpublished PhD Dissertation. Copenhagen Business School, Copenhagen.
Hyönä, J., Lorch Jr, R.F., & Rinck, M. (2003). Eye movement measures to study global text processing. In R. Radach, J. Hyona, & H. Deubel (Eds.), *The mind's eye: Cognitive and applied aspects of eye movement research* (pp. 313–334). North-Holland: Elsevier.
Jääskeläinen, R. (2011). Studying the translation process. In K. Malmkjaer & K. Windle (Eds.), *The Oxford handbook of translation studies*(pp. 123–135). Oxford: Oxford University Press.
Jakobsen, A.L. (2002). Orientation, segmentation, and revision in translation. In G. Hansen (Ed.), *Empirical translation studies: Process and product*(pp. 191–204). Copenhagen Studies in Language 27. Copenhagen: Samfundslitteratur.
Jakobsen, A.L. (2005). Instances of peak performance in translation. *Lebende Sprachen*, *50*(3), 111–116.
Jakobsen, A.L. (2011). Tracking translators' keystrokes and eye movements with Translog. In C. Alvstad, A. Hild, & E. Tiselius (Eds.), *Methods and strategies of process research: Integrative approaches in translation studies*(pp. 37–55). Amsterdam: John Benjamins.
Jakobsen, A.L., & Mesa-Lao, B. (Eds.). (2017). *Translation in transition. Between cognition, computing and technology*. Benjamins Translation Library 133. Amsterdam: John Benjamins.

Juhasz, B. J., & Rayner, K. (2003). Investigating the effects of a set of intercorrelated variables on eye fixation durations in reading. *Journal of Experimental Psychology: Learning, Memory, and Cognition*,*29*(6), 1312–1318.
Just, M.A., & Carpenter, P.A. (1980). A theory of reading: From eye fixations to comprehension. *Psychological Review*, *87*(4), 329–354.
Kliegl, R., Grabner, E., Rolfs, M., & Engbert, R. (2004). Length, frequency, and predictability effects of words on eye movements in reading. *European Journal of Cognitive Psychology*, *16*(1–2), 262–284.
Lacruz, I., & Jääskeläinen, R. (Eds.). (2018). *Innovation and expansion in translation process research* (pp. 37–54). Amsterdam: John Benjamins.
Lajoie, S.P. (2003). Transitions and trajectories for the study of expertise. *Educational Researcher*, *32*(8), 21–25.
Li, D., Lei, V., & He, Y. (Eds.). (2019). *Researching cognitive processes of translation*. New Frontiers in Translation Studies Series. Singapore: Springer.
MacArthur, C.A., Graham, S., & Fitzgerald, J. (Eds.). (2008). *Handbook of writing research*. Guilford Press.
Mandler, G. (2002). Origins of the cognitive (r)evolution. *Journal of the History of the Behavioral Sciences*, *38*, 339–353.
Marín García, A. (2017). *Theoretical hedging: The scope of knowledge in translation process research*. Unpublished PhD Dissertation. Kent State University.
Marín García, A. (2019). The opportunities of epistemic pluralism for Cognitive Translation Studies. *Translation, Cognition & Behavior*, *2*(2), 147–168.
Maturana, H.R., & Varela, F.J. (1987). *The tree of knowledge. The biological roots of human understanding*. Boston, MA: New Science Library.
Miller, G.A. (1956). Human memory and the storage of information. *IRE Transactions on Information Theory*, *2*(3), 129–137.
Miller, G.A. (2003). The cognitive revolution: A historical perspective. *TRENDS in Cognitive Sciences*,*7*(3), 141–144.
Mosenthal, P.B., & Kirsch, I.S. (1998). A new measure for assessing document complexity: The PMOSE/IKIRSCH document readability formula. *Journal of Adolescent & Adult Literacy*, *41*(8), 638–657.
Moser-Mercer, B. (1997). Methodological issues in interpreting research: an introduction to the Ascona Workshops. *Interpreting*, *2*, 1–11.
Muñoz Martín, R. (2010a). Leave no stone unturned. On the development of cognitive translatology. *Journal of Translation and Interpreting Studies*, *5*(2), 145–162.
Muñoz Martín, R. (2010b). On paradigms and cognitive translatology. In G. Shreve & E. Angelone (Eds.), *Translation and cognition*(pp. 169–187). Amsterdam: John Benjamins.
Muñoz Martín, R. (Ed.). (2014). Minding translation. Con la traducción en mente. *MonTi. Monografías de Traducción e Interpretación*, Special issue 1.
Muñoz Martín, R. (2017). Looking toward the future of cognitive translation studies. In J.W. Schwieter & A. Ferreira (Eds.), *The handbook of translation and cognition* (pp. 555–572). Hoboken, NJ: John Wiley & Sons, Inc.
Muñoz Martín, R., & Halverson, S.L. (Eds.). (2021). *Multilingual mediated communication and cognition*. London: Routledge.
Muñoz Martín, R., & Martín de León, C. (2021). Translation and cognitive science. In F. Alves & A.L. Jakobsen (Eds.), *The Routledge handbook of translation and cognition* (pp. 52–68). London: Routledge.
O'Brien, S. (2013). The borrowers: researching the cognitive aspects of translation. *Target*, *25*(1), 5–17.
Ochsner, K.N., & Lieberman, M.D. (2001). The emergence of social cognitive neuroscience. *American Psychologist*, *56*(9), 717.

Pollatsek, A., & Rayner, K. (2012). Eye movements and lexical access in reading. In *Comprehension processes in reading* (pp. 165–186). London: Routledge.
Posner, M.I. (Ed.). (1989). *Foundations of cognitive science* (pp. 183–197). Cambridge, MA: MIT Press.
Radach, R., & Kennedy, A. (2004). Theoretical perspectives on eye movements in reading: Past controversies, current issues, and an agenda for future research. *European Journal of Cognitive Psychology*, *16*(1–2), 3–26.
Rayner, K. (1978). Eye movements in reading and information processing. *Psychological Bulletin*, *85*, 618–660.
Rayner, K. (1998). Eye movements in reading and information processing: 20 years of research. *Psychological Bulletin*, *124*(3), 372.
Rayner, K., & Duffy, S. A. (1986). Lexical complexity and fixation times in reading: Effects of word frequency, verb complexity, and lexical ambiguity. *Memory & Cognition*, *14*(3), 191–201.
Rayner, K., & Pollatsek, A. (1989). The psychology of reading. New Jersey: Prentice Hall.
Risku, H. (2014). Translation process research as interaction research: From mental to socio-cognitive processes. *MonTi*, 331–353. https://doi.org/10.6035/MonTI.2014.ne1.11
Risku, H., & Rogl, R. (2021). Translation and situated, embodied, distributed, embedded and extended cognition. In F. Alves & A.L. Jakobsen (Eds.), *The Routledge handbook of translation and cognition*(pp. 478–499). London: Routledge.
Risku, H., & Windhager, F. (2013). Extended translation: A sociocognitive research agenda. *Target*, *25*(1), 33–45.
Robbins, P., & Aydede, M. (2009). A short primer on situated cognition. In P. Robbins & M. Aydede (Eds.), *The Cambridge handbook of situated cognition* (pp. 3–10). Cambridge: Cambridge University Press.
Rummelhart, D.E., & McClelland, J. (1986). *Parallel distributed processing.Explorations in the microstructure of cognition.* Cambridge, MA: MIT Press.
Scardamalia, M., & Bereiter, C. (1991). Literate expertise. In K.A. Ericsson & J. Smith (Eds.), *Toward a general theory of expertise*(pp. 172–194). New York: Cambridge University Press.
Schilperoord, J. (1996). *It's about time. Temporal aspects of cognitive processes in text production.* Utrecht: Rodopi.
Schwieter, J.W., & Ferreira, A. (2017). *The handbook of translation and cognition.* Hoboken, NJ: John Wiley & Sons, Inc.
Shanahan, T., MacArthur, C.A., Graham, S., & Fitzgerald, J. (2006). Relations among oral language, reading, and writing development. In C.A. MacArthur, S. Graham, and J. Fitzgerald (Eds.). *Handbook of writing research* (pp. 171–183). New York: Guilford Press.
Shlesinger, M. (1995). Stranger in paradigms: What lies ahead for simultaneous interpreting research. *Target*, *7*(1), 7–28.
Shlesinger, M. (2000). Interpreting as a cognitive process: how can we know what really happens? In S. Tirkkonen-Condit & R. Jääskeläinen (Eds.), *Tapping and mapping the processes of translation and interpreting*(pp. 3–15). Amsterdam: John Benjamins.
Shreve, G.M. (2002). Knowing translation: Cognitive and experiential aspects of translation expertise from the perspective of expertise studies. In A. Riccardi (Ed.), *Translation studies: Perspectives on an emerging discipline* (pp. 150-171). Cambridge: Cambridge University Press.
Shreve, G.M. (2006). The deliberate practice: Translation and expertise. *Journal of Translation Studies*, *9*(1), 27–42.

Shreve, G.M., Angelone, E., & Lacruz, I. (2018). Are expertise and translation competence the same? Psychological reality and the theoretical status of competence. In I. Lacruz & R. Jääskeläinen (Eds.), *Innovation and expansion in translation process research* (pp. 37–54). Amsterdam: John Benjamins.
Skinner, B.F. (1957). *Verbal behavior*. New York: Appleton-Century-Crofts.
Spache, G. (1953). A new readability formula for primary-grade reading materials. *The Elementary School Journal*, *53*(7), 410–413.
Sturm, A. (2016). *On the role of metacognitive proficiency in translation. Investigating the role of theory of mind in translation in terms of neural substrates, process and product data*. Unpublished PhD Dissertation. University of Geneva, Geneva.
Szpak, K.S. (2017). *A atribuição de estados mentais em atividades de Tradução: Um estudo conduzido com rastreamento ocular e ressonância magnética funcional* [The attribution of mental states in translation activities: A study carried out with eye tracking and functional magnetic resonance]. Unpublished PhD Dissertation. Federal University of Minas Gerais, Belo Horizonte, Brazil.
Szpak, K.S., Alves, F., & Buchweitz, A. (2021). Perspective taking in translation. In search of neural correlates of representing and attributing mental states to others. In R. Muñoz & S. Halverson (Eds.), *Multilingual mediated communication and cognition* (pp. 133–154). London: Routledge.
Tiselius, E. (2013a). *Same, same but different? Competence and expertise in translation and interpreting studies* (Trial Lecture for the Doctoral Degree). University of Bergen, Bergen, Norway.
Tiselius, E. (2013b). *Experience and expertise in conference interpreting* (Unpublished PhD Dissertation). University of Bergen, Bergen, Norway.
Tymoczko, M. (2012). The neuroscience of translation. *Target*, *24*(1), 83–102.
Varela, F.J., Thompson, E., & Rosch, E. (1991). *The embodied mind: Cognitive science and human experience*. Cambridge, MA: MIT Press.
Wang, M.T., & Eccles, J.S. (2013). School context, achievement motivation, and academic engagement: A longitudinal study of school engagement using a multidimensional perspective. *Learning and Instruction*, *28*, 12–23.
Watson, J.B. (1917). An Attempted formulation of the scope of behavior psychology. *Psychological Review*, *24*(5), 329.
Wernicke, C. (1874). *Der aphasische Symptomencomplex: eine psychologische Studie auf anatomischer Basis*. Cohn.
Wheeler, M. (2005). *Reconstructing the cognitive world: The next step*. Massachusetts, MA: MIT Press.

2

THE TRANSLATION PROCESS

This chapter presents an overview of research on the translation process. First, it discusses the notion of translation processes and traces the evolution of in modelling from the 1990s to the present, describing the most representative models of the translation process. It also outlines the conceptual development of research, discussing the different approaches used and highlighting the main characteristics of the translation process.

Introduction

The term *translation process* predominantly refers to the cognitive operations implemented during the execution of a translation task in real time by an individual. Over the past decades, such processes have been mapped by means of empirical-experimental research that mostly uses non-invasive tools to investigate aspects of cognitive processing performed by human subjects. However, as we shall see, this is not the only perspective found in the literature. In order to present an overview of research on the translation process carried out since the mid-1960s, this chapter builds on Hurtado Albir (2001/2011, pp. 311–375) and Hurtado Albir and Alves (2009) to account for the notion of the translation process, introduce and describe models of the translation process, discuss the disparate approaches used in their modelling and highlight the main characteristics of the translation process.

2.1 On the notion of translation processes

2.1.1 Non-cognitive approaches of the translation process

First, it is important to note that the *translation process* is not always understood as a study of the translator's mental processes. Sometimes, the term *translation process* is used to discuss issues surrounding the communicative aspects entailed in the act of translation. When this happens, the *actors* who participate in the *translation process* are described, pointing to the different subjects involved in the translation act, such as the original sender, the commissioner, the recipient of translation and so on.

DOI: 10.4324/9781003006978-3

The term *translation process* has also been used to refer to the operations performed by translators, including analysis and synthesis, without going into detail with respect to the mental processes implicated in the process. It has also been identified with the working phases of a professional translator.

Some of the descriptions of the *translation process* are anchored in linguistic approaches. This is the case of the work of Vázquez Ayora (1977) inspired by generative and transformational grammar. Vázquez Ayora (1977, p. 50) describes the process followed by the translator using the following words:

> The translation procedure consists in analysing the expression of the text in the original language in pre-nuclear sentences, in transferring the original pre-nuclear sentences into equivalent pre-nuclear sentences in the target language and, ultimately, in transforming these structures in the target language in expressions which are stylistically appropriate.[1]
>
> *[our translation]*

Vázquez Ayora's model applies generative-transformational grammar to analyse the translation process, distinguishing three levels (conceptual, nuclear and pre-nuclear), and three phases (reduction, transfer and restructuring).

Another approach also anchored in linguistics was presented by Garnier (1985), who proposed a psycho-systematic or psycho-mechanic model, based on the theories of the grammarian Guillaume (1971a, 1971b, 1973). Garnier considers the *translation process* as an activity involving recognition and defined as minimum extraction of semantic elements.

Other authors have focused on semiotic, hermeneutical and communicative aspects to discuss the *translation process*. Among these, the model proposed by Ljduskanov (1969), inspired by semiotics, conceives of translation as a process geared to the transformation of signs and sees the *translation process* as an act of extraction and reproduction of information. Ljduskanov (1969) seeks algorithms that can be used for human translation and machine translation and argues that translation theory should be considered a branch of general semiotics.

Steiner (1975) considers translation to be a transformational process and proposes a hermeneutic model of the translation process with four stages, namely, trust (a profession of faith, i.e. a stage consisting of an operating contract, which relies on prior experience), aggression (a stage of incursion and extraction), incorporation (a stage in which the translator imports semantics and formal language features within an infinite range of assimilation) and compensation (a stage to restore balance).

Nida (1964) builds on information theory and uses the terms coding, encoding and decoding to conceptualize the *translation process*. Nida postulates a three-stage process including analysis, transfer and synthesis. The phase of analysis includes grammatical, semantic and connotative aspects. During transfer, priority is given to content while structures and vocabulary are changed. Finally, there is a stage of synthesis or restructuring, which is stylistically oriented. Nida (1964, p. 146) explains this model with the following words:

> In this model, a message in a language A is decoded by the receiver to a different form of language A. A "transfer mechanism" transforms that input into a language B, and then the translator becomes the starting point for the encoding of the message into the language B.

Differently from Nida, several other authors have used the terms decoding and encoding to refer to the phases of the translation process. This is the case of Benard and Horguelin (1979), who postulate a two-stage process: decoding (a stage that includes analysis and understanding) and encoding (a stage that concerns semantic transfer, restructuring and verification).

Some other authors focus on identifying the components of the translation act, namely the sender of the source language, the recipient of the source language text in the source language, the translator, the translation, the translation receiver and so on. This is the case of Levy (1967), Diller and Kornelius (1978), Stein (1980) and Hönig and Kussmaul (1982), among others.

From another angle, Nord (1988) differentiates between two distinct yet complementary notions using the German terms *Übersetzungsvorgang* and *Übersetzungsprozeß*, which are synonymous with the English term "translation process". She refers to a type of translation process (*Übersetzungsprozeß*) that is an integral part of the main translation process (*Übersetzungsvorgang*). According to Nord (1988, p. 283), these two terms are not to be confused with the psycholinguistic notion of the translation process. She tries to clarify these differences by stating that

> I differentiate between the process of translation [*Übersetzungsvorgang*] and the translation process [*Übersetzungsprozeß*]. The translation "process" [*Übersetzungsprozeß*] is to be understood as the part of the process of translation [*Übersetzungsvorgang*] in which the translator creates a target text suitable for a specific purpose for a source text considering certain specifications, while other translation-independent factors play a role in the translation process. The term process used here is not to be confused with the psycholinguistic process term introduced into translation studies by KRINGS (1986) in particular.[2]
>
> *[our translation]*

The work of Nord (1988/1991) also deserves a special mention when she speaks of a *circular (looping) process* of translation that begins with the analysis of the translation *skopos* and consists of the following stages: analysis of the source text (and compatibility with *skopos* in terms of a detailed textual and extra-textual analysis), consideration of the relevant elements of the original for translation, transfer, synthesis and restructuring.

Still, other authors describe phases of the work carried out by professional translators. For example, Larson (1984) speaks of eight steps of translation in a translation project: preparation, analysis, transfer, first draft, revision of the first draft, final revision, refinement and preparation of the final manuscript. Gouadec (2005) organizes the translator's work into four phases of interventions; each phase including, in turn, various stages, operations and tasks. This four-phase process entails a prospective phase (previous interventions before providing a translation); a pre-translation phase (prior to the implementation of interventions in the act of translation); a translation phase (linked to the implementation of the translation, which includes pre-transfer, transfer and post-transfer); and a post-translation phase (after providing the translation). In a later work, Gouadec (2007) distinguishes a total of 156 potential sequences of operations performed in a situation of translation.

Finally, we would like to mention a distinction between the *translation process* and *translation procedures*, put forward by scholars in comparative stylistics, which entails procedures such as borrowing, calque, literal translation, transposition and so on. In our view, *translation procedures*, as conceived of by comparative stylistics, do not explain how the translator proceeds to carry out the *translation process*. As stated by Hurtado Albir (1999, p. 18; 2001, p. 314), it refers to the results of visible solutions that respond to different ways through which languages can be instantiated (and not the text). Therefore, translation procedures do not affect the *translation process* per se but have an impact on the result of the translation, thus representing a decontextualized catalogue of equivalences between language pairs.

As shown above, all these proposals can be classified as non-cognitive approaches and look at the *translation process* from disparate angles.

2.1.2 First cognitive approaches of the translation process

Since the late 1960s, however, there has been a concern in translation studies to discuss the mental process carried out by translators to produce their target texts.

Seleskovitch's (1968/1978) work entitled *L'interprète dans les conférences internationales* (*Interpreting for International Conferences*) presents a descriptive study of conference interpreting and highlights the importance of analysing the translation process to understand the act of translation/interpreting. The goal of Seleskovitch in her 1968 book was "to shed light on the mental process that make possible the virtually instantaneous transmission of an oral message into another language." (Seleskovitch, 1978, p. 9).[3]

In her work, Seleskovitch presents a first-time analysis of the process of interpretation and provides findings to open new avenues to carry out descriptive research in translation, "a great deal of scientific research and painstaking analysis will have to be done, especially on the relationship between thought and language, before a comprehensive theory can be established" (Seleskovitch, 1978, p. 146).[4]

Thirty years after Seleskovitch's first attempt, Bell (1998, p. 185) noted that

> At its simplest, translation involves the transfer of meaning from a text in one language into a text in another. This transfer constitutes a mental process which relies on sophisticated information processing skills. Since all human communication relies on the ability to process information, psycholinguistic studies of translation essentially set out to establish how translators and interpreters process information, both as distinct from other speakers and writers and as distinct from each other.
>
> *(Bell, 1998, p. 185).*

In this chapter, it is our goal to look back in time and present a detailed picture of the evolution of research about the translation process in conceptual terms, providing a concise description of 16 models that we consider to be most representative of this evolution, highlighting the approaches used and the main characteristics of these different models of the translation process.

2.2 On the evolution of investigations of the translation process

As we shall see, the evolution of investigations about the translation process can be mapped onto three distinct yet interrelated phases. In the first phase, from the late 1960s to the late 1980s, there is just a major school of thought around the interpretive theory of translation (Seleskovitch, 1968; Seleskovitch & Lederer, 1984, etc.) (see Table 2.1).

From the late 1980s to the mid-1990s, a second phase in the investigation of the translation process gave rise to a series of cognitive models of the translation process (Krings, 1986; Königs, 1987; Wilss, 1988; Bell, 1991; Gutt, 1991; Hönig, 1991; Lörscher, 1991; Alves, 1995; Kiraly, 1995). These models were developed practically in sequence to one another; portraying the translation process, mostly in flow charts, from disparate perspectives, as a special type of information processing. Most of these models have drawn on think-aloud protocols to provide evidence of their claims. We consider that these two first phases have contributed significantly to the conceptual development of translation process research.

In the third phase, models of the translation process have built on previous modelling to propose new models which carried with them hypotheses

TABLE 2.1 Evolution of research on the cognitive nature of the translation process

Phase 1: From the late 1960s to the late 1980s	Focus on the interpretive theory of translation – Seleskovitch (1968, 1975, etc.), Lederer (1981, 1994/2006, etc.), Seleskovitch and Lederer (1984/2001, etc.), Delisle (1980/1988), Hurtado Albir (1990)
Phase 2: From the late 1980s to the mid-1990s	Focus on information processing, strategies, problem-solving, decision-making and interpretive resemblance – Krings (1986), Königs (1987), Wilss (1988, 1996), Bell (1991), Gutt (1991/2000), Hönig (1991, 1998), Lörscher (1991), Alves (1995), Kiraly (1995)
Phase 3: From the mid-2000s to the late 2010s	Focus on the notion of default translation, computational modelling and post-editing – Tirkkonen-Condit (2005), Halverson (2003, 2010, 2017), Jakobsen (2011), Schaeffer and Carl (2013), Carl and Schaeffer (2017a, 2019)

that could be verified empirically. We have chosen to discuss the models developed by Tirkkonen-Condit (2005), Halverson (2003, 2010, 2017), Jakobsen (2011), Schaeffer and Carl (2013) and Carl and Schaeffer (2017a, 2019) as the most representative models of this third phase.

In a nutshell, from the mid-1980s to the present day, a series of empirical-experimental studies have been carried out, focusing on particular traits of the translation process (translation units, segmentation patterns, cognitive rhythm, phases of the translation process, etc.). These studies constitute a bulk of information in the evolution of the investigation. They have benefited from advances in the methodology of translation process research, which has incorporated the think-aloud protocols used in the second phase as well as new tools for data collection such as keylogging, eye tracking and more recently EEG, fMRI and fNIRS. We shall refer to these studies in detail in Chapter 4.

2.3 Models of the translation process

In this section, our goal is to introduce the most representative models of the translation process that approach it in light of the cognitive operations implemented in real time during the unfolding of a translation task by an individual or by a group of individuals. Thus, we describe what we consider to be the 16 most representative models of the translation process designed under a cognitive-oriented framework. These models were conceived by Seleskovitch and Lederer, Krings, Königs, Wilss, Bell, Gutt, Hönig, Lörscher, Alves, Kiraly, Tirkkonen-Condit, Halverson, Jakobsen, Schaeffer and Carl as well as Carl and Schaeffer. They are presented in chronological order in the following subsections, considering the publication date of their first presentation.

2.3.1 Seleskovitch and Lederer's interpretive theory of translation

The theory of sense or the interpretive theory of translation (ITT) is a pioneering attempt in the cognitive-oriented study of translation. ITT was developed at the *École Supérieure d'Interprètes et de Traducteurs* (ESIT) in Paris by Seleskovitch and Lederer (see especially Seleskovitch, 1968, 1975; Lederer, 1981, 1994; Seleskovitch & Lederer, 1984, 1989). Seleskovitch and Lederer based their work on an analysis of interpreters' performance and focused on the study of the interpreting process to develop a theory of translation with a phenomenological basis. ITT does not focus on a description and comparison between languages – the hegemonic paradigm in the 1960s/1970s. Instead, it offers an analysis of the cognitive processes entailed in the act of translation/interpreting to provide a cognitive-oriented account of translation. Two essential aspects play a fundamental role in ITT: (1) the fact that the translator reproduces the meaning conveyed by the source text and not the source language and (2) the whole process of meaning construal is always an interpretation.

2.3.1.1 The beginnings of a theory: The interpreter at international conferences

ITT's beginning as a theory of meaning can be traced back to Seleskovitch's first work, published in 1968, *L'interprète dans les conférences internationales – Problèmes de langage et de communication* (*Interpreting for International Conferences – Problems of language and communication [1978]*). This work, based on intuition and professional experience in conference interpreting, outlines the general ideas that would be developed later in various publications. Thus, Seleskovitch started a long history of reflection on the translation process that offered a significant change of perspective in relation to the strictly linguistic-oriented and comparative works that prevailed at that point in time. As indicated by Laplace (1994, p. 184), Seleskovitch provided evidence grounded on experience: the interpreter does not translate words but rather formulates in the other language the sense s/he has understood. The observation of interpreters' practice provided evidence for this assertion and has raised the question about the nature of sense and the process of sense construal. Thus, according to Laplace (1994, p. 184), Seleskovitch provides the outline of a phenomenology of translation and interpretation.

The work of Seleskovitch (1968) places interpretation within the scope of human communication, diminishing the role played by linguistic factors in the process. In this pioneering study, Seleskovitch describes the process of translation and interpretation (consecutive and simultaneous) in three phases: understanding, deverbalization and re-expression. The intermediate phase, known as deverbalization, has a non-verbal character that would be developed in future studies and was one of the strongest points of contention in ITT. An important element in every act of understanding, which would be developed in subsequent studies, is the role of memory. Seleskovitch emphasizes that understanding is inseparable from the retention of sense and it is automatically stored in memory. These ideas would be developed by Seleskovitch and Lederer in further works. Overall, an evolution of the essential concepts is intrinsically coupled to ITT's terminology.[5]

2.3.1.2 Translation and language: Language mechanisms viewed through translation

Laplace (1994) rightly points out that Seleskovitch's work steers clearly away from contemporary linguistic trends of the late 1960s, such as distributionalism, structuralism, glossematics, generative linguistics and so on. Seleskovitch's rejection of a purely oriented linguistic analysis is determined by a conception of translation as a discursive act and by an interest in the cognitive mechanisms that govern it. Thus, taking translation as a point of departure, her work is grounded on a reflection on language from a discursive perspective. Seleskovitch and Lederer consider simultaneous interpretation to be a paradigm case for the postulation of a theory of translation since simultaneous interpretation is an act of understanding and re-expression that takes place at the normal rate of speech production with all important elements involved in the process: the speaker, the interpreter, the audience and the communicative situation. Besides, interpretation and translation offer prime examples concerning the analysis of language mechanisms because they are linked to two fundamental processes: comprehension and expression. Thus, translation is not only subject to the operation of language mechanisms but it is also, at the same time, indicative of that operation. The unprecedented nature of equivalence in translation highlights the difference between language itself and language in use. Additionally, translation also shows that all discourse consists of units of sense that are associated with meanings (*signifiés*) contained in a visual or auditory chain (Seleskovitch & Lederer, 1984, p. 308).

In their work, Seleskovitch and Lederer have developed a conception of language as a means of communication and expression of every culture, a consideration of the dynamics of language that characterize the relationship between thought and linguistic expression.

2.3.1.3 Translating: An interpretive process in three phases

ITT conceives of the translation process as a communicative act related to the processes of comprehension and expression in monolingual communication.

Unlike other models that describe only two stages in the translation process, comprehension and re-expression, Seleskovitch and Lederer's model distinguishes three phases: understanding, deverbalization and re-expression.

Understanding: An interpretive sense-making process

According to ITT, experience in translation and interpretation shows that linguistic knowledge is not enough to understand the original text; it is necessary to incorporate a sum of knowledge: cognitive inputs (*compléments cognitifs*). These cognitive inputs are composed of encyclopaedic knowledge (*bagage cognitif*), the general knowledge of the subject, and contextual knowledge (*contexte cognitif*), i.e. mnemonic storage that builds up from the beginning of the understanding of a text.

Seleskovitch and Lederer emphasize the role of memory in the process of understanding (see Figure 2.1). This process involves an immediate memory,

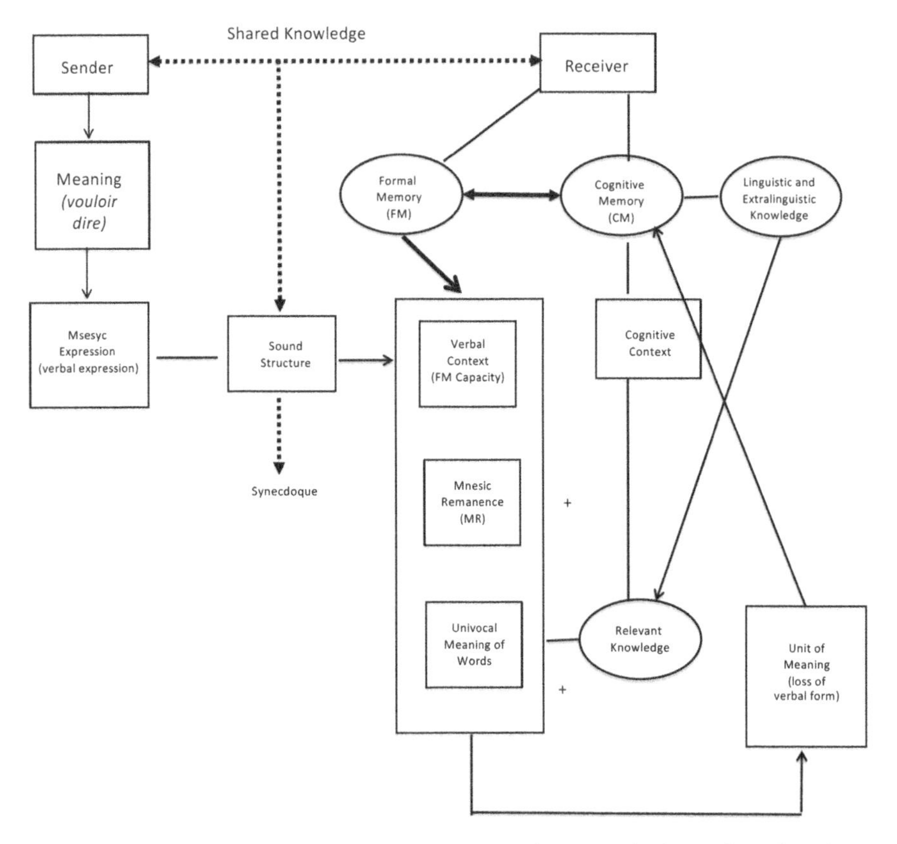

FIGURE 2.1 The process of understanding according to Seleskovitch and Lederer (Hurtado Albir, 1990, p. 57; Hurtado Albir, 2001/2011, p. 325 – our translation into English)

which retains the words for a few moments, and also a cognitive memory, which stores the set of knowledge available to individuals. There is a medium-term cognitive memory, which retains the deverbalized units that make up the cognitive context, and a cognitive long-term memory, which retains the body of knowledge acquired by individuals. During the process of understanding, memory activates the relevant linguistic and extra-linguistic knowledge needed to understand a text. Immediate memory retains sensory perceptions during the time needed for them to be identified and integrated into prior knowledge (holding capacity in adults is seven to eight words and lasting two to three seconds).

The synthesis between the semantics of an utterance and the activated knowledge produces a "state of consciousness" that is sense. This synthesis indicates the moment that understanding arises and establishes a unit of sense. Sense is the product of the mental process of understanding. It is conceived as a totality in which there is an interdependence of all elements, linguistic and extra-linguistics, that intervene in human communication (linguistic structures, cognitive inputs, etc.).

The interpretive process related to understanding generates a special type of effect that Lederer (1976, 1981) called the synecdochic effect (*effet de synecdoque*). The receiver always uses his/her knowledge to enhance the input provided by the sender. Thus, the material form of the statement is an indication rather than a description. This involves an important element: shared knowledge *(savoir partagé)* among the partners involved in the process.

Through understanding, interpreters and translators differ from normal receptors in terms of their behaviour. For them, understanding is a deliberate act, being more analytical and geared entirely to sense construal that entails the intended meaning *(vouloir dire)* conveyed by the sender of the original text. Intended meaning is the pre-verbal origin of language input; the genesis of sense comes from the sender.

Deverbalization: The non-verbal nature of sense

Seleskovitch and Lederer claim that sense is to be considered the result of understanding and has a non-verbal character. Thus, the authors define sense as a "cognitive memory". Deverbalization is the product of the phase of understanding and the beginning of the phase of re-expression. Therefore, meaning is a non-verbal synthesis resulting from the process of understanding an individual and has its locus in deverbalization. In ITT, the dissociation between linguistic form and sense is essential because it explains that the process of transfer from one language to another is affected by non-verbal sense and not by words. Central concepts for ITT are deverbalization and awareness of sense, and not linguistic awareness. Lederer highlights the importance of these concepts:

> It can be said that every act of understanding entails an awareness that persists dissociated from the stimuli that have given rise to it. The dissociation of form and sense is, in our view, the essential mechanism of language. It is present in all circumstances of human communication: forms fade and disappear, while the contents activated by the signal are associated with past memories and constitute countless meta-circuits of disparate duration, some of which are integrated into the encyclopaedic knowledge and become a part of the knowledge of the individual.[6]
>
> *(Lederer, 1981, p. 15) [our translation]*

These statements are based on Piaget's developmental psychology and on studies carried out in experimental neuropsychology, especially in the works of Barbizet (1964, 1966).

Re-expression: From intended meaning (*vouloir dire*) to linguistic formulation

Similar to what occurs in the act of understanding, re-expression mobilizes the subject's entire cognitive apparatus, resulting from an amalgamation of linguistic and extra-linguistic knowledge. The phase of re-expression in the translation process is a non-linear movement from a non-verbal level (deverbalization) to verbalization in a natural language and assimilated to the process of expression in monolingual communication – from intended meaning to linguistic expression. In any process of expression, there is a wish to communicate (intended meaning) that consciously mobilizes the necessary means of linguistic expression for its transmission. Intended meaning is a pre-verbal state of consciousness that activates speech acts; representing for the sender (speaker, writer) what is sense for the receiver. This is the origin of sense. In translation, intended meaning is the point of reference for translators/interpreters to re-express it in another language.

2.3.1.4 Written translation. The dual interpretation of the translation process: The phase of verification

In written translation, the translator, as well as the interpreter does, must understand the original text to express the same meaning in another language. The basic stages of the written translation process are the same: understanding, deverbalization and re-expression. Delisle (1980, pp. 69–86) notes that the understanding of the original text through reading is an interpretive process in itself and constitutes a process of sense construction. To grasp the sense of an original text, the translator, as well as the interpreter does, has to mobilize the entire set of cognitive inputs available to him/her. Once sense is grasped, the translator proceeds to re-express it in another language. As Delisle points out, re-expression is an analogic process of exploring the target language.

The graphic representation of the process of written translation, as proposed by Delisle, is displayed in Figure 2.2.

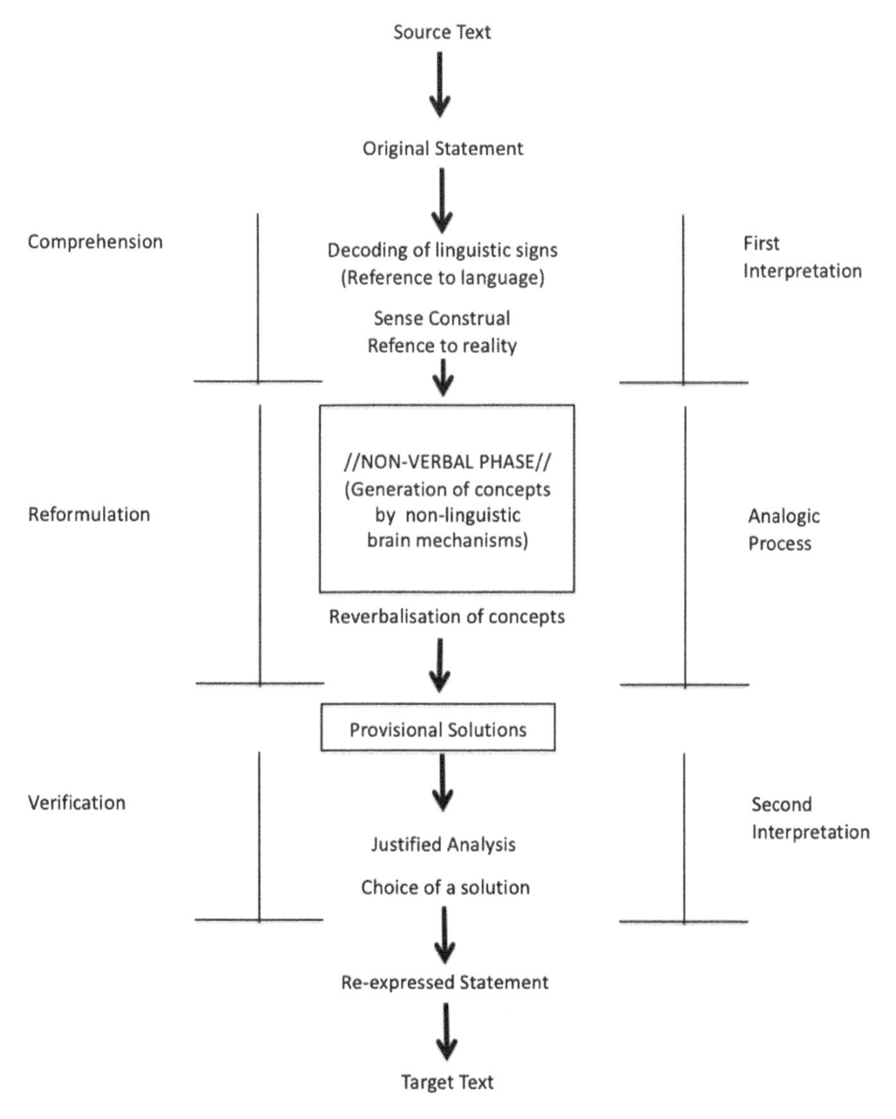

FIGURE 2.2 Delisle's heuristic process of translation

(Delisle, 1988, p. 69)[7]

Delisle also adds one last phase to the translation process which he considers to be a particular cognitive process pertaining to the process of written translation. Delisle calls this additional process a phase of verification (*analyse justificative*), namely, a phase of supporting analysis and verification, which aims to verify the accuracy of the provisional solutions found by the translators. A phase of verification is needed to ensure that the provisional solutions found in the process perfectly express the sense of the original text in the form of a new linguistic statement. Therefore, in the case of written translation, Delisle speaks of a double interpretation process.

2.3.1.5 Interpretive translation vs. correspondence (transcoding)

The interpretive nature of translation is part of a process that Lederer and Seleskovitch classify as a triangular process: signs – a non-verbal stage – reverbalization. They differentiate interpretive translation from the process of translating between languages, which they called transcoding; from 1986 onwards, Seleskovitch and Lederer started using the term correspondence, as opposed to sense equivalence. Correspondence refers to decontextualized equivalences that preserve in the target text the meaning they have at the linguistic level. Therefore, there is a difference between interpretive translation, which occurs between texts, and correspondence, which occurs between linguistic elements (words, phrases, idioms, etc.). For Seleskovitch and Lederer, sense equivalence is reserved for cases of interpretive translation only. Interpretive translation and correspondence require different processes. Every act of translation is a mixture of a coherent re-expression of textual content and the correspondence of some of its elements. However, priority is always given to interpretive translation which accounts for sense equivalence.

2.3.2 Krings's model of problem identification and translation strategies

Using think-aloud data from German university students who were advanced learners of French, Krings (1986) ushered a new trend in translation studies by conceiving of translation as a problem-solving operation that could be portrayed in a flow chart model determined by instances of yes/no decisions that would lead to the implementation of a given number of strategies. Krings innovated by using think-aloud protocols to record the translation process of translations into a second language of a simple newspaper article about a mouse in a railway dining car. Contrary to what was the norm at that time, he was not interested in the target texts but rather in the process that led to their production.

Krings's (1986) model is considered to lay the foundational stone for the development of a new phase in translation process research and is often referred to as the seminal work in modelling the translation process from an empirical perspective. The central element in the model is the concept of strategy, which is subdivided into equivalence strategies, detection strategies, evaluation strategies, reception strategies and reduction strategies.

The graphic representation of the model of the translation process proposed by Krings is displayed in Figure 2.3.

Drawing on the information-processing paradigm, Krings's model starts with a yes/no question concerning the existence of a translation problem. If there is no problem at all, a source text item would be transferred directly into a target text. If there is a translation problem, it can be identified as either a pure rendering problem, a reception problem or a reception and rendering problem.[8] Pure rendering problems will be dealt with by means of equivalence strategies, detection strategies or evaluation strategies. Once solved, translations can be rendered into a target text. Reception problems will be dealt with in two different ways: when the use of external resources (UER) is necessary or possible and when UER is unnecessary or not possible. If UER is necessary and possible, then a series of substrategies may be employed, including filter and choice strategies. If UER is unnecessary or not possible, the problem will require inferential strategies, including the use of complete meaning hypotheses or partial meaning hypotheses. If the reception problem is solved, the source text item can be rendered into the rendering problem part of the model and the relevant strategies should be applied. If, however, the reception problem cannot be solved, the source language item should be subject to reduction strategies that entail either discarding that particular item or formulating a new translation problem. The process is cyclical in nature and would unfold sequentially until the complete set of source language items is processed to give rise to a given target text.

One might say that Krings (1986) pointed to characteristics of the process of foreign language learners rather than actions performed by translators. His subjects were not translation students and showed traces of learner's patterns when, for instance, they tended to take the first choice of dictionary equivalents in cases where more than one equivalent was offered, showing shallow strategic patterns. In terms of monitoring processes, Krings observed what he called the "spot-the-difference strategy". In other words, when his subjects did not find a match between individual target-language items and source-language items, they tended to reject the item, usually without taking the context into account.

Criticisms raised against Krings's model (see Kussmaul & Tirkkonen-Condit, 1995) for a review of first-generation models of the translation process) concern the fact that his subjects were not undergoing a translator's

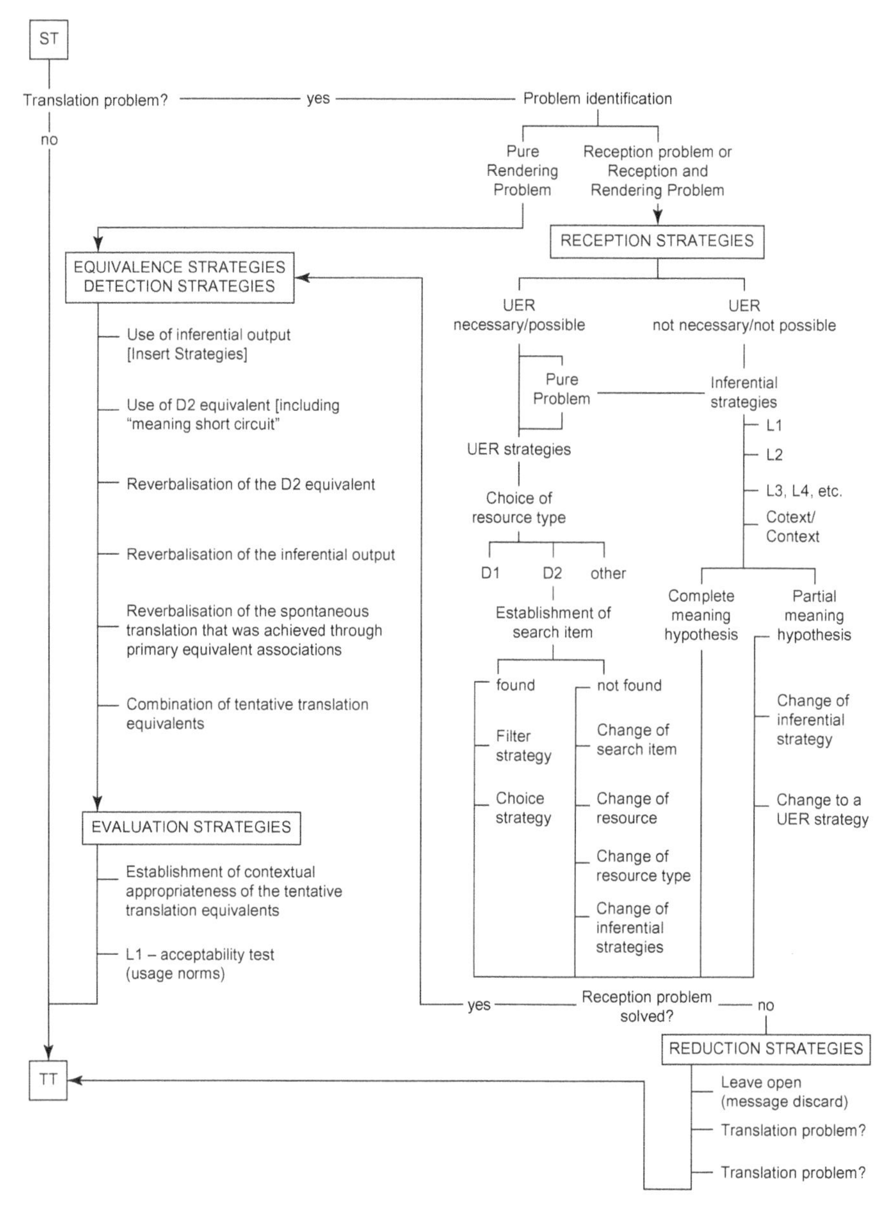

FIGURE 2.3 Krings's model of the translation process

(Krings, 1986, p. 480 – our translation into English)

training program and matters related to translation studies were not part of their academic background. Nevertheless, Krings was able to point to relevant patterns, including low metacognitive skills, low language awareness and lack of monitoring strategies. All these issues were later taken on board for furthering translation process research and giving rise to other models of the translation process.

2.3.3 Königs's Adhoc Block and Rest Block model of the translation process

Using think-aloud data from foreign language students translating from Spanish into German, Königs (1987) proposed a three-step model involving automatic and reflexive processes. In a similar fashion to Krings's model of pure lexical problems, for Königs (1987), automatic processes would be part of the so-called *Adhoc Block* while reflexive processes would occur in the so-called *Rest Block*.

Königs argues that translation takes place because a source language (L1) item must be translated as a target language (L2) item. However, this basic assumption is only a small part of the story. In fact, investigating the translation process is a matter of determining what actually happens mentally in the translator's mind from the time of the source-language text reception to the completion of the target text in an attempt to model related cognitive processes.

The fundamental differences between the *Adhoc Block* and the *Rest Block* were first introduced by Königs (1981). "In the *Adhoc Block*, the translator assigns a target language equivalent to a source language unit more or less automatically and activates an individual, mental 1:1 equivalence".[9] In contrast, the *Rest Block* contains individual translation problems that cannot be assigned to the *Adhoc Block* by the translator. First, the *Rest Block*

> does not provide an internalised or spontaneous 1:1 equivalence between the source and target language. Secondly the Rest Block includes information about the text environment (author, addressee, intention). Thirdly, the specific translator's competence, i.e. the targeted use of certain translation techniques, has its place here.[10]
>
> *(Königs, 1987, p. 164)*

To develop his model, Königs referred to earlier considerations introduced in Königs (1981) and, in particular, to a study which showed that translation units were to be defined predominantly individually. He used think-aloud protocols to record the translation processes of five subjects and analyse their problem-solving and decision-making strategies. The aim of this analysis was to describe how these participants subdivided the source text into translation units in the ad hoc and rest blocks in order to shape their target texts from a process-oriented perspective.

According to Königs, a default procedure in the translation process would be a search for equivalences between source and target text segments, which takes place in the *Adhoc Block*. Most of the time, such equivalences stem from previously made decisions and are processed automatically by translators. Königs also mentions that, given their automatic nature, such equivalences are not likely to be reassessed by translators and, thus, are not prone to be revised. As a second step, Königs argues that, whenever the default procedure fails to be implemented, translators resort to the *Rest Block* where searches for external support would be used to supplement the process of internal support in an interactive process related to problem-solving and decision-making mechanisms. As a third step, Königs postulated a separate block where interim decisions would be stored. Once a translation draft had been produced, translators would improve their work by means of revisions of different degrees and kinds (see Figure 2.4).

The results of Königs's study (1987) undoubtedly had a strong influence on the development of translation process research. Although the model was empirically validated by small-scale empirical think-aloud data from

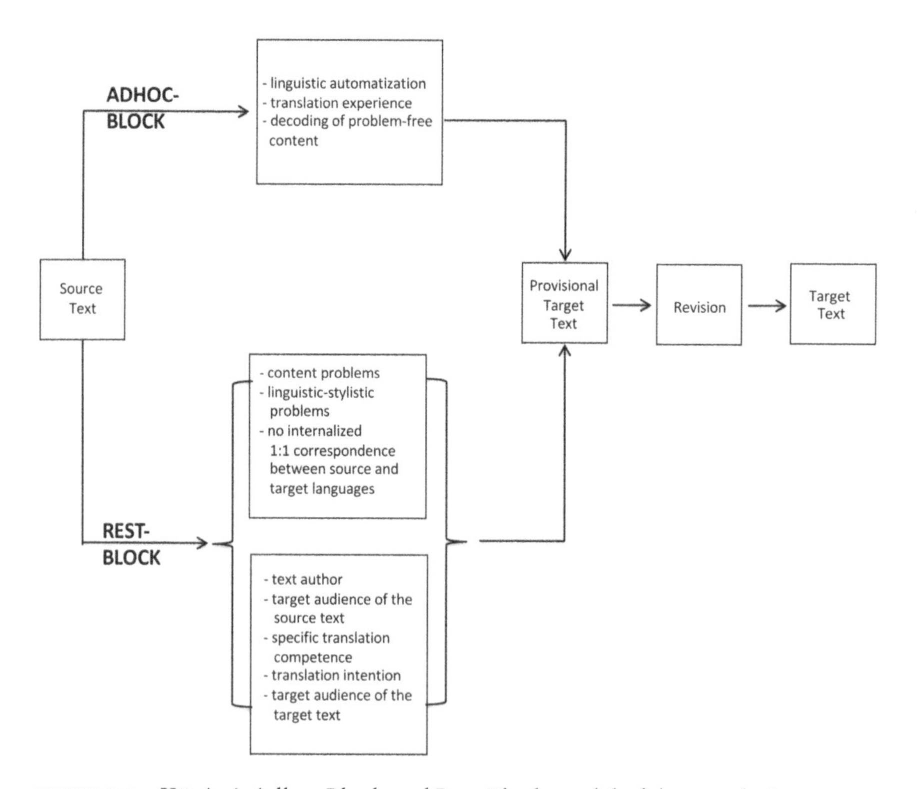

FIGURE 2.4 Königs's Adhoc Block and Rest Block model of the translation process (Königs, 1987, p. 165 – our translation into English)

foreign language students, it paved the way for a larger study carried out by Alves (1995). Königs's model also contributed to the development of considerations within the framework of translation didactics, carried out by Alves (1997, 2000), arguing that it should be of interest to combine research about mental processes and elements of translator's training, assuming that empirically inductive research on awareness raising is needed to open up new perspectives for translation didactics. Alves (2015) discusses the impact of Königs's model over three decades.

2.3.4 Hönig's model of mental schemes, expectations and beliefs

Alongside his academic career, Hönig carried out several experiments with translation students, assessing their performance during the translation of several informative texts by means of think-aloud protocol data. These studies allowed Hönig (1988a, 1988b) to describe a series of the behavioural patterns observed among his subjects and led him to propose a model of the translation process (Hönig, 1986, 1988a, 1988b, 1991, 1995, 1998). The instantiation of the model is triggered by real communicative situations and, as such, they constitute the environment in which the source text is to be situated (see Figure 2.5).

For Hönig, the reception of the source text leads the translator to make a mental projection of the text in his/her memory. Such a projection is influenced by two distinct categories of cognitive processing: mental schemes about the macro structure of the source text and the expectations and beliefs about what the target text should look like. The interaction of several cognitive processes within these two categories (schematics of the macro structure of the source text and expectations and beliefs about the target text) leads to the creation of a macro strategy that will guide the translation process and ultimately account for translation task execution. Hönig's model is organized around macro and micro strategies and controlled and non-controlled workspaces.

According to Hönig (1998), the creation of a macro strategy marks the beginning of the translation process. The main objective of a macro strategy is to reflect the translation task and allow translators to be aware of issues related to the target audience and the goals of the translation. It includes the subject of the translation and the translator's knowledge about it, even before the translator moves on to deal with linguistic and world-knowledge issues. Together, these issues can give rise to certain translation strategies such as the use of external support and strategies of transposition, among others, that are constantly monitored through a specific monitoring process. The result of the various stages of processing, including the mental projection of the text, schemes, expectations, multiple strategies and monitoring, ultimately leads to the construction of the target text.

In a nutshell, Hönig's model assumes that translational activity is a monitored process and that the translator uses macro and microstrategies to

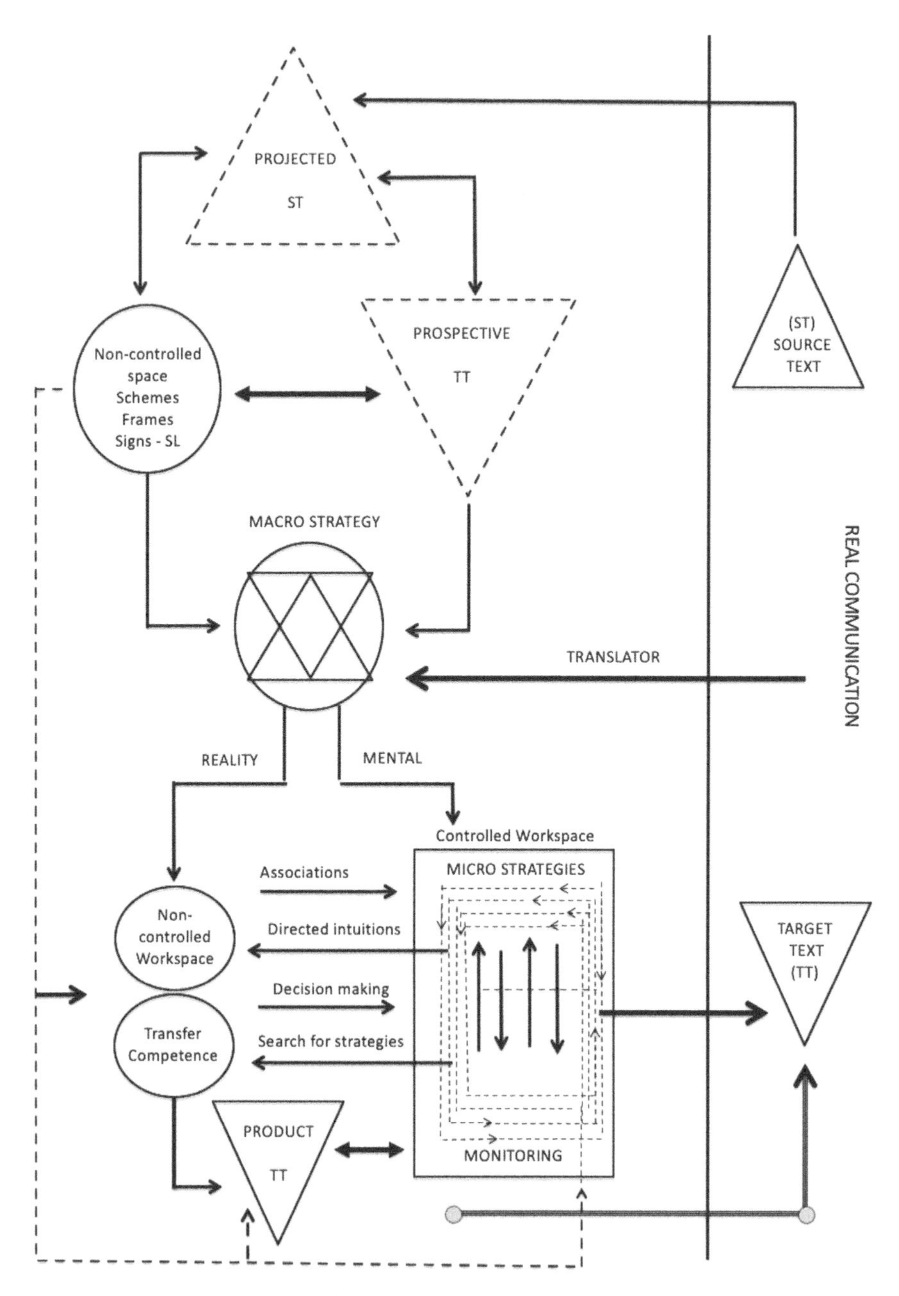

FIGURE 2.5 Hönig's model of the translation process

(Hönig, 1986, 1998, p. 29 – our translation into English)

understand the source text in its broadest sense and process with regard to the purpose of the translation task, the audience and other external factors. As shown in Figure 2.4, the arrows moving in different directions seem to suggest the non-linearity characteristics of the translation process.

2.3.5 Wilss's model of translation as a decision-making type of cognitive behaviour

Building on his previous works from 1988, Wilss (1996) considers translation as a cognitive behaviour that has two basic aspects: knowledge and skills (knowledge and experience). According to Wilss (1996, p. 37), "these are the pillars of information-processing procedures designed to determine the conditions for situationally adequate translation processes and to substantiate them evaluatively". In this sense, the author argues for a cognitive approach to translation, which, in his opinion, would help abolish the belief that translation is just a matter of the mechanical reproduction of a text in another language.

Although Wilss (1988) did not propose a descriptive model of the translation process, he clearly indicated elements that place the analysis of translation and translation competence within a cognitive perspective. His 1988 book, *Kognition und Übersetzen* [*Cognition and translation*] introduced a framework based on problem-solving and decision-making processes about the theory and praxis of human and machine translation. Wilss differentiates between human translation processes and computer transfer procedures through a comparison of multiple stage translation steps. Initially, Wilss considers the relationship between action theory and translation studies and reflects upon the role of the translator in the course of the translation process, looking at it as a problem-solving operation and a decision-making process. He also considers the role of creativity and intuition in the unfolding of the translation process. Wilss then tackles the problem of machine translation considering the state of the art in the 1980s, discussing theoretical and methodological issues as well as the possibilities and limits of disambiguation in a machine translation system. Wilss (1988) concludes his book with a reflection on the nature, possibilities and limitations of human and machine translation.

When trying to differentiate between human and machine translation, Wilss (1988) argues that flow charts are designed under strict linear and binary rules and this seems to be the only alternative available so that information processing can be carried out successfully. However, he adds that recent developments in chaos theory point to the need to reconsider how human cognitive processes unfold and conceive of non-linear processes in an account of human cognition (see Figure 2.6).

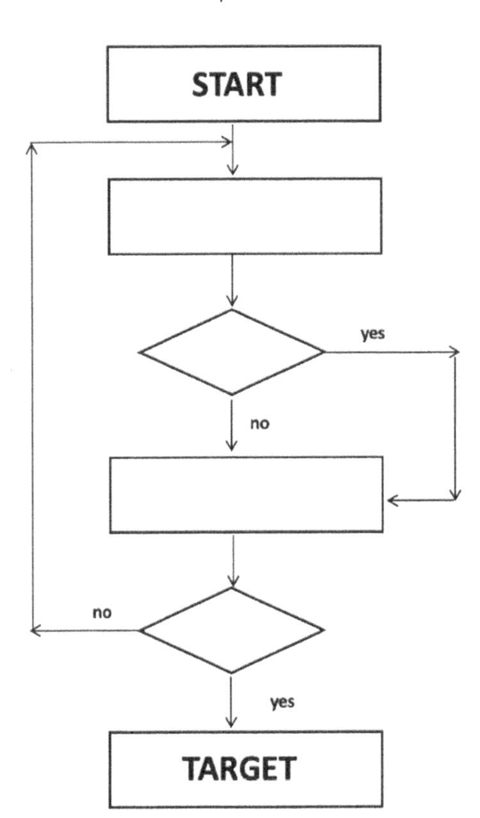

FIGURE 2.6 Wilss's model of translation as a decision-making type of cognitive behaviour

(Wilss, 1988, p. 240)

Knowledge, skills and experience in the translation process

We understand Wilss's (1996) model to be a continuation of his 1988 model. Wilss (1996) believes that translation into given a language is only the final state of a chain of mental operations resulting from the interaction of processes of analysis, interpretation, comparison, analogy, inference, balancing possibilities, planning, problem solving and so on. Thus, translation may not be represented by a linear model of decoding and encoding. According to Wilss, translation is a form of intelligent behaviour, which involves the ability to guide the translation activity based on the interaction between *knowing that* (declarative knowledge) and *knowing how* (procedural knowledge). Translation is also regarded as a problem-solving activity and as a process of decision making and choice, in which intervening factors, such as creativity and intuition, also play a role.

For Wills, cognitive psychology is a discipline that can lend an important contribution to the cognitive study of translation. Wilss argues that cognitive psychology seeks to understand mental phenomena as perceiving, thinking, remembering, problem solving, decision making and so on. Hence, translation studies should adopt approaches from cognitive psychology to carry out cognitive research in translation. Furthermore, Wilss believes that by opening up to cognitive psychology, translation studies will also open up to experimental research in order to understand the underlying cognitive mechanisms of translation. We would like to point out that these thoughts, raised in works from 1988 to 1996, foresee an avenue for research on translation as a cognitive activity that will be implemented in later years.

Translation: A knowledge-based activity

For Wilss (1996), translation is a knowledge-based activity, and, like all types of knowledge, it requires the acquisition of organized knowledge. To explain the organization of knowledge, Wilss builds on *schema theory* (Bartlett, 1932; Neisser, 1967; Tannen, 1979; Spiro, 1980, etc.). Schemas are cognitive units which enable one to cope with a situation according to cost/efficiency relations (*minimax strategies*). Schemas are complex, hierarchically structured knowledge structures that provide a scaffolding basis for knowledge. In this sense, the central task of cognitive approaches to translation research must be the mode of operation and interaction of these schemes of knowledge, and the interaction of these schemes with schematic types of knowledge (generic knowledge) and non-schematic types of knowledge (episodic knowledge).

Translator skills

Wilss also emphasizes the role of *translator skills*. He added that, although the concept of translator skills has long been used in professional circles of translation, it still needed a precise definition because there is no generally accepted consensus on what translator skills are. Wilss makes a clear difference between *ability* and *skill*. Ability is innate and cannot be observed. It is inferred from the behaviour of the individual. Skills, however, are acquired during the process of learning by doing or repetition, vary from one translator to another and are difficult to measure.

Translation as a process of decision making and choice

According to Wilss, translation consists in making decisions and choices. However, he argues that surprisingly so little has been addressed in a systematic way in the field of translation studies to discuss the issue of problem solving, and still to a lesser extent, the issue of decision making. He notes that the term *decision-making* was used with a wide range of meanings that cover a range of activities, having been employed in such diverse disciplines as economics, statistics, philosophy, psycholinguistics, mathematics, computers and so on. Wills also notes that any decision-making process is a complex activity that should satisfy four requirements: verifiability, plausibility, situational (contextual) adequacy and value orientation (weighing of decision-making factors). Decision-making processes are closely related to the activities of problem solving. For problem solving, the individual uses two types of knowledge: declarative knowledge *(knowing that)* and procedural knowledge *(knowing how)*. Wilss insists on the difference between problem solving and decision making. He states that, although it is not always possible to clearly delimit between them, they should not be mistakenly considered to be equivalent terms. Problem solving is a more complex and far-reaching concept. The decision-making process will not begin until the need for decision-making is sufficiently defined within the structure of a problem-solving operation that prepares the way for decision making. Thus, one can clearly see what factors and criteria operate in a given decision.

Based on Corbin (1980), Wilss (1996, p. 188) distinguishes six stages in the process of decision making: (1) problem identification; (2) problem clarification (description); (3) research on, and collection of, background information; (4) deliberation on how to proceed (pre-choice behaviour); (5) movement of choice; and (6) post-choice behaviour (evaluation of translation). Wilss cautions that there may be obstructions at (almost) any stage, which can disrupt or delay the process of decision making.

According to Wilss, these limits are difficult to establish in the case of translation, which leads to what is known as *not-choosing behaviour* (Corbin, 1980, p. 49). He also points out that there are two explanations for this behaviour in translation. The first explanation is related to the fact that translators may face a wide range of options and therefore they may find it difficult to make a decision. The second explanation is related to information collection; translators may have not been trained to make quick decisions with respect to documentation sources and, thus, their choice may not be optimal and require a lot of unnecessary processing time. For this reason, translators may tend to refrain from making decisions and stick to the first translation alternative that has come to mind.

Wilss indicates that having more information does not automatically lead to better results. Paradoxically, a translator, especially a novice translator, may tend to seek information even if it will be useless. Wilss notes that further research is needed, especially in the face of *cognitive simplification*, i.e. how translators reduce a complex problem to a problem-solving operation that is compatible with their processing capabilities. For Wilss, cognitive simplification can be considered as a tool to reduce uncertainty. In this sense, one must ask how much reduction of uncertainty or risk is necessary or possible in the performance of a given translator.

Finally, Wilss (1996, p. 190) cautions that "unintelligibility as a result of decision-making avoidance is probably one of the biggest sins a translator may commit". Translators should observe their behaviour to recognize that a decision must be made. Otherwise, the translation process does not go beyond the stage at which one becomes aware of a problem and stops short of providing a solution to it. That attitude adversely affects decision-making in translation and renders a translation unacceptable or stylistically unintelligible.

2.3.6 Lörscher's strategy-oriented model of the translation process

Lörscher (1991) also used verbal reports from foreign language students working from German into English in the L1 into L2 direction to design a model of the translation process in the form of a flowchart of translational problem solving. He analysed verbalizations from foreign language students with a focus on reconstructing the translation strategies that underlie their translation performance, assuming that such underlying strategies steer the unfolding of the translation process. However, they are not accessible to direct inspection.

Lörscher's model consists of two hierarchical levels, namely a lower level containing elements of translation strategies (i.e. discrete problem-solving steps) and a higher level that captures the manifestations of translation strategies. For Lörscher, interim versions captured during translation task execution can comprise several strategies and are intra- or inter-strategic phenomena. Translation versions can be located within strategies or can comprise several strategies and are thus intra- or inter-strategic phenomena. Elements of translation strategies can be distinguished as to whether they are original or potential. The former exclusively occur within strategic, i.e. problem-oriented, phases of the translation process and are thus original elements of translation strategies. The latter also occurs within non-strategic phases of the translation process.

Lörscher (1991) defines translation strategies as procedures that translators employ in order to solve translation problems. Accordingly, translation strategies have their starting point in the realization of a problem by a subject, and their conclusion in a (possibly preliminary) solution to the problem or in the subject's realization of the insolubility of the problem at a given point in time. Between the realization of a translation problem and the realization of its solution or insolubility, further verbal and/or mental activities can occur that can be interpreted as being strategy steps or elements of translation strategies. They can be formalized to yield categories of a model for the strategic analysis of the translation process.

Lörscher (2005, p. 599) considers that "translation strategies have their starting-point in the realization of a problem by a subject, and their termination in a (possibly preliminary) solution to the problem or in the subject's realization of the insolubility of the problem at the given point in time". Between the starting and end points, mental activities can be interpreted as strategy steps or elements of translation strategies. Lörscher (2005) drew on data from translations performed by foreign language students, in a first stage, and by professional translators at a later stage, and built on earlier considerations made in Lörscher (1991, 1996), to propose a model organized in two hierarchical levels. The phenomena which are considered to be elements of translation strategies are part of the first and lowest level and contain the smallest discrete problem-solving steps. The manifestations of translation strategies are part of the second level. Translation interim and final renditions can be found within several strategies, and are thus intra- or inter-strategic phenomena.

In his explanatory remarks to the flow chart of translational problem-solving, Lörscher (2005) mentions that, after realizing (RP) and possibly verbalizing (VP) a translational problem, and after a potential search for a solution (→SP), a subject may achieve a solution (SP, SPa, SPb, etc.) or a preliminary solution (PSP) immediately. In such cases, the problem-solving process may come to an end (#). This may also be the case when the subject considers a translation problem to be insoluble. Having found a preliminary solution, the subject may go on dealing with the next problem and proceed to the next decision node. The types of translation strategies used by Lörscher's subjects were schematically represented in five types. Types II, III and IV are derived from Type I, which is realizing a translational problem. Type II contains an additional phase of searching for a solution. Type III contains an additional verbalization of the translational problem. Type IV contains both an additional phase of searching and a verbalization. Type V is the most complex type of strategy and it built up of several basic and expanded structures. For Lörscher, translation strategies contain one or more of these structures.

Lörscher (2005) distinguishes between basic structures, expanded structures and complex structures of translation strategies. This is based on the fact that although translation strategies can be highly complex and thus difficult to document and describe in their manifold forms, they can be reduced to a fairly small number of simpler structures. Expanded structures of translation strategies consist of a basic structure which contains one or more expansions. Expansions are defined as additional elements of a strategy itself. Complex structures are built up of several basic and/or expanded structures.

The graphic representation of the chart of the translation process problem-solving proposed by Lörscher (2005) is displayed in Figure 2.7.

Lörscher also examines different versions of translations. Whereas translation strategies can, by definition, only occur within strategic phases of the translation process, translation versions can be located within strategic or

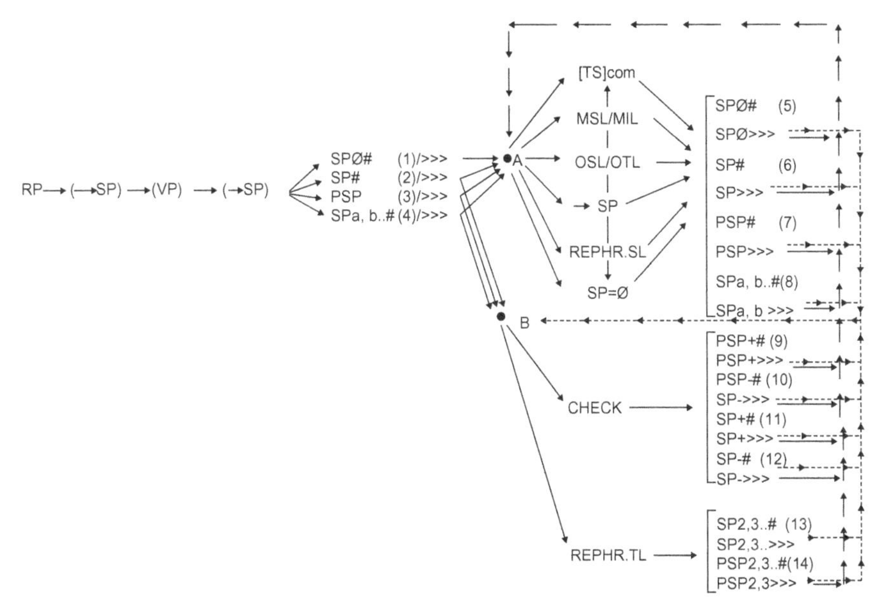

FIGURE 2.7 Lörscher's flow chart of translational problem-solving
(Lörscher, 2005, p. 607)

non-strategic phases or can extend from strategic into non-strategic phases or vice versa. When a translation version contains one or more translation strategies, these are called intra-versional strategies. When a translation strategy contains one or more translation versions, these are called intra-strategic versions.

2.3.7 Bell's linguistic and psycholinguistic model of the translation process

Bell's (1991) book, *Translation and Translating*, presents a description of the translation process that draws on contributions from other disciplines. According to Bell, a theory of translation must be able to explain: *translating*, the process carried out by the translator; *a translation*, the translated product; and *translation*, an abstract concept that encompasses both the process and the product of translation. Based on these assumptions, Bell (1991, p. 26) raises the need for: (1) a theory of translation as a process that has to borrow from psychology and psycholinguistics; (2) a theory of translation as a product linked to advances in text linguistics and discourse analysis; and (3) a theory of translation as process and product, which requires an integrated study of both process and product in the framework of a general theory of translation.

In his 1991 book, Bell's aims are twofold: to describe the specific knowledge and skills needed by the translator and to transform that description into a model of the translation process. His proposal also aims at establishing links between translation theory and linguistics, borrowing contributions from cognitive science, artificial intelligence and text linguistics. In order to build his model, Bell focuses primarily on two disciplines: linguistics and psychology. In his view, a model of the translation process requires psychological and psycholinguistic models related to memory and information processing, as well as linguistic models of meaning.

From these assumptions, Bell divides his study into three parts: model, meaning and memory. In the first part, Bell defines the translation, the translator and translation theory to propose a model of the translation process and describes the components of this process. The second part, which we consider to be the most important part of his work, is committed to meaning. For Bell, meaning plays a fundamental role in translation, including the meaning of words and clauses, semantic and communicative aspects of meaning and mechanisms, such as coherence and cohesion, related to discursive aspects of translation. Finally, in the third part of his book, Bell analyses the role of memory and knowledge in relation to the issue of text processing, storage mechanisms and information retrieval.

Bell's description of the translation process derives from work in psycholinguistics, artificial intelligence and natural language processing in real time (Harris & Coultheart, 1986; Nirenburg, 1987; Sperber & Wilson, 1986; Steinberg, 1982) and can be considered to be an adaptation of earlier proposals (Bell, 1987, 1991).

The graphic representation of the translation process proposed by Bell is displayed in Figure 2.8.

Features and components of the translation process

Bell (1991, p. 44) highlights the following characteristics of the translator process: (1) it is a special case of the more general phenomenon of human information processing; (2) it can be modelled to reflect its position within the psychological domains of information processing; (3) it occurs both in short-term and long-term memory through text-decoding mechanisms in the source language and text-encoding mechanisms in the target language, through a non-linguistic *semantic representation*; (4) it operates at the linguistic level of clause; and (5) it is both a top-down and a bottom-up process with both processes operating interactively.

Bell also considers the following features as main components in the translation process: (1) a *visual-word recognition system* and a *writing system*; (2) a *syntactic processor* that contains a *lexical search mechanism*, a

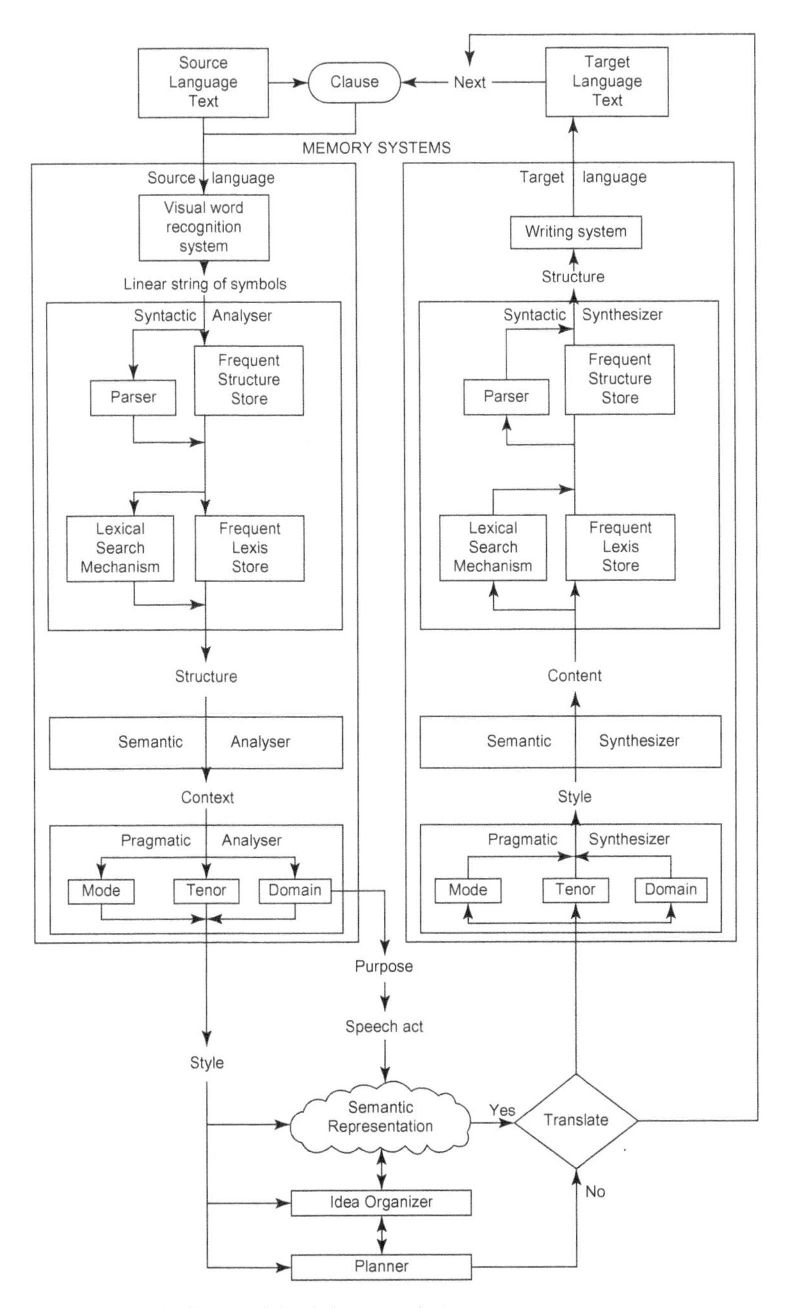

FIGURE 2.8 Bell's model of the translation process

(Bell, 1991, p. 59)

frequent structure store and a *parser*; (3) a *semantic processor*; (4) a *pragmatic processor*; (5) an *idea organizer*, which follows and organizes the progression of speech acts in the text; and (6) a *planner*, which deals with creating plans to achieve goals of all kinds; some of these plans may involve uses of language such as text processing, and may include in the translation of a text, decisions which could have been made before its first clause had been processed.

Bell distinguishes two phases in the translation process, namely analysis and synthesis. He also distinguishes three areas of operation: syntactic, semantic and pragmatic. Between the phases of analysis and synthesis, there is a *semantic representation*. For Bell, the translation process is a non-linear process with each step following another. Although the process requires processing at each phase, it is an integrated process with no fixed order in which constant revisions occur and rejections of previous decisions may take place (1991, p. 45).

Analysis

According to Bell, reading a text requires syntactic, semantic and pragmatic analysis.

Syntactic analysis requires a *visual word recognition system* capable of distinguishing words from non-words in the source language text. *Frequent lexis store* and *frequent structure store* have the function of relieving the short-term memory of unnecessary storage, thereby allowing large amounts of data to bypass the parser. The lexical search mechanism, in the case of lexis, can be directed immediately to the semantic level during analysis or the writing system during synthesis. The frequent lexis store (psycholinguistic) is a correlate of the physical glossary or terminological databases. The frequent structure store entails a set of operations involving the exploitation of structures that occur frequently and are stored in memory as lexical units. The work of the *analyser* is to analyse each sentence, when necessary. The *lexical search mechanism* has a mission to investigate and try to make sense of any lexical unit not matched by units stored in the frequent lexis store. The syntactic analyser thus has two functions: analysis of structures and allocation of lexical meaning.

Semantic analysis has the function to retrieve transitivity relations which underlie the syntactic structure of the clause. The semantic processor is used to derive content from the syntactic structure provided by the previous stage of analysis. It analyses the content of the clause, what it represents, logical relations between the participants and processes, ideational meaning, semantic sense and propositional content. Its function is, therefore, to retrieve content.

Pragmatic analysis accomplishes two tasks in relation to the information received from the previous stages of analysis: isolate the thematic structure (distribution of information whether this is marked or unmarked) and provide a register analysis (with its stylistic features, including purpose), considering three stylistic parameters: *tenor* (the relationship between the receiver and the sender), *mode* (the selected medium) and the *domain* of discourse (which includes information about what the sender intended to convey and its communicative value).

With this information, the stylistic analyser can make a provisional allocation of the clause to a given text type, which can yield several possible text-type alternatives which must wait for further information derived from later clauses in the same text in order to reach a stage when a final assessment can be made. Once a decision is made, two things happen: (1) the information on the clause moves on with the stylistic specification to form a completely language-free representation, thus forming the whole of the meaning expressed in the clause as understood by the reader; and (2) analysis draws on the two remaining stages of analysis: the idea organizer and the planner.

The *semantic representation*, is, according to Bell, a non-linguistic set of concepts and abstract, universal relations, representing all the thoughts expressed in the clause. It contains the following information: the structure of the clause, the propositional content, the thematic structure, the register features (tenor mode, and domain of discourse), the illocutionary force and the speech acts. The semantic representation is the result of the three-way analysis of the clause and the basis for a three-way synthesis of a new clause. Bell's model does not translate a clause in one language to a clause in language B but rather breaks down the A clause into its semantic representation and uses that as a basis to build an alternative clause in another language (translation) or in the same language (paraphrase).

Simultaneously, the whole analysis is fed into the *idea organizer*, whose function is to: (1) integrate the analysis with the developing overall layout of a text; (2) occasionally return to monitor the information that it accumulates; and (3) revise some semantic representations in connection with new information. The analysis is also absorbed by the *planner* and is used so that it makes it easier to achieve the objectives that precede reading. This is the time when decisions about whether it is worthwhile to keep on reading and whether to translate or not.

Bell's model applies both to the general reader and to the translator, since according to Bell, up to this point the translator is a monolingual reader. The next decision is whether or not to translate the semantic representation. If not, the process returns immediately to the beginning to start work on the next clause.

Synthesis

In the synthesis phase, Bell considers that three aspects are also involved: pragmatic, semantic and syntactic synthesis. As is the analysis phase, Bell indicates that the process is non-linear. The model now moves into the pragmatic synthesis. The pragmatic synthesizer receives all information available in the semantic representation and faces three key issues: what to do with the purpose of the original, how to deal with the thematic structure and how to deal with the style of the original.

The semantic synthesis entails the processing of indicators of illocutionary force (the purpose) to create structures that convey the propositional content in a satisfactory manner so that one can move to the next stage of the synthesis.

The syntactic processor accepts the input from the semantic stage and explores the frequent lexis storage and frequent structure store in order to produce an appropriate clause type, representing the propositional structure. If there is no appropriate clause in the frequent structure store that suits the specific meaning, the proposition passes through the parser which now functions as a syntactic synthesizer. Finally, the writing system is activated to form the clause as a string of symbols in the target language. The process concludes in the same way as it did for the monolingual reader with a return to the original text and to the next clause.

Bell concludes that the translation process can be considered as an interactive and cascading process with two major phases (a phase of analysis and a phase of synthesis) and three major stages (syntactic, semantic and pragmatic). In each phase, there are both bottom-*up* and top-*down* processes. The analysis and synthesis of the clause depend both on pattern-recognizing procedures and inference mechanisms, moving from the particular to the general and vice versa.

2.3.8 Gutt's relevance-theoretic approach to translation

According to Gutt (1991), Sperber and Wilson's (1986) relevance theory provides a framework for the study of human communication, focusing on effort rather than behaviour, and trying to account for the information-processing skills that allow humans to communicate with one another. The scope of relevance theory is mental rather than textual. Hence, it provides an ideal framework for the study of effort and effect in translation. Gutt's goal is to explain translation in terms of the communicative competence that allows human beings to express in one language what had been expressed in another language.

Gutt (1991) sees the translator as a communicator addressing a receiver and translation as part of the communication process directed to this receiver. In this sense, Gutt argues that it is not necessary to postulate a specific and independent theory to explain the act of translation. He insists that this act can be explained in the framework of relevance theory, arguing that the theory suffices to account for the intricacies entailed in the translation process. In Gutt's own words:

> The results of my research ended up surprising me. I hoped that Relevance Theory would help me formulate a general theory of translation. However, in the space of a year, I grew to see more and more clearly that Relevance Theory alone sufficed to provide an account of translation, therefore there seems to be no need to develop a general theory of translation.
>
> *(1991, p. vii)*

Relevance theory

Relevance theory aims at providing an explanatory account of human communication. It tries to explain the complexity of human verbal communication in terms of cause and effect, using an ostensive-inferential model. It advocates an inferential nature to all forms of human verbal communication and addresses the mental ability that humans have to successfully make inferences to achieve their communicative needs and goals. For relevance theory, this inferential ability is what enables human beings to communicate with one another.

For Sperber and Wilson (1986), there is a synergy between what is said and what is implicated and the former always plays a major role in the unfolding of the latter. On the one hand, the communicator wants to produce an ostensive stimulus. In relevance-theoretic terms, this is known as informative intention. On the other hand, the receiver is willing to enrich that ostensive stimulus inferentially in order to understand what is meant by the communicator.

Relevance theory presents an interactive model of human communication that is not based on mutual cooperation but rather on mutual manifestness. Context, also known as *cognitive environment*, is a mental construct that plays an important role in mutual manifestation. As a psychological concept, it is considered to be a subset of the receiver's assumptions about the world. Another important relevant-theoretic concept in the process of understanding is the notion of *contextual* or *cognitive effect*, related to the implications, contradictions and contextual reinforcement that occur in the course of inference-making and the *effort* required to achieve that end. As an act of communication, effort is required to recover contextual assumptions, depending on different degrees of accessibility. Relevance theory also considers that the interpretation of *explicatures*, i.e. analytical implications that the communicator intends to convey, and *implicatures* i.e. implicit meaning intended to convey contextual assumptions, are involved in the inferential process.

Relevance theory advocates the existence of an essential property: *the principle of relevance*, particularly information that determines what holds the attention of an individual at a given time. Sperber and Wilson define it in terms of two conditions: (1) the greater the contextual effect of an assumption, the more relevant the assumption, and (2) the lower the processing effort required to process an assumption in a given context, the more relevant the assumption is. In this sense, the main tenet of relevance theory is that human communication causes an expectation of *optimal relevance*, that is, an expectation by the receiver that his attempt to interpret an utterance yields adequate contextual effects with minimal processing effort. This is achieved through the *principle of relevance*. In other words, every act of ostensive communication conveys a presumption of its own optimal relevance. Therefore, it produces adequate contextual effects without extra processing effort.

According to Relevance Theory, relevance is a cognitive property determined by two fundamental factors, namely the necessary effort for a given stimulus to be optimally processed and the effects stemming from this optimal processing. In relevance-theoretic terms, the amount of processing effort is dependent on the effects it is capable of generating.

On the notion of interpretive resemblance

Relevance Theory assumes that cognition is a highly dynamic phenomenon which generates the mental representations used by individuals in their processes of meaning construction. In its framework, relevance theory presupposes two types of use for mental representations – descriptive and interpretive; each of them refers to a corresponding type of resemblance. Descriptive resemblance establishes a correlation between an object or state of affairs in the world and a mental representation, while interpretive resemblance does this between two mental representations.

Gutt uses the concept of interpretive resemblance to argue that two propositional forms P and Q resemble each other interpretively in context C when P and Q share analytic and contextual implications in context C. Gutt defines interpretive resemblance as the result of a contextual effect between two propositional forms which share some common properties. In his own words:

> An essential property of propositional forms is that they have logical properties: it is in virtue of these logical properties that they can contradict each other, imply each other and enter into other logical relationships

> with each other. Since all propositional forms have logical properties, two propositional forms may have some logical properties in common. Accordingly, we can say that mental representations whose propositional forms share logical properties *resemble* each other in virtue of these shared logical properties. Such resemblance between propositional forms is called interpretive resemblance.
>
> *(Gutt, 1991, p. 34)*

Relevance theory and translation: A case of optimal interpretive resemblance

According to Gutt (1991), translation is a case of interpretive resemblance. He argues that the notion of *interpretive resemblance* is apt to define translation because the translator has to produce in the target language a text that aims to inform the receiver of the same assumptions that the sender wanted to communicate to the original recipient. Given the importance of the cognitive environment, the amount of contextual effects deriving from the translation should be appropriate for the receiver to capture the same assumptions. In this sense, Gutt defines translation as a target language text that interpretively resembles the original.

Based on the notion of optimal relevance, Gutt argues that a condition of optimal similarity must comply with translation: if the translation interpretively resembles the original text and is consistent with the assumption of optimal relevance, it must produce optimal contextual effects without requiring extra processing effort.

Therefore, translation is regulated by the principle of relevance. And since it depends on the context, translation activity is also dependent on the context. These conditions determine that a translation has to resemble the original text only on those aspects that make it adequately relevant to the recipient and needs to be expressed in such a way that the target language understanding requires from the receiver the same processing effort that was required from the receiver of the original text.

Direct and indirect translation

Gutt also raises a distinction between two forms of translation called *indirect translation*, which is flexible and context-dependent, and *direct translation*, a fixed notion independent of context. Gutt shows that both indirect and direct translations stem from the notion of interpretive language use and correspond to gradual degrees of interpretive resemblance. The translator has to choose between an indirect or direct translation to determine whether there is sufficient similarity and needs to consider contextual effects and processing effort involved for the receiver. He added that there is no *theoretical* necessity that the translator follow one of two approaches rigidly, but should be aware that unexpected deviations can lead to inconsistencies in the cognitive environment that could possibly jeopardize the proper functioning of human communication.

Evolution of the theory: In search of a cause-effect relation

Gutt (2000) argues that one of the most significant contributions of relevance theory is to provide a cause-effect framework for applying this cognitive core area to research in translation. Consequently, Gutt advocates in favour of what he calls CORT, namely, competence-oriented research of translation, aiming at understanding and explicating the mental faculties that enable human beings to translate in the sense of expressing in one language what has been expressed in another.

The cause-effect framework provided by relevance theory can be used to predict problems when the stimuli and/or the audience lack ready access to certain pieces of information that are needed for consistency with the principle of relevance. Based on these assumptions, Gutt suggests that one could set up experiments to investigate cause-effect relations in translation.

More recently, Gutt (2004) has taken up the challenge to investigate translations as a higher-order act of communication (HOAC). According to Gutt, HOACs are "instances where one act of communication is about another act of communication". From this standpoint, it becomes possible to differentiate between an intended stimulus and meaning through two distinct modes of higher-order communication, namely a stimulus-oriented mode (s-mode) and an interpretation-oriented mode (i-mode). HOACs can, therefore, help translators with problem solving and decision making by providing them with strategies to choose whether s-mode or i-mode should be employed in a given situation.

Further, Gutt (2005) expands the application of relevance theory to translation by postulating that CORT operates in situations where communicator and audience do not share a mutual cognitive environment. In such cases, called secondary communication, Gutt suggests that additional sophistication is needed for communication to succeed, namely the capacity of human beings to metarepresent what has been communicated to them. According to Wilson (2000, p. 411), "metarepresentation is a representation of a representation: a higher-order representation with a lower-order representation embedded within it". Gutt (2005) claims that the capacity to generate metarepresentations is, therefore, a prerequisite for the cognitive capacity of human beings to translate (see Figure 2.9).

2.3.9 Alves's relevance-theoretic-oriented model of the translation process

Eight years after the publication of Königs's (1987) model of the translation process, Alves (1995) extended the *Adhoc* and *Rest Block* model on the

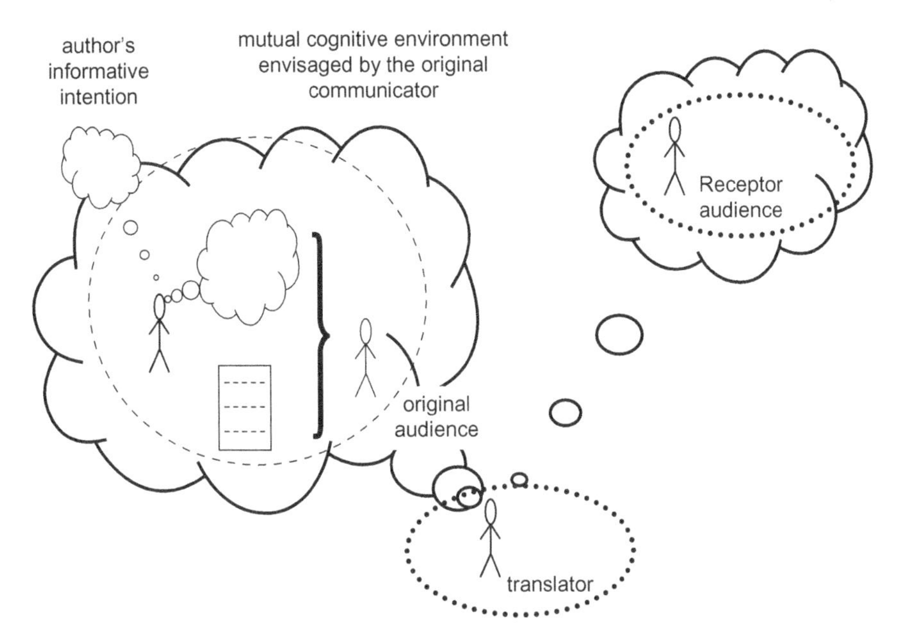

FIGURE 2.9 Gutt's model of metarepresentation in translation

(Gutt, 2004, p. 81)

basis of a larger-scale investigation in the context of the German/Portuguese language pair and examined the translation processes of 24 subjects, 12 in Brazil and 12 in Portugal, divided into four different profiles of language and translation experience. There were four subgroups with three participants in each group, namely professional translators, novice translators, translation students and bilinguals. Alves (1995) also built on Gutt (1991) to present a psycholinguistically oriented model that also draws on relevance theory. However, unlike Gutt, Alves used an empirical approach to analyse think-aloud protocols of translation process data in order to conceive a model of the translation process that aims at validating relevance-theoretic assumptions.

As a focal point for his theoretical considerations, Alves refers to relevance theory (Sperber & Wilson, 1986) in order to consider the translation process both from a cognitive perspective and also from a pragmatic angle. The departing point is the concept of the translation unit, which can be shortened or extended by translators, being constantly transformed according to the translator's needs and should be regarded as a constantly changing element. (Alves, 1995, p. 28). For Alves, translation units are controlled by their relevance, whether they are located in the *Adhoc* or in the *Rest Block*.

The model conceived by Alves (1995), displayed in Figure 2.10, is graphically similar to Bell's (1991) model in the form of a flow chart with both

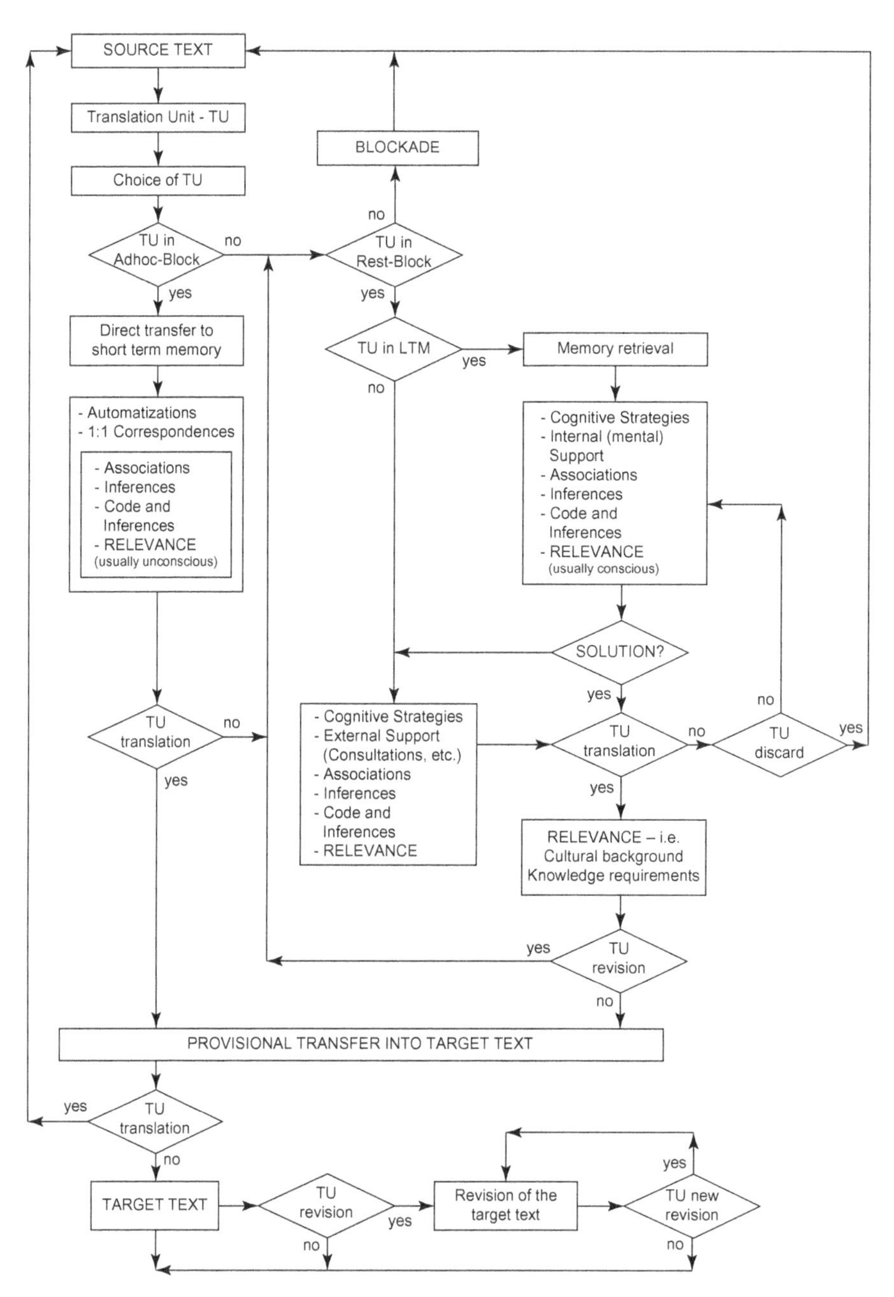

FIGURE 2.10 Alves's relevance-theoretic model of the translation process (Alves, 1995, p. 195 – our translation into English)

top-down and bottom-up processes interacting recursively. The entry point of the model was the translation unit, defined by Alves on the basis of the translator's focus of attention on the source text. This translation unit would be first processed automatically in the *Adhoc Block* as a default procedure. If a *1:1 equivalence* were produced, that translation unit would be stored in a revision block for later processing. If no *1:1 equivalence* were produced, the translation process would move into a reflexive block where mechanisms of external and internal support would interact recursively. Once a translation solution had been found, the translation unit would also be stored in the revision block for later processing.

Alves's model is also concerned with instances where processing effort would be so demanding that no cognitive effects could be produced. Such instances would generate a loop in the process and lead to a cognitive breakdown. Translation units that would enter this looping process would have to be discarded to allow the continuation of the translation process. Translators would also have the choice of consciously discarding translation units that had already been translated but failed to produce cognitive effects that were deemed to be satisfactory by the translator. Finally, a final step would lead to a fine-grained revision of previously stored translation units that would give rise to the final version of the target text.

Throughout the process, the principle of relevance would guide translators in their problem-solving and decision-making processes. The search for interpretive resemblance, as defined by Gutt (1991), would be the driving force behind the translation process and would mediate the effort/effect equation postulated by relevance theory. According to Alves (1995), translators would engage in processing effort while testing assumptions to validate their expectations of relevance. More interim renditions would be produced as long as stronger cognitive effects made up for the cost of extra processing effort. Presumptions of relevance would make translators continue with or interrupt their work.

The graphic representation of the translation process proposed by Alves is displayed in Figure 2.10.

Alves's model can be summarized in the following steps: (1) focus of attention on a given translation unit; (2) default processing in the Adhoc Block; (3) reflexive processing in the Rest Block with help of instances of internal and external support; (4) deletions to compensate for a possible breakdown resulting from a looping effect; (5) decision to translate supported by the principle of relevance and geared towards interpretive resemblance; and (6) revision phase which would incorporate all previous steps geared to the optimal maximization of relevance.

Linking cognitive strategies with the help of internal and external supports leads to solving problems and making decisions effectively. However, it may also be the case that some segments of the target text are deliberately omitted. Empirical data show that in some cases the translator is aware that there is an alternative – and even several alternatives – for a given segment. However, these potential alternatives do not provide contextualization and thus cannot be justified. Therefore, they are usually omitted from the target text. In these cases, strategies are deliberately used to contextualize the translation unit in the target text. The process concludes with the refinement of the target text filtered by expectations of relevance.

According to Alves (1997), such a detailed model offers the possibility to assess the translation process of translation students more clearly and to analyse it precisely, but also to use this model as a pedagogical tool in translators' training, which can be implemented more consciously as proposed in Alves (2000).

2.3.10 Kiraly's sociological and psycholinguistic model

Kiraly (1995) addresses the analysis of translation from two perspectives: as a communicative and social activity and as a cognitive activity. The former is considered to be an external activity while the latter is an internal process. In this regard, Kiraly (1995) proposes a dual model of the translation process: a social model based on theories conceived by Firth (1951, 1957, 1964) and a cognitive model based on psycholinguistics (Boekaerts, 1981). His multidisciplinary proposal gathers input from research in the field of communicative language teaching, psychology, psycholinguistics, sociology and translation studies.

Kiraly (1995, p. 36) attempts to link translation theory and translators' training to answer the following questions: (1) Is it possible to develop a model of translation processes to serve as a frame of reference for translation trainees and translation teaching? (2) Is it possible to identify the general and specialized components of translator competence as targets for pedagogical intervention and development? (3) What are the initial steps to take in filling the pedagogical gap in translation teaching? Thus, the aim of Kiraly's study is to investigate how translation processes can be understood, what are the competences required and how they can be manipulated for educational purposes in order to offer a more secure, creative and competent base for translators' training.

Kiraly's starting point is that translation teaching must rely on a model based on an empirical description of the translation activity. Kiraly supports his claim by means of an empirical study, more precisely by a *case study* carried out with 18 translators (nine students and nine practitioners) in inverse translation, using think-aloud protocols for data collection.

Translation as communication and social activity

From a communicative and social perspective, Kiraly aims to analyse the social implications of the communicative act that is translation. His social model of translation is based on the linguistic theories of Firth (1951, 1957, 1964). In this model, the translator is considered an active participant in three interrelated situational contexts: the *context of situation of the original text*, the *context of situation in which the target text will be embedded* and the *context of situation of the translator.*

The *context of situation of the original text* is composed of: (1) the author and the readers of the original text and the role of the relationships among them; (2) the linguistic material of the original text; (3) people, objects and events to which the text refers; and (4) the effect of the text on readers. The *context of situation of the target text* refers to the knowledge that the translator has of the addressee of the translation, the status of the text and of the translation. The *context of situation of the translator* is the amalgamation between the two previous contexts of situation and cannot be directly observed because its components are internal and mental; it is the context from which the translator identifies and chooses elements of the *context of situation of the original text* that guide the production of the translation and which elements of the *context of situation of the target text* are needed to ensure the adequacy of the choices in the target language. This context consists of competences, knowledge and understanding of the role these elements play in a particular translation.

The graphic representation of the translation process proposed by Kiraly is displayed in Figure 2.11.

An important outward manifestation of the *context of situation of the translator* is what Kiraly calls the *translator self-concept*, related to the image of the social role of the translator, the validation of the translator's competence in a given text and his/her concept of responsibility in relation to the task and to other participants in the context of translation (the author, the person making the request, the user and the reader). It is a mental construct that serves to connect the social and psychological worlds of the translator.

Translation as a cognitive activity

The psycholinguistic model proposed by Kiraly intends to represent the cognitive system that is activated during translation and is supported by evidence gathered in the case study carried out by him. In this model, the translator's mind is conceived of as an information processing system that results from the interaction of relatively uncontrolled and relatively controlled processes and in which linguistic and extra-linguistic information is used.

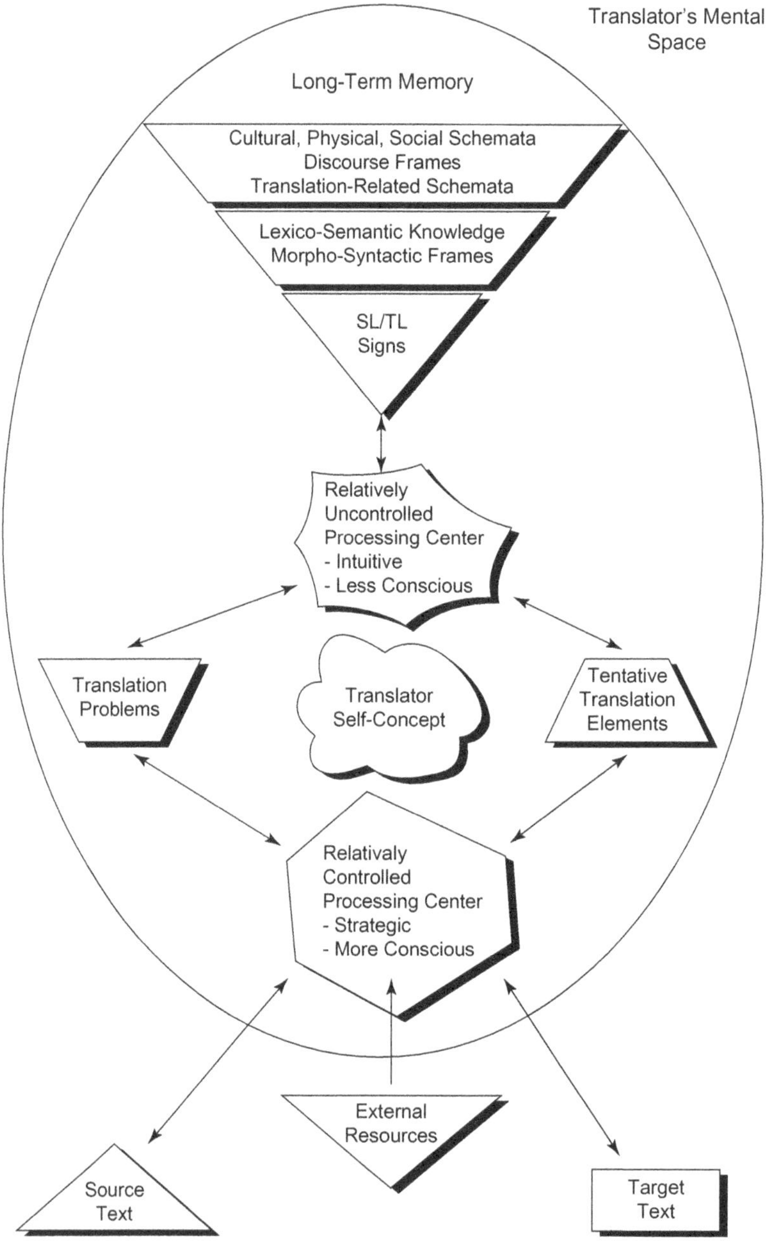

FIGURE 2.11 Kiraly's psycholinguistic model

(Kiraly, 1995, p. 101)

According to Kiraly (1995, pp. 100–105), the main components of the model are: (1) *information sources*, including long-term memory, source text input and external resources (reference books, databases, native speaker informants, subject experts); (2) the *intuitive workspace*, which is relatively uncontrolled and subconscious; and (3) the *controlled processing centre*.

Long-term memory contains knowledge of the physical world, of the source and target cultures, L1 and L2 lexico-semantic information, as well as morpho-syntactic frames and relevant source language and target language signs. It also contains information about the translator's theoretical knowledge about translation. Related schemes include knowledge of translation: translation rules, learned strategies, criteria for evaluating the quality and potential sources of error in translating. Like Lörscher (1991, pp. 268–271), Kiraly postulates the existence of an *expectation structure* of translation, i.e. a projection of what should be a translation, derived from knowledge of the translator about translation in the face of the multiple contexts. The *expectation structure* is a master plan or a set of constraints that guide text production in translation.

At a superficial level, the *input* of the original text is a linear sequence consisting of signs and co-textual elements of the original text. Signs and configurations of signs (morphemes, words, phrases and sentence groups, overall textual profile) are processed together and relate to the relevant knowledge structures of long-term memory. Unlike the process of interpretation, in the process of written translation, the source text is available to provide more information to translators. They can re-read the source text whenever they want, changing it in successive mental representations of the text. The original text is not processed as a simple linear sequence of signs, but rather simultaneously, as a form of social interaction, including a propositional structure and a complex index of shared social knowledge. Therefore, it contains all elements of the context of situation of the original text, either explicit or implicit, as well as pragmatic information inferred by the translator. These references serve to activate the elements that are relevant to the translation in the translator's long-term memory.

In addition to the information from memory and from the original text, the translator can extract information from external sources: reference works, databases, native-speaker and domain-specialist consultations and so on. Access to these sources is implemented by means of applying specific strategies. Kiraly indicates that knowing when and how to work with external resources is a crucial skill in the translation process.

Kiraly takes up the distinction made by Boekaerts (1981) between a *subconscious workspace* and a *controlled processing centre* to account for the change of subconscious processes into controlled processes without configuring an absolute dichotomy. In this sense, Kiraly proposes the existence of an *intuitive workspace* (which is *relatively uncontrolled*) where information from long-term memory is synthesized, without conscious control, together with information provided by the source text and external resources. In the intuitive workspace, two types of products emerge: the provisional translation of text elements and translation problems. The provisional translation of text elements is the product of uncontrolled spontaneous associations performed in the intuitive workspace; spontaneous association could be of a purely formal level as a result of learning or acquisition or may be functional equivalents established through an intuitive assessment of textual and situational information. The translator moves into the controlled processing centre where one of the two types of control is available: control of the target language and textual control. In control of the target language, the translator uses rules of the target language that have been stored in memory and contrasts them with elements of the provisional translation with respect to their levels of syntactic and semantic accuracy. In textual control, the translator uses a contrastive textual evaluation to assess the original text and expectation structures concerning conceptions of what the target text should be like.

Translation problems emerge from the intuitive workspace when automatic processing does not produce provisional translation elements. These problems are then considered in the controlled processing centre and a strategy is selected and applied to find a solution. For Kiraly, strategies do not solve translation problems but they help formulate plans that are being made in an attempt to solve problems. A failed strategy may cause the problem to be sent to the intuitive workspace with additional information that had not been considered previously (i.e. as a result of the subsequent implementation of the strategy of re-reading). If the intuitive workspace is unable to provide a suitable solution which matches the expectation of the translator, additional translation control will be needed. If accepted, an element of provisional translation based on inadequate information available will be produced. Otherwise, the translator can leave aside the element in question and start another search procedure.

The case study: Processing indicators

Kiraly performed his study with 18 subjects who had German as a mother tongue and English as their first foreign language: nine subjects were students in the second half of a translator training programme at a German university and nine subjects were novice translators who had recently graduated in that same program, all of them with some professional experience. The instruments used were think-aloud protocols recorded concurrently with the execution of the translation task, a German source text (therefore L1/L2 translation) taken from a tourist brochure about Frankfurt that had to be translated with a view to a similar publication for English-speaking tourists and post-task questionnaires to gather more information and evaluation of the translations (made by two reviewers outside the experiment). Subjects had to translate the text fragment and, at the same time, verbalize their thoughts as they translated. These verbalizations were recorded for later analysis.

Kiraly's study provides interesting information about the activities carried out during the translation process and describes this process as a mixture of controlled processes and (unobservable) relatively uncontrolled processes. The data provide information on the following phenomena:

1. Translation units, showing subjects seeking solutions for different types of text elements (words, word strings, supra-sentential elements, text elements).
2. Non-problem units, indicating the spontaneous production of a provisional translation solution, which are solved without verbalization by the subject.
3. Problem units, which are marked by the application of translation strategies to solve them.
4. Translation unit processing, spanning from the identification of the translation unit up to the acceptance of a decision to translate or discard the unit without translating it.
5. Translation strategy application: indicators of apparently or potentially conscious strategies.
6. Intuitive translation processes, which are inferred from the production of provisional translation alternatives without giving conscious access to the use of strategies.
7. Progression through the text. The processing of each translation unit can occur in two ways: an accepted translation decision makes the subject move on to the next unit or a not-accepted solution makes the translator move on to the next unit or return to a previous unit.

In addition, Kiraly (1995, pp. 76–78) found several indicators in the course of the translation process, which reflect states of consciousness or changes in the translator workspace (see Table 2.2).

The data obtained by Kiraly are interesting because they offer information about events and activities that occur during the translation process. However, because they were only collected by means of think-aloud protocols, as the author himself acknowledges, they tend to capture and display mostly relatively controlled processes. Furthermore, the author states that there are no significant distinctions between the performance of students and professional translators (both in terms of their translation processes and the quality of the final product). Kiraly also points out that the data cannot extrapolate all students and professional translators and should only be

TABLE 2.2 Processing indicators of the translation process according to Kiraly

1. Rephrase source text segment
2. Search monolingual dictionary
3. Employ mnemonic aid
4. Back translate
5. Break of attempt
6. Search $L_1 - L_2$ dictionary
7. Identify problem
8. Monitor for target language accuracy
9. Reduce meaning
10. Make extra-linguistic judgement
11. Recontextualize
12. Refer to the translation expectation structure
13. Make intuitive acceptability judgement
14. Attempt syntactic reconstruction
15. Accept interim solution
16. Unsuccessful dictionary search
17. Proposed dictionary solution
18. Intuition-based proposal
19. Uncertain acceptability

interpreted in the context of the case study. In addition, the sample is quite small and it is about inverse translation.

2.3.11 Halverson's model of the gravitational pull hypotheses

Building on Langacker's (1987, 1991) theory of cognitive grammar, Halverson (2003) introduced the gravitational pull hypothesis as a possible explanation for some general features of translated language, trying to make it compatible with relevant models of bilingual semantic and syntactic representation. Halverson (2003) postulated, by means of a gravitational pull hypothesis, that some patterns of activation within schematic networks would be more prominent than others due to their higher frequency of use over time.

The original gravitational pull hypothesis was further elaborated by Halverson (2010), bringing together the assumptions of cognitive grammar and the model put forward by Jarvis and Pavlenko (2008), resulting in a three-level representational system to account for patterns of translational over- and underrepresentation observed in the literature. Halverson (2010) discussed models of bilingual semantic/conceptual representation and pleas for a combined experimental and corpus-based approach in an attempt to account for patterns found in translational corpora from a cognitive perspective.

Expanding the gravitational pull hypothesis further, Halverson (2017) proposed a model of semantic structures in which, drawing on Langacker (2008), all linguistic items constitute form-meaning pairings. In such a model, both form and meaning are represented cognitively. Additionally, building on Cook's (2003) multilingual competence perspective that considers linguistic cognition as qualitatively different when bilinguals and monolinguals are compared, Halverson (2017, p. 12) argued that "in modelling linguistic categories in bilinguals, it is not sufficient to consider monolingual data alone". Particular emphasis was placed on bilingual cognition and crosslinguistic influence.

Revisiting the gravitational pull hypothesis, Halverson (2017, p. 15) mentioned that "the basic idea is that highly salient linguistic items (lexis or grammatical constructions) would be more likely to be chosen by translators and thus be overrepresented in translational corpus data". Therefore, the more established an item or phrase, the greater the chance that it will be chosen and used in translations. Thus, Halverson aimed at developing a more comprehensive and detailed cognitive linguistic model which incorporates salience phenomena in both source and target language categories and also the effects of entrenched links between translations in different language-pair combinations.

For that purpose, Halverson (2017) drew on the concept of semasiological salience in the target language, namely "a relationship among the various semantic possibilities of a given lexical item" (Geeraerts, 2009, p. 79) and split the original gravitational pull hypothesis into three types of translational effects, namely target language salience (magnetism), source language salience (gravitational pull) and link strength effects (connectivity). Magnetism (target language salience) refers to the idea that, when cognitively searching for a target language item, translators are more prone to choose target text items with high salience/frequency. Prominence or gravitational pull (source language salience) can be metaphorically understood as a true form of cognitive gravity. This can be seen as a cognitive force that hinders translators from escaping from the cognitive pull of highly salient representational elements in the source language. This phenomenon entails a kind of interference or crosslinguistic influence. Connectivity (link strength effects between source and target languages) is an additional source of translational effect stemming from the nature and strength of links between elements in the two languages mastered by bilinguals. The links between translation pairs across languages are also strengthened through the frequent activation of one member of the pairs, given the assumption of joint activation at some representational level.

Halverson (2017, p. 15) argued that "the distinction between three different potential sources of translational effects, two based on prominence and one on the entrenchment of translation pairs ('equivalents') clarifies the accounts given in Halverson (2003, 2007). She tested these three related hypotheses by developing a partial Norwegian-English bilingual schematic network using corpus data complemented by performance data. Halverson operationalized salience solely as frequency of use although she acknowledged that it may be impacted by a number of factors, including type of meaning, recency of activation and various elements of the unfolding discourse representation. The case study involved the use of three different types of data: corpus data, a sentence generation test and Translog process data, looking for evidence of frequency effects in language production tasks.

Although further larger-scale testing is still required, results obtained by Halverson (2017) provide empirical evidence to validate a cognitive-grammar-oriented model to account for how translations are rendered at product, performance and process levels. Halverson (2019) continues the discussion by revisiting the notion of default translation as a construct for cognitive translation and interpreting studies.

2.3.12 Tirkkonen-Condit's monitor model

Tirkkonen-Condit's (2005) monitor model of the translation process builds on empirical research carried out by Laukkanen (1993) and Tirkkonen-Condit (2002) to advocate that expertise in translation requires monitoring skills and self-awareness. She points to tendencies towards literal translation as a default procedure in products and processes among novice and expert translators. Tirkkonen-Condit argues that the literal translation automaton operates on a lexical as well as on a syntactic level. Its monitor becomes more and more automatic at higher levels of expertise, but even expert translators show performance traits that serve as evidence of the literal translation automaton and its monitor. Further evidence for the operation of the literal translation automaton is to be found in results concerning the so-called unique items.

For Tirkkonen-Condit, unique items are such linguistic elements in the target language that are not triggered off as formal correspondents or literal translation equivalents by any elements in the source language texts. The reason for the relative scarcity of the unique elements in translated language is that they are not generated by the literal translation automaton. They are not generated by the automaton because there is no formally corresponding material in the source text to trigger them off, and second, because there are other lexical and syntactic vehicles to convey the semantic content expressed in the source texts. Thus the unique elements find their way to translations less frequently than to texts produced in the original language. The relative scarcity of unique material in translations can be taken as indirect evidence for the literal translation automaton in operation: it generates literal or formally corresponding linguistic material as long as the material thus produced is semantically and syntactically acceptable and satisfies the equivalence requirement. The unique elements tend to be ignored as the semantic content can be conveyed by the material generated by the literal translation automaton.

Tirkkonen-Condit takes her considerations about the role of monitoring and awareness into the field of translator training. She argues that the same tools and methods that are now used in translation process research can very well be used as training tools by novices in translation as part of their translation assignments. She also suggests that think-aloud protocols and keylogging could easily be integrated into virtually any kind of take-home assignment and that these research tools might be adopted as pedagogical tools that enable the observation of one's own performance, which is a precondition for learning to monitor the performance in an expert manner.

Carl and Dragsted (2012) as well as Carl and Schaeffer (2017a) have drawn on Tirkkonen-Condit's monitor model of the translation process to discuss the role of priming, awareness and expertise in translation, strengthening her arguments with more robust evidence in favour of the importance of monitoring to the unfolding of the translation process.

2.3.13 Jakobsen's tentative computational model of human translation processes

Drawing on keylogging and eye-tracking data, Jakobsen's (2011) model conceptualizes translation production as a cycle of cognitive and motor processes. Jakobsen considers that the combined pool of eye-key data offers powerful insights into the types of cognitive and motor processes translators engage in during translation task execution. However, he cautions, having such valuable data available in a structured manner poses an analytical challenge. Researchers can scrutinize a translator's eye-key activity in detail but "to begin to make coherent sense, details have to be interpretable as constituents in a model" (Jakobsen, 2011, p. 45).

In order to propose a tentative computational model of human translation processes, Jakobsen suggests that the sequence of actions performed by human translators must be hypothetically abstracted into an algorithm, which he specifies in the following six steps (Jakobsen, 2011, p. 48):

1. Moving the gaze to read the next chunk of new source text (and constructing a translation of it).
2. Shifting the gaze to the target text to locate the input area and read the current target-text anchor word(s).
3. Typing the translation of the source-text chunk.
4. Monitoring the typing process and the screen outcome.

5. Shifting the gaze to the source text to locate the relevant reading area.
6. Reading the current source-text anchor word(s).

Jakobsen assumes that these six steps constitute a complete micro-cycle in which some of the steps (or portions of them) can be skipped or, conversely, can be repeated several times. They are not always followed strictly sequentially. Nevertheless, the six-step sequence is presented as a prototypical one. Step 1 configures the first step of the model with gaze movements reading a segment of the source text and, ideally, constructing a mental translation of it. Next, in step 2, the gaze moves onto the target text where it can find an anchor word (or not), which is meant to establish a connection between cognitively old and new text. Then, in step 3, the translation of the segment would be typed in. Jakobsen mentions that, at this stage, the gaze may shift back and forth several times between the source text word(s) being processed and the translation being typed. This accounts for the monitoring postulated in step 4. Steps 3 and 4 are to some extent concurrent and subcategories would have to be added between these steps for a fine-grained model to be implemented computationally. Jakobsen adds that while monitoring takes place concurrently with text typing, (screen) monitoring quite often continues after typing has stopped. In a nutshell, Jakobsen's model allows us to predict with a high degree of probability that step 1 will be followed by step 2, step 2 by step 3 and so on.

According to Jakobsen, a tentative computational model of human translation processes must include a model of probable reading behaviour for translation, linking, as far as possible, the recorded fixations and the words that are actually read. This should be recognizable even in a sequence characterized by repeated eye fixations and backtracking, allowing handling fixation mapping problems and diagnosing, among other things, problems with sentence parsing or meaning construction. The model also allows computationally recording the succession of new source-text segments read by a translator and automatically aligning source-text segments read and how they were translated.

To give an empirical account of his ideas, Jakobsen uses translation-process data generated in the context of the Eye-to-IT project to interpret a sequence of eye-key data as representing the following steps: eyes fixating on a succession of source-text-words (step 1), gaze shifting to the target text and identifying the target-text anchor word in a given number of eye fixations (step 2), typing the translation of the words read in the previous step (step 3), lack of gaze data indicates that eye fixation was likely on the keyboard (step 4), gaze shifting towards a new piece of the source text (step 5), a previously read segment functions as an anchor word for the reading of the next source text item(s) (step 6) and so the cyclic process continues.

Wondering about the viability of the actual implementation of a computational model of human translation, Jakobsen points out that both the quality of the recorded raw data as well as the soundness of the automatic interpretation of the data are crucially important. This includes, for instance, how eye fixations are identified in the mapping algorithm. These interpretations would be initially informed by the available knowledge of human translation processes which should provide the basis for the first computational analyses. This, however, would probably be enriched by the discovery of new patterns and regularities in large volumes of stored data containing behavioural observations of human translators' cognitive and motor processes.

Jakobsen's thoughts were ahead of his time and his insights highlighted the potential for large-scale computational analysis of translators' behaviour by means of combined eye-key data. He was sure that the necessary data was there and "the prospect of creating a computational model of how expert human translators typically execute their skill seems within reach" (Jakobsen, 2011, p. 53).

2.3.14 Schaeffer and Carl's recursive model of shared representations

Revisiting the literal translation hypothesis and the monitor model (Ivir, 1981; Tirkkonen-Condit, 2005), Schaeffer and Carl (2013/2015) empirically investigated automated processing during reading and translation tasks and found evidence that translation task execution entails the activation of shared lexico-semantic and syntactical representations of source and target language items that share one single cognitive representation. In short, they argued that the activation of shared representations facilitates automated processing.

Drawing on De Groot (1997), Schaeffer and Carl refer to two models of translation that differ in terms of their assumed cognitive processes, namely vertical and horizontal translation processes. Whereas the former consists of two monolingual systems, one for decoding the source language and the other for encoding the target language, the latter entails shared memory representations between language items in the bilingual lexicons. Revisiting Ivir (1981) and Tirkkonen-Condit (2005), Schaeffer and Carl (2013/2015) state that only by looking at translation task execution in real time can one see whether a highly literal target text was produced using vertical or horizontal processes. Thus, they propose disentangling the notion of literal translation from automatic translation processes since literal translation refers to the output observed in the target text whereas automatic translation shows how that output was generated. For Schaeffer and Carl (2015, p. 26), "priming forms the basis for the horizontal method: the influence of a previously processed item or structure on a subsequently processed item or structure forms the basis for horizontal translation". Assuming that priming is the driving force in translation task execution, Schaeffer and Carl move away from the notion of literality and suggest describing the translation process on the basis of automaticity and shared representations. Carl and Schaeffer also build on Vandepitte and Hartsuiker's (2011) evidence of more cognitive effort during translations of items with crosslinguistic differences to test their assumption that translation primes semantic and syntactical representations, suggesting that shared representations facilitate the process of translation.

In order to find evidence for their assumption, Carl and Schaeffer recruited ten translators with more than five years of professional experience, all of them having English as their L2. Six translators performed reading and translation tasks from English into German and four other translators worked similarly from English into French. The materials for both reading and translation tasks were extracts (844 and 794 words) taken from Hemingway's (1975) *The Old Man and the Sea* were presented one sentence at a time using ePrime. The task comprises producing a rough written draft of each sentence. The source text sentence was visible while participants worked on their translations. When the task was finished, participants hit the escape key in ePrime. A new sentence or a recall prompt then appeared and the previous sentence was no longer visible. The procedure during the reading for comprehension condition was exactly the same and participants did not have to translate. Recall prompts appeared every one to five sentences at irregular intervals during both conditions, instructing participants to recall as much as possible of the sentences. Schaeffer and Carl (2013/2015) used 24 recall prompts in each condition and the order of presentation of the two excerpts and tasks were counterbalanced.

Based on the data analysis, Schaeffer and Carl propose that automaticity and shared representations should be measured by comparing to what extent source text reading and target text writing cooccur in parallel. In other words, "instances of concurrent reading and writing during translation are indicative of automatic processes and shared representations" (Schaeffer & Carl, 2015, p. 36).

In their model, vertical processes act as a monitor for target text production by the horizontal processes. During decoding, horizontal and vertical processes remain equally active. Horizontal processes are early processes whereas vertical processes depend on context, which becomes available later as the translation process unfolds. Shared representations are activated during source text reading that then serve as the basis for regeneration in the target language as depicted by the circles in Figure 2.12. Translation task execution unfolds uninterruptedly on the basis of the regeneration of shared representations while the output is in line with the target norms and contextual considerations of the vertical processes. However, when the interim rendering does not comply with the criteria for acceptability, translation is adapted to target text norms by vertical encoding processes as shown in the vertical arrows in Figure 2.12. Thus, "vertical processes control the acceptability of the target text but also need to monitor equivalence" (Schaeffer & Carl, 2015, p. 38).

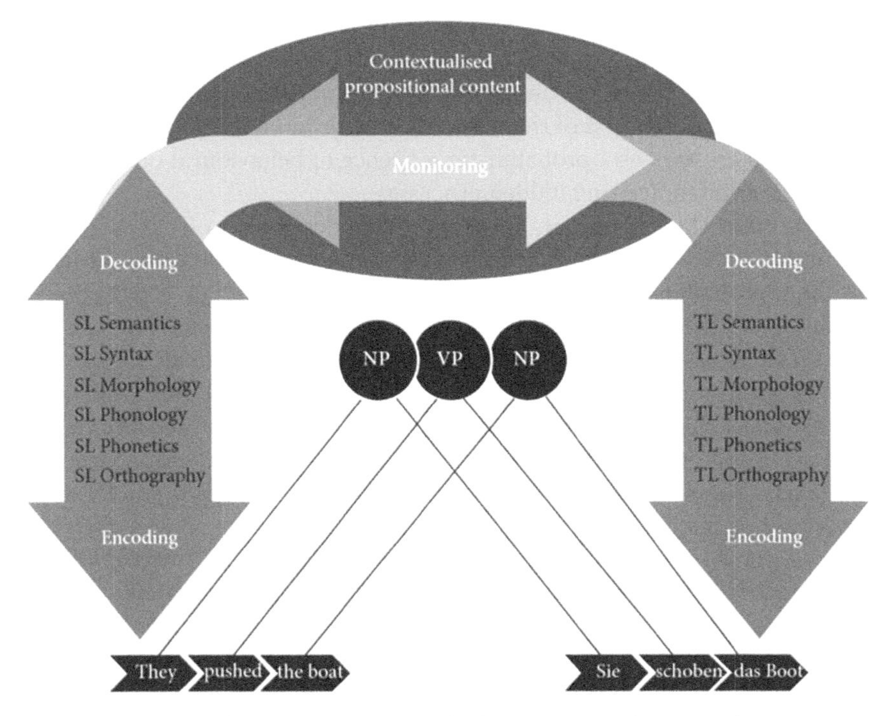

FIGURE 2.12 Schaeffer and Carl's model of vertical and horizontal processes in translation

(Schaeffer & Carl, 2013, p. 182)

The graphic representation of the translation process proposed by Schaeffer and Carl is displayed in Figure 2.12.

Schaeffer and Carl's model also highlights the recursive nature of the translation process, arguing that during translation task execution, the translator switches back and forth between the source and the target text, integrating strategic problem-solving processes with automated translation processes in a "recursive cycle which integrates horizontal and vertical source and target language processes: the monitor needs to compare whether the source is the same as the target, but it is equally important to make sure that the target is the same as the source" (Schaeffer & Carl, 2015, p. 38).

2.3.15 Carl and Schaeffer's noisy channel model for the translation process

Drawing on Shannon and Weaver's (1949) noisy channel model, which has often been used for solving non-deterministic problems in communication and computational linguistics, Carl and Schaeffer (2017a) developed a noisy channel model of the translation process aiming at predicting particular modes of behaviour through observable traces in user activity data (UAD), namely data elicited through keylogging and eye-tracking software, to uncover and understand the underlying hidden translation processes that are involved in the generation of translations. In their model, keystrokes and eye movements are seen as a probabilistic sequence of behavioural observations stemming from underlying hidden processes.

To ground their proposal, Carl and Schaeffer refer to Toury's (2004) attempt to define the notion of translation universals and his advocating in favour of probabilistic explanations in translation studies. For Toury (2004), conditioned statements would predict particular modes of behaviour or their observable results that could be verified empirically and provide a powerful framework to formalize probabilistic explanations in translation studies.

Carl and Schaeffer's noisy channel model, thus, aims at accounting for how a set of conditional probabilities that can be equivalently expressed as a particular predicted translation behaviour by means of predictor variables have an effect on and explain, at least to a certain extent, the observed behaviour in a probabilistic manner. Distinguishing between internal hidden states and early and late translation processes, Carl and Schaeffer assume that behavioural patterns are triggered through internal hidden states in the translator's mind. Such mental states, they argue, can be formalized as a hidden Markov process "in which a number of interconnected 'hidden' states emit observations with a certain probability" (Carl & Schaeffer, 2017a, p. 78).

These hidden states can be mapped on recursive networks with transition probabilities that point to the probability that one particular state should follow another given state. Early translation processes, triggered through priming mechanisms, tend to be automatic and include processes such as gaze movements observed in first fixation duration or first pass reading time. Late translation processes are deliberate, more time-consuming and involve more cognitively demanding problem-solving strategies, including processes such as source text integration or formulation of a translation hypothesis.

The graphic representation proposed by Carl and Schaeffer's noisy model for the translation process considers hidden states of early and late processes as displayed in Figure 2.13.

Carl and Schaeffer described three levels in their model.

- On the top level, there are three main types of predictors, namely linguistic models, cognitive-behavioural models and social-cultural models. Predictors stem from disparate sources and entail a huge number of variables that are prone to gear the unfolding of the translation process. The source text is also another crucial predictor that helps to determine the features of the target text. Constrained by a number of factors, the translator, represented in the centre of the model, produces a sequence of behavioural patterns during the unfolding of the translation process. In Carl and Schaeffer's model, the translator is portrayed as a network of hidden states responsible for the implementation of the actual translation processes through early and late processes.

- The mid-level of the model portrays process observations that reflect behavioural patterns also referred to as UAD. They include keystrokes, mouse clicks, eye movements and other types of behavioural data. Behavioural patterns include production units, attention units, activity units and OST units, comprised of five subcategories for orientation and revision processes. Collected UAD need to be segmented into meaningful behavioural patterns to be properly analysed.
- The bottom level of the model contains the product observations and includes changes observed in the unfolding of the translation process from the first immediate rendering to a series of successive intermediate text renditions that lead to the final output in the target text.

To test these assumptions empirically, Carl and Schaeffer drew on UAD from 95 translators, over 38 hours of work, generating 336 target texts in four target languages (Danish, German, Spanish and English) with a total of

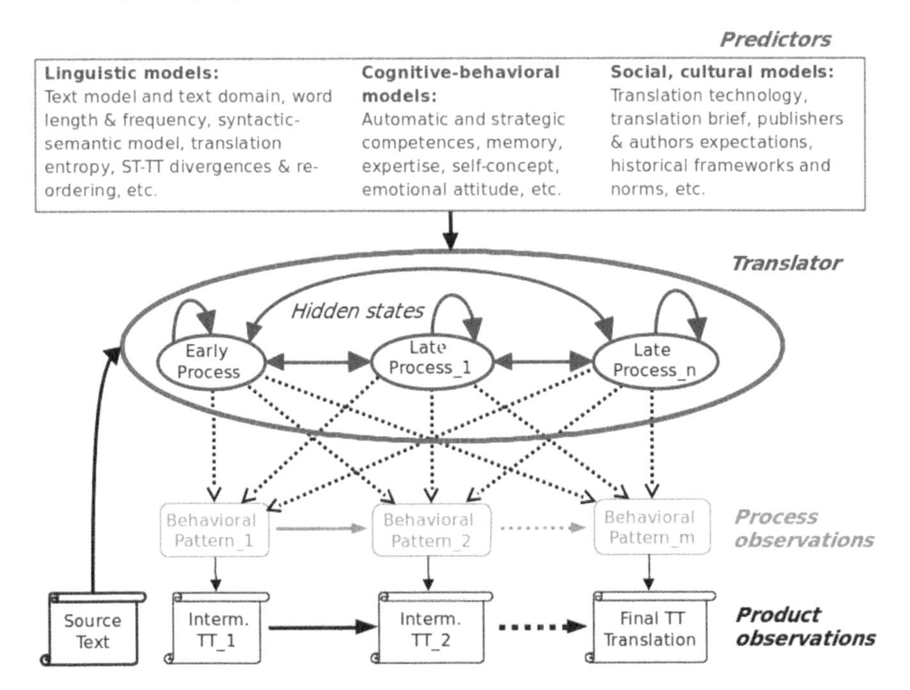

FIGURE 2.13 Carl and Schäffer's noisy model of the translation process

(Carl & Schäffer, 2017a, p. 83)

48,295 target language tokens from six different English source texts which were either translated or post-edited. Besides translations into Danish, German and Spanish, UAD also included English target texts resulting from a copying task (English to English). Carl and Schaeffer analysed the UAD by using several metrics, focusing primarily on two indicators, namely word translation entropy (HTra), related to the likely number of translation alternatives possible for a given language item, and Cross, related to the amount of crossing word alignments (inter-lingual alignment distortion) observed in the data. Assessing the results of the UAD analysis, Carl and Schaeffer pointed out that priming effects can be observed in translation as well as in post-editing of machine-translation output. However, priming effects seem to be more noticeable in post-editing, which is a task mostly carried out monolingually between the machine-translation output and the post-edited text, corroborating the fact that priming effects are generally stronger within one language than between two languages (Pickering & Ferreira, 2008).

Carl and Schaeffer also drew on the relevance-theoretic concepts of conceptual and procedural encodings (Blakemore, 2002) to investigate source text reading patterns and target text revision patterns on a set of UAD. By measuring the number of revisions as an indicator of effort in translation task execution, Carl and Schaeffer were able to show that "the generation of translations for procedurally encoded information is more difficult than that of that of conceptually heavy words" (Carl & Schaeffer, 2017a, p. 108).

Although further empirical evidence is needed, the picture emerging from the data analysis suggests the viability of using the noisy channel model to explain the translation process on the basis of hidden states in the translator's mind and through the unfolding of disparate early and late translation processes that are observable in translation task execution.

2.3.16 Carl and Schäffer's relevance-theoretical model of machine translation post-editing

Building on relevance theory (Sperber & Wilson, 1986/1995) and its application to the study of translation (Gutt, 1991/2000), Carl and Schaeffer (2019) propose a computational framework for post-editing machine translation (PEMT). However, since they consider that relevance theory has not yet been formalized to a degree that allows for rigorous quantification and predictive modelling of translation processes, Carl and Schaeffer based their relevance-theoretic framework for PEMT on the noisy channel model (Shannon & Weaver, 1949), a model also used by Sperber and Wilson (1986/1995) in their account of ostensive-inferential behaviour.

To operationalize their model, Carl and Schaeffer draw on Jakobsen's (2011) tentative computational model of human translation processes and on Carl's (2010) account of a statistical model for the production simulation of an unchallenged translation based on the ACT-R model (Anderson,

2007), breaking down the translation process into "a number of successive steps, over which the translator iterates to produce the translation" (Carl & Schaeffer, 2019, p. 51):

1. Locate-word: find physical location on the screen.
2. Attend-word: shift attention to word.
3. Encode-word: retrieve word from mental dictionary.
4. Translate-word: retrieve associated translation.
5. Type-word: serialize spelling and type word.

They caution, however, that although the ACT-R implementation correctly predicts the average translation durations, the produced sequence of keystrokes and gaze fixations is very static and hardly matches the observed variation in UAD. Carl and Schaeffer also point out that the ACT-R simulation is a stratificational model in which available cognitive resources are separately allocated either to understand the source text or to produce the target text. Drawing on Läubli's (2014) conceptualization of human translation activities as hidden Markov processes, and in line with their proposal in Carl and Schaeffer (2017a), they argue that these models can be trained by means of automatically segmenting the UAD into vectors of observations. Once the process observations are clustered, a model can be trained with cluster labels serving as output symbols of the hidden Markov model. As shown by Läubli (2014), the cluster labels are then mapped on the three basic translation processes of orientation, revision and pauses, reaching a high level of accuracy to predict the times spent on orientation, revision and pauses.

On the basis of the above-mentioned considerations, Carl and Schaeffer propose to implement the noisy channel model as a statistical model, in which any given number of variables can be introduced. These variables represent parallel or consecutive activities, low-level, automatized translation mechanisms or high-level conscious translation strategies. They also point out that "the noisy channel model does not make presumptions about the underlying architecture or representation of the bilingual mind – such as connectionist systems do" (Carl & Schaeffer, 2019, p. 52).

Focus on post-editing processes

Differentiating between translation and post-editing tasks, Carl and Schaeffer assume that translators, on the one hand, are primed either by the source or by the target texts, integrating strategic problem-solving processes with automated translation processes while post-editors of machine translation output, on the other hand, have to collaborate with a machine-translation system to produce a post-edited output. The goal of the combined human and machine translation process is to increase productivity and the overall accuracy of the translation product. In that respect, Carl and Schaeffer add that "as for any combination of two or more different systems, the underlying assumption is that the 'noise' in both channels is independent and complementary, so that the introduced errors may cancel out" (Carl & Schaeffer, 2019, pp. 54–55). Previously, Schaeffer and Carl (2013/2015) and Carl and Schaeffer (2017a) had shown that human translation is primed by entries in the bilingual mental lexicon that consist of combinatorial nodes connecting lexico-semantic and syntactical properties in the two languages.

Based on the above-mentioned works, Carl and Schaeffer (2019) argue that these combinatorial nodes are responsible for and explain priming effects in translation. In post-editing, however, the machine-translation output acts as a priming stimulus that enables the post-editor to produce translations more quickly. Based on relevance-theoretic assumptions that the goal of translation is to generate adequate cognitive effects for the target text reader without unnecessary processing effort (Gutt, 1991/2000), Carl and Schaeffer suggest a post-editing model in which the relevance-theoretic heuristics complements the "Noisy Translator Channel" by adding constraints of causal interrelation between stimulus, context and interpretation, established by the principle of relevance.

Carl and Schaeffer also argue that, when post-editing machine translation output, translators collaborate with a machine-translation (MT) system in the production of the post-edited output. The combined human and machine translation process is expected to increase productivity and the overall accuracy of the translation product. Carl and Schaeffer's model presupposes a combined system with a "Noisy MT Channel" and a "Noisy Translator Channel". The two channels compete for productivity. Such a combination may be fruitful if one system is good at finding appropriate solutions and the other one is good at correcting mistakes. In such a scenario, both systems could be combined with increased accuracy and productivity. Thus, "the more changes are introduced by the 'Noisy Translator Channel' into the MT output, the less successful must be considered the 'Noisy MT Channel'" (Carl & Schaeffer, 2019, p. 55). They also point to an underlying independence assumption and argue that translators, as post-editors, are heavily primed by the MT output.

The graphic representation of Carl and Schaeffer's model for post-editing that integrates the noisy translator channel with relevance-theoretical concepts is displayed in Figure 2.14.

The model for machine-translation post-editing assumes that an author encodes a text (S-Text) within a source language context (S-context). This text will then be read and understood by a source text reader (Reader). Understanding is reached by decoding the text and by inferences over the literal meaning (explicature) as well as by inferential processes over the intended meaning (implicature). In post-editing, the S-Text is then decoded by two different noisy channels, namely the noisy MT channel and the

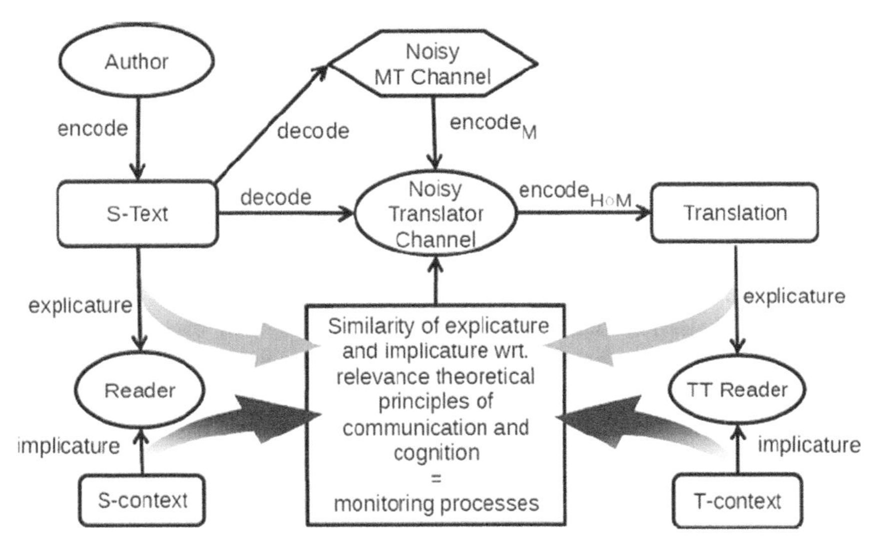

FIGURE 2.14 Carl and Schäffer's relevance-theoretical model of machine translation post-editing

(Carl & Schäffer, 2019, p. 61)

noisy translator channel. The resulting translation is then read by a target text reader (TT Reader), embedded in the target context (T-context), who draws interpretively similar inferences as those expected for the reader of the source text, both guided by relevance-theoretic principles. To ensure that interpretive resemblance is achieved, post-editors, like translators, make use of metacognitive activities through monitoring processes. Since MT systems, so far, do not have access to the context of text production and use, they lack models of optimal communicative relevance. Therefore, Carl and Schaeffer conclude, post-editors need to constantly check if the post-edited output is correctly encoded (both conceptually and procedurally) and if adequate cognitive effects can be derived by end-users of the post-edited text.

2.4 The conceptual development of research on the translation process: Approaches and main characteristics

2.4.1 Different approaches

The models we have introduced in the previous section show that translators engage in a complex cognitive process to construe meaning conveyed in the original source text into a target text counterpart. This process requires several stages, intervention by various mechanisms and cognitive operations, and the application of different types of knowledge and abilities. The models we have discussed in this chapter address the description of this complex process from different perspectives and thus highlight various mechanisms and cognitive operations.

Table 2.3 lists the central notions put forward by each model and the disciplinary framework related to it.

As we have seen, the models of the translation process presented in the previous section differ both in terms of the terminology they use as well as with respect to the conceptual framework they adopt. They also differ in terms of their theoretical frameworks and the disparate methodological approaches used to design each model. While some models favour a theoretical approach (Wilss, Gutt, Tirkkonen-Condit, Halverson) based on other disciplines, other models draw on a phenomenological perspective (Seleskovitch and Lederer) or build on experimental studies, more particularly on data from think-aloud protocols (Krings, Königs, Hönig, Lörscher, Alves, Kiraly) or a combination of keylogged and eye-tracking data (Jakobsen, Schaeffer and Carl, Carl and Schaeffer). While the earliest models arise as a result of analysis carried out from a deductive perspective, the latest models have an inductive nature and are based on observation and experience or on results of empirical data. These differences notwithstanding, there are many converging points among the models which highlight the main traits of the translation process. We will point out these traits in the next sections.

2.4.2 The specificity of the translation process

As we have noted in Table 2.3, all models of the translation process agree, one way or another, that translation is a special case of cognitive behaviour and part of the more general phenomenon of human information processing. In this sense, the translation process is related to processes involved in information processing (comprehension, expression) and their characteristics (inferential nature, interactivity of elements, the role of memory, etc.). Although the translation process is intrinsically related to general processes of human information processing, it also has its own characteristics. The basic processes of understanding and re-expression that occur in monolingual communication have their own peculiarities in translation because the translator is a special kind of receiver and sender.

Building on Danks (1991), Bell (1998, p. 186) identifies three types of constraints that characterize the translation process: (1) the translation task, including the activity that is entrusted to the translator and the context in which it is carried out; (2) the source text, including its particular linguistic and discursive features; and (3) the translators, including their skills as well as their linguistic and extra-linguistic knowledge. These constraints require translators' specific cognitive resources. Additionally, the translation task may have specific constraints depending on the mode of translation (written

TABLE 2.3 Main characteristics of translation process models

Model Authors	*Central Concepts*	*Disciplinary Framework*
Seleskovitch and Lederer's interpretive theory of translation (among others, Seleskovitch (1968, 1975, etc.); Seleskovitch & Lederer (1984/2001, etc.))	• Meaning (non-verbal synthesis) • Unit of meaning • Intended meaning (pre-verbal origin) • Phases: understanding, deverbalization, re-expression + justified analysis (written translation) • Components: memory, linguistic knowledge, cognitive input (encyclopaedic knowledge and contextual knowledge), shared knowledge • Interpretive translation vs. transcodification (correspondence)	Phenomenologicallybased theory, Genetic psychology (Piaget), Experimental neuropsychology
Krings's model of problem identification and translation strategies (1986)	• Several strategies (equivalence, discovery, evaluation, reception, reduction) • Monitoring • Cyclical nature	Psycholinguistics, Foreign language teaching
Königs's (1987) model of Adhoc Block and Rest Block	• Adhoc and Rest Block • Translation unit • Equivalence • Monitoring	Psycholinguistics, Foreign language teaching
Wilss's model of translation as a decision-making type of cognitive behaviour (1988, 1996)	• Interaction between declarative and procedural knowledge • Initial considerations about the interaction between translators and machine translation • Translator skills • Problem-solving • Decision-making	Cognitive psychology
Hönig's model of mental schemes, expectations and beliefs (1991, 1998)	• Micro and macro strategies • Controlled and non-controlled workspaces • Transfer competence • Monitoring	Psycholinguistics, Foreign language teaching

(*Continued*)

TABLE 2.3 (Continued) Main characteristics of translation process models

Model Authors	*Central Concepts*	*Disciplinary Framework*
Lörscher's strategy-oriented model of the translation process (1991)	• Importance of translation strategies for problem solving and decision-making • Five hierarchical types of translation strategies	Psycholinguistics, Foreign language teaching
Bell's linguistic and psycholinguistic model of the translation process (1991)	• Semantic representation • Phases: analysis and synthesis • Components: memory, visual word recognition system, writing system, syntactic, semantic and pragmatic processors, idea organizer, planner	Linguistics Psychology Psycholinguistics Artificial intelligence
Gutt's relevance-theoretic approach to translation (1991/2000)	• Optimal interpretive resemblance • Explicatures and implicatures • Cognitive effort • Contextual effect • Direct vs. indirect translation • Metarepresentation	Relevance theory, Cognitive science
Alves's relevance-theoretic-oriented model of the translation process (1995)	• Adhoc and Rest Block • Principle of relevance • Internal and external support • Components: translation unit, relevance-driven problem-solving and decision-making strategies	Relevance theory Cognitive science Psycholinguistics
Kiraly's sociological and psycholinguistic model (1995)	• Source context of situation, target context of situation, translation context of situation • Translator self-concept • Components: sources of information (memory, source text, external sources); intuitive workspace; controlled processing centre	Psycholinguistics Communicative language teaching Psychology

(*Continued*)

TABLE 2.3 (Continued) Main characteristics of translation process models

Model Authors	*Central Concepts*	*Disciplinary Framework*
Halverson's model of the gravitational pull hypotheses (2003, 2010)	• Salience (high-frequency use) • Magnetism (target language salience) • Prominence (source language salience) • Connectivity (link strength effects)	Cognitive grammar, Bilingualism, Second language acquisition
Tirkkonen-Condit's monitor model (2005)	• Translation automaton • Monitor mechanism • Components: literal translation, automatization, expert performance, translator training	Psycholinguistics, Expertise studies
Jakobsen's tentative computational model of human translation processes (2011)	• Monitoring processes • Recursive nature • (Tentative) computational modelling • Components: eye-key data, anchor words	Cognitive science, Computational linguistics Psycholinguistics
Schaeffer and Carl's recursive model of shared representations (2013/2015)	• Priming mechanisms • Vertical and horizontal processes • Shared representations • Recursive nature	Cognitive science, Psycholinguistics
Carl and Schaeffer's noisy channel model for the translation process (2017a)	• Noisy channel • Recursive nature • Priming mechanisms • Components: hidden states, early and late processes, behavioural patterns, interim solutions	Cognitive science, Computational linguistics
Carl and Schaeffer's relevance-theoretical model of machine-translation post-editing (2019)	• Noisy channel • Recursive nature • Priming mechanisms • Components: noisy MT channel, noisy translator channels, decoding, encoding, monitoring processes	Cognitive science, Computational linguistics

translation, consecutive/simultaneous interpreting, etc.). Dealing with the source text always involves certain lexical, syntactic and stylistic constraints. Therefore, Bell states that a model of the translation process, which inevitably shares the characteristics of a general model of human communication, must have some specific components related to translation, especially those components related to the recognition of a translation problem and to the strategies used to solve these problems. We entirely subscribe to Bell's remarks and have tried to show that the specificities of translation task execution require fine-grained descriptions of the disparate cognitive operations involved.

2.4.3 Main characteristics of the translation process

Considering the models we have discussed in this chapter, we can deduce essential features of the translation process, which account for its complexity.

2.4.3.1 The existence of basic processes in the course of the translation process

Although each model of the translation process presented in this chapter favours disparate perspectives, they all agree in pointing out two main phases, namely, understanding and re-expression. In a way, all these models consider the translation process as an interpretive process of capturing and reformulating meaning. Some authors, such as Bell and Wilss, have used the terms analysis and synthesis as an analogy for the phases of understanding and re-expression. These two phases are related to the dual role of translator as receiver of the source text and as sender of a (new) target text.

In addition, some authors agree to consider an intermediate stage of the non-verbal character called *deverbalization* by Seleskovitch and Lederer, and *semantic representation* by Bell. Gutt and Alves also point to the non-verbal nature of such as stage. Based on the principle of relevance, they call this stage *interpretive resemblance*. From this point of view, we could say that there are three key stages in the translation process: understanding, a non-verbal stage and re-expression.

As Delisle points out, in the case of written translation, there is a fourth and last stage of verification that he calls a phase of *justified analysis*; the translator produces provisional solutions which are then revised and incorporated into the target text. Along similar lines, Bell (1998) calls this phase *review*, Königs and Alves call it *improvement* (*Verfeinerung*).

2.4.3.2 The role of memory and linguistic and extra-linguistic knowledge

In one way or another, all models emphasize the role of both short-term and long-term memories as well as the importance played by the linguistic and extra-linguistic knowledge stored in memory. Seleskovitch and Lederer's interpretive theory of translation and the psycholinguistic model proposed by Kiraly point out that the translation process requires not only the intervention of linguistic knowledge in at least two languages but also extralinguistic knowledge of various kinds: encyclopaedic knowledge, thematic knowledge, cultural knowledge and knowledge of the circumstances surrounding a particular translation (including the context for the production the source text, the specifications of the translation task, etc.). For them, these different types of knowledge are stored in memory.

As Wilss points out, we must also add to these factors the need for certain skills and abilities, stored in memory, which are required to properly develop *translation competence* (see Chapter 3 on *translation competence).*

2.4.3.3 The need to integrate internal (cognitive) and external resources

It is a given fact that translators must rely on external sources for documentation. To that extent, Seleskovitch and Lederer point to the use of sources of documentation in order to enhance the cognitive inputs (linguistic and extra-linguistic) necessary to translate. Along similar lines, Königs argues that decisions made in the so-called Rest Block can benefit from external sources of documentation. Kiraly points to *internal* and *external sources of information* whereas Alves refers to *internal* and *external support.*

2.4.3.4 The existence of translation units

Most authors also agree that the translation process is carried out in smaller processing units of the source text, which are called translation units. Seleskovitch and Lederer consider that the unit of translation is the unit of meaning of a discursive nature that they identify as a unit of understanding, a mental representation, resulting from a synthesis between the semantics of linguistic expression and the translator's knowledge. Königs and Alves consider that the unit of translation stems from the translator's focus of attention triggered by instances of cognitive processing. From a different angle, Bell sees the unit of translation as the clause.

2.4.3.5 The multi-directional, non-linear nature of the translation process

Most authors point to the multi-directional nature of the translation process. On the one hand, the unfolding of the translation process does not strictly follow a linear order in which there is always a first phase of understanding followed by a phase of re-expression. These phases do not occur linearly or in isolation. This type of non-linearity varies according to the mode of translation (oral, written, etc.) and is particularly evident in the case of written translation. On the other hand, in written translation, the process does not necessarily unfold in terms of sequential units of translation. Rather, it unfolds by means of several regressions, namely, recursive movements necessary to revise what has been produced before. Last but not least, this non-linearity also refers to internal aspects within the main phases of understanding and re-expression. Both phases of understanding and re-expression entail non-linear processes within themselves in which all involved elements involved interact dynamically.

Seleskovitch and Lederer point to the non-linear movement from a non-verbal level (*deverbalization*) to verbalization in a natural language: from intended meaning to linguistic expression. Delisle shows that, in the case of written translation, this non-linearity arises in the provisional solutions produced by translators, which are then revised and appear as definite solutions in the target texts. Krings, Königs, Alves and Kiraly also take this aspect into consideration. Non-linearity is also a point of consideration for Königs who states that processes in the *Adhoc Block* are automatic and, therefore linear, whereas processes in the *Rest Block* are non-linear and require recursive movements. Wilss indicates that the translation process does not follow a linear encoding-decoding model, but rather processes of analysis and interpretation, in which the following elements interact: comparison, analogy, probability, inference, planning and so on. Wilss also indicates the existence of a *structure of expectation*, i.e. an image of the final product, which was probably constructed from the interaction between the processes of understanding the original text and the re-expression of the target text; a point which is also considered relevant by Kiraly. Bell sees the translation process as a non-linear process with each phase following another. Although the process requires processing at each phase, it is a non-linear process with no fixed order in which constant revisions occur and rejections of previous decisions may take place. Gutt also considers that the translation process is geared by higher-order metarepresentations that have an inferential nature and, thus, also point to central processes that have a non-linear nature. Alves, building on Königs and Gutt, also points to the recursive, multi-directional nature of the translation process occurring in the so-called Rest Block, supported by the higher-order metarepresentations created by the translator. Finally, Kiraly shows that translation is not processed as a simple linear sequence of signs but first and foremost through an interaction of several elements (structure, extra-linguistic knowledge, etc.).

2.4.3.6 The dynamic and interactive features of the translation process

As a consequence of its multi-directional and non-linear nature, the translation process has dynamic and interactive features. In addition to what has been said in the previous subsection, several authors highlight the importance of such dynamic and interactive features.

Seleskovitch and Lederer show that there is a dynamic interaction between linguistic expression and the processing of the cognitive inputs necessary for the construal of meaning in translation. This interaction has an impact on both processes of understanding and re-expression which require linguistic and extra-linguistic knowledge. Gutt makes a similar point in his application of relevance theory to translation. Gutt uses the concept of higher-order metarepresentation to account for the dynamic and interactive features inherent to translation and to show, through this, how translators arrive at instances of interpretive resemblance. Building on Gutt, Alves analyses experimental translation process data to consubstantiate this claim.

From a different angle, Bell sees the translation process as a dynamic, interactive and cascading process, in which both bottom-up and top-down processes (from the particular to the general and from the general to the particular) play a role. This would imply that deductive and inductive processes are integral components of the translation process.

2.4.3.7 The existence of automatized (uncontrolled) and non-automatized (controlled) processes

Translation requires a special type of cognitive processing in which automatized (uncontrolled) and non-automatized (controlled) processes interact. Seleskovitch and Lederer, for instance, note that both understanding and re-expression are the result of automatic and conscious mechanisms of an individual. Bearing this issue in mind, Kiraly's psycholinguistic model of the translation process proposes the existence of two processing centres: a *relatively controlled processing centre*, where the information provided by the long-term memory is synthesized without conscious control, and a *relatively uncontrolled processing centre*, dealing with the information provided by the text and external elements. Kiraly cautiously introduces *relative* qualifications in both centres, implying that this is not a strict dichotomy. Along similar lines, Königs and Alves use the concepts of *Adhoc Block* and *Rest Block* to account for automatic (routinized) and non-automatic (reflexive) processes.

2.4.3.8 Translation as a process of problem solving, use of strategies and decision making

As in any type of information processing, difficulties often arise in the translation process either in understanding or re-expression. Thus, operations involving problem-solving and decision-making are constantly in demand.

According to Krings and Wilss, translation requires problem solving, the implementation of strategies and techniques, geared towards decision making. Wilss adds that to implement strategies, translators use two types of knowledge: declarative knowledge *(knowing that)* and procedural knowledge *(knowing how)*. Wilss insists on the difference between problem solving and decision making. For him, decision-making processes will not begin until the need for decision making is sufficiently defined within the structure of a problem-solving operation that prepares the way for decision making. Problem-solving operations, the use of strategies, and decision making are fundamental traits in the development of the translation process. In the models we have presented, these traits have been investigated empirically by Krings, Königs, Hönig, Lörscher, Alves, Kiraly and Carl and Schaeffer.

Königs points out that the translation process starts with routinized processes that search for automatic solutions. Königs cautions that such automatic solutions are extremely resistant to modifications and may account for inadequacies observed in the target text. Additionally, whenever translators fail to find such automatic solutions, their processes move into a reflexive mode of text production (*Rest Block*) in which problem-solving, the use of strategies and decision making take place. This point is also incorporated by Alves, who builds on Königs, and insists on the importance of investigating translation processes from an inferential perspective. Kiraly also shows that whenever automatic processing does not produce provisional translation elements, these problems move away from the intuitive workspace and are then considered in the controlled processing centre: a strategy is selected and applied to find a solution.

All the above-mentioned traits are of crucial importance in the unfolding of the translation process. Differences in the unfolding of the translation process may be due to the translator's skills (level of knowledge, experience, etc.), the characteristics of the translation task (purpose, method chosen, etc.) and the mode (written, oral, audio-visual, etc.) and type (literary, technical, etc.) of translation.

2.4.4 The complexity of the translation process

The complexity of such traits has led Hurtado Albir (2001/2011, p. 375) to define the process of translation as a complex cognitive process which has an interactive and non-linear nature, encompassing automatized (uncontrolled) and non-automatized (controlled) processes, and entails processes of problem solving, the use of strategies and decision making.

Thus, translation entails a complex cognitive process in which elements of different types and kinds play a role. To this intrinsic complexity of the translation process, one must add the fact that different factors may have an impact on its unfolding, depending on the translator, the purpose of the translation and the method chosen and the type (technical, literary, legal, etc.) and modality (written, audio-visual, sight translation, etc.) of translation in question. These different factors make the study of the translation process a more difficult attempt.

However, in spite of this diversity, the translation process can only be analysed with respect to a translator's actions on one specific translation task. To that extent, rigorous empirical studies about the unfolding of the translation process in the different kinds of translation should provide reliable information about the specificities of each cognitive operation, their commonalities and their differences. In turn, it will help us to better understand the characteristics of the translation process as a whole, not only in their specificity of information processing but also in relation to the neurophysiological activities undertaken. It is the challenge that has arisen from current cognitive research on translation (see Chapter 4).

2.4.5 Lack of pedagogical applications

For decades, many authors have stressed the importance of basing the training of translators and interpreters on an adequate development of the translation processes. This has been stated, for example, by Seleskovitch (1968, 1975), Seleskovitch and Lederer (1984) and Gile (1995/2009) for the teaching of interpreting, and by Delisle (1980/1988) and Hurtado Albir (1996a, 1996b) for the teaching of written translation.

Although models of the translation process were not conceived for pedagogical purposes, the results of some empirical research and the detailed descriptions provided by researchers have had applications for the didactics of translation. Alves (2000) uses the outline of his model of the translation process to design a training program that instructs students to identify the translation unit, to use sources of internal and external support and how to link these features to problem-solving and decision-making operations. Hansen (2002) also uses think-aloud protocols in the classroom to teach students to monitor their processes with a special focus on the role of attention. Several other applications have been suggested, among other authors, by Kiraly (1995) and PACTE (2017, 2020).

However, there is a lack of pedagogical applications of the various studies carried out on the translation process to operationalize the results obtained in terms of learning outcomes, progression of difficulties, pedagogical tasks and assessment procedures. Therefore, we consider that it is necessary to continue to carry out research into the teaching of translation that aims at promoting an adequate development of the translation process.

2.5 The development of empirical research on the translation process

The models and considerations about the translation process outlined in this chapter are based either on other disciplines or on observations of translation/interpreting task execution. The intrinsic difficulty of the study of mental activities that are not directly observable, and the complexity of the translation process, create difficulties to carry out empirical studies. These difficulties, however, have been partially overcome by empirical studies that have shed light on the intricacies of the translation process (see Chapter 4).

2.5.1 From prescription to description

Already in the early 1990s, Lörscher (1991) had pointed to the danger of not providing descriptions of the translation process that were based on empirical studies. Bell (1998) also pointed to potential dangers in the inherent difficulties related to the study of mental activities, highlighting the lack of representativeness of the data or the unnatural tasks performed by subjects. However, Bell argues that, while not uniform or conclusive, results of empirical research could throw light on how translators translate, how they solve problems and how they justify their decisions. Bell's suggestions seem to foresee a trend that would gain impetus in the decades to come when a great deal of research has been carried out in order to describe, and hopefully model, the intrinsic complexity of the translation process.

2.5.2 Contributions from empirical studies

Since the mid-1980s, in parallel to the conceptual development of the study of the translation process, empirical research on the nature of the translation process has been carried out, and even more research output has been produced from the mid-1990s (see Chapter 4). From the mid-1990s, one observes the emergence of a new paradigm in research: the focus moves to the empirical description of the translation process and no longer on the conceptualization of the theoretical model of this process. These empirical studies use different instruments to collect data on the operation of the translation process: think-aloud protocols (TAPs), interviews, diaries, questionnaires, keylogging and eye tracking, as well as psychophysiological measurements, including, more recently, EEG and fMRI.

Most of these empirical studies deal with partial aspects of the translation process, such as a translation unit, lexical and syntactic problems, strategies used for problem solving and decision making, differences between professionals and students, automatic and non-automatic processes, creativity, the role of linguistic and encyclopaedic knowledge, the influence of declarative knowledge in the process of understanding, the impact of source text reading on the translation process, the processes of understanding and re-expression, the use of dictionaries, the decision-making process in inverse translation and so on. More recently, these studies have also incorporated aspects related to human-computer interaction, including issues related to the post-editing of machine-translation output. Although these studies do not address the translation process as a whole, they do contribute to highlighting the variety of mechanisms and cognitive operations involved. They also reveal that the translation process is not a monolithic process. Rather, it displays significant differences depending on whether students or professionals are involved, on the type of text, the translator's profile, the translation task, the kind of translation and so on.

All these studies highlight the complexity of the translation process and the multiplicity of factors involved in it. Chapter 4 describes in detail the evolution and the characteristics of these empirical studies.

Notes

1 Original citation: "*El procedimiento traductivo consiste en analizar la expresión del texto de Lengua Original en oraciones prenucleares, trasladar las oraciones prenucleares de Lengua Original en oraciones prenucleares equivalentes de Lengua Término y, finalmente, transformar estas estructuras de Lengua Término en expresiones estilísticamente apropiadas*"(Vásquez Ayora, 1977, p. 50).
2 Original citation: "*Ich unterscheide zwischen Translationsvorgang und Translationsprozeß. Unter Translation 'Prozeß' ist der Teil des Translationsvorgangs zu verstehen, in dem der Translator zu einem Ausgangstext unter Berücksichtigung bestimmter Vorgaben einen für einen bestimmten Zweck geeigneten Zieltext herstellt, während im Translationsvorgang noch andere translationsunabhängige Faktoren eine Rolle spielen. Der hier verwendete Prozeßbegriff ist nicht zu verwechseln mit dem vor allem von KRINGS (1986) in die Übersetzungswissenschaft eingeführten psycholinguistischen Prozeßbegriff*".
3 Original citation: "*essayer de mettre en lumière le processus mental qui rend possible la transmission quasi instantanée d'un message oral dans une autre langue*" (Seleskovitch, 1968, p. 36).
4 Original citation in: "*pour que la théorie complète puisse en être établie, il reste à faire un vaste travail de recherche objective et d'analyse systématique des mécanismes mentaux et en particulier des rapports pensée-parole*" (Seleskovitch, 1968, p. 243).
5 Seleskovitch and Lederer make a clear distinction between "sens" and "signification"; the latter term referring to words or phrases outside a given context. The authors prefer to use the contrastive pair Sense/Meaning in English to highlight the differences between the French terms "Sens'/'Signification". Seleskovitch and Lederer only refer to "meaning" when they use the original English expression "intended meaning", which the authors have borrowed from Searle (1979), when referring to the French concept of "vouloir dire".
6 Original citation: "*On peut dire que chaque acte de compréhension est une prise de conscience qui persiste, dissociée des stimulations qui l'ont provoquée. La dissociation de la forme et du sens est à nos yeux le mécanisme essentiel du langage, présent en toutes circonstances dans la communication: les formes s'estompent et disparaissent, tandis que les contenus éveillés par le signal s'associent à des souvenirs antérieurs, constituant d'innombrables métacircuits de duré variable, dont certains s'intègrent dans le bagage cognitif et deviennent une parcelle du savoir de l'individu*" (1981, p. 15).

7 Delisle (1998) is a translation into English of the first part of Delisle (1980) published in French.
8 Krings does not provide a list of the abbreviations used in his model. We have translated them as follows: R (*Rezeption*) was translated as Reception (in full) whereas W (*Wiedergabe*) was translated as Rendering (in full). HBM (*Hilfsmittelbenutzung*) was translated as UER (use of external resources). WB (*Wörterbuch*) was translated as D (Dictionary), monolingual dictionary as D1 and bilingual dictionary as D2. Finally, *Festlegung des zu suchenden Eintrags* was translated as Establishment of search item, i.e. the dictionary entry to search under.
9 Original citation: "*Im Adhoc-Block ordnet der Übersetzer einer ausgangssprachlichen Einheit mehr oder minder automatisch eine zielsprachliche Entsprechung zu. Er hat – wenn man so will – eine individuelle, mentale 1:1-Äquivalenz aktiviert*" (1987, p. 164).
10 Original citation: "*Er stellt keine internalisierte oder spontane 1:1-Entsprechung zwischen Ausgangs- und Zielsprache bereit. Zweitens gehen in den Rest-Block Informationen des Textumfeldes (Autor, Adressaten, Intention) mit ein. Drittens hat die spezifische translatorische Kompetenz, also die gezielte Anwendung bestimmter Übersetzungstechniken, hier ihren Platz*" (1987, p. 164).

References

Alves, F. (1995). *Zwischen Schweigen und Sprechen: Wie bildet sich eine transkulturelle Brücke*? Hamburg: Dr. Kovac.

Alves, F. (1997). A formação de tradutores a partir de uma abordagem cognitiva: reflexões de um projeto de ensino. *TradTerm*, *4*(2), 19–40.

Alves, F. (2000). Um modelo didático do processo tradutório: A integração de estratégias de Tradução. In F. Alves, C. Magalhães, & A. Pagano (Eds.), *Traduzir com autonomia: Estratégias para o tradutor em formação* (pp. 113–128). São Paulo: Contexto.

Alves, F. (2015). Was beim Übersetzen passiert: Der Einfluss von Königs's Modell (1987) des Übersetzungsprozesses auf die prozessorientierte Forschung im Rahmen der Übersetzungswissenschaft. In S. Hoffmann & A. Stork (Eds.), *Lernorientierte Fremdsprachenforschung und -didaktik*(pp. 123–131). Tübingen: Narr.

Anderson, J.R. (2007). *How can the human mind occur in the physical universe.* New York: Oxford University Press.

Barbizet, J. (1964). *Études sur la mémoire. Premier Série.* Paris: L'expansion Scientifique Française.

Barbizet, J. (1966). *Études sur la mémoire. Deuxième Série.* Paris: L'expansion Scientifique Française.

Bartlett, F.L. (1932). *Remembering. A study in experimental and social psychology.* Cambridge: Cambridge University Press. New edition in 1964.

Bell, R.T. (1987). Translation theory; where are we going? *Meta*, *31*(4), 403–415.

Bell, R.T. (1991). *Translation and translating.* London: Longman.

Bell, R.T. (1998). Psycholinguistic/cognitive approaches. In M. Baker (Ed.), *Routledge encyclopedia of translation studies* (pp. 185–190). London: Routledge.

Benard, J.P., & Horguelin, P.A. (1979). *Pratique de la traduction.* Montreal: Linguatech.

Blakemore, D. (2002). *Relevance and linguistic meaning: The semantics and pragmatics of discourse markers.* Cambridge: Cambridge University Press.

Boekaerts, M. (1981). Is there a direct link between the comprehension process and the production process? In M. Heid (Ed.), *New Yorker Werkstattgespräch 1980*. Munich: Goethe House.
Carl, M. (2010). A *computational framework for a cognitive model of human translation processes*. Paper presented at the translating and the computer 32, London. Retrieved from http://www.mt-archive.info/10/Aslib-2010-Carl.pdf
Carl, M., & Dragsted, B. (2012). Inside the monitor model: Processes of default and challenged translation production. *Translation: Computation, Corpora, Cognition*,*2*, 127–145.
Carl, M., & Schaeffer, M.J. (2017a). Sketch of a noisy channel model for the translation process. In S. Hansen-Schirra, O. Czulo, & S. Hofmann (Eds.), *Empirical modelling of translation and interpreting* (pp. 71–116). Berlin: Language Science Press. doi:10.5281/zenodo.1090954
Carl, M., & Schaeffer, M.J. (2017b). Models of the translation process. In J.W. Schwieter & A. Ferreira (Eds.), *The handbook of translation and cognition* (Chapter 3, pp. 50–70). Hoboken, NJ: Wiley-Blackwell. doi:10.1002/9781119241485.ch3
Carl, M., & Schaeffer, M.J. (2019). Outline for a relevance theoretical model of machine translation post-editing. In D. Li et al. (Eds.), *Researching cognitive processes of translation* (pp. 71–116). Singapore: Springer.
Cook, V.J. (Ed.). (2003). *The effects of the second language on the first*. Clevedon: Multilingual Matters.
Corbin, R.M. (1980). Decisions that might not get made. In T.E. Wallsten (Ed.), *Cognitive processes in choice and decision behaviour* (pp. 47–67). Hillsdale, NJ: Erlbaum.
Danks, J.H. (1991). *The psycholinguistics of reading and translation. Fundamental questions in translation theory*. Leipzig: University Leipzig.
De Groot, Annette M.B. (1997). The cognitive study of translation and interpretation: Three approaches. In J.H. Danks, G.M. Shreve, S.B. Fountain, & M. McBeath (Eds.), *Cognitive processes in translation and interpreting* (pp. 25–56). Thousand Oaks, CA: Sage Publications.
Delisle, J. (1980). *L'analyse du discours comme méthode de traduction*. Ottawa: University of Ottawa Press. Translated into English as Translation: An interpretive approach. (1988). Ottawa: University of Ottawa Press.
Diller, H.J., & Kornelius, J. (1978). *Linguistische Probleme der Übersetzung*. Tübingen: Max Niemeyer Verlag.
Firth, J.R. (1951). Modes on meaning. In J.R. Firth (Ed.), *Essays and studies of the English association* (Vol. 4/1, pp. 118–149). Oxford: Oxford University Press.
Firth, J.R. (1957). *Papers in linguistics*. Oxford: Oxford University Press.
Firth, J.R. (1964). *The tongues of men*. Oxford: Oxford University Press.
Garnier, G. (1985). *Linguistique et traduction. Éléments de systématique verbale comparée du français et de l'anglais*. Caen: Paradigme.
Geeraerts, D. (2009). *Words and other wonders. Papers on lexical and semantic topics*. Berlin: Mouton de Gruyter.
Gile, D. (1995). *Basic concepts and models for interpreter and translator training*. Amsterdam: John Benjamins. 2nd ed., 2009.
Gouadec, D. (2005). Modélisation du processus d'exécution des traductions. *Meta*, *50*(2), pp. 643–655.
Gouadec, D. (2007). *Translation as a profession*. Amsterdam/Philadelphia: John Benjamins.
Guillaume, G. (1971a). *Leçons de linguistique, 1948–49, Série A. Structure sémiologique et structure psychique de la langue française 1*. Québec: Klincksieck.

Guillaume, G. (1971b). *Leçons de linguistique, 1948–1949, Série B. Psychosystématique du langage: Principes, méthodes et applications 1*. Québec: Klincksieck

Guillaume, G. (1973). *Leçons de linguistique, 1948–1949, Série C. Grammaire particulière du français et grammaire générale 4*. Québec: Klincksieck

Gutt, E.-A. (1991). *Translation and relevance*. Oxford: Blackwell. 2nd ed., published by St Jerome in 2000.

Gutt, E.-A. (2004). Challenges of metarepresentation to translation competence. In E. Fleischmann, P.A. Schmitt, & G. Wotjak (Eds.), *Translationskompetenz: Proceedings of LICTRA 2001: VII. Leipziger Internationale Konferenz zu Grundfragen der Translatologie* (pp. 77–89). Tübingen: Stauffenburg.

Gutt, E.-A. (2005). On the significance of the cognitive core of translation. *The Translator*, *11*(1), 25–49.

Halverson, S.L. (2003). The cognitive basis of translation universals. *Target*, *15*(2), 197–241.

Halverson, S.L. (2007). A cognitive linguistic account of translation shifts. *Belgian Journal of Linguistics*, *21*, 105–119.

Halverson, S.L. (2010). Cognitive translation studies. Developments in theory and method. In G. Shreve & E. Angelone (Eds.), *Translation and cognition* (pp. 349–369). Amsterdam: John Benjamins.

Halverson, S.L. (2017). Gravitational pull in translation. Testing a revised model. In G. De Sutter, M.-A. Lefer, & I. Delaere (Eds.), *Empirical translation studies: New methodological and theoretical traditions* (pp. 9–46). Berlin: De Gruyter.

Halverson, S.L. (2019). 'Default' translation: A construct for cognitive translation and interpreting studies. *Translation, Cognition & Behavior*, *2*(2), 187–210.

Hansen, G. (2002). Selbstaufmerksamkeit im Übersetzungsprozess. In G. Hansen (Ed.), *Empirical translation studies: Process and product* (pp. 9–27). Copenhagen: Samfundslitteratur.

Harris, M., & Coultheart, M. (1986). *Language processing in children and adults*. London: Routledge.

Hemingway, E. (1975). *The old man and the sea*. New York: Scribner (first published in 1952).

Hönig, H.G. (1986). Übersetzen zwischen Reflex und Reflexion. Ein Modell der übersetzungsrelevanten Textanalyse. In M. Snell-Hornby (Ed.), *Übersetzungswissenschaft. Eine Neuorientierung* (pp. 230–251). Tübingen: Francke.

Hönig, H.G. (1988a). Wissen Übersetzer eigentlich, was sie tun? *Lebende Sprachen*, *33*(1), 10–14.

Hönig, H.G. (1988b). Übersetzen lernt man nicht durch Übersetzen. Ein Plädoyer für eine Propädeutik des Übersetzens. *Fremdsprachen Lehren und Lernen*, *17*, 154–167.

Hönig, H.G. (1991). Holmes' 'mapping theory' and the landscape of mental translation processes. In K. an Leuven-Zwart & T. Naajkens (Eds.), *Translation studies: The state of the art. Proceedings from the First James S. Holmes Symposium on Translation Studies* (pp. 77–89). Amsterdam: Rodopi.

Hönig, H.G. (1995). *Konstruktives Übersetzen*. Tübingen: Stauffenburg.

Hönig, H.G. (1998). Translating the constructive way. In W. Lörscher (Ed.), Special Issue Translation Studies in Germany. *Ilha do Desterro*, *33*, 11–24.

Hönig, H.G., & Kussmaul, P. (1982). *Strategie der Übersetzung*. Tübingen: Gunter Narr.

Hurtado Albir, A. (1990). *La notion de fidélité en traduction*, Col. Traductologie 5. Paris: Didier Érudition.

Hurtado Albir, A. (1996a). La enseñanza de la traducción directa 'general'. Objetivos de aprendizaje y metodología. In A. Hurtado Albir (Ed.), *La enseñanza de la traducción* (pp. 31–55). Castellón: Universitat Jaume I.
Hurtado Albir, A. (1996b). La cuestión del método traductor. Método, estrategia y técnica de traducción. *Sendebar*, *7*, 39–57.
Hurtado Albir, A. (1999). *Enseñar a traducir.Metodología en la formación de traductores e intérpretes.* Madrid: Edelsa.
Hurtado Albir, A. (2001). *Traducción y Traductología. Introducción a la Traductología.* Madrid: Cátedra. [5th Revised edition, 2011].
Hurtado Albir, A., & Alves, F. (2009). Translation as a cognitive activity. In J. Munday (Ed.), *The Routledge companion to translation studies* (pp. 54–73). London: Routledge.
Ivir, V. (1981). Formal correspondence vs. translation equivalence revisited. *Poetics Today*, *2*, 51–59.
Jarvis, S., & Pavlenko, A. (2008). *Crosslinguistic influence in language and cognition.* New York: Routledge.
Jakobsen, A.L. (2011). Tracking translators' keystrokes and eye movements with Translog. In C. Alvstad, A. Hild, & E. Tiselius (Eds.), *Methods and strategies of process research* (pp. 37–55). Amsterdam: John Benjamins.
Kiraly, D. (1995). *Pathways to translation.Pedagogy and process.* Kent: The Kent State University Press.
Königs, F.G. (1981). Zur Frage der Übersetzungseinheit und ihre Relevanz für den Fremdsprachenunterricht. *Linguistische Berichte*, *74*, 82–103.
Königs, F.G. (1987). Was beim Übersetzen passiert. Theoretische Aspekte, empirische Befunde und praktische Konsequenzen". *Die Neueren Sprachen*, *86*, 162–185.
Krings, H.P. (1986). *Was in den Köpfen von Übersetzern vorgeht. Eine empirische Untersuchung der Struktur des Übersetzungsprozesses an fortgeschrittener französischer Lernenden.* Tübingen: Gunter Narr.
Kussmaul, P., & Tirkkonen-Condit, S. (1995). Think-aloud protocol analysis in translation studies. *TTR*, *8*(1), 177–199. https://doi.org/10.7202/037201ar
Langacker, R. (1987). *Foundations of cognitive grammar. Volume 1. Theoretical prerequisites.* Stanford, CA: Stanford University Press.
Langacker, R. (1991). *Foundations of cognitive grammar. Volume 2. Descriptive application.* Stanford, CA: Stanford University Press.
Langacker, R. (2008). *Cognitive grammar. A basic introduction.* Oxford: Oxford University Press.
Laplace, C. (1994). *Théorie du langage et Théorie de la traduction*, Col. Traductologie 8. Paris: Didier Érudition.
Larson, M. (1984). *Meaning-based translation: A guide to cross-language equivalence.* Lanham, MD: University Press of America, Inc. (*La traducción basada en el significado. Un manual para el descubrimiento de equivalencias entre lenguas.* Editorial Universitaria de Buenos Aires, 1989).
Laukkanen, J. (1993). *Routine versus non-routine processes in translation: A think-aloud protocol study.* Unpublished MA Thesis, Savonlinna School of Translation Studies, University of Joensuu.
Läubli, S. (2014). *Statistical modelling of human translation processes.* Unpublished MA Thesis. University of Edinburgh, Edinburgh, UK.
Lederer, M. (1976). Synecdoque et traduction. *Études de Linguistique Appliquée*, *24*, 13–41.
Lederer, M. (1981). *La traduction simultanée.* Paris: Minard.
Lederer, M. (1994). *La traduction aujourd'hui. Le modèle interprétatif.* Paris: Hachette.

Levy, J. (1967). Translation as a decision process. In *To Honor Roman Jakobson* (Vol.2, pp. 1171–1182). The Hague: Mouton.
Ljduskanov, A. (1969). *Traduction humaine et traduction mécanique*. Paris: Centre de linguistique quantitative de la Faculté des Sciences de l'Université de Paris.
Lörscher, W. (1991). *Translation performance, translation process, and translation strategies: A psycholinguistic investigation*. Tübingen: Narr.
Lörscher, W. (1996). A psycholinguistic analysis of translation processes. *Meta*, *41*(1), 26–32.
Lörscher, W. (2005). The translation process: Methods and problems of its investigation, *Meta*, 50(2), 597–608.
Neisser, U. (1967). *Cognitive psychology*. Nueva York: Appleton.
Nida, E. A. (1964). *Toward a science of translating, with special reference to principles and procedures involved in Bible translating*. Leiden: E.J. Brill.
Nirenburg, S. (1987). *Machine translation: Theoretical and methodological issues*. Cambridge: Cambridge University Press.
Nord, C. H. (1988). *Textanalyse und Übersetzen*. Heidelberg: Julius Groos Verlag. [Translation into English. Nord, C. H. (1991). *Text analysis in translation*. Amsterdam: Rodopi].
PACTE. (2000). Acquiring translation competence: Hypotheses and methodological problems in a research project. In A. Beeby, D. Ensinger, & M. Presas (Eds.), *Investigating translation* (pp. 99–106). Amsterdam: John Benjamins.
PACTE. (2017). Defining features of translation competence. In A. Hurtado Albir (Ed.), *Researching translation competence by PACTE Group*(pp. 281–302). Amsterdam: John Benjamins.
PACTE. (2020). Translation competence acquisition. Design and results of the PACTE Group's experimental research. *The Interpreter and Translator Trainer*, *14*(2), 95–233.
Pickering, M.J., & Ferreira, V.S. (2008). Structural priming: A critical review. *Psychological Bulletin*,*134*(3), 427–459.
Schaeffer, M., & Carl, M. (2013/2015). Shared representations and the translation process: A recursive model. *Translation and Interpreting Studies*,*8*(2), 169–190. Reprinted in M. Ehrensberger-Dow, B. Englund Dimitrova, S, Hubscher-Davidson, & U. Norberg (Eds.), *Describing cognitive processes in translation: Acts and events* (pp. 21–42). Amsterdam: John Benjamins.
Searle, J.R. (1979). *Expression and meaning.Studies in the theory of speech acts*. Cambridge: Cambridge University Press.
Seleskovitch, D. (1968). *L'interprète dans les conférences internationales. Problèmes de langage et de communication*. Paris: Minard. [Translation into English. Seleskovitch, D. (1978). *Interpreting for international conferences: Problems of language and communication*. Washington: Pen and Booth].
Seleskovitch, D. (1975). *Langage, langues et mémoire. Étude de la prise de notes en interprétation consécutive*. Paris: Minard.
Seleskovitch, D., & Lederer, M. (1984). *Interpréter pour traduire*, Col Traductologie 1. Paris: Didier Érudition.
Seleskovitch, D., & Lederer, M. (1989). *Pédagogie raisonnée de l'interprétation*, Col. Traductologie 4. Paris: Didier Érudition.
Shannon, C.E., & Weaver, W. (1949). *The mathematical theory of communication*. Urbana: University of Illinois Press.
Sperber, D., & Wilson, D. (1986). *Relevance. Communication and cognition*. Oxford: Basil Blackwell. 2nd edition published in 1995.
Spiro, R.J. (1980). Constructive processes in prose comprehension and recall. In R.J. Spiro, B.C. Bruce, & W.F. Brewer (Eds.), *Theoretical issues in reading comprehension* (pp. 245–278). Hillsdale, NJ: Erlbaum.

Stein, D. (1980). *Theoretische Grundlagen der Übersetzungswissenschaft*. Tübingen: Gunter Narr.
Steinberg, D.D. (1982). *Psycholinguistics: Language, mind and world*. London: Longman.
Steiner, G. (1975). *After Babel*. Oxford: Oxford University Press.
Tannen, D. (1979). What is a frame – surface evidence for underlying expectations. In R.O. Freedle (Ed.), *New directions in discourse processing* (pp. 137–181). Norwood, NJ: ABLEX.
Tirkkonen-Condit, S. (2002). Translationese – A myth or an empirical fact? A study into the linguistic identifiability of translated language. *Target*, *14*(2), 207–220.
Tirkkonen-Condit, S. (2005). The monitor model revisited: Evidence from process research. *Meta*, *50*(2), 405–414.
Toury, G. (2004). Probabilistic explanations in translation studies: Welcome as they are, would they qualify as universals? In A. Mauranen & P. Kujamäkipp (Eds.), *Translation universals: Do they exist?* (pp. 15–32). Amsterdam: John Benjamins.
Vandepitte, S., & Hartsuiker, R.J. (2011). Metonymic language use as a student translation problem. Towards a controlled psycholinguistic investigation. In C. Alvstad, A. Hild, & E. Tiselius (Eds.), *Methods and strategies of process research* (pp. 67–92). Amsterdam: John Benjamins.
Vázquez Ayora, G. (1977). *Introducción a la Traductología*. Washington: Georgetown University Press.
Wilson, D. (2000). Metarepresentation in linguistic communication. In D. Sperber (Ed.), *Metarepresentations* (pp. 411–448). Oxford: Oxford University Press.
Wilss, W. (1988). *Kognition und Übersetzen: Zu Theorie und Praxis der menschlichen und der maschinellen Übersetzung*. Tübingen: Niemeyer.
Wilss, W. (1996). *Knowledge and Skills in Translator Behavior*. Amsterdam: John Benjamins.

3

TRANSLATION COMPETENCE AND ITS ACQUISITION

This chapter addresses the notions of translation competence and translation competence acquisition and distinguishes translators from other bilinguals who are not translators by looking into the competences required to become a translator. It also discusses the characteristics of these competences, how they are acquired, what levels of competence exist, and what are the most representative traits that distinguish the best translators, addressing the development of research on translation competence and its acquisition as well as the relationship of this development with neighbouring disciplines.

Introduction

Over the past decades, besides studying translation as a product, as a process and as a behaviour, translation studies scholars have also been busy in their attempts to describe what knowledge and abilities translators need in order to translate effectively and what enables them to be able to perform the cognitive operations necessary in the course of the translation process and the tasks required in a professional setting, namely, translation competence (TC). This competence identifies the translator as a full-fledged professional and distinguishes him/her from individuals who are not translators. Thus, the following question arises: What distinguishes translators from other bilinguals who are not translators? What are the knowledge and abilities that define translation competence? How does one acquire this competence? What levels of translation competence exist? What characterizes translators that excel in their performance and distinguishes them from other translators? This chapter builds on Hurtado Albir (2001, pp. 375–408), Hurtado Albir and Alves (2009) and Hurtado Albir (2017a, 2021).

However, before addressing the issue of TC, it is important to refer to other disciplines that have also addressed the notion of competence from their perspectives and introduce some relevant notions related to the analysis of TC.

DOI: 10.4324/9781003006978-4

3.1 The study of competences: Related notions

3.1.1 On the notion of competence

The notion of competence has a long history of analysis in other disciplines, such as applied linguistics, psychology of work and pedagogy.[1] As we shall see, while having different purposes and addressing the issue from different perspectives, there are important points of contact in their approaches.

3.1.1.1 Applied linguistics: Communicative competence

Applied linguistics has been using the concept of *communicative competence* since the mid-1960s.In order to situate and contextualize this notion within applied linguistics, one needs to refer to the distinction made by Chomsky (1965) between *competence* (intuitive, internalized and unconscious knowledge that the speaker has of his/her own native language) and linguistic *performance* (the actual use of language in concrete situations). Research arising from this distinction within applied linguistics attempts to redefine the notion of competence. These studies have broadened the scope of competence-related aspects and criticize Chomsky for not extending the scope of *competence* to incorporate aspects which he considered to be typical of *performance*, including language use abilities. Thus, the concept of *communicative competence* was coined[2] and developed within a long line of research carried out by authors such as Hymes (1971), Canale-Swain (1980), Canale (1983), Widdowson (1989), Spolsky (1989), Bachman (1990) and so on. One must also bear in mind that the concept of communicative competence is related to *Speech Act Theory* (Austin, 1962; Searle, 1969) and to early work on discourse analysis.

Canale (1983) elaborates the concept further by establishing a distinction between *communicative competence*, i.e. the underlying system of knowledge and skills required for communication, and *actual communication*, namely, its realization in certain psychological and contextual conditions. Canale considers that communicative competence consists of several interacting competences: grammar (language code), sociolinguistics (adaptation to the sociolinguistic contexts), discourse (text production) and strategic (to compensate for deficiencies and improve the effectiveness of the communication).

Bachman (1990), in turn, prefers to speak of *communicative language ability*, which is composed of knowledge (competence) and the ability to run this competence properly in language. Bachman highlights the importance of the strategic component and includes psycho-physiological mechanisms. Bachman distinguishes three components related to human communicative *ability*: (1) linguistic competence, i.e. knowledge of the language being used, consisting of an organizational competence (grammatical and textual) and pragmatic competence (related to language functions and adaptation to context); (2) strategic competence, used to assess, plan and implement communication; and (3) psycho-physiological mechanisms, i.e. neurological and psychological processes involved in actual language use.

Among several aspects related to communicative competence, the following are worth noting:

1) The distinction between *competence*, i.e. the underlying system of knowledge and skills necessary for communication, and *actual communication*, i.e. the realization of communication under determined psychological and contextual conditions.
2) The consideration that communicative competence incorporates *abilities* relevant to language use.
3) The definition of competence in terms of subcompetences.
4) The importance attached to the strategic component as a mechanism to compensate for deficiencies to plan, evaluate and improve the effectiveness of actual communication.
5) The inclusion of psycho-physiological mechanisms such as memory, attention, etc.
6) The interactive nature of all related components.

3.1.1.2 The psychology of work: Professional competences and a behavioural perspective

In the context of the workplace, there is a long history in the study of professional competences that began in the early 1970s in the United States in the field known as psychology of work. McClelland (1973) developed a behavioural approach to the study of competences in response to dissatisfaction with traditional measures used to predict work performance and methods of recruitment. McClelland tried to show that knowledge tests and a person's educational background are not, by themselves, able to predict good performance on the job. The title of McClelland's (1973) article, "Testing for competence rather than for intelligence", already highlights the change of approach in his proposal. McClelland's proposal was taken up and expanded by numerous other studies (Boyatzis, 1982, 1984; Spencer, McClelland, & Spencer, 1994, etc.), establishing models of competence (called *competence dictionaries*) for specific jobs. These descriptions were based on the study of professionals who had achieved outstanding results in the execution of tasks for these specific jobs.

McClelland's approach has also become the basis for present-day competence-based human resource management.

According to this approach, a dichotomy between competence and performance does not arise since satisfactory behaviour in work performance is also a factor to be considered. Competence is conceived as a complex know how, consisting of a set of abilities, attitudes, values and so on that ensures the effectiveness of professional practice.

3.1.1.3 Pedagogy: Competence-based training

In pedagogy, a new pedagogical model called *competence-based training* (CBT) has been advocated over the last decades.[3] According to Lasnier (2000, p. 22), CBT is the logical continuation of the previous model (*learning objectives-based training*). In CBT, competences are the core of curriculum design, which includes an integrated model of teaching, learning and assessment. The theoretical foundations of CBT draw on theories of cognitive-constructivist and socio-constructivist learning and also involve the operationalization of research carried out in the last decades, pursuing a more meaningful kind of learning among students.

There are different definitions of competence in CBT. Lasnier (2000, p. 32 – italics ours) proposes the following:

> a complex *know-how to act* resulting from the integration, mobilisation and organization of a set of capabilities and skills (which can be cognitive, affective, psycho-social or social) and knowledge (declarative knowledge) used efficiently in situations with common characteristics.
>
> *[our translation]*[4]

Yániz and Villardón (2006, p. 23), in turn, define CBT in the following terms: "a competence is the set of knowledge, abilities and attitudes needed to perform a given occupation and the capacity to mobilize and apply these resources in a given environment in order to produce a definite result" [our translation].[5]

These definitions highlight three aspects that characterize competences: knowing how to act, integration and context. First, one must define competences as a type of know how to act; it implies that competences are not just related to *know how to do* and cannot be reduced to operational knowledge. In addition, a competence involves the integration of different types of capabilities and skills (cognitive, affective, psychomotor or social), and declarative knowledge (*knowing what*). Thus, competence entails a *know* (a set of knowledge specific to a given discipline); a *know how* (skills to solve practical problems); and a *know how to be* (affective and social skills). Finally, one must consider that competence is only acquired when one is able to use it effectively in a given context.

CBT distinguishes between *discipline-related competences* (or *specific competences*) that pertain to each discipline, and *transversal* (or *generic*) *competences* which apply to all disciplines. In this sense, based on its particular professional profile, each discipline has to define what are the generic and specific competences that define this profile.

With respect to generic competences, it is worth mentioning the project *Tuning Educational Structures in Europe* (González & Wagenaar, 2003, 2005). According to González and Wagenaar (2003, p. 70), *Tuning* proposes three types of generic competences: (1) instrumental competences, which are a means to an end and can be cognitive, methodological, technological or linguistic; (2) interpersonal competences, including competences to interact well with others and to promote social interaction and communication; and (3) systemic competences, involving a combination of understanding, sensitivity and knowledge to enable the individual to understand how parts of a whole are related.

The specific competences of a university curriculum are formulated on the basis of specific knowledge and abilities commonly found in professional practice for a particular professional profile. Hence, the importance of the description of the professional profile, defined on the basis of good professional practice which are dominant and emerging practices in that particular profile. The professional profile details the main functions of a profession and the tasks through which these functions are enacted. To describe this profile, it is necessary to analyse the social needs and study the labour market for new fields of professional development (emerging practices). This definition of a professional profile helps identify the necessary competences, which, in turn, facilitates the identification of the formative elements (Yániz & Villardón, 2006, pp. 17–20).

Thus, CBT has points of contact with the study of professional competences. It is also a framework for research on TC in the context of curricula design for the training of translators.

3.1.2 Types of knowledge

Stemming from cognitive psychology, a distinction of great interest for the study of TC, including several types of knowledge, is proposed: the distinction between declarative knowledge (*knowing what*), procedural (or operative) knowledge (*knowing how*), explicative knowledge (*know why*) and conditional knowledge(*know when*) (Pozo & Postigo, 1993).

In order to understand the operation of any type of knowledge (and its acquisition), it is of paramount importance to understand the distinction between declarative knowledge and operational (or procedural) knowledge made by Anderson (1983).[6] As Pozo and Postigo (1993, p. 49) point out, these are two different types of knowledge, not always related, necessary to understand the world. According to Anderson, declarative knowledge is to know what; it is easy to verbalize, it is acquired by exposure and it is essentially controlled. Procedural knowledge, in turn, is to know how; it is difficult to verbalize, it is acquired by practice and it is largely processed automatically. Therefore, these two types of knowledge are acquired differently.

Pozo and Postigo (1993, p. 49) point out this distinction, although useful, is insufficient. The authors suggest that there may be an understanding of a particular phenomenon (cold winters) but one may not be able to explain it (why winters are cold). In this sense, Pozo and Postigo refer to a third type of knowledge suggested by Wellington (1989), namely, explicative knowledge, which would be related to *know why*. As such, explicative knowledge is identified with theoretical knowledge. Moreover, Paris, Lipson and Wixson (1983), Paris, Gross and Lipson (1984) and some other authors also distinguish another type of knowledge, i.e. conditional knowledge, which is *know when* (and why) to use declarative and procedural knowledge.

3.1.3 Expert knowledge: Expertise

Studies of expertise and expert performance (see Section 1.4.5 in Chapter 1) highlight various features of the operation of expert knowledge (see, among others, Ericsson et al., 2006) that are of interest to the study of TC. These features can be instrumental in characterizing the behaviour of translators who show a higher level of TC by consistently excelling in terms of superior performance.

Shreve (2006) highlights the following specific aspects:

1) The aggregation of specific long-term experience in domain-specific episodic memory under conditions of deliberate practice as a key factor in the development of expertise.
2) Expert performance as a demonstrably acquired skill.
3) Experts demonstrate superior performance on tasks that capture the characteristic aspects of skilled performance in a given task domain.
4) Experts overcome difficulties more efficiently and effectively than non-experts.

This implies that expertise requires a higher level of metacognitive activity. Thus, experts show greater awareness of the nature and structure of problems in their specific domains. In short, expertise involves an increase in the apparent proceduralization of domain knowledge.

Göpferich (2009, p. 25) summarizes the results of studies on expertise that are most relevant for translation process research and that have an impact on the development of TC:

1) Not only do experts possess a large amount of specialized domain knowledge, but this knowledge has also been restructured and interconnected to a higher degree in the process of its acquisition; experts possess superior analytical and creative abilities as well as practical skills; their mental processes have been automatized to a higher degree.

TABLE 3.1 Related notions to the study of competences

Discipline	*Notions*
Applied linguistics	Communicative competence Actual communication
Psychology of work	Professional competences (behavioural approach) Competence dictionaries (models of competence)
Pedagogy	Competence-based training Specific competences Transversal (generic) competences
Cognitive Psychology	Declarative knowledge (*knowing what*) Procedural (or operative) knowledge (*knowing how*) Explicative knowledge (*knowing why*) Conditional knowledge (*knowing when*)
Expertise Studies	Expertise and expert performance

2) The high degree of interconnection of knowledge in their long-term memories allows experts to retrieve it more quickly and with more precision, and to overcome the limitations of their working memories. Thus, experts are able to plan and take many different factors into account.
3) Experts have transformed their declarative domain knowledge into procedural knowledge in a given field of specialization; experts learn tactically (i.e. they store automatic sequences of actions and strategies for problem-solving needed in their domain) as well as strategically (i.e. they know how to solve problems in their domains by tackling them most efficiently). Complex mental problem representations help them to do so.

Table 3.1 presents an overview of related notions concerning the study of competences.

3.2 Translation competence[7]

As far as TC is concerned, there is no comparable research tradition in translation studies as there has been in other disciplines. Unfortunately, empirical studies related to TC are still scarce.

3.2.1 First studies of translation competence

Except for Wilss (1976) and Koller (1979), pioneers in addressing this issue within translation studies, the notion of TC only begins to be studied in the mid-1980s. It came to the fore in the 1990s, although, most of the time, the topic of TC is approached tangentially.

3.2.1.1 Lack of definitions and terminological diversity

As Orozco (2000, p. 79) points out, although many authors used the term TC in the 1980s and 1990s, only a few authors explicitly defined it. Worthy of mention are Krings (1986, pp. 501, 522); Wilss (1989, p. 140, 146); Lörscher (1991, p. 41, 1992, p. 426); Toury (1991, p. 162, 1995, p. 250); Kiraly (1995, pp. 13–19); Fraser (1996, p. 87); and so on. Most other authors do not use the notion of TC explicitly; instead, implicit definitions of TC appear in connection with the description of the competences required to successfully cover the translation process as, for example, in the work of Delisle (1980, p. 235).

In this period, the first definitions of TC are introduced. Wilss speaks of a supercompetence based on the comprehensive knowledge of the source and target languages (including a text-pragmatic dimension) and defines it as "the ability to integrate the two monolingual competences on a higher level, i.e. on the level of the text" (1977, p. 58)[8]. In turn, Bell (1991, p. 43) defines TC as the "knowledge and skills the translator must possess in order to carry it [the translation process] out". Cao defines TC as "the many kinds of knowledge that are essential to the translation act" (Cao, 1996, p. 326). In her work in the 1990s, Hurtado Albir defined TC as "the ability to know how to translate"[9] (Hurtado Albir, 1996a, p. 34, 1996b, p. 39).

Furthermore, certain terminological diversity prevails and the following terms occur: transfer competence (Nord, 1988, p. 160), translational competence (Toury, 1995, p. 250; Hansen, 1997, p. 205; Chesterman, 1997, p. 147; Pym, 1993, p. 26), translator's competence (Kiraly, 1995, p. 108), translation ability (Lowe, 1987, p. 57; Stansfield, Scott, & Mann Kenyon, 1992), translation skills (Lowe, 1987, p. 57) and translation expertise (Gile, 1995b, p. 4). In line with Hurtado Albir (1996a, 1996b), we prefer to use the term *translation competence*, drawing on the term *competence* as coined by disciplines such as applied linguistics, psychology of work and pedagogy.

3.2.1.2 First models of translation competence

In the 1980s and early 1990s, several proposals for TC models were presented. Most of them are componential models that focus on describing the components that comprise TC. Although these first studies are not TC specific, their major interest is to present first reflections on the characteristics of TC and its components and include extra-linguistic abilities. Besides, many of these proposals stem from an interest in curriculum design.

Components of translation competence

Wilss (1976, p. 120) suggests that the translator must possess three competences: *source language receptive competence*, i.e. the ability to decode and understand the source text; *target language reproductive competence*, i.e. the ability to use linguistic and textual resources in the target language; and a *supercompetence*, the ability to transfer messages across linguistic and textual systems encompassing the source and target texts and the source and target text cultures.

Although Delisle (1980, p. 235) does not use the notion of TC in his work, he proposes four competences necessary to know how to translate: linguistic competence, encyclopaedic competence, comprehension competence and reformulation competence.

Meanwhile, Roberts (1984) identifies five competences: linguistic competence, i.e. the ability to understand the source text and formulate it in a target text; transfer competence (*compétence traductionnelle*), i.e. the ability to grasp meaning and to reformulate it, thus avoiding linguistic interference; methodological competence, i.e. the ability to document and to find and assimilate the appropriate terminology; thematic competence; and technical competence, i.e. the ability to use different tools and resources to translate.

Hewson and Martin (1991, p. 52), by exposing its variational model of translation, address, although tangentially, the issue of TC. The authors distinguish three types of competences related to the translator: (1) acquired interlinguistic competence, i.e. linguistic competence in both source text and target text languages; (2) dissimilative competence, i.e. ability to generate and derive homologous statements and to define and recreate socio-cultural norms; and (3) a transferred competence, including not only what the translator knows but also what has been accumulated through the use of dictionaries, databases and other resources and tools to translate.

In two of her works, Nord (1988, 1992) shows two proposals for TC. Nord (1988, p. 161) distinguishes three components of translation competence: transfer competence, linguistic competence and cultural competence. In a 1992 paper, Nord sets out the following essential competences required by the translator: reception competence and text analysis; research competence; transfer competence; text production competence; translation quality assessment competence; and linguistic and cultural competence in both source and target languages, which she considers the main requirement for translation (Nord, 1992, p. 47).

Neubert (1994, p. 412) distinguishes three subcompetences in TC, namely linguistic competence, subject competence and transfer competence. The author stresses the importance of transfer competence as it is the transfer competence that distinguishes translators from other professionals. Transfer competence is the subcompetence that controls the other two subcompetences (linguistic and thematic).

Kiraly (1995, p. 108) proposes an *integrated model* of translator's competence based on his psycholinguistic model of translation (see Section 2.3.10 in Chapter 2). This competence model combines three types of knowledge and abilities: (1) knowledge of the situational factors that may surround a translation task; (2) translation-relevant knowledge, i.e. linguistic knowledge in the source and target languages (syntactic, lexicosemantic, sociolinguistic and textual) as well as cultural knowledge related to source and target languages; and (3) the translator's ability to initiate the psycholinguistic processes (intuitive or controlled) in order to instantiate the target text and to control its adequacy with respect to the source text.

In Hurtado Albir (1996a, p. 34, 1996b, p. 39), TC is defined as the "ability to know how to translate".[10] Five subcompetences are distinguished: (1) linguistic competence in both languages, which includes comprehension in the source language and production in the target language, both written or orally, depending on whether it concerns a translator or an interpreter; (2) extra-linguistic competence, i.e. encyclopaedic, cultural and thematic knowledge; (3) transfer competence, i.e. knowing how to steer the translation process adequately, i.e. to able to understand the source text and re-express it in the target language in compliance with the purpose of the translation and the characteristics of the audience; (4) professional competence or work style, i.e. knowing how to document, knowing how to use new technologies and knowing the job market; and (5) strategic competence, i.e. conscious and individual procedures used by the translator to solve problems encountered in the course of the translation process based on their specific needs.

Hansen (1997) distinguishes between implicit (automatic, unconscious) and explicit (conscious) knowledge and abilities. She also distinguishes three interacting subcompetences: translational competence; social, cultural and intercultural competence; and communicative competence. For Hansen, translational competence consists of two competences: an implicit competence and an explicit competence. Hansen defines implicit translational competence as being able to extract relevant information from the source text, considering the intention of whoever ordered the translation, and being able to produce a target text that meets the intended purpose. The explicit translational competence comprises explicit knowledge about translation methods and the ability to choose whichever is most appropriate; it is also related to translation strategies and strategies to recognize and solve translation problems. The social, cultural and intercultural competence comprises implicit and explicit knowledge: implicit knowledge (social and culturally conditioned) of the social and cultural environment (and other environments) as well as explicit knowledge of social norms and cultural differences. Finally, communicative competence includes linguistic and pragmatic competence.

In the 1990s, a large-scale study on TC was carried out by Risku (1998) who postulated a speculative *pragmatic-cooperative* model. Risku proposed a modular concept of TC composed of four subcomponents, all of which act in an integrated manner to construct meaning: construing a macro strategy; integrating information; planning and decision-making; and self-organization. The construction of the macro strategy serves to anticipate the communicative situation in which the translation is embedded. The integration of information helps to create representations of the source and target text and target text contextual situations, as well as evaluating the documentation. Planning and decision ensure intratextual consistency and contrastivity. Finally, self-organization provides room for reflection and continuous evaluation of decisions taken.

Translation abilities and skills

Some authors prefer to use the term *translation ability* or *translation skill*. This is the case of Lowe (1987), who uses the term *translation skill* and distinguishes eight types of knowledge and skills that draw the ideal profile of the translator: source language reading comprehension; ability to produce target language texts; understanding the source language style; mastery of the target language style; understanding of sociolinguistic and cultural aspects in the source language; mastery of sociolinguistic and cultural aspects in the target language; speed; and, finally, the *X factor*, which, according to Lowe (1987, p. 55), refers to what makes a given translation clearly superior to other translations even if the same assessment is carried out.

Meanwhile, Pym (1991, 1992), mentions two translation *skills* that make up TC. These skills include: (1) the ability to generate different options for the original text and (2) the ability to select only one option related to the specific purpose and the target text reader (1992, p. 281).

Hatim and Mason (1997, p. 205) also mention *translator abilities*. Their description is based on the model of *communicative language ability* proposed by Bachman (1990). They highlight the following subcompetences: organizational competence, pragmatic competence, and strategic competence. Hatim & Mason distinguish three stages in the translation process (processing the source text, transfer, and processing the target text) and assign a range of skills to each of them. They indicate that during the translation process such skills interact together. In the source text processing phase, and depending on the estimated effect of the source text on the reader, one must recognize traits related to intertextuality (gender, discourse, text) and situationality (register, etc.). One must also infer intentionality and analyse the organization of the texture (lexical choices, syntactic organization, cohesion) and text structure, and evaluate the informativity, depending on whether *static texts* (easy to process because they meet prescribed standards and norms, and end-reader expectations) or *dynamic texts* (difficult to process because they do not meet the standard and norms, or the expectations of the end-reader). In the transfer phase, a strategic renegotiation is developed to carry out adjustments related to efficiency, effectiveness and relevance of the communicative task of the translator in relation to the specifications of the task (brief, initiator, etc.) to fulfil a particular rhetorical

TABLE 3.2 Translator abilities according to Hatim and Mason

Source text PROCESSING SKILLS	TRANSFER SKILLS	Target text PROCESSING SKILLS
Recognizing **intertextuality** (genre/discourse/text) Locating **situationality** (register, etc.) Inferring **intentionality** Organising **texture** (lex. choice synt. arrangement cohesion) and **structure** Judging informativity (static/dynamic) in terms of estimated impact on: **source text readership**	Strategic **re**-negotiation by adjusting **effectiveness** **efficiency** **relevance** to: **audience design** (brief, initiator, etc.) in fulfilment of a **rhetorical purpose** (plan, goal)	Establishing **intertextuality** (genre/discourse/text) Establishing **situationality** (register, etc.) Creating **intentionality** Organising **texture** (lex. choice synt. arrangement cohesion) and **structure** Balancing informativity (static/dynamic) in terms of estimated impact on: **target text readership**

(Hatim & Mason, 1997, p. 205)

purpose. For target text processing, it is necessary to establish intertextuality and situationality of the target text, to create intentionality, to organize texture and text structure and a balance in informativity, depending on the impact on the target text reader (see Table 3.2).

Vienne (1998) complains that quite often there is a reduction of TC to linguistic competence (text analysis and text production) and advocates in favour of a functionalist perspective of text production for a definition of the abilities required by a professional translator in a specific situation. This proposal, aimed at the training of translators, deliberately ignores linguistic skills and focuses on four aspects: the ability to analyse different translation situations; the ability to manage and process information; the ability to discuss with the initiator of the translation project about decisions taken; and the ability to cooperate with other experts.

Epistemic knowledge and operational knowledge

Presas (1996) stresses the need to distinguish between TC and bilingual competence. For Presas, TC is considered to be a specific competence related to text reception and text production. According to the author, the basis of TC is formed by a *pre-translation competence*, consisting of knowledge of the two languages involved, cultural knowledge related to these languages, encyclopaedic knowledge, thematic knowledge and theoretical knowledge about translation. TC is built on such a basis. Presas identifies two types of knowledge that make up TC: epistemic knowledge, which is a part of bilingual competence, and operative knowledge, characterizing TC proper.

Epistemic knowledge integrates knowledge in both languages, as well as cultural, thematic and encyclopaedic knowledge. As far as operative knowledge is concerned, the author distinguishes between nuclear, peripheral and tangential knowledge. Nuclear knowledge includes reception of the source text for translation (identification of *distances* and translation problems), the development of the translation project (plans that are made to translate defining the objective and the method to be used), and production of the translation (including transfer operations and problem-solving). Peripheral skills refer to the use of specific instruments and the translator's estimation of his/her own potential to produce an acceptable text, with affordable sources of documentation and within the time available; it also includes the ability to evaluate and use documentation sources, the ability to acquire knowledge about a new or an unfamiliar topic, and the capacity to evaluate other translations. Finally, tangential knowledge refers to the ability to use tools, consisting of knowledge of text-editing technologies and desktop publishing. Presas emphasizes the importance of the relationship between all these types of knowledge.

Translation competence and translation proficiency

Cao (1996) proposes a model of translation proficiency for translation testing purposes. Departing from Chomsky's (1965) distinction between competence and performance, Cao proposes a distinction between translation and translation proficiency. In Cao's proposal, translation competence is regarded as the many kinds of knowledge that are essential to the translation act. Translation proficiency is defined by Cao (1996, p. 327) as "the ability to mobilise translation competence to perform translation tasks in context for purposes of interlingual and intercultural communication". Cao believes that translation proficiency is a global skill that entails various components for performing translation tasks.

Cao's model of translation proficiency is multi-componential, with different sets of variables that interact with each other and the context in which the translation is rendered. Based on Bachman's model of communicative language ability (see Figure 3.1), Cao proposes three components of translation proficiency: translational language competence, translational knowledge structures and translational strategic competence.

The description of translational language competence is also based on Bachman (1990) and includes organizational competence in the source

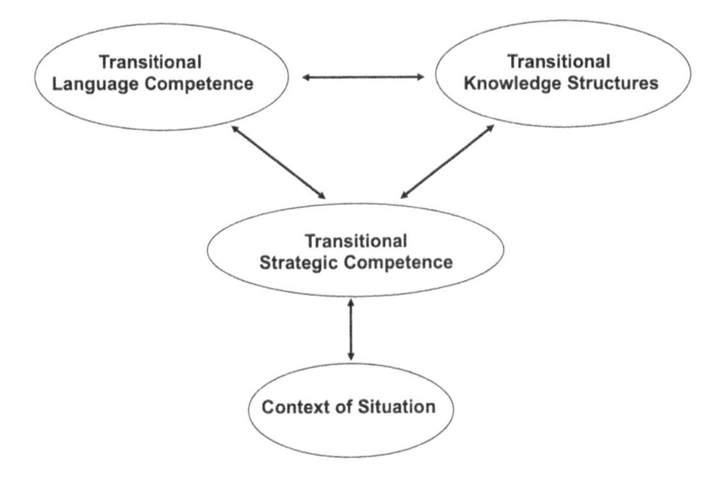

FIGURE 3.1 Cao's components of translation proficiency
(Cao, 1996, p. 328)

language and in the target language, which consists of grammatical and textual competence, and pragmatic competence in the source language and in the target language, which consists of illocutionary and sociolinguistic competence (see Figure 3.2).

Translational knowledge structures include general, special and literary knowledge (related to the prototipology in translation as proposed by Snell-Hornby, 1988). General knowledge refers to knowledge about the world: ecology, material culture, social organization and so on of both the SL and TL communities. Special knowledge includes specialist technical knowledge in different fields. Literary knowledge includes knowledge in areas including

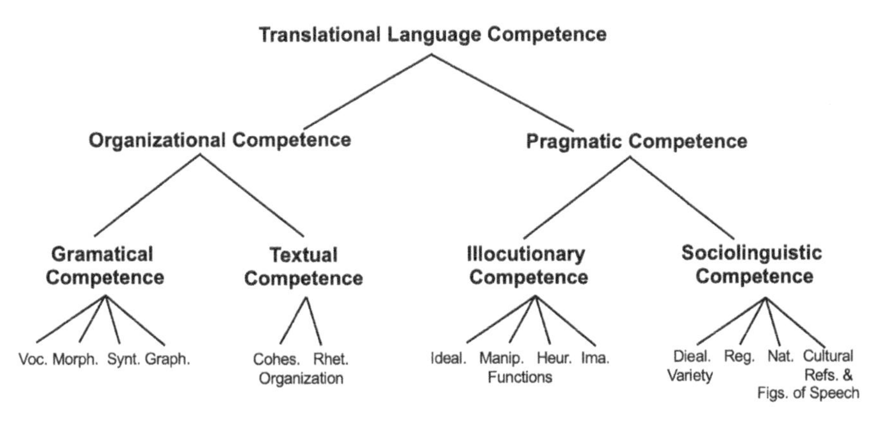

FIGURE 3.2 Cao's translational components of language competence
(Cao, 1996, p. 330)

the Bible, stage, film, lyric, poetic and literary work, cultural history and literary studies.

Translational strategic competence is a mental ability that provides the means for relating the various components of translation proficiency in the process of translation. This mental ability has a double component: the ability of assessing, planning and executing, inherent to all mental activity including language use; the skills that are demanded during the processing and non-verbal stage of reformulation and analogy by reasoning, specific to translation. It also includes psychological mechanisms: the cognitive aspect of human thought and processes of the creative aspect.

Cao emphasizes the interaction between the various components of translation proficiency and the crucial role of translational strategic competence to conclude that translation is a special area of expertise and specialization that requires knowledge in many different areas. Cao also notes that there are different levels of proficiency.

Translation competence and expert performance

Bell (1991, p. 35) asks: "What is it that translators need to know and be able to do in order to translate?" and considers that there are three possible alternatives for characterizing such a competence. The first alternative is that of an ideal bilingual competence in the Chomskyan sense, which Bell deems not suited for his purposes. The second alternative is as an expert system, i.e. generalizations based on observations of translators' work considering two basic components of this expert system: (1) a knowledge base in the source and target languages, text types, domain knowledge and contrastive knowledge; and (2) inference mechanisms to decode and code texts. The third alternative is related to the previous one and stems from a multicomponential concept of communicative competence. Building on Canale and Swain (1980), Bell distinguishes between grammatical, sociolinguistic, discourse and strategic competences. For Bell, the translator must possess linguistic competence in both languages and communicative competence in both cultures. Bell is, thus, a pioneer in linking TC with expertise and considers TC as a form of expert knowledge.

Meanwhile, Gile (1995a, pp. 4–5) refers to the components of expertise required for interpreting and translation. He distinguishes the following types of knowledge and skills: good passive knowledge of the passive working languages; good command of the active working languages; enough knowledge of the subject domain of the texts or speeches to be processed; and know how to translate, which refers to the conceptual framework and technical skills of interpreting and translation (comprehension of principles of fidelity and of professional rules of conduct, as well as techniques for knowledge acquisition, language maintenance, problem-solving, decision-making, etc.).

Along similar lines, the PACTE group, which was established in 1997 with the objective of carrying out an experimental investigation of TC acquisition, also considers TC as a development process from novice to expert knowledge (PACTE, 2000, p. 103) and proposes a holistic model of TC, which was first presented in 1998.[11] The theoretical assumptions used in the development of the first PACTE model (2001, pp. 9–45) are: (1) TC is the underlying system of knowledge and skills needed to translate; (2) TC is qualitatively different from bilingual competence; (3) TC, as every type of expert knowledge, has declarative and the source language and in the target language operative components, being basically an operational type of knowledge; (4) and TC consists of a set of subcompetences in which relationships, hierarchies and variations exist.

In this first version of the model (PACTE, 2000), six subcompetences are presented:

1) Communicative competence in two languages.
2) Extra-linguistic competence, including knowledge about translation, encyclopaedic and domain knowledge.
3) Instrumental-professional competence, including both knowledge and skills related to the tools of the trade and the profession (knowledge and use of all kinds of documentation sources and new technologies, knowledge of the market and how a translator behaves professionally, especially in relation to professional ethics).
4) Psycho-physiological competence, i.e. the ability to use all kinds of psychomotor, cognitive and attitudinal resources.
5) Transfer competence, i.e. the core competence that integrates all the others, the ability to complete the transfer process from the source text to the target text.
6) Strategic competence, including all procedures, conscious and unconscious, verbal and non-verbal, used to solve problems found during the translation process.

Although all these competences are involved in TC, in PACTE's 1998 model, transfer and strategic competences played a predominant role in the interrelation between competences.

It is important to note that in this period the terms translation competence and translation expertise were often used interchangeably without a clear distinction between these two concepts.

Translation competence in inverse translation

Some proposals refer to the specific case of translations into the foreign language (inverse translation).

Beeby (1996, p. 91) speaks of an *ideal translator communicative competence*, which, in general, consists of four ideal subcompetences:

1) Ideal translator grammatical competence, which includes linguistic knowledge and skills needed to understand and express the literal meaning of phrase (vocabulary, word formation, pronunciation, spelling and phrase structures).
2) Ideal translator sociolinguistic competence, which consists of the knowledge and abilities needed to understand and formulate solutions appropriate to the context of both cultures (socio-historical context, mode, field, tenor, status of participants, objectives of the interaction, purpose of translation, etc.).
3) Ideal translator discourse competence, which is the ability to achieve formal coherence and consistency of meaning in texts of various genres across both languages.
4) Ideal translator transfer competence, which is the ability to master communication strategies that enable the transfer of meaning from the source language to the target language and can be used to improve communication or to overcome breakdowns (caused by deficiencies in one or more components of the communicative competence or factors in actual communication).

Beeby notes, however, the specificity of translation into the foreign language (in terms of the job market and capabilities), proposing learning objectives which are characteristic of inverse translation (1996, p. 107).

Campbell (1998) also proposes a model of translation competence for inverse translation, composed of three elements with relative independence (1998, p. 152). The three elements are target language textual competence, *disposition* and *monitoring*. For Campbell, textual competence in the target language represents a central element in the case of inverse translation. *Disposition*, as he calls this non-linguistic capacity, entails how to address the task of translation. *Monitoring* refers to the ability of controlling and supervising. Campbell (1998, p. 155) adds that these three components may be reflected in the following questions: Can translators produce translations that are stylistically appropriate in the target language? Does the translator have the right personality to translate? Is the translator able to produce a text that requires minimal revisions? (see Figure 3.3).

3.2.1.3 On the lack of empirical studies

Empirical-experimental studies on written translation began in the late 1980s and developed further in the 1990s. However, these studies do not focus on a holistic approach to TC, but only address partial aspects of constituent elements.

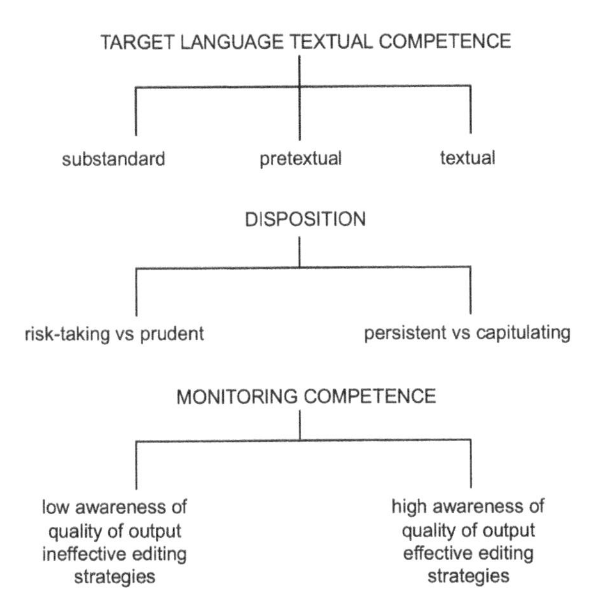

FIGURE 3.3 Campbell's translation competence model

(Campbell, 1998, p. 154)

As Orozco (2000, p. 113) notes, until the 1990s, there were only two proposals for operationalizing TC: Lowe (1987) and Stansfield, Scott, and Mann Kenyon (1992). Orozco argues that in regard to Lowe, one cannot speak of actual operationalization but rather of a proposal of elements that are indicators of TC levels. Lowe considers the possibility of adapting to the study of TC the scales proposed by the American Council's Education Testing Service (ETS) on the Teaching of Foreign Languages (ACTFL) and the Federal Interagency Language Roundtable (ILR), designed to measure the level of proficiency in a foreign language. He concludes that these scales are not sufficient to measure TC and, therefore, it would be necessary to build new instruments to measure and assess TC.

According to Orozco, the work of Stansfield, Scott, and Mann Kenyon (1992) is, in fact, the only effective attempt to operationalize TC, which these authors prefer to call *translation ability*. This research was commissioned by the FBI in order to create a measuring instrument for determining the level of TC of candidates applying for positions as translators with the FBI. The instrument they created, called the *Spanish into English Verbatim Translation Exam* (SEVTE), was tested for validity and reliability. Results confirmed that it was a valid instrument. However, the authors point out that the results cannot be generalized because of the small sample size that was submitted (seven employees of the FBI). In addition, Orozco (2000, p. 116) introduces two objections to this instrument: (1) lack of a definition of TC, therefore, one cannot tell if they measure what they wanted to measure; and (2) the characteristics of the instrument itself since only words, segments, phrases, sentences or paragraphs – but no full texts – are translated.

3.2.1.4 Main characteristics of this period

This period is characterized by:

1) These initial proposals on TC are isolated contributions that deal only tangentially with the topic.
2) They all agree that TC requires additional components beyond linguistic components and that it consists of various components (linguistic knowledge, extra-linguistic knowledge, documentation skills and skills in the use of tools, transfer competence, etc.).
3) The authors also agree that these components are of various kinds (knowledge, abilities, skills, attitudes) and that there are certain differences between the competences for direct translation and inverse translation.
4) Characteristically, early models also postulate the transfer competence as a component of TC.
5) However, it should be noted that only a few authors (Bell, Gile, Cao, PACTE) associated TC with expertise and fewer authors stressed the importance of the strategic component in TC (Hurtado Albir, Cao, Beeby, Hatim & Mason, PACTE).
6) Lack of empirical studies.
7) Lack of distinction between TC and translation expertise.

3.2.2 Consolidation of research on translation competence: Disparate perspectives and empirical validation

As we enter the 21st century, research on TC increases significantly and occupies an area of major importance in translation studies: TC is established as an object of study in its own right. It is significant to note the title of the publication edited by Schäffner and Adabs (2000), *Developing Translation Competence*, which was released at the turn of the century. Current research will further affect the consideration of the TC that requires declarative and procedural knowledge (abilities, skills, strategies) with a predominance of the latter. Moreover, a more interdisciplinary framework emerges since many TC proposals are based on research carried out in other disciplines, and one also sees attempts towards empirical validation among certain authors.

Some authors have taken up previous proposals and expanded their contents. This is, for instance, the case of Neubert (2000) who expanded his

1994 proposal in order to highlight the complexity and heterogeneity of TC. Neubert argues that TC has seven main features:

1) Complexity – translation as a complex activity different from other language-related professions.
2) Heterogeneity – involves the development of very different abilities.
3) Approximation – necessary adjustments given the impossibility of knowing all thematic fields that can be translated and the need to approach other disciplines.
4) Open-endedness – the need to remain updated.
5) Creativity – to solve certain translation problems.
6) Situationality – to adapt to new situations (purpose, commissions).
7) Historicity – the capacity to change, to be able to adapt oneself to other ways of focusing on the translation, given space-time changes.

Neubert (2000, p. 5) claims that, in order to fulfil their complex task, translators need a special type of expertise that distinguishes them from other language users. Neubert indicates five parameters that make up TC: language competence, textual competence, subject competence, cultural competence and transfer competence. As stated in his 1994 proposal, transfer competence is what differentiates translation from any other type of communicative activity.

Pym (2003) takes up the theme of TC and states that proposals from the 1970s have approached TC from four perspectives: as a form of bilingualism, subject therefore to linguistic analysis; as a result of market demands, subject to social and historical changes; as a multi-component competence, comprising linguistic, cultural, technological and professional skills; and as a vague supercompetence that transcend the other components. Pym criticizes componential models of TC and, based on his 1991 proposal, advocates in favour of a minimalist concept, based on the production and then elimination of alternatives, which includes: (1) the ability to generate a series of more than one feasible target text (TTI, TT2 ...TTN) for a pertinent ST and (2) the ability to select only one feasible target text from this series, quickly and with justified confidence (Pym, 2003, p. 489). Nevertheless, most TC models are componential and address the TC from different perspectives. In the next sections, we have included the most important proposals.

PACTE (2003) also revisits its previous TC model (PACTE, 2000) and introduces a revised model.

3.2.2.1 Didactic perspective

From a didactic perspective, Kelly (2002, 2005, 2007) proposes an integrative approach to TC to develop curricular design. Kelly (2005, p. 162) defines TC as "the set of knowledge, skills, attitudes and aptitudes which a translator possesses in order to undertake professional activity in the field". Kelly (2005, pp. 32–33) describes the components of TC as:

1) Communicative and textual competence in at least two languages and cultures.
2) Cultural and intercultural competence.
3) Subject area competence, i.e. basic knowledge of the subject areas the future translator will/may work.
4) Professional and instrumental competence, i.e. the use of documentary resources of all kinds, use of IT tools for professional practice, basic notions for managing professional activity, etc.
5) Attitudinal or psycho-physiological competence (self-concept, self-confidence, initiative, etc.).
6) Interpersonal competence, i.e. the ability to work with other professionals and actors involved in the translation process, including teamwork, negotiation and leadership skills.
7) Strategic competence, i.e. organization and planning skills, problem identification and problem-solving, monitoring, self-assessment and revision.

Kelly (2002) represents her proposal by means of subcompetences forming a pyramid-shaped TC and emphasizing the role of the strategic subcompetence, situated at the upper end of the pyramid. Her proposal is characterized by introducing interpersonal competence as a separate competence.

PACTE's research on TC stems from the group's aims to investigate TC acquisition in order to improve curriculum design and evaluation. Results from PACTE's exploratory studies (PACTE, 2002, 2003) with six professional translators led to modifications in the first version of the group's TC model, first presented in 1998, and resulted in the introduction of a revised model (PACTE, 2003). Changes in the model have an impact on the subcompetences that make up TC; besides, the subcompetences are defined in terms of declarative and procedural knowledge to indicate the predominance of either declarative or procedural knowledge in each subcompetence. As a result, PACTE (2003) adjusted the definition of the subcompetences as follows (see Figure 3.4):

1) Bilingual subcompetence. Predominantly procedural knowledge required to communicate in two languages. It comprises pragmatic, sociolinguistic, textual, grammatical and lexical knowledge in at least two languages.
2) Extra-linguistic subcompetence. Predominantly declarative knowledge, both implicit and explicit about the world in general and field-specific.

It comprises bicultural knowledge (about the source and target cultures); encyclopaedic knowledge (about the world in general) and subject knowledge (in specific domains).

3) Knowledge of translation subcompetence. Predominantly declarative knowledge. Both implicit and explicit about what translation is and knowledge about the profession. It comprises knowledge about how translation works: translation units, required processes, procedures and methods used, types of problems, knowledge about translation related to professional practice: the job market, types of translation briefs, target audiences and so on.[12]
4) Instrumental subcompetence. Predominantly procedural knowledge related to the use of documentation resources and information and communication technologies applied to translation: dictionaries of all kinds, encyclopaedias, grammars, style books, parallel texts, electronic corpora, search engines and so on.
5) Strategic subcompetence. Procedural knowledge to guarantee the efficiency of the translation process and solve problems encountered. This is an essential subcompetence that affects all the others since it creates links between the different subcompetences as it controls the translation process. Its function is as follows: to plan the process and carry out the translation project (selecting the most appropriate method); to evaluate the process and the partial results obtained in relation to the ultimate purpose; to activate the different subcompetences and compensate for errors; and to identify translation problems and apply specific procedures to solve them.
6) Psycho-physiological components. Different types of cognitive and psycho-attitudinal components and mechanisms. They include: cognitive components such as memory, perception, attention and emotion; attitudinal aspects such as intellectual curiosity, perseverance, rigour, critical spirit, knowledge about and confidence in one's own abilities, the capacity to measure one's own abilities, motivation and so on.

This model was validated in an empirical-experimental study involving 35 professional translators and 24 foreign language teachers. The full results of the study can be found in Hurtado Albir (2017b).[13]

Also within a pedagogical perspective, González Davies (2004, pp. 74–75) and González Davies and Scott-Tennent (2005, p. 162) propose six aspects a translator should know: language work (source language/s and target language/s), subject matter (encyclopaedic knowledge related to different disciplines), translation skills (problem-spotting and problem-solving, creativity, self-confidence, etc.), resourcing skills (paper, electronic and human), computer skills and professional skills (translator's rights, contracts, etc.).

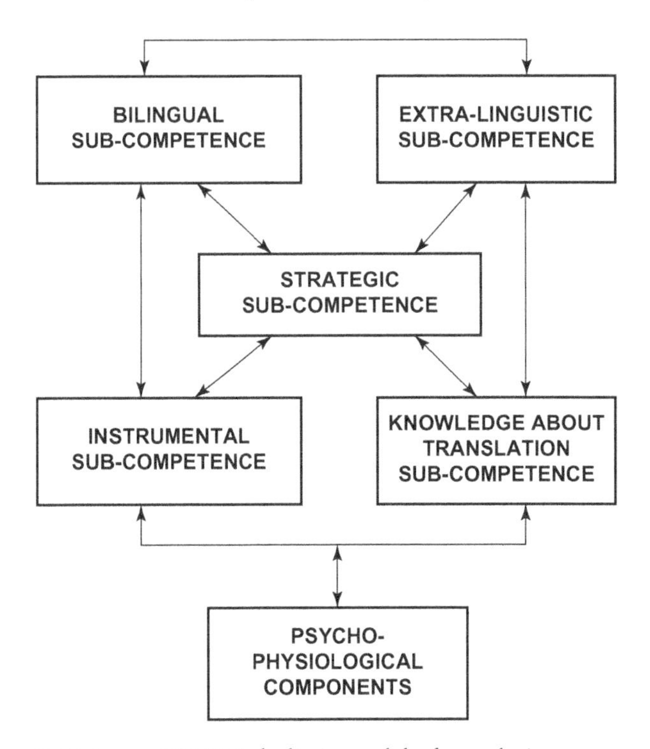

FIGURE 3.4 PACTE's holistic model of translation competence
(PACTE 2003, p. 60)

Katan (2008, pp. 133–135) proposes a multi-componential list of competences to be implemented in the teaching of specialized translation based on earlier proposals by Pym (2003), Schaffner (2004) and PACTE (2003), and organized around two large blocks: *lingua* and culture-specific competences, and translation competences. The *lingua* and culture-specific competences include competences related to textual competence (comprehension in the source language and production in the target language) and extra-linguistic competence (bicultural knowledge and knowledge of specialized topics). Translation competences include those features related to: (1) general transfer/mediation competence (knowledge of the theories of translation, the ability to decide on a translation strategy, etc.); (2) strategic transfer/mediation competence (special language related to specialist topics and linguistic/literary devices as compensation strategies, rhetorical strategies, etc.); (3) instrumental/professional competence (knowledge and skills related to professional translation practice); and (4) attitudinal competence (flexibility, creativity, etc).

In 2009, the European master's in Translation (EMT)[14] established a translator competence profile drawn up by a team of European experts.

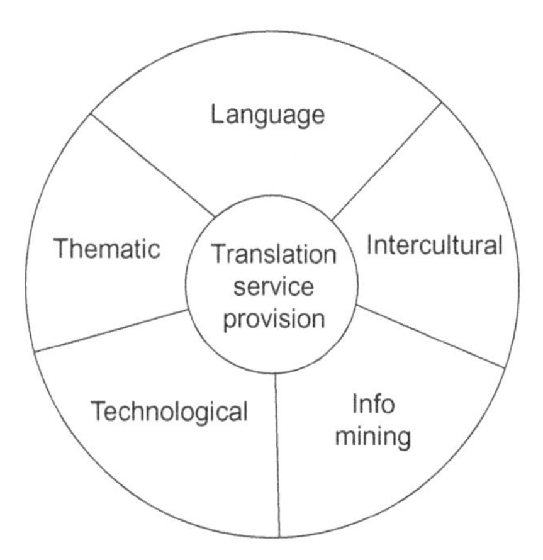

FIGURE 3.5 EMT translator competence profil
(EMT, 2009)

Figure 3.5 details the competences needed to work successfully in today's translation market. Six types of competences are distinguished and corresponding components are set out for each of them: (1) translation service provision competence (interpersonal and production dimension); (2) language competence (language A and one's other working languages B, C); (3) intercultural competence (sociolinguistic and textual dimension, in the comparison of and contrast between discursive practices in languages A, B and C); (4) information mining competence; (5) thematic competence; and (6) technological competence (mastery of tools).

In 2017, the model was revised and the following competences were proposed: language and culture (transcultural and sociolinguistic awareness and communicative skills); translation (strategic, methodological and thematic competence); technology (tools and applications); personal and interpersonal; and service provision. In 2022, the model was updated to meet current challenges, but the same competences were kept as in 2017 (see European Master's in Translation, 2017, 2022).

3.2.2.2 Relevance-theoretic perspective

Building on the tenets of relevance theory, Gutt's (1991) pioneering work postulated a relevance-theoretic perspective to the study of translation. Furthermore, expanding the application of relevance theory to translation studies, Gutt (2000) argued in favour of a competence-oriented research of translation (CORT). According to Gutt, CORT can provide a basis for research in translation which focuses on the competence of human beings to communicate with each other. The aim of CORT is to understand and explicate the mental faculties that enable human beings to translate in the sense of expressing in one language what has been expressed in another. The idea is that once these faculties are understood, it will be possible to understand not only the relation between input and output, but also, and more importantly perhaps, the communicative effects on the audience. Gutt's work is theoretically grounded and the author does not offer empirical data on how translators arrive at instances of interpretive resemblance in order to consubstantiate his claims.

Empirical-experimental evidence for the application of assumptions of relevance theory in translator's training comes from Alves (1995, 1996) and is further expanded in Alves and Gonçalves (2003), Alves and Gonçalves (2007) and Alves and Gonçalves (2013). In their 2007 work, the authors differentiate between a general translator's competence (GTC) and a specific translator's competence (STC). On the one hand, GTC (see Figure 3.6) is defined as all knowledge, abilities and strategies needed for the successful mastering of tasks that lead to an adequate performance in translation task execution.

On the other hand, STC (see Figure 3.7) is the core of a supercompetence, which is expected to coordinate a set of different subcompetences, operating mainly through metacognitive processes. Therefore, STC is situated in the more conscious layers of the human cognitive system, ranging from levels of higher procedural knowledge to metacognition.

Nevertheless, translators need to rely on other cognitive systems in order to make possible the complex transformation from a source text into a target text counterpart. Proficiency in both working languages is a prerequisite. They are represented in Figure 3.6 in the most external layers of the diagram

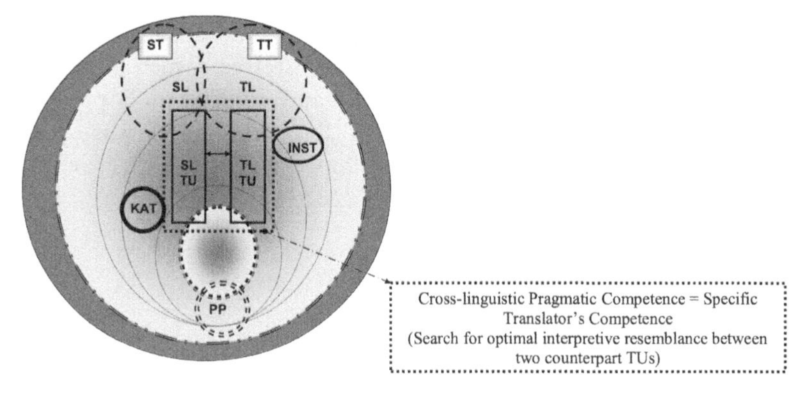

(ST = source text; SL = source language; SLTU = source- language translation unit; TLTU = target-language translation unit; TL = target language; TT = target text; KAT = knowledge about translation; PP = psycho-physiological components; INST = instrumental sub-competence)

FIGURE 3.6 Alves and Gonçalves's model of general translator's competence

(Alves and Gonçalves, 2007, p. 46)

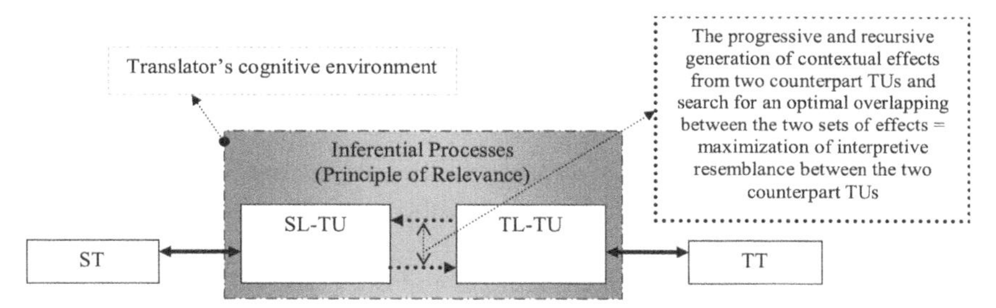

FIGURE 3.7 Alves and Gonçalves's model of specific translator's competence (Alves and Gonçalves, 2007, p. 44)

including the darkest and most external layer outside cognition where the social-interactive environment is situated. The representation of language proficiency at this level is due to the fact that language proper is mostly automated and "proceduralized". It is, at the same time, not only a cognitive phenomenon but also a social-interactive one.

Alves and Gonçalves (2007) consider the set formed by source and target languages in conjunction with STC to be the main cognitive set of TC since it is expected to function more intensively during the act of translating. Besides this main set, Alves and Gonçalves assume that there are some auxiliary subcompetences that contribute to the improvement of STC. This auxiliary set consists of three subsystems borrowed and adapted from the model developed by PACTE (2003), including an instrumental subcompetence (INST) that reflects the ability to use reference tools and to deal with several different external demands while carrying out a translation task. Being mainly procedural, INST is also related to the concept of external support proposed by Alves (1995) and can be acquired procedurally and/or declaratively. It helps translators in their search for references and, by placing constraints on STC, in their attempts to build up inferential contexts. The other auxiliary subcompetence is knowledge-about-translation (KAT). It is mainly a declarative type of knowledge and is mostly learned explicitly and/or theoretically. It helps translators gear STC towards what they believe to be the most appropriate direction for the task being performed. The last auxiliary subsystem is formed by psycho-physiological components (PPC). They include both subjective/emotional and physiological/motor aspects involved in translating and constitute an important interface between body regulation and subjective consciousness, – what, in translating, can be related to typing abilities, postural and ergonomic behaviour, emotional balance and control under psychological stress, internal motivation and so on. Despite being peripheral and less influential, the management of these aspects can either save or spoil cognitive resources that, in principle, should mostly be concentrated on the processes taking place in the specific competence system. Therefore, PP must also be considered in the study of a translator's competence.

In their model, Alves and Gonçalves (2007) argue that STC plays a similar function as that of PACTE's strategic subcompetence. Both are supposed to integrate the other subcompetences. STC, however, contributes to inferences in order to enable problem-solving and decision-making processes to take place.

The dynamic model of translator's competence proposed by Alves and Gonçalves (2007) can, therefore, be considered to embody the different aspects of GTC and STC which vary cognitively and operationally depending on the level of expertise and experience of each individual translator. As such, competence is no longer considered to be an existing component in the translator's mind but, rather, becomes an emergent cognitive property which develops gradually on the basis of the internal and external dynamics experienced by the translator. In terms of categories, they could range from a stage of pre-translation competence (Hurtado Albir, 2005; PACTE 2005), including the capacity of bilinguals to translate, to encompass the performance of novice, advanced, competent, proficient and expert translators.Alves and Gonçalves (2007) assume that the mastery of STC will be higher at the expert-end of the scale and that expert translators will draw more heavily on metacognitive processing, thus making more conscious decisions and qualitatively increasing the management of the cognitive resources available in the process of translation. On the other hand, lower levels of STC will situate the translator at the novice-end of the scale. Novice translators will draw more intensively on automatic processes, thus making fewer conscious decisions and qualitatively decreasing the management of the cognitive resources available in the process of translation. The qualitative increment of metacognitive processes will, therefore, constitute a meaningful differential aspect in the translator's competence.

3.2.2.3 Expertise studies perspective

As pointed out in previous subsections, Bell (1991) and PACTE (1998) were pioneering in associating TC as a type of expert knowledge. However, a more in-depth theoretical reflection linking TC with expertise studies was put forward by Shreve (2006) some years later. For Shreve, TC should be analysed in the scope of expertise studies and expert performance.

Consequently, Shreve (2006, p. 28) prefers to speak of translation expertise instead of TC and defines it as the multiple translation-relevant cognitive resources to perform a translation task. Shreve suggests that this competence could be seen as declarative and procedural knowledge from a variety of cognitive domains accumulated through training and experience and then stored and organized in a translator's long-term memory.

Shreve (2006, p. 40) argues that one expertise-oriented model could assume that "knowing how to translate" implies having access to: (1) L1 and L2 linguistic knowledge; (2) culture knowledge of the source and target culture including knowledge of specialized subject domains; (3) textual knowledge of source and target textual conventions; and (4) translation knowledge – knowledge of how to translate using strategies and procedures including tool using and information-seeking strategies. These four cognitive domains must be integrated to successfully complete the task translator. Shreve adds that identifying these four subcompetences implies that translation expertise can develop differently. Shreve concludes that, depending on variations of how further experience in the domain of practice is acquired, translation expertise is not "a homogeneous, uniform easily describable set of cognitive achieved by all translators' resources experts" (2006, p. 40).[15]

Göpferich (2009) also affiliates her work to the expertise paradigm. She draws on the PACTE (2003) model as her starting point and then introduces some modifications to it. Göpferich proposes a model of TC as a reference model for a process-oriented longitudinal study aimed at exploring the acquisition of translation competence in the so-called TRASCOMP project.[16]

In her model, Göpferich (2009, pp. 21–23) distinguishes six subcompetences (see Figure 3.8):

1) Communicative competence in at least two languages, which corresponds to PACTE's bilingual subcompetence.
2) Domain competence, which corresponds approximately to PACTE's extra-linguistic subcompetence.
3) Tools and research competence, which corresponds to PACTE's instrumental subcompetence.
4) Translation routine activation competence, which comprises the knowledge and the abilities to recall and apply certain (standard) transfer operations (or shifts) which frequently lead to acceptable target language equivalents (corresponding to the ability to activate productive micro-strategies as proposed by Hönig (1991, 1995).
5) Psychomotor competence, which are the psychomotor abilities required for reading and writing (with electronic tools).
6) Strategic competence, which corresponds to PACTE's strategic competence and controls the application of the other subcompetences.

Göpferich notes that the application of the subcompetences and their central control are determined by three factors: the translation brief and translation norms; the translator's self-concept and professional ethos; and the

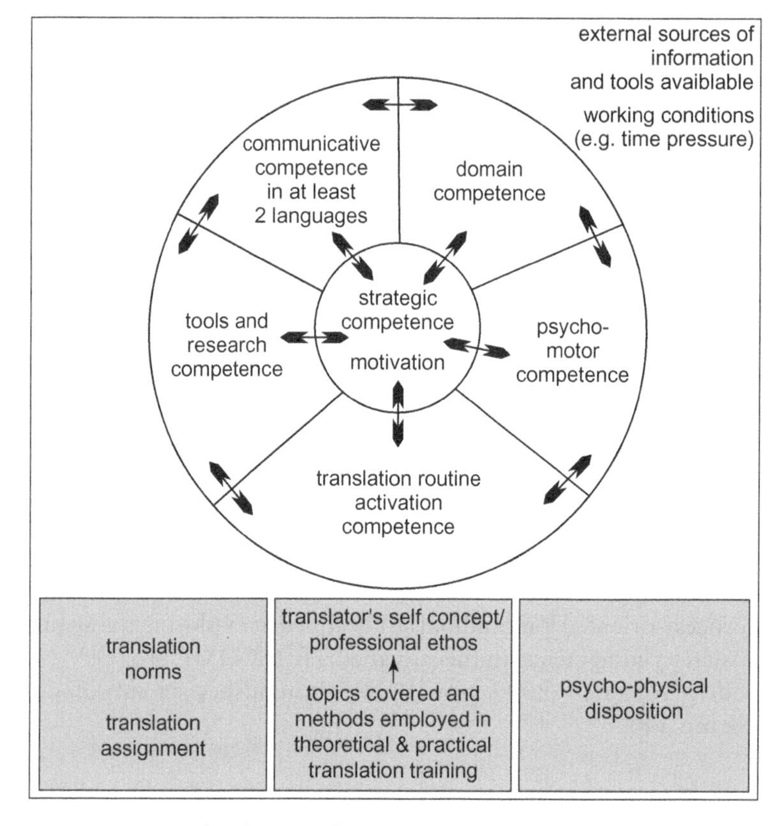

FIGURE 3.8 Göpferich's translation competence model

(Göpferich, 2009, p. 21)

translator's psycho-physical disposition (intelligence, ambition, perseverance, self-confidence, etc.).

3.2.2.4 Knowledge-management perspective

From the perspective of knowledge management,[17] and also considering translators as experts, Risku, Dickinson and Pircher (2010) emphasize the need for a new professional translator profile so that translators can take their role in knowledge management and generate intellectual capital in the knowledge society. From this perspective, Risku, Dickinson, and Pircher (2010, p. 91) classify the types of knowledge required for the translator into five categories: (1) language, linguistic, text skills and translation competence; (2) country and culture knowledge; (3) general and subject matter knowledge; (4) client and business knowledge; and (5) information technology and computer skills. For each category, the authors assigned a set of features: codifiable aspects (i.e. grammar, technology); knowledge-management

TABLE 3.3 Codifiability of relevant knowledge and knowledge-management instruments according to Risku, Dickinson and Pircher

Type of Knowledge	Codifiable Aspects	KM Instruments for Codifiable Aspects	Non-Codifiable Aspects	KM Instruments for Non-Codifiable Aspects
Language, linguistic, text skills, translation competence	Grammar, terminology, professional and regional conventions, register and writing conventions, translation methodologies and strategies, project management	Glossaries, translation memories, databases, style guides, terminology guidelines, newsletters, handbooks, ontologies	Tacit understanding of context, variations in meaning, experience of source/target languages, understanding of the purpose of the translation, instinctive, cultural or creative strategies	Mailing lists, online communities, translator associations, translation courses and collaboration tools, Communities of Practice, conferences, seminars
Country and cultural knowledge	Economic, legal, and regulatory requirements, conventional linguistic differences	Databases, websites, literature, media	Tacit knowledge of the source and target cultures, underlying knowledge of complex contexts (attitude, culture, history, etc.)	Translator associations and communities Chambers of Commerce, embassies, mentoring, storytelling, learning journeys
General and subject matter knowledge	Reference material, journals, industry guidelines	Databases, publications, knowledge portals, expert systems, knowledge and topic maps	"Education", general knowledge, constant willingness to learn, world experience, curiosity	Yellow pages, blogs, wikis, brainstorming, conferences, seminars
Client and business knowledge	Terminology, glossaries, contact, reference material, stylistic guidelines, industry information	CRM, PM tools, style guides, terminologies, translation memories, knowledge portals	Interaction strategies, long-term client-translator relationships, trust, marketing skills	Collaboration tools, yellow pages, coaching, networking, brainstorming
Information technology and computer skills	Communication, desktop publishing and translation tools, formatting guidelines	usar manuals, handbooks	Ability to solve complex problems	Courses, online forums, communities, mailing lists, conferences, seminars,

(Risku, Dickinson, & Pircher, 2010, p. 91)

instruments for codifiable aspects (i.e. glossaries, translation memories); non-codifiable aspects (i.e. tacit understanding of context, variations in meaning); and knowledge-management instruments for non-codifiable aspects (i.e. mailing lists, online communities) (see Table 3.3).

3.2.2.5 Professional and behavioural perspectives

In several of his works, Gouadec (2002, 2005, 2007) analysed translation from a professional point of view. From this perspective, Gouadec (2007, p. 150) highlights the following points, which he considers to be prerequisites and conditions of a good translator: (1) absolutely perfect mastery of the languages used, and especially the target language; (2) multi-cultural competence (in a broad sense, including technical culture, business culture, corporate culture, etc.); (3) perfect familiarity with the domains they specialize in; (4) absolute knowledge of what translation means, what it requires and what it implies; and (5) doing the job as professionally as possible.

Although it has not had much impact so far, the behavioural approach to the study of competences has also been used in some studies in translation studies.[18]

Rothe-Neves (2005) developed a proposal of an empirical study based on the behavioural approach proposed by McClelland (1973), which aimed to develop a competence model for the translation profession in its various specializations from systematic observation of the activity translators, with good results. Kuznik (2010/2012) presented an empirical study focusing on the work of in-house translators in translation companies, analysing data from ten translation companies in Barcelona.

There have also been surveys to collect opinions on what skills a good translator or interpreter should possess in their professional profile to meet the demands of their work, offering as the final result a repertoire of skills. This is the case of Mackenzie (2000), who presents the results of the project entitled *Practical Orientation studies in Translation and Interpreting* (POSI), carried out in Finland, aimed at users and providers of translation services; or Calvo Encinas (2004) who focused on the profile of community interpreters in a study carried out in the province of Toledo, Spain.

Another research focusing on exploring ergonomic issues at translators' workplaces was Massey and Ehrensberger-Dow (2011, 2014) with a study on the impact of ergonomic issues on translators' cognitive processes, the efficiency of the process and the quality of the translation product. The authors argued that organizational ergonomic factors can affect translators' job satisfaction, health and ultimately the context in which they operate. Massey and Ehrensberger-Dow (2014) suggest that the plethora of the use of translation technology at the workplace may not always enhance performance.

3.2.2.6 Main characteristics of this period

As we have seen, with the crossing over to the 21st century, research into the functioning of TC took on greater importance in translation studies. There are various proposals concerning this and various analysis perspectives. The following is a summary of the main characteristics of this period (see Table 3.4).

1. Range of approaches. TC models have been designed with various aims in mind: to be used in curriculum design; with a view to performance in the job market; and with theoretical objectives to discover the function

of the competences required of, and which identify, a translator. Most propose similar components for TC. However, they differ in their approach, the terminology used, and the distribution and importance given to these components. This disparity of criteria, however, serves to stress how complex it is to describe TC and the variety of subcomponents it comprises. Most of these models are cognitive in nature, but there are also some based on a behavioural approach. Both approaches to studying TC (what is needed to "know how to do" to be a translator and what the translators "do") are complementary when it comes to describing the workings of TC.

2. The importance of the procedural component and strategic competence. As opposed to the earlier period, most models concern the procedural nature of TC and include strategic competence as an essential component to be able to solve translation problems.
3. Linking the study of TC with expertise studies and establishing the difference between TC and translation expertise. As was the case during the previous period, some authors related TC to translation expertise (Shreve 2006; Göpferich, 2008, 2009), establishing links between studies into TC and expertise studies. However, in this period, advances are made in establishing the features that characterize translation expertise and how they differ from TC. PACTE (2017a), for instance, carried out an additional study with the best translators from the sample in their experiment on TC, which clearly demonstrated that the results from this group, in the majority of indicators, were higher than among the rest of the translators. Features in this group were also found. which, according to expertise studies, characterize experts and can serve as a basis to differentiate between TC and translation expertise (PACTE, 2017a, 2017b): superior performance; qualitative differences in the representation of knowledge; more highly developed structuring and interconnection of knowledge; more highly developed procedural knowledge; and more efficient use of documentation strategies.
4. The beginnings of empirical validation. It should be pointed out that the majority of the models proposed for TC have not been validated empirically, although there are a few cases of empirical research developed with this objective (PACTE, 2000, 2003; Gonçalves, 2003, 2005; Alves & Gonçalves, 2007).

PACTE carried out an exploratory study on TC (PACTE, 2002, 2003) with six professional translators, a pilot study with three professional translators and three foreign language teachers (PACTE, 2005a, 2005b) and, finally, an experiment with 35 professional translators and 24 foreign language teachers comparing their performance (Hurtado Albir, 2017b). The results of this study validated the proposed TC model.

TABLE 3.4 Evolution of translation competence models

Period	*Features*
Up to 2000	Emergence of early TC models • Focus on the description of components: language skills; extra-linguistic knowledge; documentation skills and use of tools; transfer competence • Inclusion of the transfer component as a specific subcompetence • Initial proposals of TC as a form of expert knowledge Lack of specific studies Lack of definition and terminological diversity Terminological confusion between TC and translation expertise Lack of empirical studies
Since 2000	Consolidation: TC as an object of study Diversity of perspectives • Minimalist perspective (Pym) • Didactic perspective (PACTE, Gonzalez Davis, Katan, Kelly) • Relevance-theoretic perspective (Alves, Alves & Gonçalves, Gutt) • Expertise studies perspective (Göpferich, Shreve) • Knowledge-management perspective (Risku et al.) • Professional and behavioural perspective (Gouadec, Kuznik, Rothe-Neves, Massey and Ehrensberger-Dow, etc.) Consideration of TC as basically comprising procedural knowledge Importance of the strategic component Linking the study of TC with expertise studies and establishing the differences Empirical validation (Alves & Gonçalves, Göpferich, PACTE)

The TC model proposed by Gonçalves (2003, 2005) and Alves and Gonçalves (2007) is assessed in various empirical studies carried out by these authors with a range of subject types: four students of English, eight translation students and four professional translators (Gonçalves, 2003, 2005); 16 translation students (Alves & Gonçalves, 2003); 17 translation students (Alves & Magalhães, 2004); three professional translators (Alves, 2005a); and four professional translators (Alves, 2005b).

In Chapter 4, we will approach the development of empirical-experimental research on TC and its acquisition in more detail and will reflect on issues pertaining to such studies.

3.3 The acquisition of translation competence[19]

Unlike the case of translation competence, there are fewer proposals of models for translation competence acquisition (TCA). Most existing models are based on observation and experience and studies in other disciplines. To the best of our knowledge, Harris, PACTE and Alves and Gonçalves are the only authors who have attempted an empirical validation of their models.

3.3.1 Models of translation competence acquisition

This section highlights the contributions of Harris, Harris and Sherwood, Toury, Shreve, Chesterman, PACTE, Alves and Gonçalves, and Kiraly.

3.3.1.1 Harris's natural translation

Harris (1973, 1977, 1980) and Harris and Sherwood (1978) indicate the existence of a *natural translation* ability as a universal innate ability possessed by any bilingual speaker. Harris attaches great importance to the study of this ability and believes that the study of natural translation provides data of great interest for translation studies.

The natural translation ability is defined by Harris (1977) as the translation rendered by bilinguals in everyday circumstances without having received special training for this. For this reason, although all bilinguals possess this ability, it is more easily observed in a primitive state, when one has not yet undergone formal teaching. According to Harris, this means that in addition to possessing bilingual competence in two languages, bilinguals have a third alternative which develops naturally with advanced competence in the two languages: the ability to translate a given languageinto another languageand vice versa. In this sense, bilingualism implies the existence of a triple competence (and not only a dual competence). Harris indicates that this issue had already been highlighted by Ljudskanov (1969), who notes that all bilingual subjects, in one way or another, translate by some form of intuition or habit. According to Harris, the main purpose of translation is the natural transmission of information. If communication works well, the linguistic expression has relative importance.

Harris (1973) only has examples of natural translation provided by the interpretation bilingual children made for their families. However, Harris and Sherwood (1978) provide an analysis of how natural translation unfolds on the basis of their own data and data collected in studies (some of them longitudinal) conducted by other researchers in North America with bilingual children and teenagers.

From the results of empirical studies, Harris and Sherwood (1978) show that natural translation is an innate ability, developed at a very early age, and subject to an evolution from a *pre-translation* stage to what they call a *semi-professional* stage.

Authors such as Toury (1986, 1995) and Presas (2000) rightly point out that this ability does not necessarily tend to create TC. Toury (1986), while accepting that there is an innate predisposition to translate related to a bilingualism, claims that TC does not develop automatically and in parallel to natural bilingualism. Besides linguistic competence, translators must create a second competence, a transfer competence which requires the transfer of text and involves structures of knowledge that are not part of bilingualism. Presas (2000), meanwhile, opposes the notion of *natural translator* to the notion of *trained translator*. Presas claims that, although she agrees with Harris that every bilingual is potentially a natural translator, the abundance of bad translations proves that this natural translation ability is not enough to allow every bilingual to become an expert translator. We agree with these authors that a natural translation ability is not enough to guarantee the emergence of TC and that a natural translation ability alone does not provide the necessary conditions to build TC (not all bilinguals are translators). To achieve the goal of TC, the development of other subcompetences is still needed. However, we agree that this rudimentary natural translation ability is one of the bases of TC.[20]

3.3.1.2 Toury's socialization of translation

Acknowledging Harris (1973), Toury (1980) suggests the concept of *native translator*, complementary to that of the linguistics notion of *native speaker*, which defines the individual who has developed translation competence progressively without any formal instruction (Toury, 1995, pp. 241–243). As noted in the previous section, Toury argues that the hypothesis of an innate translation ability, as proposed by Harris and Sherwood (1978), is not sufficient to explain the acquisition of translation competence. In this sense, the author believes that translation competence is a skill of bilinguals and develops through the acquisition of specific regulatory requirements and defends the need for an evolving model of TC in order to study translation as a separate ability in its own right.

Toury (1995, pp. 241–258) suggests a tentative development model of the process of converting a bilingual speaker into a translator and defines the process that emerging translators undergo as *socialization as concerns translating* (Toury, 1995, p. 250). This model is influenced by the notion of context from the *Manipulation School* to which the author belongs. For Toury, the crucial question is how a bilingual becomes a translator, especially if this occurs outside the formal education system. Toury argues that translation activity, even if performed by children, is a communicative production and, therefore, an interactive event, which plays an essential role in the social environment. The feedback received by the translator is essentially normative and can be received in the form of *sanction* (if there has been a bad translation) or reward (if the originator or the receiver is satisfied with the translation). This happens especially in the early stages of professional practice as inexperienced translators are discovering the functioning of the social environment and are not sure of what is expected of them. At this early stage, feedback is only external, as the inexperienced translator has no criteria for judging the suitability of various solutions or the use of alternative strategies. Subsequently, translators develop an internal control mechanism that operates during the translation act. Toury points out that during the socialization process of translation, the translator is assimilating the feedback received and therefore changing its basic competence. Thus, translation competence is, at each stage of its development, a mixture of innate, assimilated and social mechanisms.

Moreover, Toury points out that the concept of textual production can vary according to location, time, class and so on. Therefore, the initiation process may have to be repeated if the translator switches to a different subculture or goes in a completely new culture, or just when facing different translation tasks.

Another hypothesis raised by Toury is that the greater the variety of translation situations experienced by an individual, the greater the range and flexibility of the personal ability to act socially in an appropriate manner. This leads to an acquired *adaptability*, for example, the ability to adjust to changing conditions which may require different attitudes. Conversely, when there is a *specialization*, it may collide with the adaptability of the individual, lowering the level of general translation competence. Toury argues that different combinations of *specialization* and *adaptability* are important issues for empirical translation studies.

The more advanced the development of translation competence in the individual, the more he/she may be able to start *resisting* regulatory pressure without the risk of being penalized. Thus, Toury argues, a translator could not only act contrary to enforced norms but he/she could even cause changes in such norms.

3.3.1.3 Shreve: From natural to constructed translation

Shreve (1997) considers translation competence as a specialization of communicative competence. However, unlike it, not everyone has it. In this sense, translation competence is not an innate skill. Shreve notes that, unlike communicative competence, translation competence is not distributed evenly among the members of a linguistic and cultural community, not everyone can translate and those who learn to translate, achieve it by means of translation experience.

For Shreve, the development of translation competence is a continuum between natural translation and *constructed translation* (professional translation). However, this movement is not automatic, or linear, there is no set path to it. Shreve speaks of a *three-dimensional polygon*, which involves different functions and forms, experience in translation and translation situations.

In the development of translation competence, two types of changes may occur: (1) changes in individual cognitive styles and (2) changes in the history of TC acquisition. The most important thing, according to Shreve, is to identify patterns in these variations. Individual cognitive styles are variations of each individual, which are a consequence of the linguistic behaviour of the subject and, as noted by Bates and MacWhinney (1987), may be related to dimensions beyond language such as personality, temperament, social factors and so on. The history of TC acquisition is developed deliberately and can be done through education, advice from another translator or autonomously.

Shreve argues that the development of translation competence involves changes in the nature of the translation process and translation rules. There are fundamental differences in the performance of *natural* and *professional translators*. Natural translators produce no cultural or stylistically appropriate translations, translate by micro units without considering the elements of coherence and consistency, do not consider the purpose of the translation, the lexicon prevails in detriment of other elements and so on. These differences are related to the translation schemes that have been developed in relation to the communication needs of translation. Shreve emphasizes the influence of the nature, level and frequency of the translation tasks in the history of TC acquisition. This movement of restructuration of the translation competence does not occur if there are no changes in translation tasks.

In a later paper, Shreve (2006) related the acquisition of TC with the notion of *expertise trajectory* (Lajoie, 2003) (see Chapter 1). In line with expertise studies, Shreve (2006) suggests that with practice, declarative knowledge (i.e. what is known about the task) is converted into production rules which leads to proceduralization and, therefore, to less effortful processing and greater automaticity.

Shreve (2006) cautions that if such conditions are not met, i.e. if deliberate practice is absent and it lacks a critical mass of experience, then the conditions will not suffice for the cognitive changes associated with expertise to occur. On the other hand, Shreve argues, if the conditions of deliberate practice are met, it is possible to create the necessary conditions that enable the development of consistently superior performance. Experience accumulated in episodic memory will give rise to new more efficient knowledge structures capable of supporting expert behaviour.

Building on the notion of expertise trajectory, Shreve argues that TC acquisition can be developed differentially, depending on variations in how further practical experience is acquired. Shreve argues that in the case of translation, expertise trajectory must include an increase in cognitive performance in four distinct areas : (1) linguistic knowledge in L1 and L2; (2) knowledge of the source and target culture; (3) knowledge of textual conventions in L1 and L2; and (4) specific knowledge of translation. Empirical evidence suggests that these four cognitive domains need to be integrated to allow a novice translator to successfully complete their training.

Thus, there can be different kinds of translation experts, some with highly developed linguistic skills and subject area knowledge while others, compensating for their merely adequate background knowledge in a specific subject domain, excel in information-seeking skills.

3.3.1.4 Chesterman's five stages of translation expertise

Building on to the five steps proposed by Dreyfus and Dreyfus (1986), Chesterman (1997, pp. 147–149) defines the following stages in the development of translation expertise: novice, advanced beginner, competence, proficiency and expertise:[21]

- In the novice stage, one learns to recognize objective facts and predefined relevant features; rules are acquired to deal with actions related to those facts and features.
- In the advanced beginner stage, one begins to recognize traits which are difficult to define or, although relevant, not yet defined; the level of experience and recognition increases.
- In the competence stage, after having increased the levels of experience and recognition, it is necessary to develop a sense of priorities, i.e. to organize decision-making procedures in a hierarchical manner. At this stage, there is awareness of rules to be followed, how information is processed and how decisions are made.
- At the proficiency stage, most decisions are based on personal experience and, to a lesser extent, following conscious rules; this is an intuitive type of understanding and also rational action.
- Finally, at the expertise stage, expert performance is fluid and deliberate; intuition prevails and conscious actions are manifested in the form of critical reflection about one's own actions. One observes the *rational* nature and the *deliberate rationality* of expertise, in that "it gives priority to intuition but it is also characterized by 'deliberate rationality', which involves the testing and improving of intuitions" (Chesterman, 1997, p. 149).

Chesterman (1997, p. 150) defines the development of competence as a gradual process of automatization, ranging "from atomistic to holistic recognition, from conscious to unconscious response, from analytical to intuitive decisions, from calculative to deliberative rationality, from detached to involved commitment".

Acquiring translation competence must be seen as a gradual process of automatization and critical reflection over one's own intuitions. As expert knowledge advances, the ability to recognize and choose appropriate situational features increases and becomes increasingly automatized and focuses on intuitive strategies. Thus, the expert translator is someone who works largely on the basis of his/her intuition, which has a set of basic automatized, routinized procedures, and who can make deliberate use of reasoning when it is needed to solve unusual problems or in the comparison and justification of possible solutions. The degree of deliberate rationality varies according to the translation task. For example, in the translation of poetry or in the case where a translator intends to surprise readers, the translation may involve ongoing conscious control, without applying routine procedures already acquired. Chesterman wonders if, in such extreme situations, one can really refer to translation as an ability. Instead, a translator of routine documents or certificates may be able to automatically operate most of the time. According to Chesterman (1997, p. 151), a fundamental trait of expert professional is presumably the ability to judge when one needs to use deliberative rationality and how it should be done.

3.3.1.5 PACTE's dynamic model

The TC acquisition model developed by PACTE (1998, 2000, 2003, 2014, 2019a, 2020) draws on contributions of studies of learning processes. PACTE departs from the general hypothesis that TC acquisition is a process of reconstruction and development of subcompetences (bilingual, extra-linguistic, knowledge of translation, instrumental and strategic) and psycho-physiological components (see Figure 3.4).

From this point of view, PACTE considers that TC acquisition, as any learning process, is a dynamic, cyclic and spiral process that involves a process of restructuring and development from novice knowledge (pre-translation competence) to TC, requiring learning strategies and the restructuring and integration of declarative and operative knowledge as development unfolds. The development of procedural knowledge and, consequently, of the strategic subcompetence is an essential characteristic of translation competence acquisition.

There are relationships, hierarchies and variations in the process of TC acquisition. As such, in the process of restructuring and development, the following factors are at play (see Figure 3.9):

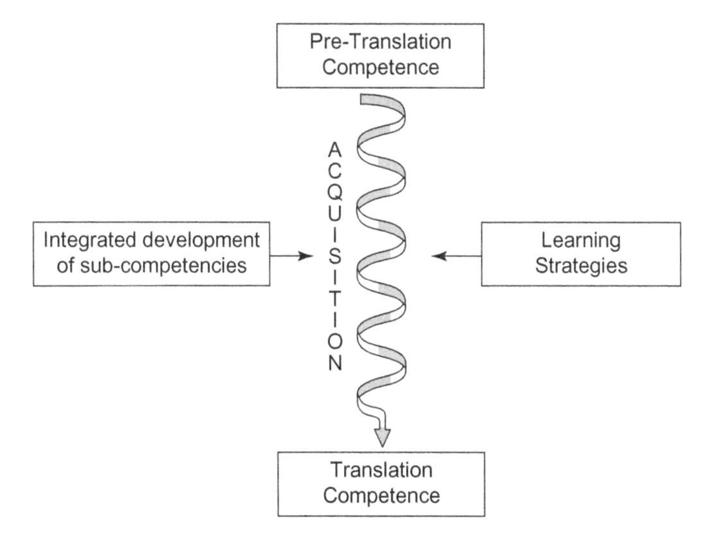

FIGURE 3.9 PACTE's translation competence acquisition model

(PACTE, 1998, 2000, p. 104,[22] among others)

1) Subcompetences interrelate and compensate for each other.
2) Its development does not occur in parallel.
3) It is essential to develop the knowledge-of-translation, instrumental and strategic subcompetences.
4) It can vary depending on directionality (direct or inverse translation), according to the language combinations in use, specialization or due to the learning environment.

Thus, PACTE considers that the process of TC acquisition cannot run in parallel in direct and inverse translation.[23] Furthermore, depending on the language combination in use, the process can be faster or slower; or depending on the domain of specialization (legal translation, literary translation, etc.), a given subcompetence may be more relevant than another. Moreover, the acquisition context (formal training, self-learning, etc.) and teaching methodology used influence the acquisition process; and, obviously, the type of training received also determines how translation competence is acquired. There are also differences at the individual level (their knowledge, abilities, cognitive styles, etc.)

3.3.1.6 Alves and Gonçalves's relevance-theoretic model

Based on connectionist approaches, Alves and Gonçalves (2007)[24] have drawn on the gradual development of cognitive networks to distinguish between two cognitive profiles:

1) *Narrow-band translators* who work mostly on the basis of insufficiently contextualized cues (i.e. dictionary-based meaning of words instead of contextualized meaning) and fail to bridge the gap between procedurally, conceptually and contextually encoded information.
2) *Broadband translators* who work mostly on the basis of the communicative cues provided by the source text and reinforced by the contextual assumptions derived from their cognitive environments.

According to Alves and Gonçalves, as shown in Figure 3.10, a translator's competence acquisition should be considered as a special type of cognitive architecture that develops through the acquisition process to allow translators "to establish a balance between the periphery and the central layers of cognitive systems and, from a situated perspective, enables them to arrive at an inferentially driven interpretive resemblance between source and target texts" (2007, p. 53).

Thus, the process of TC acquisition consists of the development of a "set of cognitive behaviours grouped around a cline that goes from the mere transfer of linguistically encoded items to the point where the translator fully integrates a more complex body of sub-competences" (Alves & Gonçalves, 2007, p. 53). Alves and Gonçalves also add that "narrow-band and broadband translators share potential cognitive characteristics. However, one observes changes of degree and kind in the levels of translator's competence as this competence develops and matures and procedural and declarative knowledge about translation become forms of specialised knowledge" (Alves & Gonçalves, 2007, p. 53).

3.3.1.7 Kiraly's four-dimensional model

Kiraly (2013, 2015) criticizes the two-dimensional TC models as they are unable to capture the complexity involved. He proposes a three-dimensional TC model to which he adds the time factor to turn it into a four-dimensional model of the emergence (rather than acquisition) of translator competence.

Kiraly's model reflects the complex interplay of competences and their non-parallel emergence over time and represents uniqueness in that each individual's competence development is different. In his emergence model, the author describes TC as a complex network and subcompetences as subnetworks; however, he refuses to propose a list of specific subcompetences and justifies this by arguing there is no consensus on which ones actually exist. He does underline the fact that a range of aspects influence the competence acquisition process, which is in constant evolution. Among these aspects, there are the translation tasks and projects in which the translator engages and learns, their personal and interpersonal attitude towards translating, human and material resources available and employed and the

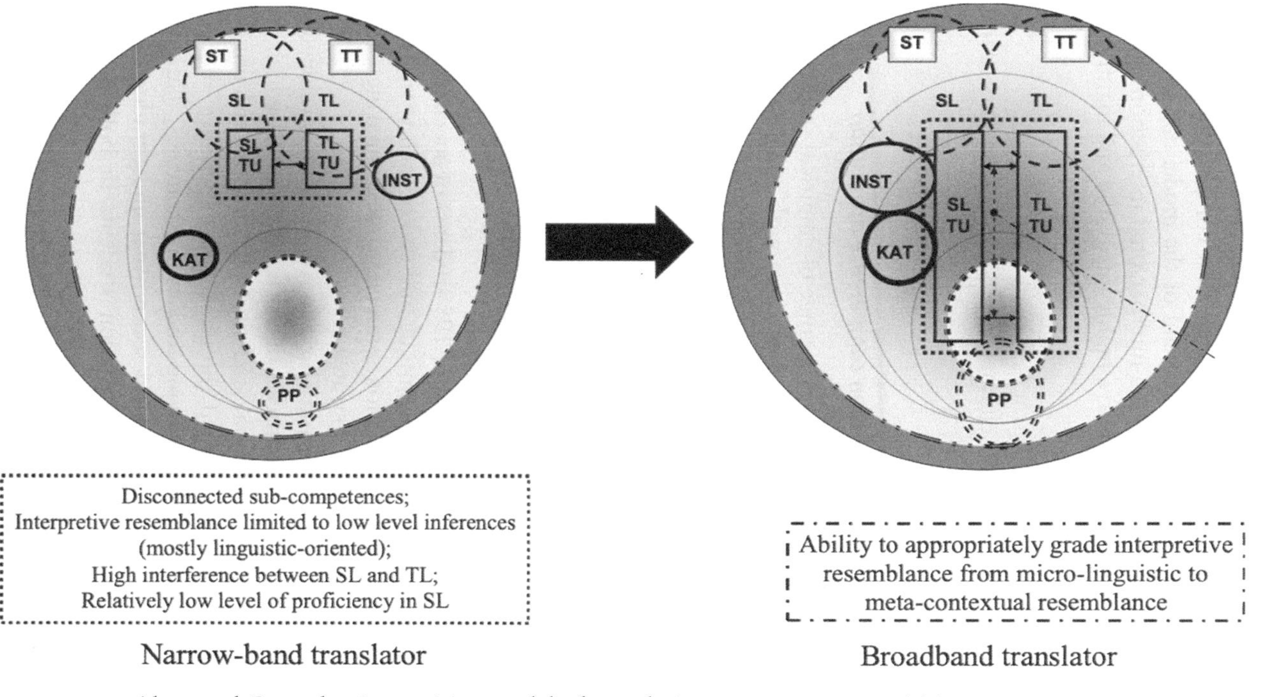

FIGURE 3.10 Alves and Gonçalves's cognitive model of translation competence acquisition

(Alves & Gonçalves, 2007, pp. 51–52)

influence of the learning environment (2013, p. 212). The translator's disposition for learning, abstracting from experience, using language in a creative manner, adapting to norms and so on are also included among the influential elements that can have a bearing on TCA and make every process unique.

In Kiraly's model, each subcompetence would appear near the lower (novice) level as a separate dynamic vortex but show complex links throughout the system towards the upper (expert) end of the model due to experience and learning, including learning from interpersonal interaction. Finally, the separate subcompetences merge into a highly integrated and mainly intuitive supercompetence (2015, p. 29).

Table 3.5 summarizes the main characteristics of the models of translation competence acquisition.

3.3.2 Empirical studies on translation competence acquisition

Since the 1980s, there has been a wide range of empirical studies on issues related to the acquisition of TC, most of them with small samples. These studies focus on the performance of students in translation or compare the performance of professional translators and translation students or translation students at different levels of their training, addressing issues such as creativity, process automatization, the use of translation strategies, the process of understanding, the use of sources of documentation and processes of decision-making. See Massana Roselló (2016, pp. 39–67) for a review of such studies up to 2015 and PACTE (2020, pp. 7–9).

The following studies are noteworthy as regards large sample groups:

- Séguinot (1991) analysed a total of 195 students of specialized translation, who were tested at the beginning and end of each year. This study focused on analysing translation strategies and comparing the differences between native and L2 strategies.
- Orozco (2000) and Orozco and Hurtado Albir (2002) developed instruments to measure the TCA process in written translation, which drew on a sample group of 235 first-year students from three Spanish universities.
- Lachat Leal (2003) concerned the impact of experience and learning in the process of problem-solving and using strategies. This was carried out on a sample group of 111 second-year undergraduate students, 98 fourth-year students – translation students in both cases – and 12 professional translators.

TABLE 3.5 Characteristics of translation competence acquisition models

Model Authors	*Disciplinary Framework*	*Key Features*
Natural translation Harris (1973, 1977, 1980), Harris and Sherwood (1978)	Linguistic approaches Ljudskanov (1969)	**Basic concepts:** • *Natural translation:* an innate ability in bilingualism. • Phases of natural translation: *Pre-translation, self-translation and transduction.* **Description of TCA process:** Not specified.
Socialization of translation Toury (1980, 1995)	Manipulation school	**Basic concepts:** • *Native translator:* bilingual who acquired translation ability progressively without formal instruction. • *Socialization of translation:* importance of feedback, essentially normative, of the social environment in acquiring translation competence. **Description of TCA process:** • Internal mechanism of gradual control. • From an initial stage to the *socialization of the translation.*
From natural to constructed translation Shreve (1997)	Cognitive approaches	**Basic concepts:** • *Natural translation.* • *Constructed translation:* professional translation. • Translation competence as a specialization of communicative competence. • *Tridimensional polygon:* different translation forms and functions, experience in translation and translation situations. **Description of TCA process:** • TCA is developed deliberately. • Continuum from natural translation to constructed translation (professional translator).

(*Continued*)

TABLE 3.5 (Continued) Characteristics of translation competence acquisition models

Model *Authors*	*Disciplinary Framework*	*Key Features*
Expertise-performance approach Shreve (2006)	Expertise studies (Lajoie 2003)	**Basic concepts:** • *Expertise trajectory:* development through deliberate practice. **Description of TCA process:** • Process of automation and proceduralization. • Existence of different sequential processes depending on how TC is acquired.
Five stages of translation expertise Chesterman (1997)	Cognitive psychology (Dreyfus & Dreyfus, 1986)	**Basic concepts:** • Five steps of Dreyfus and Dreyfus: novice, advanced beginner, competent, proficiency and expert. **Description of TCA process:** • Gradual internal process of automation, evolving from novice to expert knowledge.
A dynamic TCA model PACTE (1998, 2002, 2003, 2017c, 2020, etc.)	Cognitive psychology, Psychology of learning	**Basic concepts:** • *Pre-translation competence:* novice knowledge. • Components of TC: bilingual, extra-linguistic, knowledge-of-translation, instrumental and strategic subcompetences; psycho-physiological components. **Description of TCA process:** • Dynamic, cyclic and spiral-shaped. • Restructuring and development from novice knowledge (pre-translation competence) to TC. • Requires learning competence (learning strategies). • Restructured and integrated development of declarative and procedural knowledge (subcompetences of translation competence). • Importance of acquiring procedural knowledge (strategic subcompetence).

(Continued)

TABLE 3.5 (Continued) Characteristics of translation competence acquisition models

Model *Authors*	*Disciplinary Framework*	*Key Features*
A relevance-theoretic model Alves and Gonçalves (2007)	Relevance theory, connectionist approaches	**Basic concepts:** • Translator's *competence*. Focus on interpretive resemblance. • General translation competence (GTC) and specific translation competence (STC). • *Narrow-band translator:* predominantly use of automatized processes; lower levels of metacognitive activity. • *Broadband translator: ability* to self-regulate cognitive effort in terms of problem-solving and decision-making; higher levels of metacognitive activity. **Description of TCA process:** • From narrow-band to broadband translator; cognitive cline towards expertise. • Gradual, systematic and recursive processes.
A four-dimensional model Kiraly (2013, 2015)	Cognitive and constructivist approaches	**Basic concepts:** • TC as a complex network. • Four-dimensional emergence of translator competence. **Description of TCA process:** • The TCA process is in constant evolution. • A range of aspects influence the process: experience (translation tasks), learning, interpersonal interaction. • The separate subcompetences (novice) merge into a highly integrated and mainly intuitive supercompetence (expert).

- Gregorio Cano (2014) analysed the development of strategic competence for resolving problems of a cultural nature, with 1,046 undergraduate translation students from five Spanish faculties of translation and interpreting: 655 first-year students and 391 fourth-year students. It included a longitudinal study with 37 students who were given the same test in their first and fourth years.

- Quinci (2014) carried out a longitudinal study over three years with 53 undergraduate and master's students of translation (one group of BA students and two of MA students). This study also included ten professional translators. The aim of this study was to observe whether different levels of competence reflected different linguistic patterns.
- Massana (2016) performed an experimental study on TCA as regards resolving false friends (Portuguese-Spanish) with 30 undergraduate translation students from the second, third and fourth years at two Spanish universities and ten professional translators.
- Olalla-Soler (2017) performed an experimental study on the acquisition of translator cultural competence with a sample group of 38 undergraduate translation students taking German as a second foreign language in the BA in translation and interpreting from the first, second, third and fourth years and ten professional translators.

However, these studies deal with partial aspects of TCA and research into comprehensive monitoring of TCA as a whole is in short supply. Only three of the TCA proposed models have incorporated empirical validation:

- Harris and Sherwood (1978) based their analysis of how natural translation functions on data taken from studies of bilinguals (some of which are longitudinal), from birth to the age of 18, carried out in the US.
- Alves and Gonçalves (2007), in turn, worked from empirical studies with translation students and professional translators (see Alves & Gonçalves, 2003; Alves & Magalhães, 2004; Alves, 2005a, 2005b) for their proposal of two TC profiles: narrow-band translators and broad-band translators.
- PACTE (2014, 2015, 2017c, 2019a, 2020) carried out a study with 129 undergraduate students in translation and interpreting from the first, second, third and fourth years and those recently graduated (approximately 30 subjects from each of these groups). The results were compared with the group of translators from the TC experiment. The results have allowed for the identification of four types of "evolution" that vary according to the various competences (PACTE, 2019a, 2020): (1) non-evolution, no difference in the values between successive groups between the first year and the end of training; (2) rising evolution, values rise between the first year and the end of training, with each value between successive groups being higher than or equal to the previous one; (3) falling evolution, values fall between the first year and the end of training, with each value between successive groups being lower than or equal to the previous one; and (4) mixed evolution, a combination of rising and falling evolution between the first year and the end of training.

There are two noteworthy research projects that have carried out longitudinal studies on TCA:

- The TransComp project (2008–2011, University of Graz) monitored the performance of 12 students of translation over a period of three years and compared it to the performance of ten professional translators (see Göpferich, 2009).
- The Capturing Translation Processes (CTP) project (2009–2011, ZHAW Institute of Translation and Interpreting), which compared translation students at various stages in their training (194 beginners and 112 advanced students) and 39 professional translators (see Massey & Ehrensberger-Dow, 2011; Ehrensberger-Dow & Massey, 2013; Ehrensberger-Dow, 2014).

3.4 Characteristics of translation competence and its acquisition: Objectives and difficulties in the investigation

As we have seen, there are several proposals for the operation of translation competence and several perspectives of analysis. Such difference highlights the complexity of TC and has an impact on its description and the variety of subcomponents that are part of TC.

Over two decades ago, Campbell (1998, p. 18) proposed some requirements that should be part of a model of translation competence:

- To show whether translation competence is divisible into components, and, if so, to describe such components and their relationships.
- To describe the developmental pathway taken in learning how to translate.
- To include means for describing the differences between the performance of different translators.

Therefore, one needs to collect not only data related to the operation of the TC but also data related to TCA. Similarly, Waddington (2000, p. 135) considered several problems for TC modelling:

- It is difficult to know the number of components, clearly identifying them and the relationship between them.
- A model that has been developed for a given level of competence is not necessarily valid for another.
- Any competence model is therefore incomplete without a model of competence development.

3.4.1 Difficulties in the investigation of translation competence and translation competence acquisition

It should be noted that most TC models have not been validated empirically and only a few authors have drawn on empirical-experimental research in order to validate their models. Thus, there is no history of empirical research that could be used as a basis in order to define TC and its acquisition, and this is the first major difficulty concerning the study. Other difficulties in the investigation of TC and TCA stem from their complexity, procedural nature, heterogeneity and diversity. As described below, these factors create difficulties in carrying out empirical-experimental research into TC and TCA as a whole:

1) The complex nature of TC and TCA and the complexity of the relationship of their components. It should first be pointed out that research into TC is problematic because of its inherent complex nature given the wide range of cognitive areas and activities involved and the complexity of the corresponding relationships.
2) The procedural and automatized nature of TC and TCA. Proceduralization and automatization, characteristics that affect both the functioning of TC as well as its acquisition, make it difficult to analyse them since procedural knowledge is more difficult to verbalize and observe.
3) The heterogeneous nature of TC and TCA is another aspect that poses problems to research since this implies a very diverse range of abilities, which in addition can vary depending on the subject.
4) The diversification of TC and TCA. How TC functions and the relationships between its components are particularly difficult to observe given the differences depending on the individual characteristics of the subjects (knowledge, experience, cognitive styles, etc.) and the way TC is acquired (guided, via teaching-learning; autonomously, through practice outside the teaching system). There are also differences depending on the translation direction (into L1 or L2). Furthermore, each specialized professional profile has its own specific characteristics.

3.4.2 Main characteristics of translation competence and its acquisition

3.4.2.1 Translation competence: A collection of knowledge, abilities and attitudes

The proposed models and emerging empirical research leave us with the following noteworthy essential TC characteristics:

- TC is a collection of knowledge, abilities and attitudes necessary in order to translate. It comprises declarative and operative knowledge, and is essentially operative knowledge since it integrates the abilities to perform translation tasks.

- TC is comprised of a set of interrelated subcompetences: linguistic competence in at least two languages; extra-linguistic competence (encyclopaedic, cultural and thematic knowledge); knowledge of translation competence (principles that govern translation and professional aspects); instrumental competence (use of all kinds of documentary sources and ICTs applied to translation); and strategic competence.
- Strategic competence plays a fundamental role in order to be able to guarantee the translation process efficacy and solve translation problems appropriately.
- TC affects the development of the translation process and its product (the quality of translations).
- There are differences in the functioning of TC depending on directionality (into L1 or L2) and the area of translation specialization in question (legal, technical, scientific, literary, audio-visual, localization, etc.), as well as differences of an individual nature.
- TC is an acquired competence that is different from bilingual competence.

3.4.2.2 The acquisition of translation competence: A cyclical and non-linear process

Being a cyclical process, various phases are indicated in the acquisition of the TC, which vary according to the authors. We lack, however, more empirical knowledge of these different phases of TCA. Detailed knowledge of these phases could provide input to levelling competences in translation in a similar way to what takes place in other neighbouring disciplines (i.e. language acquisition), which are vital for the teaching of translation.

However, based on the proposed models and the empirical studies already carried out, one can highlight the following traits of TCA:

- TCA is a process in which TC subcompetences are developed and restructured.
- TCA is a process in which it is essential to develop procedural knowledge and strategic competence in order to make progress in one's capacity to solve translation problems.
- TCA implies a gradual process of automatization. Some authors (Alves and Gonçalves, Chesterman, PACTE, Shreve) assimilate this acquisition process with the process of acquiring any knowledge and underline the gradual process of proceduralization and automatization.
- TCA involves a different process depending on the subcompetence. The results of PACTE's empirical research have demonstrated that not all subcompetences are developed in parallel and there are different types of development depending on the case (non-evolution, rising evolution, falling evolution, mixed evolution).

- TCA is not a linear process. Some authors (Kiraly, PACTE, Shreve) give importance to the fact that, given the complexity of the TCA process, it does not develop in a linear fashion. The mixed evolution identified by PACTE in their TCA experiment serves as an illustrative example.
- TCA affects the translation process and its product, bringing about an evolution as regards the functioning of the translation process and the quality of translations.
- There are variations in the TCA process. Some models (PACTE, Shreve, Kiraly) stress that TCA is a complex process in which we can find different types of variations according to: the way it is acquired (naturally and self-taught, guided by means of teaching-learning); the pedagogical context; directionality (towards L1 or L2); and professional profile (legal, technical, literary translator, etc.). Of course, there are also variations at an individual level depending on the characteristics of each subject.

3.4.3 Perspectives for the further investigation of translation competence and its acquisition

Although much has been achieved, there is still a long way to go in research on TC and TCA. Research should develop along the following major lines:

1) Empirical research on TC and TCA. As we have seen, most of the TC and TCA models have not been validated empirically and there is a shortage of empirical research on TC and TCA as a whole. These studies should be based on large and representative samples so that the results can be generalizable. Furthermore, studies already carried out should be replicated (e.g. those by PACTE on TC and TCA, TransComp on TCA) in different contexts so that the results can be compared in each case, and we can deduce common and generalizable characteristics. As regards studying TCA, it is important to carry out longitudinal studies that, solving the inherent difficulties performing this kind of study (controlling confounding variables, development of parallel instruments for each measuring, subjects dropping out, etc.), are able to control all the possible external influences that could distort the results.
2) Research on the competences acquired in each professional profile and how they are acquired. Most studies into TC and TCA refer to generalist translator competences. So, what is lacking is advances in research into the competences required in each professional translation area and the process by which they are acquired: legal, business-finance, technical, scientific, literary, audio-visual, accessibility, localization and so on.
3) Research on possible variations that can crop up in TC and in TCA. It would be helpful to carry out studies that compare performance depending on translation direction (into L1 and into L2) and according to the

context (social, pedagogical), the language pair and the characteristics of the subjects, so that consistencies and differences can be identified.

4) Research on the functioning of TC and TCA in the age of artificial intelligence. TC is not static, and its characteristics have changed throughout history (i.e., the discovery of the printing press, the widespread use of computers and translation memories, etc.). The increasing presence of technology and artificial intelligence in translation task execution makes it essential to study empirically what changes are taking place in TC and its impact on TCA in today's changing society.
5) Establish levels of competences. As opposed to other disciplines, in translation, there is no common base for describing levels of competences (see next section). This requires research into the TCA process, with large and representative samples, and also in different contexts in order to better understand the different phases in the TCA process.

3.5 Translation competence levels

As pointed out in the previous section, in translation studies, differently from other disciplines, there is no common base for describing levels of competences as it happens, say, in foreign language teaching (for example, CEFR, Council of Europe, 2001, 2018). A description of this kind would provide a common framework that would be of great use in the education and professional sectors of translation.

3.5.1 Proposals for competence levels in translation

In the case of translation, very few attempts have been made to develop scales of competence level descriptors. Moreover, none of the proposals have been empirically validated, their categories and levels are not described in sufficient detail and most of them do not describe competences. Hurtado Albir, Kuznik and Rodriguez-Inés (2022, pp. 43–52) describe some proposals from the professional sector and from academia that we present below.

3.5.1.1 Proposals from the professional sector

In some countries, there are professional accreditation or regulation bodies for translation. In most cases, certification is based on a translation test, which is a requirement for admission to the body itself or for official recognition. The following bodies are cited in Hurtado Albir, Kuznik and Rodriguez-Inés (2022).

In Australia, the National Accreditation Authority for Translators and Interpreters (NAATI) offers a certification system that considers the knowledge, skills and attitudes required to work as a translator or interpreter.

It offers 11 certifications for interpreting and two for translation (called "Recognised Practising" and "Certified Translator").

In Brazil, the Associação Brasileira de Tradutores e Intérpretes (ABRATES) has a system of level accreditation for its members, consisting of the translation of three short texts, in direct (into L1) and inverse (into L2) translation, and proposes correction criteria, although it does not differentiate between levels.

In Canada, the Canadian Translators, Terminologists and Interpreters Council (CTTIC) conducts national translation level certification tests, although it does not provide information on the skills it assesses or whether it discriminates between levels.

In China, the Accreditation Test for Translators and Interpreters (CATTI), promoted by the Language Service Competence Accumulation and Training, offers test preparation services, examinations and computerized marking. In addition, the Translators Association of China (TAC) offers translation assessment and recognition.

In the Netherlands, the Vertaalacademie Maastricht and the PsTEVIN platform (which brings together the professional associations of translators in the Netherlands) developed in 2011 a competence matrix and three levels of competence, which have been revised from 2016 onwards. The proposed competences are translation competence, linguistic and textual competence, documentation and research competence, cultural competence, technological competence and business competence.

In the United Kingdom, there are several bodies:

- The Institute of Translation and Interpreting (ITI) provides certification as a qualified translator. The certification test consists of the translation of a text which, according to the ITI, must be of professional quality, technically correct and faithful to the meaning of the original text.
- The Chartered Institute of Linguists (CIOL) has developed a system of assessment and certification for different levels, profiles (translation, interpreting and bilingual skills) and language combinations. CIOL builds on the scale of levels of the Regulated Qualifications Framework (RQF), which is the framework for creating and accrediting qualifications in England, Wales and Northern Ireland.
- Instructus (formerly Skills CFA) sets national occupational standards that define the knowledge, skills and attitudes that a worker must possess to carry out a particular occupation, as well as the work expected to be carried out in that occupation. In 2007, Skills CFA updated the national occupational standards for translation; these standards distinguish between the categories of professional translator and advanced professional translator, with the difference that the latter can handle texts with complex subject matter and act as mentors to colleagues or translation students.

In the USA, there are two bodies:

- The American Translators Association (ATA) provides certification for 30 language combinations and has a detailed grading scale but it does not set out various competences or distinguish levels. Obtaining its certificate is equivalent to a minimum level 3 of the Interagency Language Roundtable.
- The Interagency Language Roundtable (ILR) proposes five levels: levels 0 and 1 correspond to minimum performance, level 2 corresponds to limited performance and levels 3, 4 and 5 correspond to professional performance. The ILR identifies skills that the translator must have, although they are not presented as competences or descriptors; it is specified that the complexity of the translation task increases with text complexity.

Another example of certification is the AVT Pro Certification, promoted by the platform and directory of audio-visual translation and localization professionals known as The Poool. It aims to certify linguistic and technical knowledge and skills to provide quality language services to the audio-visual industry (subtitling, captioning and spotting).

These are some examples of translation accreditation or regulation bodies, which highlight the lack of proposed levels and descriptions of competences.

3.5.1.2 Proposals from academia

There have been several initiatives regarding the description of competence levels for translation training. Hurtado Albir, Kuznik and Rodriguez-Inés (2022) cite the following contributions.

In Spain, the *Libro Blanco del Título de Grado en Traducción e Interpretación* (Muñoz Raya, 2004) was drawn up in 2004 with the collaboration of the Spanish National Agency for Quality Assessment and Accreditation after consulting various agents in the world of translation (graduates, employers, authorities from the academic and professional world of translation). It includes a list of general and specific competences. The specific competences proposed are command of foreign languages, knowledge of foreign cultures and civilizations, command of one's own language both written and oral, command of specialized translation techniques and terminology, command of computer tools, command of assisted translation and localization techniques, information and documentation research skills, knowledge of economic and professional aspects, ability to work in a team, ability to design and manage projects and broad cultural background.

At the European level, as mentioned before, the EMT (European master's in translation)[25] competences proposal, drawn up in 2009, significantly revised in 2017 and again in 2022, aims to facilitate assessment at master's level. The first proposal included six competences, namely, translation service provision, linguistic, intercultural, documentation, thematic and technological. The second proposal reduced them to five competences and introduced modifications. The five competences are language and culture, translation, technological, personal and interpersonal, and service provision. In April 2022, the key competences and skills were adjusted to meet current challenges. Different levels are not established.

In the Competence Awareness in Translation (CATO), an initiative created within the EMT, an empirical study was carried out at the European level to find out the perception of master's students regarding their acquisition of the competences described in the 2017 EMT model; ten universities participated and responses from 310 informants were obtained (Froeliger, 2019).

The proposal by Cnyrim, Hagemann and Neu (2013) consists of two categories, that of translation competence and that of competence in translation studies (knowledge of translation theory, metalanguage, etc.). Five levels are distinguished in both: level 1 or lay competence, level 2 or basic functional competence, level 3 or conceptual and procedural competence, level 4 or multidimensional competence and level 5 or autonomous and progressive competence.

In specialized areas, two European research projects have proposed competences:

- The eTransfair project has drawn up a proposal of competences for specialized translation, including translation, linguistic, inter- and transcultural, revision and proofreading, specific field, technological, documentation and terminological, and professional competences. However, it neither establishes levels of performance nor does it describe the different areas of specialization.
- The PETRA-E project has developed a framework for literary translation with five levels. The competences proposed are transfer, linguistic, textual, heuristic, literary-cultural, professional, evaluative and research. Five levels are distinguished, namely, beginner, advanced learner, beginner professional, advanced professional and expert.

The Translation and Interpreting Competence Questionnaire (TICQ)[26] (Schaeffer et al., 2020) is a questionnaire to collect qualitative and quantitative data from subjects and facilitate the identification and classification of profiles. The results group subjects who have responded in a similar way. However, the TICQ does not establish levels of performance.

Finally, with regard to cultural competence in translation, three proposals can be mentioned: (1) the intercultural competence curriculum framework resulting from the European PICT (Promoting Intercultural Competence in Translators) project (Tomozeiu, Koskinen & D'Arcangelo, 2016); (2) the dimensions of intercultural competence proposed by the INCA (Intercultural Competence Assessment) project; and (3) the intercultural competence model proposed by Yarosh (2012, 2015), which includes learning outcomes for each subcompetence.

3.5.2 The NACT project[27]

The NACT project, abbreviated according to the project's name in Spanish (*Nivelación de competencias en la adquisición de la competencia traductora/Establishing competence levels in the acquisition of translation competence*), was carried out by the PACTE group and aimed at establishing competence levels in the acquisition of translation competence in written translation. It is a continuation of the experimental investigations of the PACTE group about TC and TCA. See PACTE (2018, 2019b) and Hurtado Albir and Rodriguez-Inés (2022c).

Purpose and development of the research

The aim of the NACT project was to describe performance levels in translation competence acquisition in order to advance towards a common European framework of reference in the educational and professional sectors of written translation. These levels should be comparable to the Common European Framework of Reference (CEFR) for languages. It is therefore a matter of defining scales of descriptors around descriptive categories with levels of performance that establish a progression, as is typical in the development of level scales. The descriptive categories used in the NACT project are specific competences that make up translation competence.

The project was developed in three phases:

- Phase 1 (2015–2017): Development of a first proposal of level descriptors. In this first phase, the following aspects were compiled and analysed: curricular documentation (bachelor's and master's degrees) from 18 European translation training centres; proposals of competences required for translators from the academic and professional sectors. Subsequently, a bilingual document in Spanish (*Nivelación de competencias en traducción. Propuesta 1 revisada*) and in English (*Establishing competence levels in translation. Proposal 1 revised*) was drawn up by PACTE in June 2017. This document contains a first proposal of level descriptors, with a three-level scale (with sublevels) and five descriptive categories: language competence; cultural, world knowledge and

thematic competence; instrumental competence; translation service provision competence; translation problem-solving competence; 23 European translation training centres from 15 countries participated in the first phase of the project,
- Phase 2 (2017–2018): Evaluation of the proposal for level descriptors. In this phase, the first proposal for level descriptors was evaluated by experts from the academic and professional translation world from 16 European countries through an evaluation questionnaire with closed and open questions, which allowed for the collection of quantitative and qualitative data. The evaluation involved 65 translation teachers, 23 professional translators and 11 representatives of professional translation associations.
- Phase 3 (2018–2019): Analysis of the data obtained through expert judgement and formulation of a second revised proposal.

Second NACT proposal for level descriptors

This proposal, like the first one, consists of a three-level scale with sublevels organized around five descriptive categories. See Hurtado Albir and Rodríguez-Inés (2022b).

The descriptive categories are the same as in the first proposal, with two small name changes and greater clarification of their content: language competence; extra-linguistic competence; instrumental competence; service provision competence; and translation problem-solving competence (see Table 3.6).

Three levels of translation are proposed:

- Translation level C: Translator specialist in at least one professional area of translation specialization. This is the consolidation of the professional fields of specialization in translation and includes the competences corresponding to each professional profile. It focuses on the following key professional areas: legal, economic-financial, technical, scientific and humanistic.
- Translation level B: Non-specialist translator. This is an introduction to professional areas of specialization in translation and includes skills for translating semi-specialized texts.
- Translation level A: Pre-professional translator. This is an introduction to translation and includes skills for translating non-specialized texts.

Translation levels A and B are divided into two sublevels (A1 and A2; B1 and B2) and descriptors are proposed for each level. In the case of translation level C, it is described only in general terms and no sublevels have been

TABLE 3.6 Descriptive categories and performance levels in translation competence acquisition (Second NACT proposal)

	Language competence	*Extra-linguistic competence*	*Instrumental competence*	*Service provision competence*	*Translation problem-solving competence*
Translation level C (specialist translator)	Can do…	Can do…	Can do…	Can do…	Can do…
Translation level B2 (non-specialist translator)	Can do…	Can do…	Can do…	Can do…	Can do…
Translation level B1 (non-specialist translator)	Can do…	Can do…	Can do…	Can do…	Can do…
Translation level A2 (pre-professional translator)	Can do…	Can do…	Can do…	Can do…	Can do…
Translation level A1 (pre-professional translator)	Can do…	Can do…	Can do…	Can do…	Can do…

Second NACT proposal (Hurtado Albir & Rodríguez-Inés, 2022b).

proposed. Such sublevels would need to be established in the future as it requires further research.

Additionally, the proposal contains:

- A global scale with descriptors defining the essential features of each level for each competence.
- Three annexes with examples for each level:
  - Text genres expected to be translated.
  - Cultural and encyclopaedic knowledge.
  - Documentation and technological resources and functionalities.
- A glossary, with 37 entries defining 77 concepts used in the description of the levels.

3.5.3 Continuation of the NACT project

Research that began with the NACT project was continued in two other related research projects, namely the EFFORT and EACT projects that are described below.

The EFFORT project

The EFFORT project (Towards a European framework of reference for translation)[28] is a European Erasmus+ project with a duration of three years (2020–2023). A consortium of 10 translation training institutions from nine European countries, led by the Universitat Autònoma de Barcelona, was created to carry out the project. In addition, the project has involved 32 associated partners from academic and professional translation and language institutions, with a total of 32 languages and 31 countries. The aim was to cover different geographical and linguistic areas and different fields of specialization in translation in order to ensure the greatest possible number of language combinations and specializations among the members.

The aim of the EFFORT project has been:

- To revise the description of levels for the non-specialist translator (translation levels A and B) proposed in the NACT project (Second NACT Proposal) and to design a methodological guide for using the framework. The review of the Second NACT Proposal used a questionnaire and involved 20 lecturers (two from each centre of the consortium). The analysis of the results, and input from members of the EFFORT project, led to modifications of the Second NACT Proposal. Thus, a Third NACT Proposal was drafted. The Methodological Guide includes, besides a guide for using the framework, examples of texts for each translation level (A1, A2, B1, B2), a glossary, and a self-assessment tool.

- To establish a first proposal of descriptors for the higher translation performance level (level C) in five key areas of specialization: literary, economic and financial, legal, scientific and technical translation. For each area, descriptors are proposed in terms of competences with a characterization of the area including a definition for each area; main areas of specialization; textual genres; professional contexts; relevant resources; and typical translation problems.

The EACT project[29]

The EACT project, abbreviated according to the project's name in Spanish (*Evaluación en la adquisición de la competencia traductora/Evaluation in the acquisition of translation competence*), was a research project funded by a Spanish Ministry, carried out from 2019 to 2022. Researchers from five Spanish universities and from a university in the United Kingdom, led by the Universitat Autònoma de Barcelona, participated in the project.

The aim of the EACT project was to establish assessment procedures for each level of translation competence in the framework of undergraduate translation training in Spain. The EACT project has focused on the translation levels A1, A2 and B1 described in the NACT project (Second NACT Proposal); direct translation from German, French and English (first foreign languages of Spanish translation training centres); and translation between first languages that are official languages in Spain (Spanish-Catalan, Spanish-Basque, Spanish-Galician). The target languages were Catalan, Galician, Spanish and Basque.

Two studies were carried out for this purpose:

- A survey on the current situation of evaluation in translation and interpreting degrees in Spain, aimed at translation teachers; 97 lecturers from various Spanish universities took part in this study.
- Design and evaluation of assessment procedures. In this study, translation level tests have been designed for translation levels A1, A2 and B1; the design of each test includes several assessment tasks to collect information on the descriptors of each competence, translation grading scales and rubrics for assessing each task. Subsequently, data were collected from students and teachers to evaluate the design of the tests. A total of 103 students and 42 translation teachers from five Spanish translation training centres took part in the evaluation of the proposal.

3.5.4 Perspectives for the further investigation of translation competence levels

Although the studies carried out so far represent progress towards the development of scales of level descriptors in translation and their evaluation, further research is needed in order to achieve reference frameworks comparable to those that exist for languages.

Many issues remain to be addressed, such as the following: the need for large-scale validation of the proposals made; establishing scales of descriptors for other varieties of translation; and establishing learning outcomes, pedagogical tasks and assessment procedures for different levels of translation competence and so on.

In addition to the intrinsic complexity of the relationship between all the components of translation competence and the insufficient empirical studies on TC as a whole and its acquisition, there is a lack of tradition in translation studies of developing scales of level descriptors.

Furthermore, the rapid pace of current technological changes, with consequent impact on the development of TC, makes it difficult to establish an adequate progression for the use of technology and artificial intelligence in the different levels of TCA.

Moreover, a scale of level descriptors in translation must be useful for the academic and professional field of translation. Consequently, it is necessary to involve all the implicated sectors so that a consensus can be reached.

Notes

1 For a previous discussion on the notion of competence, the reader is referred to Hurtado Albir (2017a).
2 The creator of the term is the anthropologist Hymes in 1966 in a paper entitled "On communicative competence" (published in 1971).
3 For more information on competence-based training and its application in translator's training cf. Hurtado Albir (2007, 2008, 2015a, 2015b, 2015c, 2018, 2019, 2022).
4 Original citation: "Une compétence est un savoir-agir complexe résultant de l'intégration, de la mobilisation et de l'agencement d'un ensemble de capacités et d'habiletés (pouvant être d'ordre cognitif, affectif, psychomoteur ou social) et de connaissances (connaissances déclaratives) utilisées efficacement, dans de situations ayant un caractère commun".
5 Original citation: "Una competencia es el conjunto de conocimientos, habilidades y actitudes necesarios para desempeñar una ocupación dada y la capacidad de movilizar y aplicar estos recursos en un entorno determinado, para producir un resultado definido".
6 Anderson's distinction rests on the distinction of Ryle (1949) between *knowing what* and *knowing how*.
7 The reader is referred to Hurtado Albir (2001, pp. 378–393, 2017a, 2021, pp. 389–414) for a previous account concerning the evolution of the study of translation competence.
8 Original citation: "die Fähigkeit, die beiden einsprachigen Kompetenzen auf einer höheren Ebene zu integrieren, d. h. auf der Ebene des Textes".
9 Original citation: "la habilidad de saber traducir".
10 Original citation: "la habilidad de saber traducir".
11 This model was first presented on the poster "La competencia traductora y su aprendizaje" *in IV International Congress on Translation*, held at the Universitat Autònoma de Barcelona, May 1998.

12 Other aspects intervene, such as knowledge of translation associations, tariffs and taxes.
13 PACTE has carried out empirical-experimental research on TC which is presented in Chapter 4.
14 The EMT project (http://ec.europa.eu/emt) is a partnership project between the European Commission and European institutions of higher education offering master's level translation programmes. The project has established a quality label for university translation programmes that meet agreed professional standards and market demands. EMT is a registered EU trademark and universities in the EMT network are entitled to use the logo (see EMT website).
15 For a more recent discussion, the reader is referred to Shreve, Angelone and Lacruz (2018).
16 This project, whose principal investigator was Göpferich, was launched in October 2007 and held at the University of Graz, tracking the performance of 12 students of translation over a period of three years and comparing it to the performance of ten professional translators.
17 Knowledge management promotes an integrated approach to identify, capture, evaluate, retrieve and share all of an enterprise's information assets. Such assets may include databases, documents, policies, procedures and previously uncaptured expertise and experience in single workers (Duhon, 1998).
18 For applications of behavioural approach in translation studies, cf. Kuznik and Hurtado Albir (2015).
19 For previous related work, the reader is referred to Hurtado Albir (2001, pp. 401–406, 2021, pp. 389–314); PACTE (2020, pp. 96–102).
20 Since there are different types of bilingualism, one can assume that the operation of the natural translation will be different depending on the degree of development of the two languages.
21 Dreyfus and Dreyfus identify five stages but do not provide a precise term for each stage; we therefore use the terms proposed by Chesterman for each stage.
22 This model was first presented on the poster entitled "La competencia traductora y su aprendizaje" in *the IV International Congress on Translation*, held at the Universitat Autònoma de Barcelona, May 1998.
23 PACTE has carried out empirical-experimental research on the acquisition of translation competence (PACTE 2020, among others), which is presented in Chapter 4.
24 Alves and Gonçalves have carried out empirical-experimental research to validate their approach to the acquisition of translation competence, which is presented in Chapter 4.
25 https://ec.europa.eu/info/sites/default/files/emt_competence_fwk_2017_en_web.pdf
26 https://traco.uni-mainz.de/ticq/?fbclid=IwAR3p0amyNQRfy4rQ_ig4Eo8YBrtDQBRf_NGMoUbqrIbZh7csX-kdoRTndTc
27 https://ddd.uab.cat/record/273075
28 https://www.effortproject.eu
29 https://pagines.uab.cat/eact/es

References

Alves, F. (1995). *Zwischen Schweigen und Sprechen: Wie bildet sich eine transkulturelle Brücke? Eine psycholinguistisch orientierte Untersuchung von Übersetzungsvorgängen zwischen portugiesischen und brasilianischen Übersetzern.* Hamburg: Dr. Kovac.

Alves, F. (1996). Veio-me um 'click' na cabeça: The theoretical foundations and the design of a psycholinguistically oriented, empirical investigation on German-Portuguese translation processes. *Meta*, *41*(1), 33–44.
Alves, F. (2005a). Bridging the gap between declarative and procedural knowledge in the training of translators: Meta-reflection under scrutiny. *Meta*,*50*(4), CD-ROM.
Alves, F. (2005b). Ritmo cognitivo, meta-função e experiência: parâmetros de análise processual no desempenho de tradutores novatos e experientes. In F. Alves, C. Magalhães, & A. Pagano (Eds.), *Competência em tradução: cognição e discurso* (pp. 109–169). Belo Horizonte: Editora UFMG.
Alves, F., & Gonçalves, J.L. (2003). A relevance theory approach to the investigation of inferential processes in translation. In F. Alves (Ed.), *Triangulating translation: Perspectives in process oriented research* (pp. 3–14). Amsterdam: John Benjamins.
Alves, F., & Gonçalves, J.L. (2007). Modelling translator's competence: Relevance and expertise under scrutiny. In Y. Gambier, M. Shlesinger, & R. Stolze (Eds.), *Translation studies: Doubts and directions* (pp. 41–55). Amsterdam: John Benjamins.
Alves, F., & Gonçalves, J.L. (2013). Investigating the conceptual/procedural distinction in translation: A relevance-theoretic analysis of micro and macro translation units. *Target*, *25*(1), 107–124.
Alves, F., & Magalhães, C. (2004). Using small corpora to tap and map the process-product interface in translation. *TradTerm*, *10*(1), 143–162.
Anderson, J.R. (1983). *The architecture of cognition*. Cambridge: Harvard University Press.
Austin, J.L. (1962). *How to do things with words*. Oxford: Oxford University Press.
Bachman, L.F. (1990). *Fundamental considerations in language testing*. London: Oxford University Press.
Bates, E., & MacWhinney, B. (1987). Competition, variation, and language learning. In B. MacWhinney (Ed.), *Mechanisms of language acquisition* (pp. 157–193). Mahwah, NJ: Lawrence Erlbaum Associates, Inc.
Beeby, A. (1996). *Teaching translation from Spanish to English* [Didactics of Translation Series 2]. Ottawa: University of Ottawa Press.
Bell, R.T. (1991). *Translation and translating*. London: Longman.
Boyatzis, R.E. (1982). *The competent manager: A model for effective performance*. New York: Wiley.
Boyatzis, R.E. (1984). *Identification of skill requirements for effective job performance*. Boston: Mcber.
Calvo Encinas, E. (2004). La administración pública ante la interpretación social: toma de contacto en la provincia de Toledo. *Puentes*, *4*, 7–16.
Canale, M. (1983). From communicative competence to communicative language pedagogy. In J.C. Richards & R.W. Schmidt (Eds.), *Language and communication* (pp. 2–27). London: Longman.
Campbell, S. (1998). *Translation into the second language*. London: Longman.
Canale, M., & Swain, M. (1980). Theoretical bases of communicative approaches to second language teaching and testing. *Applied Linguistics*, *1*(1), 1–47.
Cao, D. (1996). Towards a model of translation proficiency. *Target*, *8*(2), 325–340.
Chesterman, A. (1997). *Memes of translation*. Amsterdam: John Benjamins.
Chomsky, N. (1965). *Aspects of the theory of syntax*. Cambridge, MA: MIT Press.
Cnyrim, A., Hagemann, S., & Neu, J. (2013). Towards a framework of reference for translation competence. In D. Kiraly, S. Hansen-Schirra, & K. Maksymski (Eds.), *New prospects and perspectives for educating language mediators* (pp. 9–34). Tübingen: Gunter Narr Verlag.

Council of Europe. (2001). *Common European Framework of Reference for Languages (CEFRL)*. Strasbourg: Languages Policy Division.
Council of Europe. (2018). *Common European Framework of Reference for Languages: Learning, teaching, assessment. Companion volume with new descriptors*. Strasbourg: Language Policy Programme.
Delisle, J. (1980). *L'Analyse du discours comme méthode de traduction [Cahiers de Traductologie 2]*. Ottawa: University Press. Translated into English as Translation: An interpretive approach. (1988). Ottawa: University of Ottawa Press.
Dreyfus, H.L., & Dreyfus, S.E. (1986). *Mind over machine*. Oxford: Blackwell.
Duhon, B. (1998). It's all in our heads. *Inform*, *12*(8), 8–13.
Ehrensberger-Dow, M. (2014). Challenges of translation process research at the workplace. *MonTi*, *1*, Special Issue, 355–383.
Ehrensberger-Dow, M., & Massey, G. (2013). Indicators of translation competence: Translators' self-concepts and the translation of titles. *Journal of Writing Research*, *5*(1), 103–131.
Ericsson, K.A., Charness, N., Feltovich, P.J., & Hoffman, R.R. (Eds.). (2006). *The Cambridge handbook of expertise and expert performance*. Cambridge: Cambridge University Press. 2nd ed., 2018.
European Master's in Translation. (2009). *Competences for professional translators, experts in multilingual and multimedia communication*. Brussels: European Master's in translation (EMT).
European Master's in Translation. (2017). *Competence framework*. Brussels: European Master's in translation (EMT). Retrieved from https://commission.europa.eu/system/files/2018-02/emt_competence_fwk_2017_en_web.pdf
European Master's in Translation. (2022). *Competence framework*. Brussels: European Master's in translation (EMT). Retrieved from https://commission.europa.eu/system/files/2022-11/emt_competence_fwk_2022_en.pdf
Fraser, J. (1996). Mapping the process of translation. *Meta, Journal des Traducteurs*, *51*(1), 84–96.
Froeliger, N. (2019). Are we getting it right for our translation programs… A tentative method to measure if we are. In M. Koletnik & N. Froeliger (Eds.), *Translation and language teaching – Continuing the dialogue* (pp. 215–237). Cambridge: Cambridge Scholars Publishing.
Gile, D. (1995a). *Regards sur la recherche en Interprétation de conférence*. Lille: Presses Universitaires de Lille.
Gile, D. (1995b). *Basic concepts and models for interpreter and translator training* (2nd ed., 2009). Amsterdam: John Benjamins.
Gonçalves, J.L. (2003). *O desenvolvimento da competência do tradutor: investigando o processo a través de um estudo exploratório-experimental*. Unpublished PhD Dissertation. Universidade Federal de Minas Gerais.
Gonçalves, J.L. (2005). O desenvolvimento da competência do tradutor: em busca de parâmetros cognitivos. In F. Alves, C. Magalhães, & A. Pagano (Eds.), *Competência em tradução: cognição e discurso* (pp. 59–90). Belo Horizonte: Editora UFMG.
González Davies, M. (2004). Undergraduate and postgraduate translation degrees: Aims and expectations. In K. Malmkjaer (Ed.), *Translation as an undergraduate degree* (pp. 67–81). Amsterdam: John Benjamins.
González Davies, M., & Scott-Tennent, C. (2005). A problem-solving and student-centred approach to the translation of cultural references. *Meta*, *50*(1), 160–179.
González, J. & Wagenaar, R.G. (Eds.). (2003). *Tuning educational structures in Europe. Final report. Phase one*. Bilbao: Universidad de Deusto.

González, J., & Wagenaar, R.G. (Eds.). (2005). *Tuning educational structures in Europe II*. Bilbao: Universidad de Deusto.
Göpferich, S. (2008). *Translationsprozessforschung: Stand- Methoden-Perspektiven*. Translationswissenschaft 4. Tübingen: Gunter Narr.
Göpferich, S. (2009). Towards a model of translation competence and its acquisition: The longitudinal study 'TransComp'. In S. Göpferich, A. L. Jakobsen, & I.M. Mees (Eds.), *Behind the Mind: Methods, models and results in translation process research* (pp. 11–37). Copenhagen: Samfundslitteratur.
Gouadec, D. (2002). *Profession: Traducteur*. Paris: La Maison du Dictionnaire.
Gouadec, D. (2005). Modélisation du processus d'exécution des traductions. *Meta, Journal des Traducteurs*, *50*(2), 643–655.
Gouadec, D. (2007). *Translation as a Profession*. Amsterdam/Philadelphia: John Benjamins.
Gregorio Cano, A. (2014). *Estudio empírico-descriptivo del desarrollo de la competencia estratégica en la formación de traductores*. Unpublished PhD Dissertation. Universidad de Granada.
Gutt, E.-A. (1991). *Translation and relevance: Cognition and context*. Oxford: Basil Blackwell.
Gutt, E.-A. (2000). Issues of translation research in the inferential paradigm of communication. In M. Olohan (Ed.), *Intercultural faultlines. Research models in translation studies 1: Textual and cognitive aspects* (pp. 161–179). Manchester: St. Jerome.
Hansen, G. (1997). Success in translation. *Perspectives: Studies in Translatology*, *5*(2), 201–210.
Harris, B. (1973). La traductologie, la traduction naturelle, la traduction automatique et la sémantique. *Cahiers de Linguistique*, *10*, 11–34.
Harris, B. (1977). The importance of natural translation. *Working Papers on Bilingualism*, *12*, 96–114.
Harris, B. (1980). How a three-year-old translates. In A. Evangelos & A. Afrendas (Eds.), *Patterns of bilingualism* (pp. 370–393). Singapore: National University of Singapore Press.
Harris, B., & Sherwood, B. (1978). Translating as an innate skill. In D. Gerver & H. W. Sinaiko (Eds.), *Language, interpretation and communication* (pp. 155–170). Oxford: Plenum Press.
Hatim, B., & Mason, I. (1997). *The translator as communicator*. London: Routledge.
Hewson, L., & Martin, J. (1991). *Redefining translation. The variational approach*. London: Routledge.
Hönig, H.G. (1991). Holmes' 'Mapping Theory' and the landscape of mental translation processes. In K. van Leuven-Zwart & T. Naajkens (Eds.), *Translation studies: The state of the art. Proceedings from the first James S. Holmes symposium on translation studies* (pp. 77–89). Amsterdam: Rodopi.
Hönig, H.G. (1995). *Konstruktives Übersetzen*. Tübingen: Stauffenburg Verlag.
Hurtado Albir, A. (1996a). La enseñanza de la traducción directa 'general'. Objetivos de aprendizaje y metodología. In A. Hurtado Albir (Ed.), *La enseñanza de la traducción* (pp. 31–55). Castellón: Universitat Jaume I.
Hurtado Albir, A. (1996b). La cuestión del método traductor. Método, estrategia y técnica de traducción. *Sendebar*, *7*, 39–57.
Hurtado Albir, A. (2001). *Traducción y traductología. Introducción a la traductología* (5th Rev. ed., 2011). Madrid: Cátedra.
Hurtado Albir, A. (2005). A aquisição da competência tradutória: aspectos teóricos e didáticos. In F. Alves, C. Magalhães & A. Pagano (Eds.), *Competência em tradução: cognição e discurso* (pp. 19–57). Belo Horizonte: Editora UFMG.

Hurtado Albir, A. (2007). Competence-based curriculum design for training translators. *The Interpreter and Translator Trainer*, *1*(2), 163–195.
Hurtado Albir, A. (2008). Compétence en traduction et formation par compétences. *TTR (Traduction, Terminologie, Rédaction). La formation du traducteur: pédagogie, docimologie, technologies*, *21*(1), 17–64.
Hurtado Albir, A. (2015a). The acquisition of translation competence. Competences, tasks, and assessment in translator training. *Meta*, *60*(2), 256–280.
Hurtado Albir, A. (2015b). *Aprender a traducir del francés al español. Competencias y tareas para la iniciación a la traducción.* Serie *Aprender a traducir.* Castellón de la Plana: Edelsa – Universitat Jaume I.
Hurtado Albir, A. (2015c). *Aprender a traducir del francés al español. Competencias y tareas para la iniciación a la traducción. Guía didáctica: Serie aprender a traducir.* Castellón de la Plana: Edelsa – Universitat Jaume I.
Hurtado Albir, A. (2017a). Translation and translation competence. In A. Hurtado Albir (Ed.), *Researching translation competence by PACTE Group* (pp. 3–33). Amsterdam: John Benjamins.
Hurtado Albir, A. (Ed.). (2017b). *Researching translation competence by PACTE Group*. Amsterdam: John Benjamins.
Hurtado Albir, A. (2018). Training. In Y. Gambier & L. D'Hulst (Eds.), *A history of modern translation knowledge* (pp. 415–428). Amsterdam: John Benjamins.
Hurtado Albir, A. (2019). La investigación en didáctica de la traducción. Evolución, enfoques y perspectivas / Research on the didactics of translation. Evolution, approaches and future avenues. *MonTI*, *11*, 47–76.
Hurtado Albir, A. (2021). Translation competence and its acquisition. In F. Alves & A.L. Jakobsen (Eds.), *The Routledge handbook of translation and cognition* (pp. 389–414). London: Routledge.
Hurtado Albir, A. (2022). Didáctica de la traducción/Didactics of Translation. *ENTI, Enciclopedia de traducción e interpretación.* AIETI. https://doi.org/10.5281/zenodo.6382950
Hurtado Albir, A., & Alves, F. (2009). Translation as a cognitive activity. In J. Munday (Ed.), *The Routledge companion to translation studies* (pp. 54–73). London: Routledge.
Hurtado Albir, A., Kuznik, A., & Rodríguez-Inés, P. (2022). Marco conceptual de la investigación sobre descriptores de nivel en traducción / Conceptual framework for research on level descriptors in translation. In A. Hurtado Albir, & P. Rodríguez-Inés (Eds.), *Hacia un marco europeo de niveles de competencias en traducción. El Proyecto NACT del Grupo PACTE* / Towards a European framework of competence levels in translation. The PACTE Group's NACT project. *MonTI*, 7, Special Issue, 41–68 / 45–72.
Hurtado Albir, A., & Rodriguez-Inés, P. (2022a). Perspectivas de la investigación / Future avenues of research. In A. Hurtado Albir, & P. Rodríguez-Inés (Eds.), *Hacia un marco europeo de niveles de competencias en traducción. El Proyecto NACT del Grupo PACTE* /Towards a European framework of competence levels in translation. The PACTE Group's NACT project. *MonTI*, 7, Special Issue, 204–209 / 208-213.
Hurtado Albir, A., & Rodríguez-Inés, P. (2022b). Segunda propuesta de descriptores de nivel / Second proposal. Resulting level descriptor proposal. In A. Hurtado Albir & P. Rodríguez-Inés (Eds.), *Hacia un marco europeo de niveles de competencias en traducción. El Proyecto NACT del Grupo PACTE* / Towards a European framework of competence levels in translation. The PACTE Group's NACT project. *MonTI*, 7, Special Issue, 119–203 / 123–207.
Hurtado Albir, A., & Rodríguez-Inés, P. (Eds.). (2022c). *Hacia un marco europeo de niveles de competencias en traducción. El Proyecto NACT del Grupo PACTE /*

Towards a European framework of competence levels in translation. The PACTE Group's NACT project. *MonTI*, *7*, Special Issue.
Hymes, D.H. (1971). *On communicative competence.* Philadelphia: University of Pennsylvania Press.
Katan, D. (2008). University training, competencies, and the death of the translator. Problems in professionalizing translation and in the translation profession. In M.T. Musacchio & G.H. Sostero (Eds.), *Tradurre: Formazione e professione* (pp. 113–140). Padova: CLEUP.
Kelly, D. (2002). Un modelo de competencia traductora: bases para el diseño curricular. *Puentes*, *1*, 9–20.
Kelly, D. (2005). *A handbook for translator trainers.* Manchester: St. Jerome.
Kelly, D. (2007). Translator competence contextualized. Translator training in the framework of higher education reform: In search of alignment in curricular design. In D. Kenny & K. Ryou (Eds.), *Across boundaries: International perspectives on translation studies* (pp. 128–142). Cambridge: Cambridge Scholars Publishing.
Kiraly, D. (1995). *Pathways to translation.Pedagogy and process.* Kent: The Kent State University Press.
Kiraly, D. (2013). Towards a view of translator competence as an emergent phenomenon: Thinking outside the box(es) in translator education. In D. Kiraly, S. Hansen-Schirra, & K. Maksymski (Eds.), *New prospects and perspectives for educating language mediators* (pp. 197–224). Tubingen: Günther Narr Verlag.
Kiraly, D. (2015). Occasioning translator competence: Moving beyond social constructivism toward a postmodern alternative to instructionism. *Translation and Interpreting Studies*, *10*(1), 8–32.
Koller, W. (1979). *Einführung in die Übersetzungswissenschaft.* Heidelberg: Quelle und Meyer.
Krings, H. P. (1986). *Was in den Köpfen von Übersetzern vorgeht. Eine empirische Untersuchung zur Struktur des Übersetzungsprozesses an fortgeschrittenen Französischlernern.* Tübingen: Narr.
Kuznik, A. (2010/2012). *El contenido de los puestos de trabajo de los traductores. El caso de los traductores internos en las empresas de traducción de Barcelona.* PhD. Thesis, Universitat Autònoma de Barcelona [Saarbrücken, AV Akademikerverlag GmbH & Co. KG/ Editorial Académica Española, 2012].
Kuznik, A. & Hurtado Albir, A. (2015). "How to define good professional translators and interpreters:applying the behavioural approach to studying competences in the field of TranslationStudies". *Across Languages and Cultures*16 (1): 1–27.
Lachat Leal, C. (2003). *Estrategias y problemas de traducción.* Unpublished PhD Dissertation, Universidad de Granada.
Lajoie, S.P. (2003). Transitions and trajectories for the study of expertise. *Educational Researcher*, *32*(8), 21–25.
Lasnier, F. (2000). *Réussir la formation par compétences.* Montréal: Guérin.
Lörscher, W. (1991). *Translation performance, translation process, and translation strategies. A psycholinguistic investigation.* Tübingen: Narr.
Lörscher, W. (1992). Investigating the translation process. *Meta*, *37*(3), 426–439.
Lowe, P. (1987). Revising the ACTFL/ETS scales for a new purpose: Rating skill in translating. In M.G. Rose (Ed.), *Translation excellence: Assessment, achievement, maintenance* (pp. 53–61). New York: Suny Binghamton Press.
Ljudskanov, A. (1969). *Traduction humaine et traduction mécanique.* Paris: Dunod.
Mackenzie, R. (2000). Positive thinking about quality in translator training in Finland. In A. Beeby, D. Ensinger, & M. Presas (Eds.), *Investigating translation: Selected papers from the 4th International Congress on Translation* (pp. 213–222). Amsterdam: John Benjamins.

Massana, G. (2016). *La adquisición de la competencia traductora portugués-español: un estudio en torno a los falsos amigos*. Unpublished Ph.D. Thesis. Universitat Autònoma de Barcelona.

Massey, G., & Ehrensberger-Dow, M. (2011). Investigating information literacy: A growing priority in translation studies. *Across Languages and Cultures*, *12*(2), 193–211.

Massey, G., & Ehrensberger-Dow, M. (2014). Cognitive ergonomic issues in professional translation. In J. Schwieter, & Ferreira, A. (Eds.), *The development of translation competence: theories and methodologies from psycholinguistics and cognitive science* (pp. 58–86). Cambridge, MA: Cambridge Scholars Publishing.

McClelland, D.C. (1973). Testing for competence rather than for "intelligence". *American Psychologist*,*28*(1), 1–14.

Muñoz Raya, E. (Ed.). (2004). *Libro Blanco. Título de grado en traducción e interpretación*. Agencia Nacional de Evaluación de la Calidad y Acreditación, y Universidad de Granada. Retrieved from http://www.aneca.es/var/media/150288/libroblanco_traduc_def.pdf

Neubert, A. (1994). Competence in translation: A complex skill, how to study and how to teach it. In M. Snell-Hornby, F. Pöchhacker, & K. Kaindl (Eds.), *Translation studies. An interdiscipline* (pp. 411–420). Amsterdam: John Benjamins.

Neubert, A. (2000). Competence in language, in languages and in translation. In C. Schäffner & B. Adab (Eds.), *Developing translation competence* (pp. 3–18). Amsterdam: John Benjamins.

Nord, C. (1988). *Textanalyse und Übersetzen*. Heidelberg: J. Groos Verlag. [English edition. *Text analysis in translation*. 1991. Amsterdam: Rodopi].

Nord, C. (1992). Text analysis in translator training. In C. Dollerup & A. Loddegaard (Eds.), *Teaching translation and interpreting* (pp. 39–48). Amsterdam: John Benjamins.

Olalla-Soler, C. (2017). *La competencia cultural del traductor y su adquisición. Un estudio experimental en la traducción alemán-español*. Unpublished PhD Dissertation. Universitat Autònoma de Barcelona.

Orozco, M. (2000). *Instrumentos de medida de la adquisición de la competencia traductora: Construcción y validación*. Unpublished PhD Thesis, Universitat Autònoma de Barcelona.

Orozco, M., & Hurtado Albir, A. (2002). Measuring translation competence acquisition. *Meta*, *47*(3), 375–402.

PACTE. (1998). *La competencia traductora y su aprendizaje: Objetivos, hipótesis y metodología de un proyecto de investigación*. Poster, IV Congrés Internacional sobre Traducció. Barcelona: Universitat Autònoma de Barcelona.

PACTE. (2000). Acquiring translation competence: Hypotheses and methodological problems in a research project. In A. Beeby, D. Ensinger, & M. Presas (Eds.), *Investigating translation* (pp. 99–106). Amsterdam: John Benjamins.

PACTE. (2001). La competencia traductora y su adquisición. *Quaderns*, *6*, 39–45.

PACTE. (2002). Exploratory tests in a study of translation competence. *Conference Interpretation and Translation*, *4*(2), 41–69.

PACTE. (2003). Building a translation competence model. In F. Alves (Ed.), *Triangulating translation. Perspectives in process oriented research* (pp. 43–66). Amsterdam: John Benjamins.

PACTE. (2005a). Primeros resultados de un experimento sobre la competencia traductora. In R. García & M. Luisa (Eds.), *Actas del II Congreso Internacional de la Asociación Ibérica de Estudios de Traducción e Interpretación* (pp. 573-587). Madrid: AIETI.

PACTE. (2005b) Investigating translation competence: Conceptual and methodological issues. *Meta*, *50*(2), 609–619.
PACTE. (2014). First results of PACTE group's experimental research on translation competence acquisition: The acquisition of declarative knowledge of translation. *MonTI*, Special Issue, *1*, 85–115.
PACTE. (2015). Results of PACTE's experimental research on the acquisition of translation competence: the acquisition of declarative and procedural knowledge in translation. The dynamic translation index. *Translation Spaces*, *4*(1), 29–35.
PACTE. (2017a). The performance of the top-ranking translators. In A. Hurtado Albir (Ed.), *Researching translation competence by PACTE Group* (pp. 269–280). Amsterdam: John Benjamins.
PACTE. (2017b). Conclusions. In A. Hurtado Albir (Ed.), *Researching translation competence by PACTE Group* (pp. 281–302). Amsterdam: John Benjamins.
PACTE. (2017c). The second stage of PACTE Group's research. Experimental research into the acquisition of translation competence. In A. Hurtado Albir (Ed.), *Researching translation competence by PACTE Group* (pp. 303–308). Amsterdam: John Benjamins.
PACTE. (2018). Competence levels in translation: Working towards a European framework. *The Interpreter and Translator Trainer*, *12*(2), 111–131.
PACTE. (2019a). Evolution of the efficacy of the translation process in translation competence acquisition. Results of the PACTE Group's experimental research. *Meta*, *64*(1), 242–265.
PACTE. (2019b). Establecimiento de niveles de competencia en traducción. Primeros resultados del proyecto NACT. *Onomazein*, *43*, 1–25.
PACTE. (2020). Translation competence acquisition. Design and results of the PACTE Group's experimental research. *The Interpreter and Translator Trainer*, *14*(2), 95–233.
Paris, S.G., Gross, D.R., & Lipson, M.Y. (1984). Informed strategies for learning: A program to improve children's reading awareness and comprehension. *Journal of Educational Psychology*,*76*, 1239–1252.
Paris, S.G., Lipson, M.Y., & Wixson, K.K. (1983). Becoming a strategic reader. *Contemporary Educational Psychology*, *8*, 293–316.
Pozo, J.I., & Postigo, Y. (1993). Las competencias de aprendizaje como contenido del currículo. In C. Monereo Font (Ed.), *Estrategias de aprendizaje* (pp. 47–64). Barcelona: Domènech.
Presas, M. (1996). *Problemes de traducció i competència traductora.Bases per una pedagogia de la traducció*. Unpublished PhD Dissertation. Universitat Autònoma de Barcelona.
Presas, M. (2000). Developing Translation Competence. In C. Schäffner & B. Adabs (Eds.), *Bilingual competence and translation competence* (pp. 19–31). Amsterdam: John Benjamins.
Pym, A. (1991). A definition of translational competence, applied to the teaching of translation. In M. Jovanovic (Ed.), *Translation: A creative profession. Proceedings of the 12th World Congress of FIT*(pp. 541–546). Belgrade: Prevodilac.
Pym, A. (1992). Translation error analysis and the interface with language teaching. In C. Dollerup & A. Loddegaard (Eds.), *Teaching translation and interpreting. Training, talent, and experience* (pp. 279–290). Amsterdam: John Benjamins.
Pym, A. (1993). *Epistemological problems in translation and its teaching*. Teruel: Caminade.
Pym, A. (2003). Redefining translation competence in an electronic age: In defence of a minimalist approach. *Meta*, *48*(4), 481–497.
Quinci, C. (2014). *Translators in the making: an empirical longitudinal study on translation competence and its development*. Unpublished PhD Thesis. Università degli studi di Trieste.

Risku, H. (1998). *Translatorische Kompetenz. Kognitive Grundlagen des Übersetzens als Expertentätigkeit.* Tübingen: Stauffenburg.
Risku, H., Dickinson, A., & Pircher, R. (2010). Knowledge in translation practice and translation studies: Intellectual capital in modern society. In D. Gile, G. Hansen, & N.K. Pokorn (Eds.), *Why translation studies matters* (pp. 83–96). Amsterdam: John Benjamins.
Roberts, R.P. (1984). Compétence du nouveau diplômé en traduction. In G.-M. Boivin (Ed.), *Traduction et qualité de langue. Actes du colloque société des traducteurs du Québec/Conseil de la langue française* (pp. 172–184). Québec: Éditeur Official du Québec.
Rothe-Neves, R. (2005). A abordagem comportamental das competências. Aplicabilidade aos estudos da tradução. In F. Alves, C. Magalhães, & A. Pagano (Eds.), *Competência em tradução: cognição e discurso* (pp. 91–107). Belo Horizonte: Editora UFMG.
Ryle, G. (1949). *The concept of mind.* Chicago: The University of Chicago Press.
Schäffner, C. (2004). Developing professional translation competence without a notion of translation. In K. Malmkjaer (Ed.), *Translation as an undergraduate degree* (pp. 113–125). Amsterdam/: John Benjamins.
Schäffner, C., & Adabs, B. (Eds.). (2000). *Developing translation competence.* Amsterdam: John Benjamins.
Schaeffer, M., Huepe, M., Hansen-Schirra, S., Hofmann, S., Muñoz, E., Kogan, B., Herrera, E., Ibáñez, A., & García, A.M. (2020). The translation and interpreting competence questionnaire: An online tool for research on translators and interpreters. *Perspectives*, *28*(1), 90–108.
Searle, J.R. (1969). *Speech acts: An essay in the philosophy of language.* Cambridge: Cambridge University Press.
Séguinot, C. (1991). A study of student translation strategies. In S. Tirkkonen-Condit (Ed.), *Empirical research in translation and intercultural studies*: Tübingen: Günther Narr Verlag.
Snell-Hornby, M. (1988). *Translation studies. An integrated approach.* Amsterdam: John Benjamins.
Spencer, L.M., McClelland, D.C., & Spencer, S.M. (1994). *Competency assessment methods: History and state of art.* New York: Hay/McBer Research Press.
Spolsky, B. (1989). Communicative competence, language proficiency, and beyond. *Applied Linguistics*, *10*(2), 138–156.
Shreve, G. (1997). Cognition and the evolution of translation competence. In J.H. Danks, G. Shreve, S.B. Fountain, & M. McBeath (Eds.), *Cognitive processes in translation and interpreting* (pp. 120–136). Thousand Oaks: Sage.
Shreve, G. (2006). The deliberate practice: Translation and expertise. *Journal of Translation Studies*, *9*(1), 27–42.
Shreve, G., Angelone, E., & Lacruz, I. (2018). Are expertise and translation competence the same? Psychological reality and the theoretical status of competence. In I. Lacruz & R Jääskeläinen (Eds.), *Innovation and expansion in translation process research* (pp. 37–54). Amsterdam: John Benjamins.
Stansfield, C., Scott, M.L., & Mann Kenyon, D. (1992). The measurement of translation ability. *The Modern Language Journal*, *76*(4), 455–467.
Tomozeiu, D., Koskinen, K., & D'Arcangelo, A. (2016). Teaching intercultural competence in translator training. *The Interpreter and Translator Trainer*, *10*(3), 251–267.
Toury, G. (1980). *In search of a theory of translation.* Tel Aviv University: The Porter Institute for Poetics and Semiotics.
Toury, G. (1986). Monitoring discourse transfer: A test-case for a developmental model of translation. In J. Housey & S. Blum-Kulka (Eds.), *Interlingual and*

intercultural communication: Discourse and cognition in translation and second language acquisition studies (pp. 79–94). Tübingen, Günther Narr Verlag.
Toury, G. (1991). Experimentation in translation studies: Achievements, prospects and some pitfalls. In S. Tirkkonen-Condit (Ed.), *Empirical research in translation and intercultural studies* (pp. 45–66). Tübingen: Gunter Narr Verlag.
Toury, G. (1995). *Descriptive translation studies and beyond.* (2nd ed., 2012). Amsterdam: John Benjamins.
Vienne, J. (1998). Vous avez dit compétence traductionnelle? *Meta*, *43*(2), 187–190.
Waddington, C. (2000). *Estudio comparativo de diferentes métodos de evaluación de traducción general (inglés-español).* Madrid: Universidad Pontificia de Comillas.
Wellington, J.J. (1989). *Skills and processes in science education. A critical analysis.* London: Routledge.
Widdowson, H.G. (1989). Knowledge of language and ability for use. *Applied Linguistics*, *10*(2), 128–137.
Wilss, W. (1976). Perspectives and limitations of a didactic framework for the teaching of translation. In R.W. Brislin (Ed.), *Translation: Applications and research* (pp. 117–137). New York: Gardner.
Wilss, W. (1977). *Übersetzungswissenschaft: Probleme und Methoden.* Stuttgart: Klett.
Wilss, W. (1989). Towards a multi-facet concept of translation behavior. *Target*, *34*(1), 129–149.
Yániz, C., & Villardón, L. (2006). *Planificar desde competencias para promover el aprendizaje.* Bilbao: Universidad de Deusto.
Yarosh, M. (2015). Translator intercultural competence: A model, learning objectives, and level indicators. In Y. Cui & W. Zhao (Eds.), *Handbook of research on teaching methods in language, translation and interpretation* (pp. 160–178) Hershey: IGI Global.
Yarosh, M. (2012). *Translator intercultural competence: The concept and means to measure the competence development.* Unpublished PhD Thesis. Universidad de Deusto.

4

EMPIRICAL-EXPERIMENTAL RESEARCH ON COGNITIVE ASPECTS OF TRANSLATION

This chapter discusses the tenets of empirical-experimental research and describes the evolution of research on cognitive aspects of translation. The chapter is divided in three sections. Section 1 addresses the principles of empirical-experimental research and their relevance for the study of translation as a cognitive activity. Section 2 describes methods and data collection procedures to carry out research in translation as a cognitive activity. Section 3 presents the evolution of empirical-experimental research on cognitive aspects of translation divided into five distinct temporal phases. In short, it aims to offer a comprehensive overview of the principles, practices and results, spanning from the mid-1980s to the present date.

Introduction

Throughout the three previous chapters, we have considered first the importance of disciplinary approaches to the study of translation as a cognitive activity and then seen how research has evolved from the mid-1960s to the present date. We have looked at conceptual aspects related to translation process research as well as to the characteristics of translation competence and its acquisition and levelling. In this chapter, we look at the evolution of empirical-experimental research on cognitive aspects of translation. The chapter is divided into three sections, each one dedicated to a particular aspect related to the empirical investigation of translation as a cognitive activity. Section 4.1 looks at tenets of empirical-experimental research and its relevance for the study of translation as a cognitive activity. It discusses the need to use the scientific method as a basis for the types of research carried out in this particular subdiscipline and expands the discussion to encompass disparate research methodologies and to reflect critically on criteria for accuracy in empirical research in translation. Section 4.2 describes data collection procedures of empirical-experimental research in translation whereas Section 4.3 assesses the evolution of empirical-experimental

DOI: 10.4324/9781003006978-5

research on cognitive aspects of translation in five distinct temporal phases, spanning from the mid-1980s to the present date.

For the first four phases, we have described the types of research designs used, the samples and subjects, the data collection procedures and the most important methodological approaches and results. For the fifth emerging phase, we have highlighted the trends and pointed to future avenues for cognitive research in translation. The reader will notice a progressive increase in complexity in each one of these five phases as the field matures and research manages to incorporate more techniques, tools and instruments to tap into the intricacies of translation as a cognitive activity.

In the fifth phase, we address a concern with the importance of an interdisciplinary approach that has been discussed in depth in Chapter 1. In that light, we insist on the relevance of considering publications that have tried to bridge the gap between studies of translation as a cognitive activity and related works in neighbouring disciplines. We refer to these works in Section 4.3.5. Thus, we have pointed towards the need for a stronger interdisciplinary dialogue.

The chapter closes with a critical appreciation of the evolution of empirical-experimental research in translation as a cognitive activity.

4.1 On empirical-experimental research

Empirical-experimental research in translation studies has been carried out not only but particularly by researchers with an interest in translation as a cognitive activity. This kind of research allows the gathering of data on translation processes and translation competence and thus enables their study from either a deductive or an inductive perspective. However, empirical-experimental research in translation as a cognitive activity does not yet have a long-standing tradition and this has a negative impact on the development and validity of research designs and practices. This calls for a reflection on the scientific basis upon which research can be built and this necessarily leads to critical considerations about the methodological principles underlying research in this area of study.

4.1.1 On the need to use the scientific method

When a scientific field undergoes a qualitative leap such as that observed in research on translation as a cognitive activity, this change usually poses a challenge for research. Over the past decades, several authors have insisted that translation studies should focus on empiricism (Toury, 1995; Gile, 1998; Chesterman, 1997; Neunzig, 2001, 2002, among others). In this sense, some authors have pondered on how to use the scientific method in translation studies.

In several works, Neunzig (2001, 2002, 2011, 2017) as well as Neunzig and Tanqueiro (2007) present some of the main methodological issues that emerge when applying empirical research methods to translation. Neunzig looks at the issues raised when closely examining the postulates that have defined the natural sciences and which have been integrated into the social sciences. Additionally, Neunzig also discusses the main steps to consider in the research process when designing a scientific study. He, thus, proposes a research procedure shaped by the intelligibility and transparency of the scientific process, as well as by the relevance of its aims, evidence and results, a proposal we subscribe to in this book.

Hurtado Albir (2001, pp. 169–199) insists on the need to develop a specific methodological framework within translation studies and the relevance to carry out empirical-experimental research in the field. Hurtado Albir raises questions related to methodological perspectives in general and, in particular, with respect to methodologies to be used in translation studies. To assert her position, she introduces a general overview of empirical-experimental research in translation studies and points to problems and perspectives in that type of research.

Williams and Chesterman (2002) focus on the interdisciplinary nature of translation studies to provide a step-by-step introduction to how to carry out research in a field that encompasses a vast array of topics and methodologies. They provide an overview of 12 research areas in translation studies as a point of orientation – a *Map* – for researchers willing to set out to explore the discipline. Williams and Chesterman (2002) also provide instructions about how to work from an initial idea to plan a research design, how to choose among different research approaches and how to elaborate and develop a research project (formulation of hypotheses, relations between variables, selection and analysis of data, etc.).

Saldanha and O'Brien (2013) build on Williams and Chesterman (2002) to describe in detail when and how to apply different methodologies within translation studies. They also discuss principles and ethics in research and provide a distinction between product-oriented, process-oriented, participant-oriented and context-oriented research, suggesting tools and instruments to be used in each particular type of research. Saldanha and O'Brien also differentiate between qualitative, quantitative and mixed methodological perspectives and insist that the methodological approach one should take depends on one's research questions and how best they might be addressed.

Rojo López (2013) also presents a proposal geared to those who are learning how to carry out research in translation studies. By means of first-step suggestions, Rojo focuses on qualitative and quantitative approaches, placing them along a cline and highlighting the importance of a multi-methodological perspective that draws on both qualitative and quantitative approaches. Rojo highlights the main traits of each perspective and introduces relevant work that has been carried out within translation studies for each perspective. The author also focuses on ethical issues that she considers to be relevant for carrying out empirical-experimental research in translation studies.

Mellinger and Hanson's (2017) work is a comprehensive overview of quantitative research methods in translation and interpreting studies. The book is divided into five parts, encompassing all stages of the research process. Part 1, preparing, focuses on research questions, hypotheses, design, sampling and ethics, and measurement. Part 2, describing, contains detailed information about descriptive statistics, probability distributions, statistical terminology and one-sample tests. Part 3, analysing differences, discusses issues such as comparing groups and testing categorical data. Part 4, analysing relationships, addresses correlation, reliability and linear regression. Part 5 deals with the interpretation of results. Mellinger and Hanson also provide references to additional resources and a reference table for specific tests is included in the appendix.

All of these authors, as well as others not mentioned here, have highlighted the need to anchor the basis of empirical-experimental research on cognitive aspects of translation on the principles of the scientific method. In the next sections, we will look into disparate research methodologies, quantitative and qualitative alike, as well as the specific choice of methodological approaches, leading the discussion in the direction of what we believe to be needed in order to carry out empirical-experimental research in this field of study.

4.1.2 Research methodologies

There are several types of research and various ways of classifying them according to authors and disciplines.

4.1.2.1 Theoretical and empirical research

Drawing on Gile (1998), we believe it is important to distinguish, first, between theoretical research, centred on an intellectual process with speculative activities, often occurring in disciplines in the humanities, such as the case of philosophy, and empirical research, aimed at collecting and analysing data by means of different research methods.

Williams and Chesterman (2002), in line with Gile, distinguish between conceptual and empirical research, whereas the former has a focus on ideas while the latter is concerned with data. According to Williams and Chesterman (2002, p. 58), conceptual research "aims to define and clarify concepts, to interpret or reinterpret ideas, to relate concepts into larger systems, to introduce new concepts or metaphors or framework that allow a better understanding of the object of research" and empirical research "seeks new data, new information derived from the observation of data and from experimental work; it seeks evidence which supports or disconfirms hypotheses or generates new ones".

There are several proposals for the classification of empirical research. To that extent, Gile (1998) distinguishes two large blocks in empirical research: observational and experimental.

Observational research consists of the rigorous observation of a situation as it occurs, through observations, questionnaires, surveys and so on. Gile distinguishes three kinds of observational research: the exploratory approach, with its own objectives that can lead to hypothesis development; the analytic-punctual approach, when specific phenomena are studied; and the demonstration of hypotheses, similar to the experimental method, but the data are extracted from a real situation. Gile also differentiates between interactive and non-interactive observation, depending on the observer's role in collecting, analysing and evaluating data.

Experimental research, according to Gile (1998), is the result of a systematic observation of situations deliberately provoked by the researcher to be studied under predefined, controlled conditions. Gile differentiates between experimental investigations in which a statistical demonstration of a hypothesis is made and the open experiment, when there is no hypothesis.

Therefore, there are multiple types of empirical research. There is also a diversity of classifications around it, depending on the object of study. In our opinion, the most fundamental distinction occurs between qualitative and quantitative types of research.

4.1.2.2 Qualitative and quantitative research

Research designs can be qualitative, quantitative and mixed (qualitative and quantitative). Qualitative research focuses on quality and aims at understanding, describing and discovering new findings that can be used to build hypotheses. It has a holistic perspective and researchers tend to carry out inductively driven analyses. On the other hand, the focus of quantitative research is quantity (how much, how many) and its purpose is to predict, control, describe, test and confirm hypotheses by means of deductive analyses carried out through statistical methods. As mentioned by Saldanha and O'Brien (2013, p. 27), qualitative research is generally associated with an interpretivist stand whereas quantitative research is usually associated with a positivist epistemological position.

We understand that there is no radical opposition between these two methodological blocks but rather a continuum. Accordingly, most instruments used in research designs are either qualitative or have a focus on quantification. Although quantitative and qualitative modes of investigation have been frequently presented in dichotomous and even antagonistic terms, the past decades have seen the emergence of a unified approach and a reconciliation that seeks the compatibility and the complementarity between both qualitative and quantitative research methodologies. Therefore, both approaches should be seen as a methodological continuum and not as opposing polarities. Moreover, it should also be considered that they are not exclusive methodologies and the suitability of one or the other mode always depends on the object of study and the goals of research.

Qualitative research

Qualitative research is used in various disciplines (humanities, social sciences, physics, etc.) in which a multitude of perspectives, approaches and procedures converge. Thus, there is no single qualitative research approach but rather different approaches that differ in terms of research criteria, data collection techniques, research tools and so on. Rodríguez-Gómez, Gil Flores and García Jiménez (1996, pp. 32–59) identify the following types of qualitative research:

- Phenomenology: emphasizing individual and subjective experiences.
- Ethnography: seeking to describe the forms of human organization in social groups.
- *Grounded theory*: seeking to discover theories, concepts and hypotheses directly driven from available data and not from a priori assumptions.
- Ethnomethodology: focusing on practices through which members of social groups coordinate, structure and understand their daily activities.
- Biography or life story: interpreting one or several life stories with a view to interpreting global aspects of social life (social mobility, immigration, employment structure, etc.).
- Action research: focusing on social situations in order to improve quality of action (for example, teacher-centred research on educational practices with the aim to transform it).

Although Rodríguez-Gómez, Gil Flores and García Jiménez (1996) consider action research to be a type of qualitative research, we share with other authors the assumption that action research can combine qualitative with quantitative procedures.

The sources of data collection for qualitative research are of various types, including direct observation, introspection and retrospection, interviews, questionnaires, discussion groups, recordings of conversations, field notes, journals and so on.

Quantitative research

As we have already pointed out, quantitative research is deductively driven, more structured than qualitative research and requires greater intervention on the part of the researcher. In regular terms, hypotheses are formulated and then contrasted empirically by means of objective instruments and through statistical analysis.

Orozco (2000) distinguishes three different types of quantitative research: the selective method, the quasi-experiment and the experiment. The goal of the selective method is the description of characteristics or attributes of a population through instruments such as interviews and questionnaires. The quasi-experiment shares similarities with the experiment but falls short of completely controlling the study variables. Finally, the experiment is designed in a controlled fashion with the researcher artificially generating a situation that is similar to reality, and creating an environment where the variables are controlled.

Neunzig (2001) refers to the characteristics of the experimental design in translation studies and distinguishes between the exploratory experiment (in which research questions are verified) and the experiment per se based on hypotheses that are confirmed or rejected by means of empirical observation. The experimental design approach can also be of different types: observation of a representative sample, follow-up of a representative sample, comparison between samples, measurement before and after an intervention and so on.

Therefore, quantitative research can be of different types and use different sources of data collection, including interviews, questionnaires, think-aloud protocols (TAPs), online recordings of the translation process and so on (see Section 4.2.)

Type of research and methodological choice: The triangulation approach

The different types of research described here are neither good nor bad in the abstract sense. The suitability of one or the other approach will always depend on the object of research (*what* is being investigated) and its purpose (*for what* it is being investigated). The quality of the results of a given study is dependent on the strict application of the research approach.

Moreover, an investigation does not have to be based on a single technique or instrument. According to its object of study and the goals pursued, it can combine the types of research that are considered pertinent for the case in point (*triangulation*). In such a sense, the triangulation approach within the social sciences (Smith, 1975; Denzin, 1978; Jick, 1979, etc.) can be seen as a multi-methodological perspective that has great advantages for research in human and social sciences. It promotes the use of various techniques and instruments, seeking to explain more fully the complexity of human behaviour, studying it from more than one point of view and combining different types of data (qualitative and quantitative). It also allows researchers to contrast data from different perspectives and overcome limitations such as possible distortion of results, artificiality and so on. Jakobsen (1999, 2002) and Alves (2003) build on the triangulation approach within the social sciences to postulate on the empirical use of the triangulation paradigm in cognitive-oriented research in translation.

In this context, we would like to emphasize the importance of methodological pluralism when it comes to investigating complex objects of study, as is the case of translation, since it is difficult, not to say practically impossible, for a single methodological procedure alone to provide reliable answers.

4.1.3 The three levels of the scientific method

Neunzig (2011, 2017) postulates three different levels that can be applied to empirical-experimental research in translation studies, namely a theoretical-conceptual level, a methodological level and an analytical level:

- On a theoretical-conceptual level, one must define the problem to be studied and formulate testable hypotheses.
- On a methodological level, one chooses an approach, designs and plans the research and then gathers data that can be used to validate hypotheses.
- On an analytical level, one analyses empirical data and contrasts them with initial hypotheses.

Figure 4.1 presents a graphic illustration of the three levels of scientific research.

4.1.4 Criteria for accuracy in empirical research

According to Neunzig (2011, 2017), despite inherent difficulties, there are guidelines and procedures to be followed in common with all scientific fields that have opted for an empirical approach to solving research problems. Neunzig (2017, pp. 48–49)[1] proposes that research problems associated with each field arise, in particular, at a methodological level, which would require the following criteria.

Objectivity. As far as objectivity is concerned, the research design has to guarantee that the approach and instruments used are independent of the researcher who will use them. In other words, should the study be carried out by other researchers, then equivalent, or very similar, results would be obtained. Neunzig (2011) contends that the problem with objectivity is that researchers can manipulate (consciously or unconsciously) the stimulus and the results. A solution to this problem could consist of standardizing the instructions, interventions and instruments used for measurement in such a way that other researchers would attempt to obtain the same results, or, at the very least, ensure clarity, transparency, intelligibility, comprehensibility and logic in a methodological approach, so that other researchers would be in a position to understand the procedures that led to the results under scrutiny.

Reliability.[2] This criterion refers to internal consistency in the approach. It demands that the research design guarantees control of all factors that

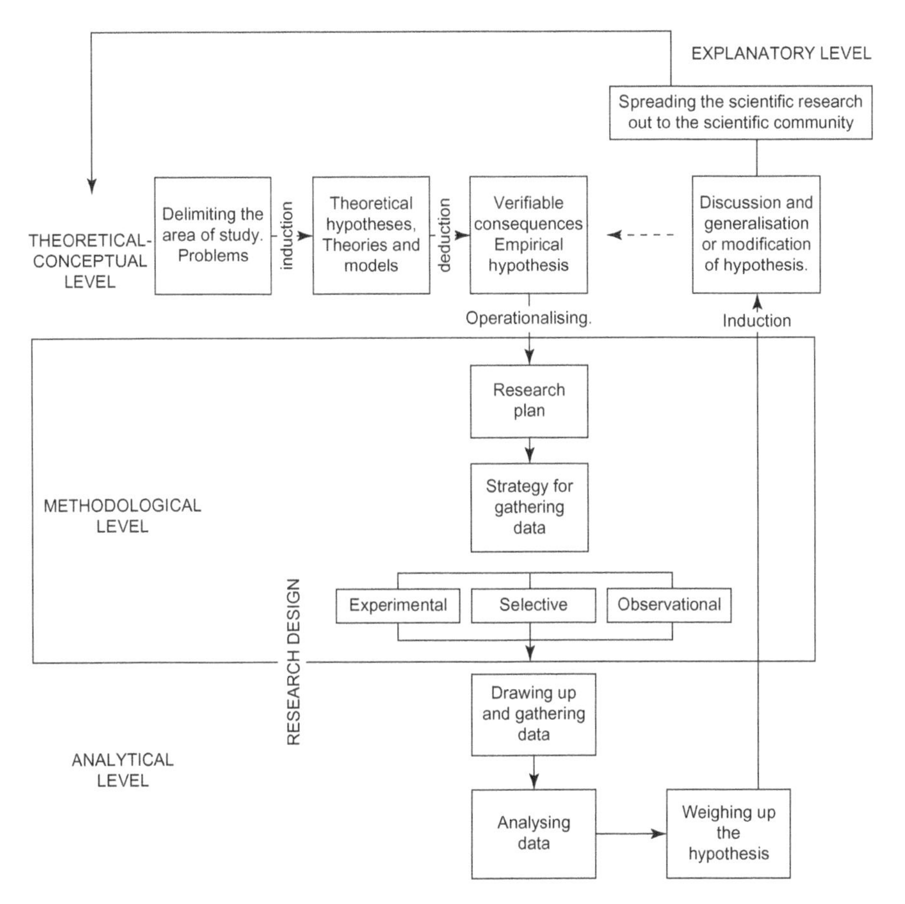

FIGURE 4.1 Three levels of scientific research according to Neunzig (Neunzig, 2011, p. 18)

could distort the results. In other words, all confusing elements (in our case these would be linguistic knowledge and general awareness of culture, previous experience, pedagogical input, time, etc.) and the accuracy of the instruments measuring them.

Repeatability (or *reproducibility*). With respect to repeatability, the design must guarantee that the results obtained in a particular experiment can be repeated in parallel experiments with other subjects, which implies complete transparency when selecting the sample, choosing the instruments for data collection or drawing up indicators.

Validity.[3] It presupposes that measures should be taken to ensure that results are reliable indicators for the objectives that one wishes to achieve. In other words, it is essential to ensure that one is indeed measuring what one set out to measure. This is a crucial requirement in an empirical approach to research in general as well as for cognitive research in translation in particular. Problems can emerge not only when designing the instruments for measuring what one wishes to measure, but also when operationalizing constructs as well as when defining the environment (population, corpus of texts) from which the sample will be taken. A solution lies in justifying the relevance of the selected corpus or subjects.

Extrapolability (or *generalizability*). The experiment has to be designed in such a way that the results obtained can be extrapolated into other situations, or, at least, can serve as a basis for formulating a working hypothesis for later research.

Quantifiability. This criterion refers to the idea that the data obtained must be quantifiable (in other words, expressible in numbers). Many researchers erroneously believe that results that are not the fruit of statistical tests have no explanatory strength whatsoever. However, in our field of study, categorical or qualitative analyses can be equally appropriate.

Ecological validity (or *environmental validity*). The experiment should reflect a real situation. In other words, it should represent the least artificial circumstances possible. Obviously, this is the most serious problem for all laboratory experiments, since laboratories, by definition, are artificial. It is difficult to design a situation in which the subjects, for example, translators, are not influenced by the environment itself or by the mere fact that they know they are involved in an experiment. It is here where data collection procedures of cognitive translation studies have their greatest weakness (TAPs, interviews, surveys, physiological measurements).

In addition to the prerequisites already mentioned, Neunzig (2011, 2017) reminds us that the research design must respect other criteria, which he calls *experimental pragmatics*, among which he particularly notes *practicability* or *scientific economy*, criteria described by Giegler (1994) demanding that research be designed in the simplest way possible to avoid overloading the subjects, as well as ensuring that they are manageable as a whole and that the analysis of the results does not imply excessive effort by the researchers (see Table 4.1).

4.1.5 Steps of the empirical research process

Building on Bunge (1972) and on Neunzig and Tanqueiro (2007), Neunzig (2011, 2017) presents a series of ten steps in order to guarantee transparency and ensure intelligibility of translation research procedures. These steps are as follows.

1) Justifying the relevance of a study. Neunzig recalls that Popper (1963) insisted that the starting point for all scientific work is the delimitation of the problem and not the gathering of data. Neunzig quotes Tausch

TABLE 4.1 Criteria for accuracy in empirical research according to Neunzig

Criteria	To ensure that [...]
Objectivity	*The approach and instruments used are independent of the researcher.*
Reliability	*Internal consistency in the approach*
Repeatability	*Results obtained in a particular experiment can be repeated in parallel experiments with other subjects*
Validity	*Results are reliable indicators for the research objectives*
Extrapolability (or generalizability)	*Results obtained in a study can be extrapolated into other situations*
Quantifiability	*Data obtained must be quantifiable*
Ecological validity (or environmental validity)	*The experiment reflects a real situation*
Practicability (scientific economy)	*Research is designed in the simplest possible way*

(Neunzig, 2017, pp. 48–49).

and Tausch (1991) who insisted that the importance of a study should derive from the relevance of the problem it deals with. So, for Neunzig (2011), the first step in any research should be enunciating well-formulated and credibly fertile questions and justifying interest in the topic, in short, stressing its relevance.

2) Introducing the referential framework. To state a problem, Neunzig (2011) suggests that one should start with a bibliographical analysis so that the referential framework is established and the antecedents of the study are described. This framework helps to systemize the research questions and helps to draw up models as well as to decide on the research focus.
3) Formulating hypotheses. The next step is to develop well-defined hypotheses formulated as a statement describing a fact in the scientific field susceptible to being compared and contrasted in order to obtain data that confirms or rejects the hypothesis. Hypotheses structure the relationships between variables of study (i.e. everything which, from a quantitative or qualitative point of view, one is going to measure) that can be observed using deductive or inductive methods. The following criteria should be applied for systematic research:

- Compatibility. This refers to the fact that hypotheses should be compatible with scientific knowledge and previous objective knowledge.
- Verifiability. This refers to the fact that hypotheses are not mere speculations and should be able to be verified or rejected by means of empirical studies.

- Intelligibility. This means that others can intellectually assimilate the reasoning used.
- Verisimilitude. This means that hypotheses must be logical.
- Relevance. This means there should be an obvious point to the exercise; it should have some scientific or professional interest.

Following the phase model, Neunzig (2017) recommends that one should draw up hypotheses on three levels:

- Theoretical hypotheses, namely, presumptions or suppositions derived directly from an established theoretical model. They are formulated in a general way and cannot be directly verified using systematic observations (empirically).
- Empirical hypotheses, namely, deductions based on a theoretical hypothesis referring to the variables one wishes to study.
- Operational hypotheses (or working hypotheses) referring to concrete studies of the indicators that have been developed and are aimed at confirming or rejecting empirical hypotheses, and, indirectly, the theoretical hypotheses behind a given model. Operational hypotheses predict the result of the behaviour of the variables in a particular study and they are derived from the experimental approach.

4) Deciding the research focus and the strategy for gathering data. Depending on the problem one wants to investigate, one decides on a given empirical focus. Either choose an empirical-observational investigation or design an experiment. This decision should be based on the aims and objectives of the research.

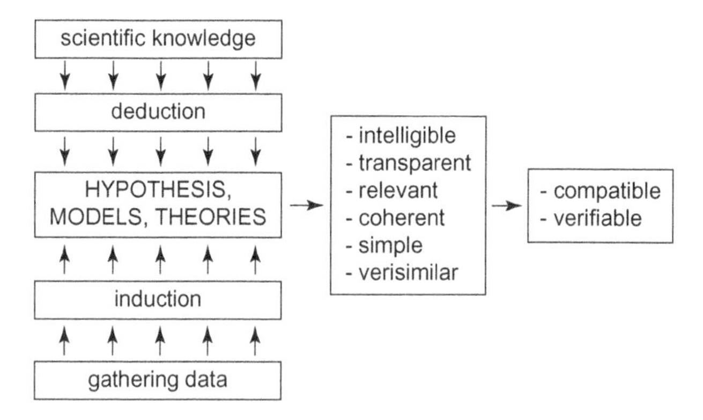

FIGURE 4.2 Hypothesis in empirical studies according to Neunzig

(Neunzig, 2011, p. 24)

Neunzig (2011) notes that quite a few renowned researchers in empirical translation studies have opted for case studies precisely because they argue that the act of translation is so complex that research into a wide range of samples leads to researchers getting lost amidst too much information.

Within the field of translation studies, exploratory studies are also very common. These attempt to verify if a conviction, or an idea, that a scholar has extracted from his or her own professional experience is verifiable in reality and observable on a more general level and whether the tendencies observed can be extrapolated to other similar cases, in other words, if there is any foundation for them.

In recent years, there has been an increase in the designing of experiments in which experimental conditions are controlled, offering the possibility of eliminating confusing variables and manipulating those variables in which we are interested, while, in addition, offering more accurate measurement. The main problem here is the possible lack of environmental validity, i.e. the very artificiality of the situation in which data is obtained. Nevertheless, carrying out measurements in a natural environment (fieldwork) where subjects perform in a natural context is rare in our research (except in didactic situations) because it requires a great deal of effort by the researcher.

Figure 4.2 describes the relationship between data, hypotheses and their operationalization according to Neunzig (2011).

5) Definition of study variables and its indicators. Neunzig (2011) insists on the need to define the variables of a study and its indicators. According to him, variables in experimental research, or in an observational study, can be defined as everything which, from a quantitative or qualitative point of view, one is going to measure, control or study – everything that is in close relationship with the hypotheses of a study. These include independent variables, dependent variables and confusing variables.

- Independent variables are those variables that can be selected or manipulated. They are understood to have the capacity to influence, have a bearing on or affect the phenomenon that we are observing.
- Dependent variables reflect the result of an action by the independent variables. They can be defined as the observable consequences of the manipulation, or selection, of an independent variable by the researcher. Finding one or more dependent variables that are valid for measuring what we really wish to measure is of major importance in the design of a study. In order to make a variable measurable, it is crucial to start from the theoretical definition already drawn up and define the proportions into which the variable can be broken down. These *proportions*, which

correspond to the theoretical concepts we are interested in, are the indicators of the variables we are trying to measure.

- Confusing variables are external influences that can distort the results obtained in the study (the influence of a confusing variable is often attributed erroneously to an independent variable). They should be eliminated or controlled when designing the study.

Figure 4.3 illustrates the relationship between variables in experimental research.

6) Defining of the universe of the study and extracting a sample population. For Neunzig (2011), the next step in the empirical research process is to define the universe of the study and extract a sample. This implies determining *who* or *what* one wishes to observe. The universe (the population or the collective) is a set of reference elements – whether subjects (e.g. professional translators) or objects (e.g. self-translated works) – that are subject to observations. It is defined by a distinctive common characteristic, which is what is going to be studied. Defining the universe (and with it the drawing up of a sample) is vital when it comes to interpretation (always subjective) and extrapolation (only valid within a defined universe) of data gathered. As it is not possible to observe the entire population (the universe) that we are interested in analysing, a representative sample of the universe we wish to analyse is taken. The most common way of obtaining such a sample is by random selection, which is not very common in our field.

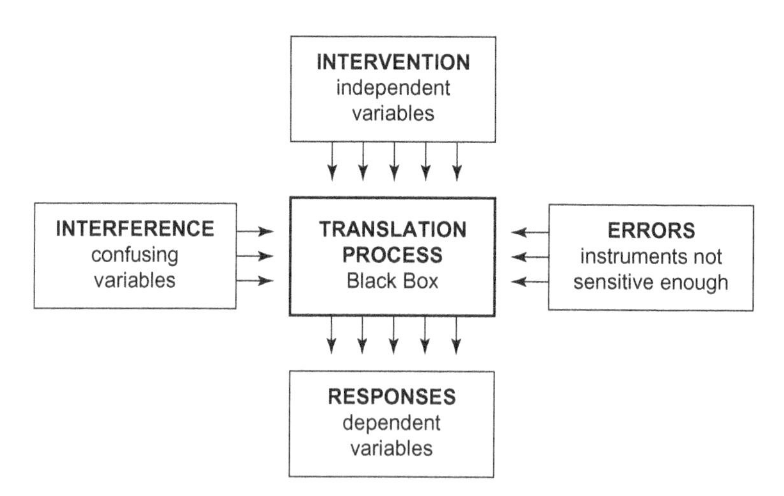

FIGURE 4.3 Variables in experimental research according to Neunzig

(Neunzig, 2011, p. 28)

7) Determining the instruments for data gathering. Next, according to Neunzig (2011), one should determine the instruments for gathering data. To ensure the objectivity, reliability, extrapolability and environmental validity of the empirical approach and, especially, the relevance of the results obtained, it is of vital importance to have effective instruments for gathering data and measuring it accurately.

   One of the main problems in our discipline is the lack of previous experience along with the above-mentioned lack of standardized instruments. That is why researchers usually limit themselves, essentially, to using instruments that could be called "classic" (translations, questionnaires, and interviews) and verbal protocols.
8) Gathering data. As far as gathering data is concerned, Neunzig (2011) suggests that one should limit the data to what is relevant for the study to be carried out to abide by the principle of practicability or scientific economy as described by Giegler (1994) (see Section 4.1.4).
9) Carrying out a statistical analysis of the data.

   Neunzig (2011) also recommends carrying out a statistical analysis of the data. For him, statistics puts at our service procedures and techniques that allow us to describe and analyse any data obtained. Descriptive statistical methods should coincide with the basic characteristics of the population, the universe from which the sample has been taken and inferential statistical methods, which are those based on calculations of probabilities and which attempt to extend or extrapolate to the entire population the information obtained from a representative sample. This will allow the objective interpretation of results.
10) Interpreting the results and communicating them to the scientific community. Finally, Neunzig (2011) argues that the last step in scientific work is to compare the results with hypotheses in order to corroborate or reject them. The latter would oblige one to modify hypotheses, a theory or a model. This modification would in turn be validated in an empirical process, bringing full circle the *wheel of science*.

Figure 4.4 summarizes the steps and criteria proposed by Neunzig (2011) in order to assure scientific transparency in translation research procedures.

4.2 Data collection procedures of empirical-experimental research in translation

This section presents some of the data collection procedures that can be used in research on translation as a cognitive activity. We have listed the procedures that we consider to be more representative of research in our field and divided this section into eight subsections, each one dealing with a particular function, according to the type of data to be collected and analysed.

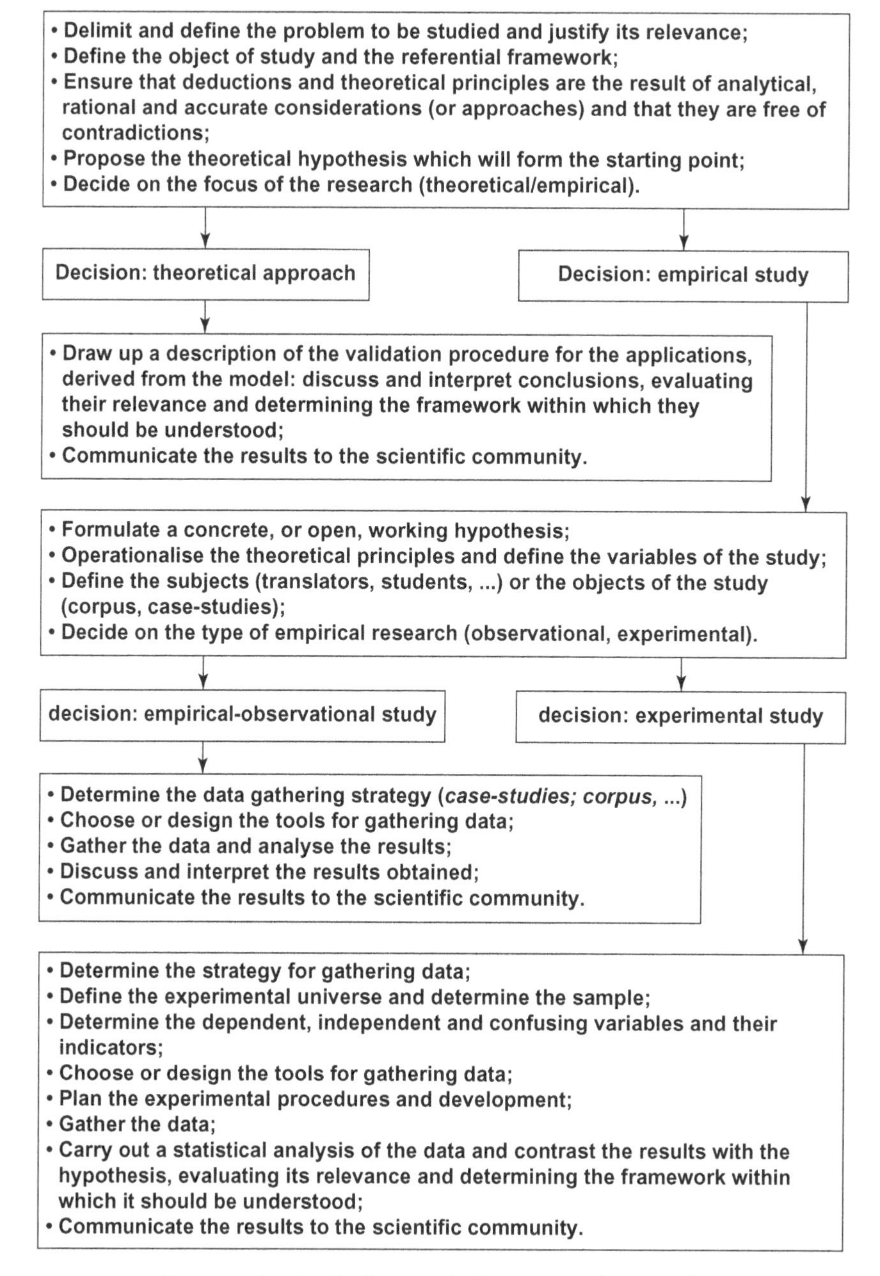

FIGURE 4.4 Steps and criteria in translation research procedures according to Neunzig

(Neunzig, 2011, p. 35)

We also focus both on quantitative and qualitative methods to collect and analyse data that we consider to be useful and representative for research in our field and provide a list of software we consider relevant for research purposes.

A detailed description of most technological tools and software mentioned below can be found on the website of the TREC network (Translation, Research, Empiricism, Cognition) available at https://ddd.uab.cat/pub/pagweb/2016/trec/.[4]The TREC website has been updated and is now available at https://www.trecwebsite.com.

4.2.1 Collecting introspective data

Introspective data provide information concerning the participants' knowledge about their own mental states. The first technique used in research on translation as a cognitive activity consisted of collecting introspective data, which provided researchers with verbalizations related to introspections and/or retrospections of participants' subjective impressions of a given translation task. In this subsection, we list the ones which we consider to be more representative of research in our field.

4.2.1.1 Verbal reports

There are various types of verbal introspective data (concurrent, retrospective, dialogued verbalizations, etc.) which can be used solely or in conjunction with data collected by means of other instruments and tools.

Think-aloud protocols, also known as verbal or introspective protocols, is a data-collection technique stemming from psychology (Ericsson & Simon, 1984) that consists in the recording and further transcription of verbalizations produced during the execution of a given task. TAPs are said to provide information about what goes on in the subject's mind as he/she verbalizes what happens as he/she translates a text. It is expected that information about the nature of cognitive processes is made available in the course of a translation task execution.

TAPs have been used in research on cognitive aspects of translation for a series of case studies involving different types of subjects (language students, translation students, bilinguals, professional translators and other language professionals), different language combinations and directionality (L2-L1 or L1-L2 translation) and different topics (aspects related to problem-solving and decision-making factors, the role of creativity, etc.). However, TAPs also proved to be problematic for many different reasons, the strongest objections being that: (1) TAPs showed what the subjects believed to have happened during the translation process and are not necessarily what actually occurred; (2) subjects knew that they were being observed and were performing two tasks simultaneously (translation and verbalization) that could compromise the level of ecological validity (artificial translation situation) and, thus, somehow distort the data they provided; and (3) TAPs did not provide access to unconscious or automatic processes and interfered in the flow of text production.

Similar to TAPs, retrospective protocols are carried out in a similar manner. However, reports are recorded after task execution is completed. Sometimes, retrospection is performed from memory alone whereas in some forms of retrospection, information from data collection can be provided to enhance memory retrieval.

Dialogued protocols are usually carried out while experimental tasks are being performed and, as such, share methodological similarities with TAPs. However, dialogued protocols can also be carried out after task execution is completed and, as such, are more similar to retrospection.

Due to the lack of other data collection procedures, verbal protocols, including TAPs, retrospective and dialogued reports, remained the main source of process-oriented information until the mid-1990s.

4.2.1.2 Journals

Journals are personal activity reports in which a subject can set out their thoughts, concerns, feelings, opinions, hypotheses and explanations. As such, journals also provide researchers with some sort of introspective data.

Translation journals, conceived as personal reports provided by subjects when performing translation tasks (problems encountered, decisions taken, documentation used, errors made, etc.), can also be a tool for collecting introspective data. Translation journals can be used in several cases: with students (for example, to collect data on their process of acquiring translation competence), professional translators (for example, to collect data on difficulties in performing a certain translation task) and so on.

4.2.2 Collecting data about subjects

One important source of data for research purposes consists of information related to participants' personal characteristics, subject profiling and participants' opinions about different issues related to translation. This includes assessment of linguistic proficiency, personal preferences, beliefs, habits and so on. Various types of instruments can be used for data collection: interviews, questionnaires, tests and so on.

4.2.2.1 Interviews

Interviews can provide information of various types related to translation: opinions on a certain aspect of the translation, retrospective interviews on problems and strategies encountered in the performance of a translation task and so on. As indicated by Neunzig and Tanqueiro (2007, p. 51), interviews after having performed a translation have the advantage (like the questionnaire) of not influencing the moment of data collection (the translation), as in the case of TAPs. However, interviews can sometimes measure something that is not intended to be measured, for example, if the interviewee adapts to the researcher's expectations. In addition, the problem of standardization arises. The standardization of the interview is important when, for example, several subjects are interviewed or several interviewers are involved in the same investigation.

Interviews can be open (unstructured), structured (through interview guides or questionnaires used by the interviewer) or semi-structured (more flexible, combining open and closed questions).

4.2.2.2 Questionnaires

A questionnaire is "(1) a list of questions each with a range of answers; (2) a format that enables standardized, relatively structured, data to be gathered about each of a (usually) large number of cases" (Matthews & Ross, 2010, p. 201, also mentioned in Saldanha & O'Brien, 2013, p. 151). It is an instrument that can be used for various purposes and is the instrument of data collection when using the survey technique. This needs to be well-structured; the participation of the researcher in its administration is less required than in the case of the interview, especially when data are collected online.

Questionnaire questions can be opened or closed. In the case of closed questions, it is a question of choosing a response from a list of options. These options can be put on a dichotomous (yes/no, agree/disagree, etc.) or multiple (with several possible options) scale, or on a Likert scale (specifying the level of agreement/disagreement with respect to a statement: nothing, little, enough, totally).

Neunzig and Tanqueiro (2007, p. 52) summarize in the following steps the process of elaborating a questionnaire: (1) compilation of items that could appear in the questionnaire; (2) selecting appropriate items; (3) determination of the measurement scale; (4) conducting a test of the questionnaire; (5) elimination of inappropriate items; (6) determination of the final questionnaire; and (7) validation of the questionnaire.

Questionnaires can be designed with a specific objective to collect information on a specific aspect or you can use questionnaires already used and validated. This is a problem in the case of translation studies research because, due to the lack of empirical tradition, we lack validated questionnaires of their own.

In the case of translation, questionnaires can be used to collect information of different types: profile of subjects, beliefs or knowledge about a topic, opinions after having performed a translation task and so on. Subject profiling is used to analyse intra-individual differences, that is, variability in terms of research participants' profiles.

Online questionnaires are an effective alternative to traditional paper surveys administered in person or by mail. Their advantages include the speed with which data can be collected, its cost-effectiveness relation and the confidential and anonymous treatment of responses.

We add below a concise list of software available for that purpose.

Software available:

- JORFORM (DROPBOX FORMS) – http://www.jotform.com/
- ENCUESTAFACIL – http://www.encuestafacil.com/
- GOOGLE FORMS – https://www.google.com/forms/about/
- LIMESURVEY – http://www.limesurvey.org
- SURVEYMONKEY – https://www.surveymonkey.com

Recently, Schaeffer et al. (2020) developed the Translation and Interpreting Competence Questionnaire (TICQ), which is an online tool purposefully designed to collect quantitative and qualitative data to profile participants in experiments with respect to their prospective levels of competence in translation and interpreting. TICQ, available at https://bit.ly/33otWeY, has three sections. Section A asks questions related to demographic data and aspects of language history and multilingual abilities. The other two sections are directly focused on either aspects of translation (Section B) or interpreting (Section C) competence. They use self-rating scales on modality-specific skills and questions about procedural, declarative and otherwise professional factors. TICQ is available in three languages (English, German and Spanish). It is fully customizable, and it can be used online or in a printed version. Schaeffer et al. (2020) contend that TICQ provides translation and interpreting studies with a tool to enhance sample selection, between-study comparisons and meta-analytic research. Thus, the authors encourage translation and interpreting scholars to use TICQ as a means to standardize practices and raise the levels of convergence in subject profiling.

4.2.2.3 Subject profiling

In addition to TICQ, there are several other tools to profile subjects. Research in the cognitive aspect of translation has seen an increasing need to investigate how participants' individual differences influence translation task execution and performance. This is also particularly important to allow replications of empirical studies. Subject profiling is carried out by means of questionnaires (see above) or tests, which can be used for several purposes: to measure intelligence, assess memory capacity, determine levels of linguistic competence, outline core personality traits and so on. Tests are used predominantly to assess subjects' profiles. They make data collection more coherent and usually aim at creating more homogenous samples. To that extent, multiple-choice questions can be used to help identify personality traits or correctly answered questions can be used to assess intelligence levels.

Below we list some tests available to help researchers identify intelligence levels, personality traits, language skills and translation competence levels, among other relevant features.

Software available:

- DIALANG TESTS – http://www.lancs.ac.uk/researchenterprise/dialang/about
- MYERS-BRIGGS TYPE INDICATOR (MBTI) – http://www.myers-briggs.org/my-mbti-personality-type/
- TEST OF ENGLISH AS A FOREIGN LANGUAGE (TOEFL) – http://www.ets.org/toefl
- WECHSLER ADULT INTELLIGENCE SCALE (WAIS) – https://www.pearsonassessments.com/
- EFFORT SELF-ASSESSMENT TOOL FOR TRANSLATION COMPETENCE LEVELS – https://www.effortproject.eu/framework-for-translation-levels-a-b/self-assessment-tool/

4.2.3 Collecting behavioural data

Behavioural data consists of information related to participants' actions directly related to translation task execution. The most basic form of data collection is direct observation. Technological developments have allowed the collection of behavioural data by means of electronic tools such as screen recordings and remote monitoring, keylogging and eye tracking.

4.2.3.1 Direct observation

Direct observation is a technique that consists of carefully observing a phenomenon to collect information and record it for later analysis. Through the technique of direct observation, the researcher can directly collect information on the behaviour of subjects. In the case of translation, the observable behaviours can be of different types: external actions of the subjects when translating (for example, external queries to the computer), the behaviour of translation students before a pedagogical input and so on.

Instruments for recording information related to direct observation can be of different types: journals of the researcher, field notes, observation templates and so on. In order not to influence the observed subjects, it is important for observers to act with discretion and not to let their presence affect the behaviour of the subjects they are studying.

4.2.3.2 Screen recording and remote monitoring

Screen-recording software is used to capture on-screen activity during translation task execution in video format (usually .avi or flash). Most screen recording applications can also capture keystroke and mouse click data when these tools are being used for research. Thus, they serve as a complementary source of data collection. Screen recordings can be replayed, rewound or fast-forwarded in real time or at an accelerated pace. As such, they can be used to visualize logged actions and help subjects retrieve memories related to the actions they performed or guide researchers in their analyses of translator styles, problem-solving strategies, use of documentation sources and revision patterns. A major advantage of screen recording as a research tool is its non-invasive nature and the relative preservation of ecological validity. When recordings are made, subjects are not required to do anything different from what they would do while translating.

Software available:

- BLUEBERRY FLASHBACK EXPRESS – http://www.bbsoftware.co.uk/BBFLASHBACK_FREEPLAYER.aspx
- CAMTASIA – http://www.techsmith.com/camtasia.html
- A POWER REC – https://www.apowersoft.es/grabador-de-pantalla-gratis

4.2.3.3 Keylogging

Keystroke logging is a type of translation process data that is elicited by means of recording (or logging) in real time the keys struck on a keyboard by a translator. There are several types of keylogging software (Writelog, Inputlog, Translog) that use different approaches to record data. Researchers make frequent use of keystroke logging tools to describe online writing or translation processes in detail.

In our field of research, the most used keylogging software is Translog, a computer program first developed at the Copenhagen Business School by Jakobsen and Schou (1999). There have been several versions of the software named Translog DOS, Translog 2000, Translog 2006; and Translog II. Differently from Writelog or Inputlog, Translog was developed specifically to be used for analysing translation process data, having a window displaying the source text and a window in which the target text is typed. Translog II is a completely different software than the earlier Translog versions. In addition to the keylogging features, Translog II can record the position of the eyes on the computer monitor during a translation process. Translog II is compatible with EyeLink and Tobii's eye-tracking hardware systems.

Software available:

- TRANSLOG – https://sites.google.com/site/centretranslationinnovation/translog-ii
- INPUTLOG – http://www.inputlog.net
- WRITELOG – https://writelog.com/

4.2.3.4 Eye tracking

Eye tracking is a type of data elicited by means of an eye tracker, a device that records eye movements on a computer screen. Most eye-tracking systems typically use infrared light beams to create a foveal refraction that is recorded by the eye-tracking software. The recorded eye-movement data allow researchers to calculate fixation count and duration, saccades, regressions and pupil dilation. Differently from eye trackers with a chin rest, remote eye-tracking systems allow participants to freely move their heads and keep visual access to the keyboard. Thus, remote eye-tracking systems are less invasive and more adequate for eliciting translation process data. Eye movements can be analysed in particular areas of interest (AOI), thus allowing separate screening of source and target text areas as well as transitions between them.

Software available:

- TOBII – http://www.tobii.com
- EYE LINK (SR Research) – http://www.sr-research.com

4.2.3.5 Integrating keylogging and eye-tracking data

The integration of keylogging and eye-tracking data, using the same time stamp, has been made possible with the advent of Translog II (Carl, Jakobsen, & Jensen, 2008). The software allows researchers to generate tables with joint data and progression graphs that map the unfolding of keystroke actions and visual activity in the course of text production in translation. Thus, researchers are able to identify to what extent typing activity (writing, deleting, revising) occurs in parallel to reading or whether one action precedes or follows the other.

4.2.4 Collecting neurophysiological data

Neurophysiological data is obtained by means of hardware that captures neurophysiological reactions resulting from brain activity activation. This includes electroencephalography (EEG), electrocardiography (ECG) and functional magnetic resonance imaging (fMRI). The latter technique has been used in translation research to locate areas of brain activation as participants perform translation-related tasks inside the scanner.

4.2.4.1 Electroencephalography

EEG is the recording of electrical activity along the scalp. Different EEG techniques are used to investigate cognitive processing. In principle, they all record data while participants are performing translation-related tasks and attempt to measure the electrical signals and locate brain activation related to translation task execution.

4.2.4.2 Electrocardiography

An ECG is used to measure the rate and regularity of heartbeats and attempts to establish a connection between neuro-vegetative activity and cognitive processing. The ECG technique records data while participants are performing translation-related tasks and attempts to measure heartbeats in relation to translation task execution with respect to the level of alertness, emotion, physical implication and cognitive processing.

4.2.4.3 Functional magnetic resonance imaging

Functional magnetic resonance imaging is a neuroimaging technique that identifies changes in metabolism and oxygenation in specific areas of the brain. Different frequencies make it possible to distinguish the signals emitted by the grey matter from the white matter in the brain and also from the cerebrospinal fluid, generating an image of great spatial precision. Using fMRI, brain signals can be visualized and interpreted in terms of where activity is taking place in the brain and what is the specificity of neural processing in that region. For translation purposes, actions have to be performed inside the scanner and restriction of movement hinders the manual execution of translation tasks. Thus, translation-related actions (such as reading for translation) rather than translation task manual execution per se are usually used as stimuli when fMRI is used.

Hardware and software available:

- BESA – http://www.besa.de/
- g.MOBIlab+ – https://www.gtec.at/
- AFNI – http://afni.nimh.nih.gov/

4.2.5 Preparing oral data for speech recognition

Speech recognition (SR) is the automatic conversion of spoken input into written text by means of a computer application. Speech recognition allows researchers to generate written text through verbal dictation. In principle, it can reduce the amount of time used to produce a text or a translation. However, there are limitations in terms of system efficiency and users have to be trained to use the speech-recognition system. For translation purposes, translators would have to perform a task that is similar to sight translation, reading silently in source language input and verbalizing the target language output, which is then captured and generated in writing by the SR system. The quality of the written output is thus heavily dependent on the translator's skills and on training the SR system to recognize the output verbalized by the translator.

Software available:

- DRAGON NATURALLYSPEAKING – http://www.nuance.com/dragon/
- WINDOWS SPEECH RECOGNITION – http://windows.microsoft.com/en-us/windows7/set-up-speech-recognition

4.2.6 Analysing corpus-driven data (product and process)

A collection of texts in electronic form, assembled according to a particular set of criteria, is defined as a corpus in corpus linguistics. Such text collections, or corpora, can be tagged electronically to allow robust analyses of larger quantities of language data. Process data can also be assembled to make up a corpus, building on the same principles of corpus linguistics. The combination of product and process data allows researchers to make inquiries into the product/process interface and attempt to answer questions related not only to the characteristics of translated texts but also to how such translations are rendered in the course of a translation task execution.

4.2.6.1 Tagging texts

The most frequent form of corpus annotation is in electronic format. It usually refers to part-of-speech (PoS) tagging in order to identify grammatical markers in language data so that they can be retrieved by search engines developed by computational linguists. Tagged texts contain identification fields (tags) usually in XML format. Tagged segments are generally enclosed between the symbols < and />, referring to the specific part of a text assigned to a particular PoS segment. There are several taggers available for free on the web. CLAWS, PetraTAG, JDTAG, INCEpTION and YAWAT have been specially designed for tagging translation process data.

Software available:

- CLAWS – http://ucrel.lancs.ac.uk/claws/
- PetraTAG (for Spanish) – http://sourceforge.net/projects/petrapostagger/

- JDTAG – https://sites.google.com/site/centretranslationinnovation/tpr-db
- YAWAT – https://sites.google.com/site/centretranslationinnovation/yawat
- INCEpTION – https://morbo.ukp.informatik.tu-darmstadt.de/?9

4.2.6.2 Aligning texts

Text alignment aims at establishing links between linguistic units of at least two texts, representing such links on a computer screen, and storing them for future access. Some text aligners work at subsentential levels but most of them are designed to align sentences. As a rule, text-aligning software imports files with (almost) identically formatted texts and connects them in a new file. Results are presented in columns or on a split screen. An editing function usually allows users to correct the automatic alignment and merge and split aligned sentences, or leave empty slots. Aligned texts can be analysed, searched and manipulated for research or professional purposes and used in concordancers and translation memory systems. Professional translators often use them to build translation memories from stored translations.

In translation research, text aligners are used to contrast an original with various translations, compare alternative translations of a given source text, and study bilingual terminology and phraseology.

Software available:

- PARACONC – http://www.athel.com/para.html
- WINALIGN – http://www.sdl.com/products/sdl-trados-studio/
- WORDSMITH TOOLS – http://www.lexically.net/wordsmith/index.html
- YOUALIGN – http://www.terminotix.com/?lang=en

4.2.6.3 Analysing corpora

Corpora of translated texts can be analysed by comparing originals and their translations, a set of different translations for a given source text or translated texts as compared with original texts. As a rule, analyses build on text alignment between source and target texts in search of the intrinsic characteristics of translated material. There is a wide range of software packages to help researchers tag and analyse texts by means of concordances (software which allows the retrieval of all occurrences of a particular word or phrase in a corpus, together with the segment of text in which they are located) and wordlists (listing a set of data in alphabetical order).

Software available:

- ANTCONC – http://www.antlab.sci.waseda.ac.jp/software.html
- WORDSMITH TOOLS – http://www.lexically.net/wordsmith/index.html
- SKETCH ENGINE – https://www.sketchengine.eu/

4.2.7 Analysing audio and audio-visual data

As far as audio data (e.g. from interviews, think-aloud commentaries, retrospective commentaries) and audio-visual data (e.g. from screen recordings with voice-overs, video recordings, films) are concerned, data can be segmented and then encoded and grouped into categories. Several applications are available to analyse audio-visual data collected in translation process research to carry out statistical analyses.

Software available:

- ATLAS.ti – http://www.atlasti.com/index.html
- EdEt – http://www.etnologia.uw.edu.pl/etno/dlaStudentow/edet
- ELAN – http://tla.mpi.nl/tools/tla-tools/elan/
- HyperRESEARCH – https://www.researchware.com/products/hyper-research.html
- NVivo – https://www.nvivo.de/en/

4.2.8 Managing statistical data

In order to analyse large amounts of quantitative data, researchers need to draw on statistics and carry out analyses to obtain predictive or confirmatory results and validate them. For studies that are only looking for general tendencies, descriptive statistics may be enough. On the other hand, however, inferential statistics may be necessary in order to find out the statistical relevance of differences studied in a sample or the exact magnitude of relation between parameters, and to be able to extrapolate our findings to a whole population. The use of descriptive or inferential statistics will depend on the goals and the characteristics of research designs. There are different programmes to help researchers organize and validate quantitative databases, providing a wide range of tools to perform descriptive and inferential statistical analyses and generate graphs.

Software available:

- GNU PSPP – http://www.gnu.org/software/pspp/
- IBM SPSS – http://www-01.ibm.com/software/analytics/spss/products/statistics/
- R – https://www.r-project.org/

4.3 The evolution of empirical-experimental research on cognitive aspects of translation

Describing cognitive traits of translation task execution has been a long-time challenge for researchers with an interest in studying translation as a cognitive activity.

Neunzig (1999) distinguished between two opposite methodological approaches in research of translation: (1) a more general approach that builds on the humanities to understand what happens from a somewhat subjective perspective using text analysis or self-observation; and (2) a more focused approach that draws on the methods and techniques used in the social sciences (particularly on psychology) to explain from an objective standpoint what happens in the course of the execution of a translation task by means of an empirical-experimental perspective.

Neunzig (1999) argued that given the complexity inherent to the task of translating and the amplitude of its object of scrutiny, methodological approaches vary greatly. Neunzig also pointed out that the still incipient character of the discipline in the late 1990s accounted for the lack of an empirically driven research tradition that already existed in other disciplines such as psychology, pedagogy and applied linguistics. The lack of such an empirical tradition resulted in the absence of criteria and instruments specially designed and validated in order to carry out research in translation. Neuzing's (1999) remarks can be considered as a call for action that would take shape in the ensuing years.

From the 1990s onwards, one observes the introduction of new methodologies that foster the development of empirical-experimental research in translation. This development is particularly noticeable in research on cognitive aspects of translation.

In this section, we look at the evolution of empirical-experimental research in cognitive aspects of translation and divide it into five phases, starting in the mid-1980s with disparate attempts to investigate cognitive-related aspects of translation to present-day research that encompasses a unified product/process approach and the use of strong computational tools to model translation task execution. In short, the five phases can be summarized as follows:

- *First phase* (mid-1980s to mid-1990s). Predominance in the use of TAPs. The first phase consists mostly of works that draw on data collected by means of think-aloud protocols to analyse translation process data.
- *Second phase* (late-1990s to the mid-2000s). Introduction of technological tools and a multi-methodological paradigm (triangulation). It begins with the use of keylogging and screen-recording software as an

attempt to track writing processes in real time through pauses, regressions and editing procedures. Building on the paradigmatic approach known as triangulation, studies carried out in this second phase also draw on questionnaires, interviews and analyses of verbal protocols to foster the paradigm of data triangulation. Additionally, some researchers also include an analysis of the translation product to triangulate it with translation process data.

- *Third phase* (mid-2000s to 2010). Consolidation of the multi-methodological paradigm (triangulation) and the introduction of eye-tracking data as a means to tap into reading processes. The third phase is defined by the consolidation of the multi-methodological paradigm (triangulation) through the introduction of new technological tools for data collection. This new trend is spearheaded by the use of eye-tracking technology, the emergence of more robust experimental designs and the use of statistics to assess the significance of results.
- *Fourth phase* (early 2020s to present date). Focus on interdisciplinarity and convergence of tools. This fourth phase is marked by a stronger interface with translation technology and the development of interactive translation tools as well as by enhancing the dialogue with computational linguistics, computer science, studies of human-computer interaction (HCI) and machine translation (MT) as well as (interactive) post-editing and neuroimaging studies at the interface with neuroscience. This fourth phase is also marked by the further integration of data collected by means of keylogging and eye-tracking software using the same time stamp, creating what Carl (2009) calls user activity data (UAD).
- *Fifth phase* (early 2020s to present date). The incipient nature of this phase suggests that it still needs to be asserted in its own right. Progress in human-computer interaction and artificial intelligence has been a driving force to guide research into a new paradigm in which the interaction between humans and machines will be of paramount importance in empirical-experimental investigations of translation

In the next subsections, we will describe in detail the main studies carried out on cognitive aspects of translation in each one of the first four phases and highlight the most important achievements as well as the shortcomings observed. Due to its incipient nature, the fifth phase will be treated only prospectively. We do not aim to bring together the whole body of research carried out in each phase but rather point to those studies which we consider to be the most relevant ones in order to trace the evolution of research and highlight the paradigmatic changes that have occurred as research grew and developed.

4.3.1 *First phase: Predominance in the use of think-aloud protocols*

Starting in the mid-1980s, research in this first phase drew extensively on TAPs to tap into the translator's "black box" with a line of inquiry based primarily on the work of Ericsson and Simon (1984) with the analysis of verbal protocols. Sandrock's (1982) pioneering study was followed by the seminal work of Krings (1986) and, among several others, by the works of Königs (1987), Gerloff (1988), Jääskeläinen (1987, 1989), Séguinot (1989, 1991), Tirkkonen-Condit (1989, 1991), Lörscher (1991, 1992), Fraser (1993, 1994), Alves (1995) and Kiraly (1995). The scope of these pioneering works ranged from practical aspects concerning translators' training to attempts to establish cognitive profiles observed in the performance patterns of foreign language students as well as novice and professional translators. The most substantial differences among such studies was in the way in which data were analysed and presented, according to the researchers' goals (see Fraser (1996) for a complete account of this phase).

4.3.1.1 Types of research designs

This first phase was marked by a variety of approaches concerning the choice of subjects, data collection procedures and methodological frameworks.

Subjects

According to Fraser (1996), subjects used in this first phase of research on translation as a cognitive activity fall into three categories: foreign language and translation students (the majority), a mixed sample of students and professional translators – both categories without proper subject profiling in experimental samples – and professional translators (the minority).

As far as subjects are concerned, Krings (1986) uses only foreign language students as subjects. Königs (1987) also uses foreign language students as subjects. However, although his results focus almost exclusively on students' performance, he also includes one professional translator among his subjects. Jääskeläinen (1987) uses more and less experienced translation students while Gerloff (1988) studies a mixed sample of bilinguals, intermediate-level translation students and professional translators. Séguinot (1989) focuses her work on an in-depth investigation of the performance of one single professional translator. Jääskeläinen (1987) and Tirkkonen-Condit (1989) use advanced students who were not yet practising translators. Lörscher (1991) analyses the performance of foreign language students. Jääskeläinen (1989) investigates the work of translation students, professionals and non-translators with a high level of competence in the source language (English). Fraser (1993, 1994) focused solely on professionals, including community interpreters. Alves (1995) uses a combination of professional translators, non-translators with a high level of competence in the source and target languages (German/Portuguese) and advanced and novice translation students. Kiraly (1995) uses novice and professional translators in the German/English language pair.

Altogether, the number of subjects in these studies is almost always quite small and samples vary greatly from over a handful of six informants (Königs 1987) to a larger sample of 24 subjects (Alves, 1995). As stated above, subject profiling varies greatly in such studies (foreign language students, translation students, bilinguals and professional translators) and a heterogeneous non-representative sample is usually the norm.

Data collection procedures

Think-aloud protocols, also known as introspection or verbal reports, are the most important technique for data elicitation in the first phase of empirical-experimental research. Nevertheless, the use of TAPs varies greatly among researchers. Königs (1987) states explicitly that he did not intervene at all in the introspection process; a procedure which is seconded by Alves (1995). Krings (1986) also prefers not to intervene and points out that introspective data are more valid when there has been no pressure to verbalize. Gerloff's (1988) subjects responded only to direct questions but otherwise remained silent during the protocols whereas Fraser (1994) prompted subjects when they fell silent for more than a few seconds.

Another important procedure is the use of a translation brief in research designs. Gerloff (1988), Jääskeläinen (1987, 1989), Séguinot (1991) and Fraser (1994) state that they assigned a brief, whereas Fraser (1993) did not. Königs (1987) and Alves (1995) simply instructed subjects to translate so that they produced an acceptable version of their source texts. Other studies carried out in this phase do not seem to be concerned with a translation brief when reporting research designs and results.

Methodological approaches

Methodologically speaking, the main orientation in the first phase seems to build on the information-processing paradigm and draw on a psycholinguistic approach to translation process research. Krings (1986) and Lörscher (1991), and to some extent Königs (1987), Alves (1995) and Kiraly (1995), have a strong psycholinguistic orientation, while Fraser (1993, 1994), Séguinot (1991) and Tirkkonen-Condit (1991) seem to be more oriented towards observation of online behaviour using verbal protocols. Although studies use TAPs are their main source of data, the methodologies used differ greatly among researchers. Differences between concurrent and retrospective verbal protocols are seemingly not considered for the purposes of designing experiments and the choice of subjects is dependent on the availability of participants rather than on the needs of subject profiling with respect to the object of study.

During this first phase, samples used in research were not always representative of the performance of professional and expert translators since studies quite often used language students or translation students as subjects. Experimental designs lacked systematization and clear objectives, used small samples (case studies) and were, therefore, unable to provide robust evidence and generalization of results. Additionally, research designs differed significantly both conceptually and methodologically among researchers.

4.3.1.2 Objects of study and main results

As far as objects of study are concerned, the first phase of research on cognitive aspects of translation has focused on identifying segmentation patterns, describing translation strategies used by subjects, assessing sources of external support involved in the process, such as the use of dictionaries and other reference materials, reflecting on metacognitive aspects of the process and applying results to translator's training by means of evidence generated through TAPs.

Segmentation patterns

Königs (1987) shows that text segmentation in the course of the translation process can occur in an automatic fashion (*Adhoc Block*) or in a more reflexive mode (*Rest Block*). Gerloff (1988) points out that students seem to segment their translation processes in smaller language units (translation units) and at lower levels of processing while professionals segment translation units in larger chunks of text, which are processed at higher linguistic levels. Séguinot (1989, 1991) is especially concerned with editing patterns. Alves (1995) builds on Königs (1987) to identify segmentation patterns of novice and professional translators at word, phrase, sentence and text levels.

Translation strategies

Krings (1986) uses a detailed and highly structured framework for analysing translation strategies. Königs (1987) focuses on two distinct processes placed in what he calls the *Adhoc Block* and the *Rest Block*, the former consisting of routinized, automatic actions and the latter encompassing conscious decisions geared by problem-solving and decision-making processes. Gerloff (1988) looks at the number of problem-solving activities, time spent on solving particular problems or the number of times each translator worked through the entire text. Tirkkonen-Condit (1989) focuses on decision-making criteria. Séguinot (1989, 1991) points out that her only professional informant explicitly accounts for the strategies used in the translation process and seems to focus in particular on what is perceived as the ultimate goal of the translation task, a first indication of the role of metacognition in translation task execution. Jääskeläinen (1989) defines strategies in terms of goal-oriented procedures rather than problem-solving activity and points to the relevance of the former type of procedures in the translation process of more advanced subjects. On the other hand, Lörscher (1993) assesses the procedures employed by subjects in order to solve translation problems (translation strategies) and shows that such strategies differ considerably between foreign language learners and professional translators. Alves (1995) and Kiraly (1995) look at automatic and reflexive types of cognitive behaviour as indicators of translation strategies.

Metacognitive activity

Jääskeläinen (1989) attempts to identify the subjects' focus of conscious attention aiming to investigate both problematic and unproblematic (but conscious) processing. Alves (1995) and Kiraly (1995) both argue that higher levels of metacognitive activity differentiate novice from more advanced, professional subjects.

Use of external support

There are also striking differences in terms of subjects' use of dictionaries and other reference materials. Gerloff (1988) found that professional translators used dictionaries more often than students. Jääskeläinen (1987) and Tirkkonen-Condit (1989) report marked differences in this respect with advanced students preferring monolingual dictionaries whereas younger students used bilingual dictionaries for the same purpose. Jääskeläinen (1987) also highlights the differences between more and less experienced subjects with a special reference to professional behaviour in the use of dictionaries and with respect to the translation brief.

Impact factors on translator's training

Another object of study in this first phase is the impact of evidence generated by means of TAPs on translator's training. The findings of studies that compare the behaviour of different groups can be directly relevant to the teaching of translation. Séguinot (1989, 1991) and Tirkkonen-Condit (1989) focus primarily on what protocols can tell about the way in which learners approach their task. On the one hand, Séguinot (1991) expresses doubts about the extent to which knowledge of professional practice is transferable to the teaching process. Jääskeläinen (1989), on the other hand, argues that while translation process analysis is largely descriptive, she supports the view that its findings could be of use in translation teaching.

4.3.1.3 Overview

In a thorough review of research carried out in this first phase of research on translation as a cognitive activity, Fraser (1996, p. 77) concludes that "translation process studies have, in fact, relatively little in common and present very different pictures of the translation process they all set out to investigate", a conclusion we agree with. Due to the incipient nature of this type of research, studies in this first phase are disparate in scope and kind and emerge in a myriad of topics and approaches (see Table 4.2).

Indirectly, since TAPs have been the primary technique for these works, Fraser's remarks also lead to a reflection on the role played by TAPs in the course of these endeavours. According to Fraser (1996), introspection is only partially explored in this range of studies and none of the researchers appears to have tried to compare think-aloud data with retrospective data.

As we have seen, the spectrum of studies in this first phase is quite wide. They range from attempts to produce a detailed psycholinguistic account of language learners' performance and processing capabilities (Lörscher, 1991,

TABLE 4.2 First phase of the evolution of empirical-experimental research in cognitive aspects of translation

First phase (mid-1980–mid-1990) *Predominance in the use of think-aloud protocols*
Characteristics • Lack of systematic rigour in research designs • Predominance in the use of TAPs • Varied disparate studies that lack convergence among them • Small and non-representative samples **Objects of study** • Segmentation patterns (Königs, 1987; Gerloff, 1988; Séguinot, 1989, 1991; Alves, 1995) • Translation strategies (Krings, 1986; Königs, 1987; Gerloff, 1988; Tirkkonen-Condit, 1989; Séguinot, 1989, 1991; Jääskeläinen, 1989; Lörscher, 1993; Alves, 1995; Kiraly, 1995) • Metacognitive activity (Jääskeläinen, 1989; Alves, 1995; Kiraly, 1995) • Use of external support (Gerloff, 1988, Jääskeläinen, 1987; Tirkkonen-Condit, 1989) • Impact factors on translator's training (Tirkkonen-Condit, 1989; Séguinot, 1989, 1991; Jääskeläinen, 1989)

1992) to attempts to identifying best practices in a professional context and apply them to translators' training (Fraser (1993, 1994). Fraser (1996) insists on the need to systematically extend research to involve professional translators or at least subjects with optimal levels of competence in translation.

According to Fraser (1996), mixed studies involving subjects with varying levels of translation experience (bilinguals, foreign language and translation students, professional translators), which were carried out in this first phase, tend to (1) highlight the effects of experience in translation; and (2) provide evidence of a shift from comprehension difficulties and a more literal translation towards an awareness of higher-level criteria of text production in translation. Fraser (1966) also indicates that one of the most significant findings of this first phase of research was the identification of novice subjects' inadequate levels of awareness with respect to translation problems.

As shown by Fraser (1996), the picture emerging from studies carried out in this first phase was quite varied and results could not be generalized. Therefore, Fraser pleaded for more systematic and rigorous studies; a plea the research community was willing to embrace in the following years and gave rise to the second phase of research on translation as a cognitive activity.

4.3.2 Second phase: Introduction of technological tools and of a multi-methodological paradigm (triangulation)

In our understanding, Fraser (1996) calls for a more systematic and rigorous study of cognitive aspects of translation marked the end of the first phase and also the beginning of the second phase of empirical-experimental research in translation, spanning over a period of ten years from 1996 to 2006. The main feature of this second phase is the introduction of information technology to support empirical research (Neunzig, 1999), including the use of the keylogging software Translog (Jakobsen & Schou, 1999) to track writing processes in real time and the use of screen-recording software (PACTE, 1998, 2001) to capture screen actions, including web consultations and dictionary look-ups. This second phase is also characterized by the emergence of the triangulation paradigm (Jakobsen, 1999; Neunzig, 1999, 2002; Alves, 2001, 2003) as a multi-methodological approach to collect and analyse data. The scope of research ranges from investigating topics already present in the first phase – such as segmentation patterns and translation strategies – as well as new objects of study, including identifying phases of the translation process, tapping into translators' cognitive rhythm and monitoring skills, assessing the impact of translation technology on cognitive processing, mapping translation competence, looking into the process/product interface, investigating issues related to declarative and procedural knowledge and defining indicators of expert performance in translation.

4.3.2.1 Types of research designs

The second phase is marked by a noticeable change in the choice of subjects, new data collection procedures and the refinement of methodological frameworks.

Subjects

As far as subjects are concerned, in this second phase, one notices an increase in the number of studies that use professional translators as subjects (PACTE, 2001, 2002, 2005; Alves, 2005; Dragsted, 2005). Novice translators are still favoured as subjects but they are now mostly used to contrast performance traits with professional translators and to account for differences in terms of expert performance (Jakobsen, 2005, 2006). Differently from the random choice of participants in the first phase, foreign language students are no longer used as primary source for subjects in this second phase. However, foreign language teachers now play a role as informants to contrast their behaviour with professional translators' performance (PACTE, 2001, 2002, 2005). Altogether, although higher than in the first phase, the number of subjects in studies of the second phase continues to be relatively small in most studies.

Data collection procedures

The main novelty in this second phase of research is the advent of keylogging as a tool for data collection, offering a new methodological avenue to research on cognitive aspects of translation.

Jakobsen (2006) mentions that the idea to develop the keylogging software Translog was sparked by a small experiment carried out by Tommola and reported by Wollin and Lindqvist (1986), showing a sequence of keystrokes and some indication of the lengths of pauses occurring between words. According to Jakobsen (2006), the original purpose was to create an automatic, subject independent tool for collecting hard data to supplement softer process data collected by means of verbal protocols. Jakobsen's idea was to provide researchers with access to the various stages a target text passed through before reaching its final state, and to make available information about the partial and total timings of this process, thus showing real-time text segmentation and reflecting underlying cognitive processes. With keylogging, subjects could read the source text displayed on a computer screen according to the specification in the project environment and type in a translation. Researchers could then track keystrokes and the points in time at which they occur. It was then possible to perform simple operations to establish pauses, regressions, deletions and additions and analyse such actions.

Different measurements allow more refined calculations such as the overall number of segments in a given translation task, segment duration and segment length (in terms of the number of keystrokes), as well as the calculation of phases of initial orientation, drafting and revision. By replaying the log files, researchers could track the unfolding of the translation process at different speeds and relate it to stretches of verbalizations collected by means of verbal protocols or contrast pauses with stretches of screen recordings to map instances of external support not recorded by the keylogging software.

In parallel to the use of keylogging software, screen-monitoring and recording software, implemented by means of software such as Proxy[5] or Camtasia, was also introduced in this second phase (PACTE, 2001, 2002, 2003, 2005).

Screen-recording software was primarily used to provide complementary input to keylogged process data, mostly for sources of external support, including consultations, such as dictionary look-ups, the use of other reference materials, such as web searches, and the use of parallel texts for translation purposes.

Direct observation is also used by some researchers (PACTE, 2001, 2002, 2003, 2005) as an alternative to register or confirm actions related to cognitive aspects that were not recorded online by means of computer tools. Questionnaires and interviews were also considered as supplementary forms of data collection.

Introspection, in the form of concurrent or retrospective verbal reports, is now used as complementary input to data triangulation (PACTE, 2002, 2003, 2005; Alves, 2003, 2005). There is a debate about what type of verbalization technique would be most suitable for research (Jakobsen, 2003).

Finally, there was also increased concern with the ecological validity of experiments so that subjects worked in more natural environments, similar to the spaces used for the execution of regular translation tasks (PACTE, 2003, 2005; Alves, 2005).

Altogether, one could summarize data collection procedures in this second phase of research as a multi-methodological approach consisting primarily of keylogged data, screen recordings of online performance visualized in computer monitors and verbalizations of either concurrent or retrospective nature. Additionally, to a smaller extent, direct observations and the use of questionnaires and interviews were also used to provide additional information to online data. This phase also marks the beginning of data collection geared to a combined analysis of product and process data (PACTE, 2002, 2003, 2005; Alves, Magalhães, & Pagano, 2004).

Methodological approaches

The main methodological focus in the second phase of empirical-experimental research in translation is the introduction of a multi-methodological approach to data collection and data analysis.[6]

Initially, building on the triangulation metaphor used in the social sciences (Smith, 1975; Jick, 1979), Jakobsen (1999) proposes the joint use of different data elicitation techniques as a way to capture translation processes. The introduction of the software Translog, developed by Jakobsen and Schou (1999), paved the way to the online tracking of translation processes and allowed the study of pauses and regressions, including deletions and insertions in the course of text production in translation. The approach spearheaded by the advent of keylogging also allowed a series of measurements of online data and, as a result, strengthened the potential to carry out more robust experimental designs and to triangulate data.

Further on, Jakobsen (2002) builds on Schilperoord (1996), which was inspired by the seminal psycholinguistic research carried out by Goldman-Eisler (1972), to investigate the temporal course of text production processes. The keylogging software Translog is used to record the temporal course of the typing process in text production across a computer keyboard. In other words, the temporal course of the typing process is an observable and recordable reflection of underlying cognitive processes. Jakobsen (2006) argues that one key assumption is that by analysing recordings of this process, in particular of its temporal patterning by pauses, it was possible to arrive at a clearer understanding of the dynamic, real-time interaction of cognitive processes, not only in translation but also more generally in language.

However, keylogging alone proved to be unable to yield data related to sources of external support. The software only recorded keystrokes within its own online environment. Therefore, the need for a complementary tool arose and screen recordings began to be used in conjunction with keylogging (Alves, 2003). At the same time, other research groups preferred to draw on input generated by *Proxy* (PACTE, 2002, 2003, 2005), arguing that this would provide a more naturalistic setting and increase the ecological validity of experiments.

Keylogging, screen recordings and direct observations, in conjunction with data from verbal reports, questionnaires and analyses of the translation product, provided fertile ground for more robust experimental designs. Thus, hypotheses could be formulated and tested under new experimental conditions. Experimentation also allowed the control of variables and paved the way for the replication of studies. Progressively, the second phase enabled researchers to come together under a more consolidated methodological framework and build research groups targeting research questions of crucial importance for the development of research on translation as a cognitive activity. As a consequence, one observes the emergence of a multi-methodological approach to data collection and analysis that progresses steadily as more research output is produced (see, among others, Hansen, 2002; Jakobsen, 2002; Alves, 2001, 2003; PACTE, 2002, 2003, 2005).

In parallel to developments in translation process research, research on translation competence also draws a multi-methodological approach (direct observation, questionnaires, retrospective interview, electronic corpora) and fosters the recording of online data by means of screen-monitoring software (PACTE, 2000, 2001, 2002, 2003, 2005).

One also observes an interest in mapping the process-product interface in translation (see, among others, Hansen, 2002; PACTE, 2001, 2002, 2003, 2005; Alves, Magalhães, & Pagano, 2005).

4.3.2.2 Objects of study and main results

As far as objects of study are concerned, the second phase of research on cognitive aspects of translation continued to work on segmentation patterns and translation strategies, including assessments of internal and external support. It has also focused on new objects of study such as identifying the impact of verbalization on processing effort, accounting for phases of the translation process and tapping into translators' cognitive rhythm, mapping cognitive effort and monitoring processes, assessing the impact of translation technologies on cognitive processing, mapping translation competence, looking into the process/product interface and the role of declarative and procedural knowledge in translation and defining traits of expert performance.

Segmentation patterns

Investigation of segmentation patterns focuses predominantly on how the translation process unfolds in real time and at which level (word, phrase, sentence, etc.) translation is processed. Dragsted (2004, 2005) demonstrated that novice and professional translators show different segmentation patterns when dealing with easier or more difficult source texts and suggested that long-term working memory features may have an influence in segmentation patterns. Alves and Magalhães (2004) showed that segmentation patterns of novice translations occur mainly at word level due to their lack of awareness of discursive features.

Phases of the translation process and cognitive rhythm

Jakobsen (2002) built on Schilperoord's (1996) notion of cognitive rhythm, namely rhythmical patterns (pauses, regressions, segmentation patterns, etc.) observed in the production of textual material, to analyse different phases of the translation process in the English/Danish language pair. Thus, Jakobsen (2002) was able to identify clear, distinct phases (orientation, drafting and revision) that were mapped empirically onto translation process data and was able to show that these phases display different patterns when comparing the performance of novice and professional translators. Alves (2005) drew on Jakobsen's findings to show evidence of similar patterns across other language pairs (German/English/Portuguese/Spanish). In applied terms, Lorenzo (2002) used keylogging to foster awareness raising of segmentation patterns in translators' training and showed that translation students were not able to deal with revision as an independent phase.

Translation strategies

As far as translation strategies are concerned, Alves (2003, 2005) and Alves and Gonçalves (2003) used keylogging whereas PACTE (2002, 2003, 2005) used *Proxy* recordings and direct observation to provide accounts of problem-solving and decision-making processes in translation and looked at instances of internal and external support as translation specific strategies. Other authors, such as Livbjerg and Mees (2003) and Barbosa and Neiva (2003) used keylogging to analyse the use of dictionaries in the process of translation and related their use to translation strategies.

Cognitive effort and monitoring processes

Alves and Gonçalves (2003) used keylogging in conjunction with retrospective verbal protocols to account for aspects of inferential processes and to tap into issues related to conceptual and procedural encodings and the type of cognitive effort they require. They also argued that the analysis of metacognitive aspects related to inferential processing was a key to mapping effort and effect in translation. Alves and Gonçalves (2003) also showed that lower levels of metacognitive activity lead to weaknesses in inferential processing. Alves (2005) looked into instances of cognitive effort in the performance of novice and professional translators from English, German and Spanish into Portuguese and showed evidence of distinct cognitive effort patterns between novice and professional translators. Alves argued that increased metacognitive activity leads to successful problem-solving and decision-making processes and reveals a more balanced relation between processing effort and cognitive effects.

As far as monitoring is concerned, Tirkkonen-Condit (2005) revisited the concept of a monitor model to assess the *literal translation default hypothesis*, namely the tendency to produce a first draft based on the linear structure of the source text, and the role of cognitive monitoring as an impact factor in terms of problem-solving and decision-making processes in translation, a hypothesis she was able to confirm.

Impact of verbalization on processing effort

Jakobsen (2003) was the first study that provided evidence of the negative impact of the concurrent think-aloud condition on cognitive processing in translation. He showed that subjects working under this condition took longer to translate and had an increase in the number of segments in text production irrespective of language direction. Jakobsen found evidence of stronger cognitive effort, or even cognitive overload, registered under exceptional circumstances, and recommended caution with respect to the use of the think-aloud procedure. Corroborating previous criticisms raised within translation studies, Jakobsen recommended retrospection as a preferable form of collecting verbal data for investigating cognitive aspects of translation. As a result, the use of retrospective verbal protocols became more frequent than concurrent think-aloud protocols.

Impact of translation technologies on processing effort

Dragsted (2004, 2005) investigated the impact of translation technology, in particular of translation memory systems, on cognitive processing and was able to show that lack of familiarity with such tools had an impact on translation performance.

Issues related to the process/product interface

PACTE (2003, 2005), Alves, Magalhães and Pagano (2004) and Alves (2005), among others, looked into the process/product interface to expand the scope of research in order to assess the relationship between cognitive performance (through process data) and translation quality (through product data). The overall goal of these works was to establish a relation between the characteristics of the translation product and the type of cognitive processes it entails.

Declarative and procedural aspects of cognitive processing

Kiraly (2000), in his socio-constructivist approach to translators' competence, and Hurtado Albir (2005) in her cognitive-constructivist approach to the acquisition of translation competence, highlighted the importance of analyses related to the integration of procedural and declarative knowledge in translation. Schäffner and Adab (2000) and Gonçalves (2003) as well as Alves, Magalhães and Pagano (2004) also discussed such aspects and insisted on analyses of procedural and declarative knowledge in translation in order to map these types of knowledge onto cognitive-related aspects of translation performance.

Translation competence

PACTE (2001, 2002, 2003, 2005) used *Proxy* to record and monitor translation processes and, thus, analyse phases, pauses, corrections and so on in an attempt to account for characteristics of translation competence. PACTE proposed such a combined approach, thus strengthening the multi-methodological perspective for data collection and analysis related to cognitive aspects of translation. The PACTE group also spearheaded the combined analysis of product and process data.

Traits of expert performance

Building on Ericsson (2002), Jakobsen (2005) is perhaps the first author in the field of cognitive translation studies who tries to identify indicators of expert behaviour in translation. Like Dragsted (2004, 2005), Jakobsen sees instances of expert performance in terms of the development of long-term working memory and believes that expert behaviour in translation is generally manifested in instances of peak performance, namely longer stretches of text production in translation not interrupted by pauses or regressions, which are enabled by complex mediating mechanisms acquired through many years of *deliberate practice*.

Englund Dimitrova (2005) examined expertise in translation in relation to explicitation processes. Alves (2005) also showed an incipient interest in the characterization of expertise in translation. All these authors agree that expert performance in translation is a type of expert knowledge and they inquired into the nature of expertise in translation. However, none of them makes a clear difference between translation competence and traits of expert performance and they seem to erroneously equate one to the other.

4.3.2.3 Overview

Altogether, a series of innovative actions promoted the development of empirical-experimental research on translation as a cognitive activity. Results arising from research carried out from the mid-1990s to the mid-2000s presented a wide variety of characteristics. Altogether, features that differentiated the performance of novice and professional translators emerged as the most significant results in this second phase. During this second phase of research, samples used in experimental designs became more representative of the performance of professional translators and attempted to provide indications of translation competence and expert performance in translation. Experimental designs grew in strength and became more systematic with hypotheses being formulated on the basis of more precise and controlled variables. Besides, researchers started comparing research designs both conceptually and methodologically. The picture emerging from studies carried out in this second phase was still quite varied. However, we would like to argue that studies became more systematic and rigorous, the generalization power of results increased and replication of studies, although still incipient, became potentially possible (see Table 4.3).

Finally, one interesting aspect in the unfolding of this second phase is the creation or consolidation of research groups, such as TRAP (Copenhagen Business School, 1995–2003), EXPERTISE (University of Oslo, 1999–2005), PACTE (Universitat Autònoma de Barcelona, created in 1997 and active until 2022), LETRA (Universidade Federal de Minas Gerais, created in 2000 and currently active) and PETRA (Universidad de Granada and Universidad de Las Palmas de Gran Canaria, created in 2001 and active until 2019),[7] which have brought together researchers committed to and engaged in the development of research in translation as a cognitive activity.

TABLE 4.3 Second phase of the evolution of empirical-experimental research in cognitive aspects of translation

Second phase (mid-1990–mid-2000)
Introduction of technological tools and of a methodological paradigm (triangulation)

Characteristics

- Introduction of a multi-methodological paradigm (triangulation)
- Introduction of technological tools (keylogging and screen recordings) to track translation processes in real time
- Greater rigour and consistency in research designs (formulation of hypotheses and definition of variables, introduction of statistical analyses, etc.)
- Further development of research

Objects of study

- Segmentation patterns (Dragsted, 2004, 2005; Alves & Magalhães, 2004)
- Phases of the translation process and cognitive rhythm (Jakobsen, 2002; Lorenzo, 2002; Alves, 2005)
- Translation strategies (Livbjerg & Mees, 2003; PACTE, 2002, 2003, 2005; Alves, 2003, 2005, Alves & Gonçalves, 2003, Barbosa & Neiva, 2003)
- Cognitive effort and monitoring processes (Alves & Gonçalves, 2003; Alves, 2005; Tirkkonen-Condit, 2005)
- Impact of verbalization on processing effort (Jakobsen, 2003)
- Impact of translation technologies on processing effort (Dragsted, 2004, 2005)
- Issues related to the process/product interface (PACTE, 2003, 2005; Alves, Magalhães & Pagano 2004; Alves, 2005)
- Declarative and procedural aspects of cognitive processing (Hurtado Albir, 1999, 2005; Kiraly, 2000; Schäffner & Adab, 2000; Gonçalves, 2003; Alves, Magalhães & Pagano, 2004)
- Translation competence (PACTE, 2000, 2001, 2002, 2003, 2005)
- Traits of expert performance (Dragsted, 2004, 2005; Alves, 2005; Englund Dimitrova, 2005; Jakobsen, 2005)

4.3.3 Third phase: Consolidation of a multi-methodological paradigm (triangulation) and introduction of eye-tracking data

Starting in the mid-2000s and spanning over the next five years, until 2010, the third phase of research on cognitive aspects of translation consolidated the multi-methodological paradigm (triangulation) introduced in the second phase through the combined use of several complementary techniques, instruments and tools. Keeping the use of tools and instruments of data collection introduced in the previous phase (keylogging, screen recording, questionnaires, interviews, etc.), the main methodological novelty was the introduction of eye-tracking technology in data collection (O'Brien, 2006). This phase also sees the first attempts to integrate keylogged and eye-tracking data using the same time stamp (Carl, 2009). Another important characteristic of this phase is the increasing relevance of statistical analyses based on larger data samples (Balling, 2008). The scope of research ranged from investigating topics already present in the previous phase – such as the impact of translation technology on cognitive processing, defining indicators of translation competence and expert performance, and looking into the process/product interface in translation – as well as other objects of study, including modalities of translation, complexities in the translation process, time pressure, translation unit and user activity data, directionality, creativity, metalinguistic awareness and metacognitive activity and the acquisition of translation competence.

Altogether, the third phase is marked by a more consistent approach concerning the choice of subjects, data collection procedures and methodological frameworks.

4.3.3.1 Types of research designs

In general, almost all research designs in the third phase adopt the paradigm of data triangulation. Most of the eye-tracking-related research carried out in this phase draws on the methodological procedures pioneered by O'Brien (2006), which was further developed at the Centre for Research and Innovation in Translation and Translation Technology (CRITT), then at the Copenhagen Business School (CBS).[8] Investigations of the translation process were carried out by means of research designs aimed at aligning keylogged and eye-tracking data using the same time stamp (Carl, 2009). Research on translation competence acquisition saw the emergence of research designs that built on the tradition of competence-oriented research that had been developed by PACTE (2000, 2002, 2003, 2005).

Subjects

As far as subjects are concerned, one of the most important characteristics is a significant increase in the number of participants in experiments in the scope of research on translation competence research. PACTE's (2008) study used 35 professional translators and 24 foreign language teachers. Almost all other empirical studies, including those drawing on eye-tracking data, still used a relatively small number of subjects in their experimental designs.

For instance, O'Brien's (2006) study used only six professional translators experienced in the use of translation memory systems. Similarly, Jakobsen and Jensen (2008) only used eight professional translators as subjects, the same number used by Dragsted and Hansen (2008) while Pavlović and Jensen's (2009) had data from ten professional translators. Sharmin, Špakov, Räihä and Jakobsen (2008) attempted to recruit a somewhat larger cohort of participants and had 18 translation students reported in their results.

Altogether, the number of professional translators used as subjects increased significantly from those experiments carried out in the previous phases, which mostly used students and novice translators in their experiments. By using more professional translators as subjects, researchers were able to better capture and analyse characteristics of translation competence and expertise in translation more systematically.

Additionally, one notices a greater awareness concerning the importance of subject profiling, a concern expressed by Muñoz (2009a), who points out that not enough attention had been paid to variations in subjects' mental abilities and language skills, variations that could seriously affect results. Muñoz suggested that subjects could be classified by means of the WAIS (Wechsler Adult Intelligence Scale) and TOEFL (Test of English as a Foreign Language) subtests and corroborated his proposal with the results of an experiment in which 17 subjects who translated four texts using Translog were profiled on the basis of their performance in the above-mentioned tests.

Data collection procedures

Data collection procedures were built on achievements from the second phase and consolidated the combined use of various techniques, instruments and tools of data collection.

As far as the use of eye tracking is concerned, data collection focused on identifying eye fixations in specifically targeted areas of interest (AOIs) found in source and target texts in order to investigate processing effort in terms of reading and writing for translation.

The most innovative aspect of data collection in the third phase was the integration of keylogging and eye-tracking data using the same time stamp which was made possible by the advent of the software Translog II (Carl, Jakobsen, & Jensen, 2008), a revamped and substantially more powerful version of the original version of the keylogging software Translog developed by Jakobsen and Schou (1999).

Methodological approaches

As far as methodological approaches are concerned, the most important characteristic of this third phase was the consolidation of the triangulation paradigm. The use of eye tracking was also a fundamental new feature incorporated into the methodological approaches.

From the outset, the use of eye-tracking data in the research on cognitive aspects of translation was built on two assumptions that attempted to establish a link between eye movements and the interpretation of data:

- The first assumption is called the *immediacy assumption*. It assumes that a reader tries to interpret each content word of a text as it is encountered. In other words, "there is no appreciable lag between what is being fixated and what is being processed" (Just & Carpenter, 1980, p. 331).
- The second assumption, also postulated by Just and Carpenter (1980), assumes that the eye remains fixated on a word as long as the word is being processed. Thus, the time taken to process a newly fixated word is directly indicated by the gaze duration.

Although the two assumptions also consider backwards and forwards eye movements (saccades), the basic overall assumption, or rather a guiding metaphor, is that the eye is a window into the mind; the so-called *eye-mind assumption* (Just & Carpenter, 1980) that gives support to applying the eye-mind analogy to the interpretation of eye-tracking data for the purpose of analysing cognitive effort in translation (Rayner, 1998).

Most authors drawing on the above-mentioned assumption argue that eye-tracking data can be interpreted as correlates of ongoing cognitive processing of source and/or target texts. Under the eye-mind assumption, the allocation of cognitive resources in translation is essentially an information-processing task. The works of Göpferich, Jakobsen and Mees (2008), Jakobsen and Jensen (2008), Carl (2009), Alves, Pagano and Silva (2009), Pavlović and Jensen (2009) and Alves, Pagano, Neumann, Steiner and Hansen-Schirra (2010), among others, built on this overall assumption.

The establishment of CRITT at the CBS in 2007 was instrumental in the development and consolidation of methodological approaches in this third phase. CRITT obtained funding from the EU FP6 programme to carry out the *Eye-to-IT* project, which aimed at exploring the possibility of combining eye-tracking and keylogging data in order to create new research opportunities for studying translation processing, particularly with respect to how source-text comprehension and target-text production were coordinated. An additional applied goal of the *Eye-to-IT* project was to determine the feasibility of developing a translation tool based on online interpretation of a user's gaze behaviour across a computer screen. The Eye-to-IT project developed a tool known as Gaze-to-Word Mapping (GWM) that allowed the automatic identification of words on the basis of gaze fixations.

Methodological and technical issues, testing the reliability of the eye-tracker and pointing out the advantages of certain statistical techniques over others when engaged in process research were major methodological achievements in this phase. Such advances provided the structure for a new probabilistic methodological framework to deal with user activity data (Carl, 2009).

It is also relevant to note that substantial progress was made in this third phase with respect to testing the methodology employed in eye-tracking studies. Earlier studies had shown that there were certain problems with the accuracy of remote eye-tracking equipment. Studies emerging in this phase tested the accuracy of eye-tracking equipment for linear and non-linear reading tasks and the use of filters from different software in the same data sample (see Section 4.3.3.2).

Another important methodological development was the introduction of more robust statistical analyses. Besides the emphasis on ecological validity observed in the second phase, experiments in the third phase stressed the importance of employing statistical tests that could deal with naturalistic data (Balling, 2008). In this context, Balling (2008) discussed the advantages of multiple regression designs over the factorial designs traditionally used in many psycholinguistic experiments and highlighted the advantages of employing regression techniques when analysing language process data obtained by eye tracking and keystroke logging.

4.3.3.2 Objects of study and main results

Results arising from research carried out from the mid-2000s to 2010 present a wide variety of characteristics. Below, we highlight some relevant findings that we consider to be representative of the whole body of research carried out within this five-year period.

Impact of translation technology on processing effort

O'Brien (2006) investigated instances of cognitive effort when translators deal with different types of matches provided by translation memory systems and also tried to answer the question of whether eye-tracking data could be useful to investigate translators' interaction with computer-assisted tools. Her results suggest that the cognitive effort for exact matches in translation memory systems is much lower than for other match types.

Alves and Liparini Campos (2009) carried out a battery of experiments to investigate the way in which a translation memory system and time pressure affect the types of support used by professional translators. The translation processes of professional translators were analysed in terms of internal and external support used for orientation, drafting and revision of a number of texts that were translated into Brazilian Portuguese either from English or German. The text samples, language direction, subjects' experience as professional translators and their familiarization with the translation memory system were controlled variables. The findings illustrated the predominant role of internal support in all tasks. All translators consulted the internet, dictionaries and a spell checker but the experiments showed that they predominantly relied on their own internal knowledge to solve translation problems.

Dragsted, Gorm Hansen and Sørensen (2009) used speech recognition as a technological alternative to help translators perform tasks. They carried out an exploratory study of the processes and products of three expert translators who were to a greater or lesser extent familiar with speech recognition technology. The participants were given five tasks: a reading task, a reading-for-the-purpose-of-translation task, a sight translation task, a sight translation task with the use of speech recognition and a written translation task. Results showed that familiarity with speech technology is fundamental to the effective use of speech recognition as an alternative for translators.

Impact of eye tracking data in measurements of processing effort

To the best of our knowledge, O'Brien (2006) was the first study that used eye-tracking data in translation studies. O'Brien's pioneering study demonstrated that eye-tracking data, including pupil dilation measurements and gaze replays, in association with retrospective protocols, offered a very effective methodology for carrying out research on cognitive aspects of translation. For O'Brien, one of the most interesting aspects of using eye-tracking data for research in translation was the associations that could be established between cognitive effort and eye movements and, in particular, correlations between cognitive effort and pupil dilation.

Previous studies (Rayner, 1998) have shown that there were certain problems with the accuracy of remote eye-tracking equipment. It was not always possible to identify what words were fixated, which meant that it was not always possible to draw reliable conclusions about eye-movement behaviour and assumed cognitive processing. To meet that challenge, Jensen (2008) attempted to investigate the extent to which the eye-tracker and associated software could detect fixated words in various reading tasks ranging from normal linear reading to non-linear reading (such as the type employed when engaged in translation). Jensen's results showed that, contrary to expectations, the same degree of accuracy could be achieved in non-linear reading tasks as in linear reading tasks.

Alves, Pagano and Da Silva (2009) looked at the impact of filters from different eye-tracking software (Clear View and Tobii Studio) on the accuracy of eye-tracking data and showed that the use of filters from different software yielded different results in the same data sample.

Impact of task modality on the translation process: Reading for different purposes

Jakobsen and Jensen (2008) examined differences in reading for different purposes, namely reading for understanding, translating, sight translation and written translation. Their results indicated that, as measured in terms of fixation duration, translators allocate more cognitive effort to target text processing rather than to correlated instances in source texts. They also showed that there was a significant increase in cognitive effort as different reading modalities became more complex and, therefore, more demanding. Reading for a general understanding is less effortful than reading for translation. Sight translation is more effortful than reading for translation whereas reading and translating in parallel demand increasingly more cognitive effort. Jakobsen and Jensen suggested that there is some evidence, although preliminary, that target text processing requires more cognitive effort than source text processing.

Issues related to the comprehension/production interface

Dragsted and Hansen (2008) employed a combination of eye-tracking and keystroke logging technologies to explore how translators coordinate comprehension and production processes. Results obtained for the eye-key span and fixation duration from a small sample of eight translators indicated that difficult words were fixated longer and attracted attention long before they were translated.

Dragsted, Gorm Hansen and Sørensen (2009) undertook a preliminary analysis of the translations produced in the written and speech-recognition conditions in order to detect potential differences in the quality of the spoken and written output.

Denver (2009) included both product and process data from two groups of students and a group of professional translators in her analysis of translating logical-semantic relations across sentence boundaries.

Issues related to the process/product interface

Alves et al. (2010) used a corpus-linguistics orientation and drew on the results of the CroCo project (Neumann & Hansen-Schirra, 2012) to look into phenomena such as empty links (when there is no alignment between source and target language segments in translation) or crossing lines (when alignment between source and target language segments refer to dislocations within structures in the source and target texts). The authors compared process-driven data with product-driven data to show correlations between the translation process and the translation product with large variation depending on the types of textual input and conditions for translation task execution.

Consequences of textual complexity in the translation process

Jensen (2009) aimed to determine textual complexity in translation and investigated how texts of varying levels of complexity affect the gaze behaviour of professional translators and their translations. Using readability indexes, word frequency and non-literalness as indicators to measure the complexity of three different texts, Jensen suggested that readability indicators could be used to estimate the production effort during a translation process. Word frequency could imply that the less common a word is, the more effort is needed to translate it, whereas indicators of non-literalness (i.e. the presence of idioms, metaphors and metonyms) suggest that non-literal expressions are expected to involve a greater processing effort than literal expressions.

Faber and Hjort-Pedersen (2009) used concurrent introspection together with keylogging to study the complexity of cognitive processing in legal translation. They argued that legal texts are notoriously difficult and it is often necessary during the comprehension process to make explicit information that is only implicit in the source text. On the other hand, legal translators sometimes choose to omit elements in their translation, making implicit text that is explicit in the source. Faber and Hjort-Pedersen borrowed two concepts from relevance theory, namely *reference assignment* and *enrichment*, and offered some tentative results on the correlation between mental explicitation processes and resulting instances of linguistic explicitation or implicitation.

Denver (2009) also addressed the issue of inferencing in translation using a combination of think-aloud and keylogging to examine the complexity of translating logical-semantic relations across sentence boundaries. She drew on both the *explicitation hypothesis* and the *unique items hypothesis* to argue that the use of explicitations by means of unique itemswould be markedly lower than when the same connectors are used at the propositional level with alternative, disjunctive or conditional meaning.

Jensen, Sjørup and Balling (2009) also looked into translation complexity by conducting an eye-tracking experiment with the purpose of establishing whether segments requiring a change in the word order in the translation had an effect on participants' eye behaviour. Assessing translations from Danish (L1) into English (L2), Jensen, Sjørup and Balling showed that participants gazed significantly longer at segments for which the word order had to be reversed even though there was no significant word order effect on pupil dilation.

Directionality in the translation process

Pavlović and Jensen (2009) investigated directionality in translation by observing the performance of professional translators and final year translation students working in the English/Danish language pair. They employed three eye-movement indicators (total gaze time, fixation duration during source and target text processing, and pupil dilation) to measure cognitive effort and were able to show that, irrespective of directionality, target text processing requires more cognitive effort than source text processing. They were also able to partially confirm that, in both directions, translation students invested more cognitive effort in translation tasks than professional translators.

Time pressure and the translation process

Sharmin et al. (2008) analysed the eye movements of translation students who translated three different texts, an easier text and two difficult ones, under three different time conditions. Time pressure was found to affect the average duration of fixations on the source text, so that when less time was available, fixations were shorter. In terms of text difficulty, fixations were more frequent if the text was more complex, but not longer.

Alves and Liparini Campos (2009) also assessed time pressure in their experimental design and showed that time pressure appeared to reduce the number of revision pauses both in the drafting and revision phases. Time pressure also increased the need to rely on solutions offered by the translation memory systems and it did not have an impact on the types of support used.

Segmentation patterns: User activity data

Carl, Jakobsen, and Jensen (2008) proposed an approach based on a probabilistic framework of fixation modelling during reading in which fixations on textual objects were directly computed from the gaze sample points. Carl (2009) also suggested a strategy and a set of tools for cross-validating and triangulating process and product data. He introduced into translation process research the computational alignment of translation units, which refers to translation equivalences in the source and target texts. Once source and target texts have been fragmented into alignment units, keylogged and eye-tracking data could be mapped onto them. This new approach gave rise to what Carl called *user activity data*, namely "any kind of data which is consulted or generated by a translator during a translation session" (Carl, 2009, p. 101).

Alves and Vale (2009) revisited the concept of translation units to develop *Litterae*, an online tool designed to map keylogged data onto translation segments and proposed to characterize such segments as micro and macro translation units. A micro translation unit is defined as the flow of continuous target text production separated by pauses during translation that can be correlated to a source text segment that attracts the translator's focus of attention at a given moment. A macro translation unit, in turn, is defined as a collection of micro translation units that comprises all the interim text productions that follow the translator's focus on the same source text segment from the first tentative rendering to the final output that appears in the target text. Their distinction allowed a more detailed mapping of online target text production and offered a more refined alternative for a combined process/product account of translation task execution.

Building on Alves and Vale (2009), Alves et al. (2010) carried out an exploratory study in the language pairs English/German and English/Portuguese to map micro and macro translation units onto translation process data. They aimed at identifying standard alignments, empty links and crossing lines (Neumann & Hansen-Schirra, 2012) observed in corpora of translated texts with similar occurrences in translation process data. The methodology proposed by Alves and Vale (2009) to identify micro and macro translation units in the translation process was corroborated in terms of correlations between product and process-driven data in translation.

Creativity in translation

Bayer-Hohenwarter (2009) presented a new approach to measure creativity in translation and aimed at describing how such an elusive ability develops in students of translation as compared with professional translators. Bayer-Hohenwarter suggested that translational creativity can effectively be analysed by adopting the creative procedures of *abstraction*, *modification* and *concretization*, which represent cognitive shifts between source and target texts as opposed to mere reproduction. These procedures were tested on a sample of translations rendered by translation students and professional translators. Bayer-Hohenwarter's study found modest confirmation for the hypothesized lower creativity in first-year students as opposed to that of professional translators.

Bayer-Hohenwarter (2010) was an attempt to draw an assessment matrix to measure process and product creativity in translation. She suggested that creativity could be measured by using indicators of acceptability, flexibility and novelty and looked into the routine behaviour of 12 subjects (five professionals, three third-semester students and four first-semester students) by means of indicators of routine performance such as automaticity and short translation time and contrasted them with indicators of creative behaviour.

Metalinguistic awareness and metacognitive activity

Alves, Pagano and Da Silva (2009) pointed out that a fine-grained linguistic analysis of translation problems might also shed light onto relevant aspects of cognitive processing in translation. They claimed that such analyses required an account provided by a pertinent linguistic theory and advocated the need to analyse both product and process data, a plea that had already been made in the second phase of research. The innovative aspect in the third phase relates to the role of metacognitive activity assessed in conjunction with eye-tracking data. Alves, Pagano and Da Silva (2009) were able to show, through the combined analysis of retrospective verbal reports and eye movements, that the higher the level of translation expertise, the higher the metacognitive ability of their subjects.

Ehrensberger-Dow and Künzli (2010) delved into the issue of how one can access translators' metalinguistic awareness. They compared the quality of the data obtained by means of concurrent verbalization and cue-based retrospection of students translating into their L1 (German) or L2 (English) and focused on the impact of these methods on the translation process, the metalinguistic data and the target text itself. Their results suggest that think-aloud protocols are more revealing with respect to providing information about revision practices, while retrospection is a better means of obtaining explicit information on translators' use of resources and their reflections on strategies.

Muñoz (2009b) put forward a hypothesis that typographical errors may not be caused only by imperfect typing skills, keyboard size and the like, but also by shifts or lapses in attention. Muñoz also argued that attention drops may sometimes represent situations where cognitive resources have been reallocated to support other mental activities such as problem-solving.

Translation competence

Based on the results of an experiment specially designed to assess translation competence using a large sample of 59 subjects, PACTE (2008) presented results concerning knowledge of translation and the efficacy of the translation process while PACTE (2009) presented results on acceptability and decision-making. Both studies contribute to validating PACTE's translation competence model (PACTE, 2003).

Traits of expert performance in translation

Shreve (2006) is a theoretical paper that looks at expert performance in translation from the perspective of expertise studies (Ericsson, 2002). Shreve insists on the distinction between translation competence and expertise in translation from a theoretical point of view and indicates that this distinction should be assessed empirically, a discussion that had already been initiated by Jakobsen (2005) in the second phase of research on translation as a cognitive activity.

Drawing on a series of empirical studies they had previously carried out, Alves and Gonçalves (2007) developed an account of expertise in translation using the concepts of narrow-band and broadband translators that distinguish the two different profiles based on the translator's ability to assess higher levels of metacognitive activity and self-regulate cognitive processing when confronted with task complexity.

Translation competence acquisition

Göpferich's (2009) longitudinal study assessed the development of translation competence among a group of translation students investigated over a period of three years and compared their behaviour with the performance of professional translators. Translation processes were analysed using a wide range of methodologies, including think-aloud data, keylogging, screen recordings, webcam recordings,retrospective interviews and questionnaires.

Pavlović (2009) dealt with the use of a special type of verbal reporting, namely collaborative translation protocols (CTP), a procedure based on concurrent verbalization of a pair or group of people translating the same source text together, basing their decisions on mutual consensus. Pavlović worked with an experimental group of translation students and a control group of students. They all performed direct and indirect translation tasks. Pavlović also compared the process of translation students and professionals working into and out of their first language (Croatian) with respect to problems, solutions, resources and decision-making. She pinpointed the difficulties encountered by translation students and how they solve problems, thus offering novel insights into the acquisition of translation competence and thereby improving translator education.

4.3.3.3 Overview

Altogether, the studies carried out in this third phase can be directly related to substantial progress made in understanding the complexities entailed in research on cognitive aspects of translation. During this third phase of research, one notices a significant change of degree and kind in rigorous attempts to carry out more complex and better designed experiments. The number of objects of study increased, research designs became more robust, samples used in experiments became more representative of the performance of professional translators and the methodology used in experiments became more objective, reliable and prone to replication. Yet, there were shortcomings to be addressed. Jakobsen and Jensen (2008) insisted that a word of caution still seemed necessary since most studies still used relatively small samples of eye-tracking data. In general, the statistical analyses they provided were based on very small populations. As Jakobsen and Jensen (2008, p. 108) point out "with such small samples, any free variable can cause havoc in the data". They argued that future studies should thus use larger population samples to increase the statistical significance of their results. This is a trait that will emerge in the fourth phase of research.

All in all, the picture emerging from studies carried out in this third phase is more consistent and robust, revealing attempts from different research groups to work under similar principles (see Table 4.4).

4.3.4 Fourth phase: Focus on interdisciplinarity and convergence of tools

Starting in the early 2010s and spanning until the early 2020s, research grew exponentially and new aspects became relevant, including the increasing role of interdisciplinarity in research, issues related to human-machine interaction and the impact of computational linguistics and machine translation as alternatives to enhance the relationship between humans and machines in translation as well as a concern about neurophysiological aspects of translation as a cognitive activity.

4.3.4.1 Types of research

The fourth phase is marked by a variety of approaches concerning the choice of subjects, data collection procedures and methodological frameworks.

Subjects

The number of subjects in studies of the fourth phase still varied greatly. However, one notices a tendency to an increase in the number of subjects. PACTE, for instance, used 129 students as subjects in their experiment on translation competence acquisition.

Perhaps the most striking difference concerning subjects in the fourth phase of research consists in the possibility of using data from subjects from files stored in databases. Stored data allowed researchers to use subjects for different analyses as well as for control groups in new experiments. The CRITT Translation Process Research Database (henceforth CRITT TPR-DB), available at https://sites.google.com/site/centretranslationinnovat

TABLE 4.4 Third phase of the evolution of empirical-experimental research in cognitive aspects of translation

Third phase (mid-2000–2010)
Consolidation of a multi-methodological paradigm (triangulation) and introduction of eye tracking data

Characteristics
- Consolidation of the multi-methodological paradigm (triangulation)
- Introduction of eye-tracking data in translation process research
- Beginning of integration of data (keylogging + eye tracking) using the same time stamp
- Emergence of more robust designs
- Increasing the use of statistics to assess the significance of results

Objects of study
- Impact of translation technology on processing effort (O'Brien, 2006; Alves & Liparini Campos, 2009; Dragsted, Gorm Hansen & Sørensen, 2009)
- Impact of eye-tracking data in measurements of processing effort (O'Brien, 2006; Jensen, 2008; Alves, Pagano & Silva, 2009)
- Impact of task modality on the translation process: *reading for different purposes* (Jakobsen & Jensen 2008)
- Issues related to the comprehension/production interface (Dragsted & Hansen, 2008; Dragsted, Gorm Hansen & Sørensen, 2009; Denver, 2009)
- Issues related to the process/product interface (Alves et al., 2010)
- Consequences of textual complexity in the translation process: word frequency; word order; idioms, metaphors and metonymy; reference assignment; logical semantic relations (Jensen, 2009; Faber & Hjort-Pedersen, 2009; Denver, 2009; Jensen, Sjørup & Balling, 2009)
- Directionality in the translation process (Pavlović & Jensen, 2009)
- Time pressure and the translation process (Sharmin et al., 2008; Alves & Liparini Campos, 2009)
- Segmentation patterns; user activity data (Carl, Jakobsen, & Jensen, 2008; Alves & Vale, 2009; Carl, 2009; Alves et al., 2010)
- Creativity in translation (Bayer-Hohenwarter, 2009, 2010)
- Metalinguistic awareness and metacognitive activity (Alves, Pagano & Silva, 2009; Muñoz, 2009a, 2009b; Ehrensberger-Dow & Künzli, 2010)
- Translation competence (PACTE, 2008, 2009)
- Traits of expert performance in translation (Shreve, 2006; Alves & Gonçalves, 2007; PACTE, 2008, 2009; Göpferich, 2008, 2009)
- Translation competence acquisition (Göpferich, 2009; Pavlović, 2009)

ion/tpr-db, stores a huge amount of data gathered in different experiments designed and carried out by several researchers at disparate locations. It gives researchers access to a pool of keylogged and eye-tracking data involving different language pairs and a variety of subject profiles. The CRITT TPR-DB contains studies of translation, post-editing, revision, authoring and copying tasks, recorded with Translog II.

LETRA also has a similar database, called CORPRAT, available at http://letra.letras.ufmg.br/corprat. However, it only contains data from experiments carried out by the Brazilian research group. Data stored in repositories such as the CRITT TPR-DB and CORPRAT allows researchers to have access to standardized user activity data in order to replicate experiments or to use them in cross studies of different kinds.

Data collection procedures

Translog II and the TPR-DB offered new possibilities of data collection procedures and paved the way for standardizing analyses under a unified paradigm. While Translog II allows the simultaneous collection of keylogged and eye-tracking data, the TPR-DB contains tables with an array of features that can be easily processed by various visualization and analysis tools. Carl, Schaeffer and Bangalore (2016) described the structure of the CRITT TPR-DB and presented a selection of papers that drew on input from the CRITT TPR-DB.

As mentioned previously, the most striking change in data collection procedures in the fourth phase was related to the creation of repositories that can serve as a data pool for several studies. These repositories consolidate the multi-methodological paradigm of data triangulation with most researchers now collecting data using similar tools and sharing methodological guidelines that allow studies to be replicated and cross-validated.

It is also worth noting the development of interactive platforms that allow machine-translation output to be processed in real time and logged in for the purposes of empirical investigation. The CASMACAT workbench (http://www.casmacat.eu/) provides an interesting opportunity for investigating human and computer-assisted translation processes carried out by novice and advanced users and, thus, offers input and insights for the automatic modelling of translation and post-editing task execution.

Methodological approaches

As far as the convergence of tools and methodologies are concerned, the fourth phase of research shows new proposals for consolidating and standardizing research designs and methodological procedures. Methodologies developed in the previous phase become consolidated and three new yet incipient trends become relevant for research purposes, namely (1) a new approach to the interpretation of eye-tracking data; (2) the emerging role of human-computer interaction in translation; and (3) the use of neuroimaging techniques to map translation activity in the brain.

As far as the interpretation of eye-tracking data is concerned, *the eye-mind assumption* postulated in the third phase, is challenged by Von der Malsburg and Vasishth (2011). They argue that, if taken literally, this assumption is clearly false due to two facts. First, the cognitive processing of a given word can start even before the eyes fixate it for the first time (Rayner, 1998). Second, cognitive processing initiated at one given word can continue even after the eyes have moved on to fixate on another word (Rayner & Duffy, 1986). In principle, these two facts contradict the strict formulation of the *eye-mind assumption*. Von der Malsburg and Vasishth (2011) warn us, however, that if we were to assume that the *eye-mind assumption* was completely false, then we would be unable to interpret recordings of eye movements because fixation durations would have no straightforward relationship with processing difficulty. Clifton, Staub and Rayner (2007) presented a review of empirical results in sentence comprehension that showed that the interpretation of largely replicable findings is possible. Von der Malsburg and Vasishth argued that such evidence leaves us with an intermediate version of the *eye-mind assumption* in which fixation durations reflect processing difficulty but lags in processing and constraints arising from oculo-motor control (Rayner, 1998) have the potential to complicate the interpretation of the eye movement recordings. These conclusions have brought about more cautious interpretations of eye tracking data in research on translation as a cognitive activity and generated increased awareness among researchers about the methodological potential as well as the methodological shortcomings of analyses drawing on eye tracking data.

The emerging role of human-computer interaction in translation also has striking methodological implications for research. The CASMACAT workbench offered enhanced technological procedures to investigate human-computer interaction, particularly for post-editing tasks. It presented researchers with an interface that provided enriched information about translator types and translator styles and contributed to the design of a cognitive model of human-computer interaction for translation purposes. Interactive translation prediction and interactive editing seem to be promising features for the development of human-computer interaction in translation. Additionally, the CASMACAT workbench provides input to foster the conceptualization of adaptive translation models derived from supervised machine learning in interaction with human translators. Such an interface allows the system to update and adapt its models instantly based on the translation choices made by the user and, thus, increases the quality of human-computer interaction and, consequently, of machine-translation output.

The third methodological novelty in this fourth phase of research, still incipient in terms of empirical evidence, attempts to bring together standard methodological tools, such as eye tracking, in conjunction with neuroimaging techniques (García, 2019). The studies of Annoni, Lee-Jahnke and Sturm

(2012), Sturm (2016) as well as Szpak (2017), Alves, Szpak and Buchweitz (2019) and Szpak, Alves and Buchweitz (2021) have put forward research designs proposing the development of two studies in parallel, one with a behavioural focus drawing on eye-tracking data and another one using neuroimaging data from fMRI to account for neuro-physiological processes in translation. These studies are still in their infancy and one should wait and see to what extent they shall bear fruit.

4.3.4.2 Objects of study and main results[9]

Results arising from research carried out from the early-2010s to the early 2020s encompass a wide variety of characteristics. Below, we highlight some relevant findings that we consider to be representative of the whole body of research carried out over recent years.

Methodological and technological issues to improve research

Hvelplund (2014) discusses key methodological issues involved in the use and interpretation of eye-tracking data in translation process research. Hvelplund identifies four types of methodological issues that have implications for research: (1) preparatory steps that precede the actual recording of eye-tracking data; (2) a critical assessment of general assumptions linking eye movements to cognitive processing in the context of translation research; (3) accurate measurements of eye tracking data, including the relevance of measuring fixation count/duration and pupil size; and (4) a method to evaluate the quality of eye tracking data. Together, these four issues provide a robust method to evaluate the quality of eye-tracking data and validate their use in empirical-experimental studies.

Da Silva (2015) puts forward a robust methodological proposal to triangulate keylogging with retrospective protocols with the aim of increasing reliability. According to Da Silva (2015), the percentage of subjects' respective protocols that refers to a particular cognitive aspect could shed light on the development of translation expertise. Da Silva's proposal involves exploring the notions of representation (Chi, 2006a, 2006b) and segmentation (Dragsted, 2005) as two related variables that can be explored by using retrospective protocols and keylogging data, respectively. By singling out the performance traits of subjects who excel in specific aspects of translation task execution, Da Silva's approach offers a promising avenue for defining more precise indicators of metacognitive behaviour in relation to expert performance in translation.

Hvelplund (2017) looks at cognitive efficiency in translation and aims at investigating cognitive mechanisms that underlie the efficient allocation of cognitive resources during the translation process. He points to three indicators of efficient resource allocation that are considered as correlates of translation expertise, namely, flexibility, automaticity and processing flow. By comparing data from students and professional translators, Hvelplund shows that pupil-size analyses reveal lighter cognitive load on the professional translators' cognitive systems. He argues that, from a methodological perspective, measures of flexibility, automaticity and processing flow can be used as a testing ground for further explorations into cognitive translation efficiency.

Finally, in terms of methodological advances, the development and implementation of the CRITT TPR-DB (Carl, Schäffer & Bangalore, 2016) has offered researchers worldwide a platform to explore jointly translation process data. Recorded process data as well annotated information assembled in seven kinds of simple and compound process/product units provide empirical input to the investigation of human and computer-assisted translation processes and advanced user modelling.

Differences in cognitive processing between novice and professional translators

Hvelplund (2011) builds on the concept of attention units to investigate the allocation of cognitive resources in translation in different settings. He measures fixation duration and pupil dilation to gain insights into the allocation of cognitive effort in translation between professional and novice translators and finds out that cognitive effort was higher for the latter than for the former group during source-text and target-text processing. Hvelplund's results indicate that cognitive load is higher for student translators than for professional translators and that professional translators rely more on automatic processing than novice translators. The results also show that professional translators show a lower cognitive cost of switching attention between source-text processing and target-text processing and between their subprocesses (ST reading, source-text comprehension and target-text reformulation, target-text typing and target-text reading, respectively).

Carl and Kay (2011) reported that a production pause of more than 1000ms in text production is likely to represent a shift of attention towards another translation segment. They also analysed shifts of attention with respect to the segment being processed and segments that lie ahead. Their results show that professional translators are capable of typing a translation while already reading ahead in the source text (parallel mode), whereas novice translators often resort to a sequential mode and can only carry out one activity at the same time, thus alternating between actions related to reading and writing (alternating mode).

Segmentation patterns: Attention units, production units, alignment units, translation units and user activity data

Several concepts, such as attention units, production units, alignment units, translation units and user activity data are postulated or revisited and offered new insights to open new research avenues.

Hvelplund (2011) defined attention units as a time measurement unit of uninterrupted cognitive processing, as indicated by eye movement data (fixations and saccades) and typing events, relating them to the eye-mind and immediacy assumptions proposed by Just and Carpenter (1980).

Carl and Kay (2011) defined a production units as sequences of coherent typing activity. For them, a production unit boundary contains a pause of 1000ms or more without keyboard activity. Beyond this pause duration, Carl and Kay assume that coherent typing is interrupted, with a likely shift of attention towards a different text segment. Carl and Kay (2011) claim that, as a coherent temporal/textual segment, production units have a temporal beginning and a duration, and they may cover one or more insertion or deletion keystrokes, an editing procedure that contributes to building up one or more target text tokens.

Alves and Vale (2009, 2011) revisit the concept of translation unit and refer to recurring editing activities of the same word or segment as translations as micro units, defined as "the flow of continuous target text production separated by pauses during the translation process" (Alves & Vale, 2011, p. 107). Together, a set of micro translation units can make up a macro translation unit, defined as a collection of micro units "that comprises all the interim text productions that correspond to the translator's focus on the same ST segment" (Alves & Vale, 2011, p. 107).

Carl, Schäffer and Bangalore (2016) built on Alves and Vale (2011) to consider these units of continuous target text production as production units and created a mechanism in the CRITT TPR-DB to compute and classify such production units.

Altogether, attention units, production units, alignment units and translation units can be understood to make up what is considered to be UAD as proposed in Carl (2011) and assessed by Carl and Kay (2011) and Carl and Dragsted (2012). In experimental terms, these concepts allow the investigation of the translation process under a new perspective with the potential to map instances of local and distributed effort in the course of translation task execution.

Issues related to the process/product interface

Building on work that started in the third phase of empirical research on the process-product interface in translation, drawing particularly on Alves et al.

(2010), the Tricklet project[10] carried out empirical-experimental research that aimed at developing an empirically grounded model of translation by analysing observable features of translation task execution elicited by means of translation-process data and complemented with a corpus-linguistics-oriented account of the final product and its interim renditions.

The Tricklet project's long-term goal was to analyse a range of linguistic, cognitive, social and workflow-related factors that resulted in specific translation outcomes. The overall results indicate that automaticity in translation task execution can be more adequately characterized as one of the elements in a cline leading to the routinization of cognitive processing. From a corpus-linguistics perspective, the results suggest that the prestige of the languages involved in a translation task may have an impact on whether translations display linguistic similarities with the source language or not. The project also developed computational solutions for processing experimental data to designing, testing and analysing translation process-product data and yielded robust empirical evidence of multiple dimensions that probabilistically constrain translation in terms of linguistic, cognitive and social factors.

As far as linguistic factors are concerned, Serbina et al. (2017) investigated changes of word class during translation task execution and found that verb-to-noun shifts are the most frequent type of change in translations from English to German and they are often immediately implemented in the process, shifting complexity from the clause to the phrase level and showing that translation shifts generally require cognitive effort. Serbina et al. (2017) also showed that first solutions tend to be kept, suggesting that translators may decide on grammatical structures before starting to write a translation.

In terms of cognitive factors, Heilmann, Serbina and Neumann (2018) found no processing differences between grammatically complex and simple stimuli but identified differences in the number and length of eye fixations for reading and translation tasks. The results suggest that automaticity should be considered as a continuum reflected through different behavioural patterns. Heilmann, Serbina and Neumann (2018), for instance, showed that register awareness might play a role in the routinization of the entrenchment of constructions. Freiwald et al. (2020) looked at the role of automaticity by analysing different strategies for the translation of German post-finite subjects into English. The results suggest that salient known differences between English and German are quickly recognized and solved automatically, indicating a degree of routinization that, depending on the level of translation experience, may even become entrenched. Heilmann et al. (2021) showed that, although there are contrastive differences in inanimate subjects between English and German, the translation of inanimate subjects in agentive constructions is not contrastively challenging and does not show increased cognitive effort in terms of keystrokes or eye fixations.

Heilmann (2021) investigated syntactic complexity of the source text in structural terms with the help of an innovative corpus of unfolding texts elicited during various translation experiments and the respective final products. He found that complexity shifts depend on the level of text structure. For instance, complexity increases in the number of chunks per sentence even when complexity is reduced by a lower number of clauses.

Heilmann et al. (2022) also showed that the impact of frequency seems to affect the translation process only at word level. The results reinforce the assumption that automaticity is better seen as part of a cline rather than as a dichotomy between literal and functional translation types. These findings also reinforce the assumption that entrenchment does play a role in the unfolding of translation task execution. Building on Muñoz (2012), the members of the Tricklet project prefer to use a weaker concept of routinization since translational strategies, on the whole, encompass a wide range of cognitive activities at different degrees of automaticity.

In terms of social factors, Evert and Neumann (2017) focused on the translation property of "shining-through" proposed by Teich (2003), showing that normalization is observed in translations into German. Their results also showed that translators may prefer to use linguistic features that are typical of English not only in translations into English but even in translations into German, indicating that it may be related to the fact that a given language is considered to be more prestigious than another one.

Finally, in terms of computational and methodological results, Serbina et al. (2015) developed a computational solution for reassembling individual keystrokes into words for creating a keystroke-logged translation corpus. Couto-Vale, Neumann and Niemietz (2016) developed an automatic identifier of unfolding words, aligning writing and typing behaviour in relation to cognitive effort. This work allowed Heilmann and Neumann (2016) and Couto-Vale (2017) to show that indicators that build on individual typing speed and keyboard layouts are more accurate for analysing the process-product interface in translation. Heilmann, Serbina and Neumann (2018)tested different lengths of stimuli to determine a window placement that allowed efficient eye-tracking data processing without affecting translation behaviour. Heilmann et al. (2019)provided novel insights into the ecological validity of stimulus materials and found that single-sentence stimuli tend to be translated more literally while paragraph-sized sequences of three sentences are comparable to longer texts. This finding has important implications for the ecological validity of translation experiments.

Summing up, Neumann and Serbina (2021) point out that features of translations are probabilistic in nature and, as such, they are more specifically conditional rather than deterministic. Consequently, linguistic choices in translation task execution are probabilistic in nature and conditioned by linguistic, cognitive, social and workflow-related factors. These factors, they argue, interact in complex ways and need to be conceptualized in a cline as shown for processes of routinization.

Impact of post-editing tasks on cognitive processing

Enhanced dialogues with computational linguistics, computer science, studies of human-computer interaction and machine translation as well as (interactive) post-editing become increasingly frequent in this fourth phase of research.

In one of the first studies ever published about cognitive processes related to post-editing tasks, Carl et al. (2011) analysed the performance of seven translators. None of them had significant experience with post-editing. Their lack of experience notwithstanding, results indicated that translation times were lower for the post-editing tasks when compared with the amount of time dedicated to standard translation tasks. The authors also found that post-editing involved notable differences in gaze behaviour and showed that post-editing resulted in a modest improvement in quality as compared with manual translations.

More robust results were derived from analysis carried out within the CASMACAT project, an acronym for cognitive analyses and statistical methods for advanced computer-aided translation. The CASMACAT project was developed within the Seventh Framework Program of the European Union between 2012 and 2014 with a view to building a next generation translator's workbench to improve productivity, quality and work practices in the translation industry. The project proponents argued that conventional computer-assisted translation systems were not able to learn from user feedback, repeating errors when translating the same or similar sentences contained in a given document. One of the main goals of the CASMACAT project was to design and implement techniques to effectively deal with this problem. As the user types the translations, the interactive machine-translation system suggests alternative translations which a post-editor can interactively accept or overwrite, in contrast to the traditional post-editing condition where no aids are provided to the user while editing the raw MT output. A workbench was developed with a view to putting the proposal to the empirical test. Results of the validation of the CASMACAT workbench were published in a special volume edited by Carl, Schäffer and Bangalore (2016).

Bangalore et al. (2016) investigated the role of syntactic variation in translation and post-editing tasks and looked at whether co-activation of both source and target language has an influence on translators' behaviour. The authors compared five data sets comprising translation and post-editing data of the same English source texts translated into Danish, German,

Spanish and Hindi, together with data from monolingual copying of the same English source texts, to test whether syntactic variation had an effect on cognitive effort. The results point to positive correlations between syntactic variation and total reading time per source word, and between syntactic variation and production time during translation. However, no influence of syntactic variation on source text reading could be detected in the post-editing data, suggesting that the post-editors were primed by the machine-translation output, as syntactic variation also had no effect on behavioural measures during copying.

Carl, Gutermuth and Hansen-Schirra (2015) used keylogging, eye tracking and retrospective interviews to track back different (un)conscious cognitive processes and problems to compare post-editing strategies to translation strategies. The authors investigated efficiency, strategies and revision processes in professional translation settings in both tasks and showed that, although incipient, the quality of machine translation output was sufficient to serve as an informative translation for users without any knowledge of the source language but not for the purpose of professional translation.

Schmaltz et al. (2016) used keylogging and eye tracking to carry out an exploratory study on cohesive relations in text comprehension and production in the Chinese/Portuguese language pair, comparing the processes of translation and post-editing tasks. Their results point to an impact on target text reading and production which varies depending on the type of cohesive relations at play. In conjunction with Sekino (2016), who investigated translation and post-editing processes for the Japanese/Portuguese language pair, Schmaltz et al. is one of the few studies involving languages with logographic scripts.

Nitzke and Oster (2016) also compared translation and post-editing tasks. The authors introduced an annotation schema of translation process data and compared process data from general language and domain-specific English-to-German translation and post-editing tasks with respect to total production times, text production activity and text elimination activity (as measured by keystroke logging) and total reading times on source text and on target text (as measured by eye-tracking data). The results support the hypothesis that post-editing is faster than translation from scratch for both domain-specific and non-domain-specific text types.

Alves et al. (2016) analysed the impact of interactive machine translation on the post-editing of two specialized texts under certain experimental conditions and correlated the effort with 13 Translation Edit Rate (TER) scores. Using the CASMACAT workbench as a post-editing tool in conjunction with a Tobii T60 eye tracker, subjects with some training in post-editing were asked to carry out post-editing tasks under two different conditions: standard post-editing and interactive post-editing, namely a human-computer type of interaction in which the machine-translation (MT) system contains a learning algorithm that uses human input to improve the quality of MT output. Results showed that interactive post-editing had significantly lower fixation duration in comparison with traditional post-editing, thus indicating less processing effort and a facilitating effect for interactive post-editing.

Daems, Carl, Vandepitte, Hartsuiker and Macken (2016) looked at the effectiveness of consulting external resources during translation and post-editing of general text types. The authors presented a novel way to capture screen-recording data by combining the functionalities of CASMACAT with those of the keylogging software Inputlog. The authors used post-editing data to compare the types of resources used and the time spent on external resources. Although strategies for external resources seemed to be more successful for translating than for post-editing tasks, post-editing was faster than regular translation and the quality of the final product was comparable in both tasks.

Impact of translation technology on cognitive processing

As in the previous phase, research in this fourth phase examined the impact of translation memory systems and speech recognition tools on cognitive processing. Some studies focused on the impact of such tools on revision processes whereas others looked into instances of self-correction and revision of translations carried out by others.

Angelone (2011) had participants document their original translations using Integrated Problem and Decision Reporting (IPDR) logs, think-aloud protocols and screen recordings and used this documentation to assist self-revision. He found a significant improvement in error detection overall in six discrete error categories when participants used screen recordings to assist their self-revision.

Shreve, Angelone and Lacruz (2014) attempted to partially replicate Angelone's findings concerning the efficacy of screen recording in translation revision. However, instead of focusing on self-revision, the authors investigated revisions of output that had been translated by other translators, assuming that error analysis would show that screen recording could be a more efficacious process than IPDR logs. The results obtained by Shreve, Angelone and Lacruz (2014) partially confirmed Angelone's (2011) results with screen recordings being significantly more efficacious than IPDR logs in overall error mitigation.

Mees et al. (2013) compared data from oral translations carried out with the assistance of speech recognition software with data from sight translations and written translations. Keylogging was used to measure overall task times. The number and types of misrecognitions were identified by a phonetician when speech recognition was used. Their results suggest that oral translation with speech recognition could provide a potentially useful supplement to written translation or at least offer an alternative to it.

Mellinger and Shreve (2016) built on the assumption that computer-assisted translation is a means of increasing translator productivity and improving translation quality while decreasing the amount of effort required to complete certain translation and localization tasks. Drawing on Angelone's (2010) notion of *uncertainty management* in translation, Mellinger and Shreve explored how professional translators behave when presented with translations offered by a translation memory system. They argue that the editing behaviour observed during an experimental task highlighted a mismatch between the translation memory match and the participant's internal conception of what an optimal translation (a match) should be, resulting in a tendency to over-edit. Mellinger and Shreve's (2016) results confirm that professional translators are prone to over-edit proposed translation segments.

Impact of task modality on the translation process: Copying, reading for different purposes, paraphrasing

A series of experiments carried out helped shed light on the impact of task modality on the translation process through experiments that looked into differences between copying and translating, different reading tasks and paraphrasing.

Carl (2011) compared text copying and translation in terms of typing speed and the number of fixations on the source text. Although typing speed showed no significant differences, the distribution of eye fixations was different in copying and translating. Carl also showed that translators tend to look further ahead into the source text than copyists.

Carl and Dragsted (2012) proposed an extension of Tirkkonen-Condit's (2005) *monitor model* to investigate to what extent comprehension and production activities in translation may occur in parallel. According to Tirkkonen-Condit (2005, pp. 407–408), "literal translation is a default rendering procedure, which goes on until it is interrupted by a monitor that alerts about a problem in the outcome. The monitor's function is to trigger off conscious decision-making to solve the problem". The authors used eye-tracking data to investigate differences between copying and translation tasks and showed that, differently from copyists, translators often resort to sequential reading and writing patterns that seem to be triggered through target text production problems. Carl and Dragsted (2012) also found evidence of more processing effort during translation than during copying tasks. Finally, whereas parallel reading and writing activities appeared to be more prevalent during copying tasks, sequential reading/writing processes prevailed in translation tasks.

Alves, Pagano and Silva (2011) attempted to replicate Jakobsen and Jensen's (2008) study about the impact of reading modalities on translation task execution. Using the same source texts as input, the authors had participants read for understanding, translating and sight translation. Their results differed from those presented by Jakobsen and Jensen (2008), showing a lower count for the number and duration of eye fixations. What seemed to be a refutation of the previous studies, turned out to be explained by differences in subject profiling. Whereas Jakobsen and Jensen's subjects were familiar with sight translation tasks, participants in this study had little experience with sight translation.

Whyatt, Kajzer-Wietrzny and Stachowiak (2016) looked into processes of translating and paraphrasing and compared cognitive effort in both tasks. They argued that paraphrasing, as a form of intralingual translation, can be researched using the same tools and methodologies successfully applied to study translation processes. Their results are tentative due to the incipient nature of the exploratory study but nevertheless suggest that similarities between translating and paraphrasing outweigh the differences in terms of the cognitive effort they require.

Consequences of textual complexity in the translation process

As in the previous phase, textual complexity was a relevant object of study in the fourth phase of research. One finds a series of cognitive-oriented studies concerned with the translation of metonymy, metaphor, (de)metaphorization, subjectivity markers, types of *conceptual and procedural encodings* and syntactic variance as well as language variation and entropy in translation.

Vandepitte and Hartsuiker (2011) designed a controlled psycholinguistic experiment in which metonymic language use was tested as a student translation problem. They showed how the translation of a particular metonymic language construction that differs across languages constitutes a translation process problem, both among untrained and trained students.

In a further study, Vandepitte, Hartsuiker and van Assche (2015) investigated whether metonymic language constitutes a translation problem for translators. Their results showed that subjects took more time to translate metonymic than their non-metonymic constructions. Subjects also required more processing effort to produce a non-metonymic construction if the source text was metonymic than if it was non-metonymic.

Rydning and Lachaud (2011) also designed a psycholinguistic experiment to investigate the cognitive processing of metaphor comprehension. Building on Lakoff and Johnson (1980, 1999), Rydning and Lachaud inquired whether primary metaphors are easier to translate than complex metaphors. Their results seem to corroborate Lakoff and Johnson's assertions, showing greater conceptual clarity in the translations of primary metaphors than complex metaphors, and pointing out that translators are prone to face different cognitive challenges depending on the type of metaphor to be understood for translation purposes. Working on the English/Portuguese language pair, Koglin (2016) also found similar results which corroborate Rydning and Lachaud's (2011) assumptions.

Schäffner and Shuttleworth (2013) used keystroke logging, eye tracking and verbal data to explore metaphor comprehension and translation, looking into a wide range of different languages to assess both the number and generality of examples available for analysis and to explore the potential benefits of closer interaction between metaphor studies and translation process research.

Alves and Gonçalves (2013) drew on relevance theory (Sperber & Wilson, 1986/1995) to account for processing effort in translation to examine instances of *conceptual and procedural encodings*, namely the encoding of conceptual information prone to inferential interpretation and the encoding of procedural information that constrains inferential processing. Alves and Gonçalves used keylogged data to identify translation units related to issues of *conceptual and procedural encodings* that were annotated and analysed in terms of the linguistic complexity and relative distance of editing procedures. Their results suggest that processing effort in translation is greater in instances of *procedural* than *conceptual encodings*.

In a further study, Alves, Gonçalves and Szpak (2014) also built on the *conceptual/procedural* distinction postulated by relevance theory to investigate processing effort in translation task execution, drawing on eye-tracking data. The authors showed that there are statistically significant differences when fixation durations related to *conceptual and procedural encodings* are analysed in selected areas of interest, with instances related to *procedural encodings* requiring more processing effort to be translated.

Behrens (2016) looked at the task of structuring information in translation and compared three studies taking a syntactic, a functional and a conceptual approach respectively. She argued that structuring operations go beyond syntax and include a redistribution of content within phrases and clauses that is not captured by the syntactic measures alone. For Behrens (2016), syntactic operations as well as *procedural encoding* operations are likely involved in the cognitive task of structuring information in translation. However, *procedural encodings* seem to be a stronger indicator of higher processing effort than shallow syntactic annotation.

Bangalore et al. (2016) looked at syntactic variance and *priming* effects in translation. They suggested that priming is a default setting in translation, a special case of language use where source and target languages are constantly co-activated. For them, such priming effects are not restricted to lexical elements but also occur on the syntactic level. These hypotheses were tested with translation process data from the CRITT TPR-DB using Danish,

English and Spanish. Results showed that response times are shorter when syntactic structures are shared due to strongly co-activated network activity, which triggers a priming effect.

Schaeffer et al. (2016) looked at word translation entropy in an attempt to find evidence of early target language activation during reading for translation. Their study reported on the effect of word order differences between source and target texts. Results showed that the number of translation alternatives for a single word and differences between source and target text in terms of word order have an effect on very early and late eye movement measures. Their findings support the *literal translation hypothesis* (Tirkkonen-Condit, 2005).

Directionality in the translation process

Ferreira, Schwieter, Gottardo and Jones (2016) examined the translation performance of four professional translators with the aim of exploring the amount of cognitive effort involved in direct and inverse translation. Eye-tracking data was used to analyse the total time spent on each task as measured by fixation count, fixation time and average fixation time. Fixation count in two selected areas of interest (source and target texts) showed that more effort was directed towards the source text in both direct and inverse translation tasks. Although the number of subjects was quite small, the study indicated that while more traditional measures for translation difficulty (e.g. total time) point to more effort in the inverse translation task, eye-tracking data shows that differences in the effort applied in both directions must be carefully analysed, mostly regarding the areas of interest. The authors argue that language dominance for the translator can also potentially play a role in translation performance as determined by the direction of translation and should continue to be tested in future studies.

Ferreira, Gottardo and Schwieter (2018) analysed metacognitive aspects of decision-making processes in the performance of eight professional translators who translated related and unrelated texts from L2 (English) into L1 (Portuguese) and also from L1 into L2. Retrospective protocols were recorded and transcribed after each translation task and classified into two categories (problem identification and prospective solution) and each one was divided into several subcategories. The data analyses evaluated metacognitive activities during decision-making processes. Results suggest that noteworthy differences between direct and inverse translation can be assessed via retrospective protocols and that translator performance and behaviour might be closely related to the source text.

Whyatt (2019) analysed the impact of directionality including text type as an external factor. She investigated the performance of 26 professional translators in the language pair Polish (L1)/English (L2). The study also included assessments by proofreaders who were native speakers of the respective target languages. The analysis of corrections made by the proofreaders shows that different aspects of translation quality are affected by directionality.

Issues related to the impact of ideology and emotions on cognitive processing

Rojo and Ramos (2014) carried out an experiment designed to measure the influence that a translator's political stance may exert on the time needed to find a translation solution when working with ideologically loaded concepts. To that extent, positive and negative prompting conditions were designed to evaluate whether words and expressions that are contrary to the translator's ideology may slow down the translation process, making translators take longer to find an adequate translation. Their results showed that negative prompts yielded longer reaction times and differences in reaction times between two groups of translators with different ideological viewpoints provided evidence suggesting that translators' behaviour may be influenced by their ideological views.

Rojo and Ramos (2016) investigated the impact of emotions and certain probability traits on translation performance. Their study replicates Lehr's (2014) methodology but also explores the influence of personality factors on the induced emotional impact. Results point to a differential impact of emotions on different facets of translation performance, suggesting that different emotions may activate different processing styles. Their study corroborates evidence also found by Lehr (2014) and highlights the role of emotions in the cognitive study of translation.

Issues related to ergonomics and the technologized knowledge work

Ehrensberger-Dow (2014) looked at the challenges of translation process research in the workplace. Using empirical data collected in office spaces and home offices, Ehrensberger-Dow analysed ergonomic aspects that favour or hinder efficiency in terms of effort in translation task execution. She compared her results using ergonomic-related data with data collected under controlled conditions such as the classroom or the lab and pointed to problems deriving from lack of attention to ergonomic concerns. As a result of her observations, Ehrensberger-Dow (2014) introduced solutions for research designs that were developed for a workplace study and suggested that these solutions may prove useful in other types of investigations.

Ehrensberger-Dow and O'Brien (2015) investigated ergonomic issues at the professional translation workplace and looked into the impact of physical conditions on the translation process and more specifically on the ergonomics of the translation workplace, inquiring into the potential for cognitive friction. They identified indicators of cognitive friction that might be attributable to the cognitive, physical and organizational ergonomics of translators' workplaces and introduced the design of a follow-up international survey.

By using a multi-method approach, including screen and video recordings, interviews and ergonomic assessments, Ehrensberger-Dow and Hunziker Heeb (2016) investigated the ergonomics of a technologized translation workplace. The results of their case study indicated that apparently minor disturbances can have a major negative effect on the efficiency of the translation process and potentially impact job satisfaction and even health.

Issues related to cognitive effort in audio-visual translation (subtitling, dubbing)

By means of a study on innovative sub- and surtitling, which combined eye-tracking and retrospective on-screen questions intended to assess the reception capacity, Künzli and Ehrensberger-Dow (2011) tested the legitimacy of a subtitling norm that a subtitle should only be one or two lines long and have a maximum of 80 characters. Eye tracking measured fixation duration and percentage of gaze time in the various areas of interest, whereas the questionnaire assessed accuracy on questions about movie content and audience perception and satisfaction. Their results showed no significant differences in accuracy between the two conditions, indicating that viewers of subtitled audio-visual productions are able to process more information than established subtitling norms suggest.

Shreve, Lacruz and Angelone (2011) investigated sight translation in comparison with written translation to assess cognitive disfluency, namely disruptions that will manifest not just as errors or deficiencies in rendering but as speech disfluencies in the oral performance of sight translation tasks. The authors found significant information about cognitive phenomena associated with sight translation such as visual interference, as well as about cognitive processes associated with the solution of lexical, syntactic and strategic translation problems.

Hvelplund (2015) used eye-tracking data to investigate the process of dubbing translation. He used measures of fixation duration, visual transitions and pupil size to investigate the participants' distribution of attention in different areas of interest, the processing flow in dubbing translation and the cognitive effort during the translation process. Hvelplund (2015) found that the target text manuscript in dubbing translation attracts the majority of visual attention during dubbing translation. He also showed that fixations were considerably longer when the dubbing translators worked with the target text, an indication of more intense processing during target text processing. However, Hvelplund also found that mechanical operations related to typing and that working with the audio-visual material were more cognitively demanding than any other part of dubbing translation. To that extent, pupil sizes were considerably larger when translators worked with the film sequence.

Kruger et al. (2017) aimed to investigate the impact of subtitles on the processing of audio-visual texts by assessing levels of self-reported engagement with the text. They investigated the neural processing of subtitles using EEG and psychometrics to show that by establishing beta coherence between prefrontal and posterior regions, one can determine whether the effect of subtitles can be captured through EEG, and how this is related to psychological immersion. By means of two experiments, one using psychological immersion and the other using beta coherence indicators, the authors showed that adding the same language subtitles results in statistically significantly higher levels of immersion and enjoyment, lending support to a view that subtitles facilitate (dis)embodied cognition.

Neurophysiological aspects of translation

Annoni, Lee-Jahnke and Sturm (2012) looked into neurocognitive aspects of translation from a neuroimaging perspective and suggested that, since cognitive neurosciences have unravelled some brain mechanisms in the bilingualism domain, it is quite logical to transfer such knowledge to the field of translation as well as the learning of translation. This assumption had already been discussed from a theoretical perspective by Tymoczko (2012) and spearheaded by the pioneering work of Buchweitz (2006). Progress in neuroimaging studies now allows refined experimental designs that can deal with the challenges imposed by technical constraints and offers the possibility of parallel investigations of behavioural and neurophysiological aspects of translation task execution.

García (2014, 2015a, 2015b, 2019) reviewed psycholinguistic research on lexical translation equivalents to account for the development of successive models of interlingual processing and drew attention to the main findings and highlighted their methodological implications for empirical research within cognitive translatology.

In a complementary fashion, García, Mikulan and Ibáñez (2016) reviewed and discussed the implications of a neuroscientific approach to investigate the biological embeddedness of interlingual reformulation. They presented a relevant overview of research using neuroimaging (positron emission tomography, functional magnetic resonance imaging) and electromagnetic (electroencephalography, direct electrostimulation) techniques in cognitive neuroscience and focused on a discussion relevant for the purposes of reembbeding translation process research by offering a neuroscientific toolkit for cognitive translation studies.

More recently, Szpak (2017), Alves, Szpak and Buchweitz (2019) and Szpak, Alves and Buchweitz (2021) have put forward a proposal to investigate neurophysiological aspects of translation by means of a theoretical approach that combines presuppositions from theory of mind, as proposed by Premack and Woodruff (1978), and assumptions from relevance theory as proposed by Sperber and Wilson (1985/1995). According to Alves, Szpak and Buchweitz (2019) both theory of mind and relevance theory offer a potential theoretical path to correlate the results of neurophysiological studies using fMRI and behavioural studies drawing on eye-tracking data.

Translation competence and translation expertise

As empirical-experimental results related to characteristics of translation competence are published, one notices a difference in degree and kind in the overall performance of professional translators and in the performance of a selected group of participants that stand out among a pool of subjects with respect to their expertise, reflecting about indicators that could account for clear traits expert performance in translation – a feature that will be more clearly defined in the fourth phase of research.

A compilation of the PACTE group's research on translation competence was published in Hurtado Albir (2017). It includes the conceptual and methodological framework of the research, as well as the research design and its development (exploratory test, pilot studies), and the procedures of data collection and analysis. The results of PACTE's final experiment are presented with data from 35 translators and 24 foreign language teachers and a comparison of the performance of the two groups of participants. The results encompass analyses of the six dependent variables (knowledge of translation, translation project, identification and solution of translation problems, decision-making, efficacy of the translation process and use of instrumental resources) and the acceptability of the subjects' translations as a transversal indicator. The results also included the Dynamic Translation Index (obtained by crossing the results of the variables knowledge of translation and translation project), and a corpus analysis of the translations produced in the experiment. In addition, appendices with the data collection and analysis instruments and a glossary (with methodological terms and statistical terms) are included. The results highlight the traits that characterize translation competence. Finally, the perspectives for future empirical research in translation competence are outlined.

Besides, as part of PACTE's overall analysis of translation competence, the results of a study on the performance of top-ranked translators are presented (PACTE, 2017). In this study, the performance traits of nine subjects who stood out for the quality of their performances were analysed.

The performance indicators of this group of nine translators were higher than that of the group of 35 translators, highlighting that these top-ranked translators excelled in their translation expertise and reached the highest indicators among all the translators who participated in the PACTE's Group research sample on translation competence. The superior performance levels of this group of nine subjects are in line with the characteristics reported in the literature on expert performance (Ericsson et al., 2006).

Shreve, Angelone and Lacruz (2018) discussed whether expertise in translation and translation competence are conceptually related with respect to the psychological reality and the theoretical status of the two terms. They suggest that the notion of translation competence should be reconsidered and argue that the concept of expertise could be a robust and more enlightening substitute.

Aiming to offer a revised account of expertise in translation, Alves and Da Silva (2021) drew on the expert performance approach developed by Ericsson (2000) and applied to translation by Shreve (2002, 2006) to revisit the issue of expertise in translation. They also drew on Da Silva's (2021) metanalysis of expertise in translation. Alves and Da Silva (2021) took into consideration the current debates over translation as an embedded, extended, emergent, embodied and affective activity that has challenged the status quo of the EPA either because of its primary focus on accounting for expertise solely under laboratory conditions (Muñoz, 2014, 2017) or because of the need of epistemological criticisms related to the notion of expertise (Marín García, 2017, 2019). To take the discussion a step further, Alves and Da Silva (2021) propose to reconcile the expert performance approach with a sociologically oriented approach, namely the interactional expertise approach, that builds on the notions of language and socialization as important aspects of expertise (Collins & Evans, 2007) and propose to approach translation as a skill to focus on absolute expertise (Alves & Da Silva, 2022). The resulting framework is expected to provide cognitive translation studies with the necessary basis to investigate translation under laboratory conditions and real-life situations. It is also expected to advance our understanding of expertise by grounding it on an epistemological basis, which is expected to be both cognitive translation studies consistent and inter/transdisciplinary, that is, capable of working with and providing feedback to other disciplines also concerned with expertise.

Translation competence acquisition

Building on research on translation competence developed in the second and third phases, the fourth phase in research of translation as a cognitive activity saw a series of studies examining the acquisition of translation competence from an empirical-experimental perspective.

Massana-Roselló (2016) provided an overview of previously carried out research of translation competence acquisition. In her review of the literature, she listed a series of works published from 2010 onwards.

However, if we consider empirical-experimental results that appeared during the fourth phase of research in translation competence acquisition, the most conclusive evidence comes from work carried out by PACTE. The study consisted of an experiment involving 129 participants and used a methodological design that simulated a longitudinal study with simultaneous measurements from five groups, namely first, second, third and fourth-year translation students and a group of recent graduates. The experiment was conducted in November 2011, when the first-year subjects had just begun their degree course. The graduates had completed their studies in June 2011. The results produced by the translation students were compared with those obtained in the translation competence experiment, carried out by the PACTE group in 2005/2006 with 35 professional translators. The results were published in PACTE (2014, 2015, 2019a, 2020) and Kuznik and Olalla-Soler (2018).

PACTE (2014) presented the first results concerning the acquisition of declarative knowledge about translation. A questionnaire with 27 items was used to obtain data about subjects' knowledge of translation and related concepts. Indicators used included a "dynamic index" and a "coefficient of coherence". The dynamic index showed whether a subject's implicit knowledge about how translation works was more dynamic or more static, whereas the coherence coefficient pointed to the subject's vision of different aspects of translation was coherent.

PACTE (2015) presented the results related to knowledge of translation and the translation project. The former is a type of declarative knowledge while the latter is related to procedural knowledge. These two indicators are related to the acquisition of declarative and procedural knowledge in translation competence.

Kuznik and Olalla-Soler (2018) presented results about the acquisition of the instrumental subcompetence and analysed five indicators related to L2/L1 and L1/L2 translation processes. These indicators consisted of the number of resources used, the overall time taken on searches, the time taken on searches at each stage and the number and variety of searches. These indicators were then correlated with the quality of the final product of the translation process: translation acceptability.

PACTE (2019a) presented the results for the variable "efficacy of the translation process". This is one of the variables that provides information about the acquisition of the strategic subcompetence. Translation process efficacy is based on an optimal relationship between solution acceptability and time, i.e. achieving maximum acceptability in minimum time.

PACTE (2020) presented the results of all the study variables. These variables consisted of knowledge of translation, translation project, identification and solution of translation problems, decision-making, efficacy of the translation process and use of instrumental resources. Besides describing the conceptual and methodological framework as well as the measurements used, PACTE also used translation acceptability as a transversal indicator with results that were compared with those of most of the other indicators. In short, PACTE (2020) highlighted the defining features of translation competence acquisition and also included six online appendices containing the hypotheses, the main instruments used in the project, the statistical test results and a glossary of key terms from the research.

Translation competence levelling

PACTE (2018, 2019b; Hurtado Albir & Rodríguez-Inés, 2022a) reported on the NACT project to establish competence levels in the acquisition of translation competence in written translation. The NACT project was a continuation of the empirical-experimental investigations of the PACTE group about translation competence and translation competence acquisition.

Further, the NACT project was continued in two other related research projects, namely the EFFORT and EACT projects. The EFFORT project attempted to revise the description of levels for the non-specialist translator (translation levels A and B) proposed in the NACT project (Second NACT Proposal) and to design a methodological guide for using the framework. The EACT project aimed at establishing assessment procedures for each level of translation competence in the framework of undergraduate translation training in Spain.

4.3.4.3 Overview

Altogether, the studies carried out in this fourth phase showed that research on cognitive aspects of translation has come of age. During this fourth phase of research, one notices that the number of objects of study increased significantly and encompassed issues related to ergonomics and emotions that were not present in the previous phases. One also notices a greater concern with an interdisciplinarity approach, not only borrowing from but also lending to neighbouring disciplines. The interface with computational linguistics, machine translation and human-computer interaction gained prominence in terms of interdisciplinarity interest. Statistical analyses were now based on larger populations (see Table 4.5).

Engagement in interdisciplinarity

Around 2015, a series of collected volumes began to appear, highlighting the need to engage in an interdisciplinary dialogue with neighbouring disciplines to strengthen research in translation and cognition. We understand

TABLE 4.5 Fourth phase of the evolution of empirical-experimental research in cognitive aspects of translation

Fourth phase (early-2010s to early-2020s) *Focus on interdisciplinarity and convergence of tools*
Characteristics • Focus on interdisciplinary approaches to translation as a cognitive activity • Stronger interface with translation technology • Convergence of tools and methodological procedures among members of the research community • Enhanced dialogue with computational linguistics, computer science, studies of human-computer interaction (HCI), machine translation (MT) and (interactive) post-editing • Increase in the number of objects of study • Increase in the number of replications of previous studies • Increase in the number of publications **Objects of study** • Methodological and technological issues to improve research (Hvelplund, 2014, 2017; Da Silva, 2015; Carl, Schäffer, & Bangalore, 2016) • Differences in cognitive processing between novice and professional translators (Carl & Kay, 2011; Hvelplund, 2011) • Attention units, production units, alignment units, translation units and user activity data (Alves & Vale, 2009, 2011; Hvelplund, 2011; Carl & Kay, 2011; Carl, 2011; Carl & Dragsted, 2012; Carl, Schäffer, & Bangalore, 2016) • Issues related to the process/product interface (Serbina, 2015; Serbina et al., 2017; Evert & Neumann, 2017; Heilmann Serbina & Neumann, 2018; Freiwald et al., 2020; Neumann, 2020; Heilmann et al., 2021, 2022) • Impact of post-editing tasks on cognitive processing (Carl et al., 2011; Carl, Gutermuth, & Hansen-Schirra, 2015; Alves et al., 2016; Bangalore et al., 2016; Daems et al., 2016; Nitzke & Oster, 2016; Schmaltz et al., 2016; Sekino, 2016) • Impact of translation technology on cognitive processing (Angelone, 2010, 2011; Mees et al., 2013; Shreve, Angelone, & Lacruz, 2014; Mellinger & Shreve, 2016) • Impact of task modality on the translation process: copying, reading for different purposes, paraphrasing (Carl, 2011; Alves, Pagano, & Silva, 2011; Carl & Dragsted, 2012; Whyatt, Kajzer-Wietrzny, & Stachowiak, 2016) • Consequences of textual complexity in the translation process: metonymy, metaphor, (de)metaphorization, subjectivity markers, types of conceptual and procedural encodings, syntactic variance, language variation and entropy (Rydning & Lachaud, 2011; Vandepitte & Hartsuiker, 2011; Schäffner & Shuttleworth, 2013; Alves & Gonçalves, 2013; Alves, Gonçalves & Szpak, 2014; Vandepitte, Hartsuiker, & van Assche, 2015; Behrens, 2016, Koglin, 2016; Schaeffer et al., 2016) • Directionality in the translation process (Ferreira et al., 2016; Ferreira, Gottardo, & Schwieter, 2018; Whyatt, 2019) • Issues related to the impact of ideology and emotions on cognitive processing (Lehr, 2014, 2021; Rojo & Ramos, 2014, 2016)

(Continued)

TABLE 4.5 (Continued) Fourth phase of the evolution of empirical-experimental research in cognitive aspects of translation

- Issues related to ergonomics and the technologized knowledge work (Ehrensberger-Dow, 2014; Ehrensberger-Dow & O'Brien, 2015; Ehrensberger-Dow & Hunziker Heeb, 2016; Ehrensberger-Dow, 2021; Lacruz & Jääskeläinen, 2018; O'Brien, 2013b, 2021)
- Issues related to cognitive effort in audio-visual translation (subtitling, dubbing) and in sight translation (Künzli and Ehrensberger-Dow, 2011; Shreve, Lacruz, & Angelone, 2011; Hvelplund, 2015; Kruger et al., 2017)
- Neurophysiological aspects of translation (Tymoczko, 2012; Annoni, Lee-Jahnke, & Sturm, 2012; García, 2015a, 2015b; García, Mikulan, & Ibáñez, 2016; García & Muñoz, 2021; Sturm, 2016; Szpak, 2017; Alves, Szpak, & Buchweitz, 2019; Szpak, Alves, & Buchweitz, 2021)
- Translation competence (PACTE, 2011a, 2011b; Hurtado Albir, 2017)
- Traits of expert performance in translation (Alves and Gonçalves, 2007; PACTE, 2017; Shreve, Angelone, & Lacruz, 2018; Da Silva, 2021; Alves & Da Silva, 2021, 2022)
- Translation competence acquisition (PACTE, 2014, 2015, 2019a, 2020)
- Translation competence levelling (PACTE, 2018, 2019b; Hurtado Albir & Rodriguez-Inés, 2022a, 2022b)

that this new trend was spearheaded by O'Brien (2013b) when she reminded us that cognitive-oriented studies of translation should not only borrow but also try to lend to other disciplines.

O'Brien, Ehrensberger-Dow and Göpferich (2013/2015) was perhaps a first special issue explicitly dedicated to enhancing interdisciplinary exchanges in translation process research. This interdisciplinary dialogue was fostered by ensuing publications. Ehrensberger-Dow, Englund Dimitrova, Hubscher-Davidson and Norberg (2013/2015) addressed translation as an act and an event and included the social situation in the study of translation as a cognitive activity. Ferreira and Schwieter (2015) offered contributions discussing cognitive aspects of translation at the interface with psycholinguistics and cognitive science while Alves, Hurtado Albir and Lacruz (2015) contained contributions interfacing with linguistics, psycholinguistics and ergonomics.

Muñoz (2016) looked at new angles in the relationship between translation and cognition and aimed at re-situating the complex interaction between translation, cognition and the environment in which it is embedded. Ehrensberger-Dow and Englund-Dimitrova (2016/2018) explored the dynamics of the interface between the cognitive and situational levels of translation as a cognitive activity.

Jakobsen and Mesa-Lao (2017) focused on the developments of cognitive-oriented research of translation, scrutinizing the relationship between cognition, computing and technology. Schwieter and Ferreira (2017) showed an overarching account of translation and cognition. Li, Lei and He (2019) covered a myriad of different approaches and disparate research tools to explore theoretical, methodological issues and pedagogical implications at the interface between translation and cognition.

Improvement in methodologies

Balling and Hvelplund (2015) outlined an approach to good practices in quantitative research, including the formulation of research questions, data treatment and statistics analyses and focused on the nature of the variables involved, both in terms of their scale and their role in the design. The concerns raised by Balling and Hvelplund (2015) seem to be shared by most researchers who carried out investigations in this fourth phase. Robust evidence about local and distributed effort in translation and post-editing, including temporal, technical and cognitive effort, is presented together with novel research at the interface between behavioural and neurophysiological studies, between machine translation and human-computer interaction and between metacognitive activity and expert performance in translation. Research on translation competence and translation competence acquisition also showed conclusive evidence.

Carl, Bangalore and Schaeffer (2016) provided a comprehensive introduction to the Translation Process Research Database (TPR-DB) compiled by CRITT, focusing on usability issues and details of implementing interactive machine translation, discussing the use of external resources and addressing the cognitive and statistical modelling of human translation processes.

Hansen-Schirra, Czulo and Hofmann (2017) approached the empirical modelling of translation and interpreting, addressing multi-method as well as product- and process-based perspectives to gain insights into model and theory building.

Beginning of neurophysiological-oriented research

Although the investigation of neurophysiological aspects of translation is still in its infancy, there seems to be an enormous potential for this new research strand. Until now, research of translation as a cognitive activity has primarily used observational or behavioural data in experiments. Neuroimaging techniques can offer the field the opportunity to look at translation performance directly in the human brain and, thus, answer questions that researchers were unable to tackle.

All in all, the picture emerging from studies carried out in this fourth phase is even more consistent and robust than in the three previous phases, pointing to the consolidation of research on translation as a cognitive activity.

4.3.5 *Fifth phase: Enhanced focus on interdisciplinarity and on human-computer interaction*

Already in the fourth phase, some authors hinted that the time was ripe for a new phase in the evolution of research in cognitive aspects of translation. We consider that around the early-2020s a new fifth phase started. This fifth phase is still incipient to allow for a detailed description. Here we present an overview of some particular aspects, which, we believe, pave the way for a fifth phase in the evolution of research. Besides a large number of research articles, a series of collected volumes at the interface between translation and cognition have also appeared in recent years, highlighting the growth of this field of study. In this chapter, we present some of them to discuss future avenues for the study of translation as a cognitive activity (see Table 4.6).

Interaction with language industry studies

Angelone, Ehrensberger-Dow and Massey (2020) is a collected volume that provides a comprehensive overview of key issues at the interface between the

TABLE 4.6 Fifth phase of the evolution of empirical-experimental research in cognitive aspects of translation

Fifth phase (early-2020s to present date) *Focus on enhanced interdisciplinarity and on human-computer interaction*
Characteristics • Enhanced interdisciplinarity • Grounding of paradigmatic approaches • Focus on technological developments that impact human-computer interaction • Stronger interface with translation technologies and artificial intelligence • Increase in the number of collected volumes **Objects of study** • Interdisciplinary accounts of translation and cognition (Alves & Jakobsen, 2021; Muñoz Martín, Sun & Li, 2021; Halverson & Marín García, 2022) • Developments in the empirical modelling of the translation process (Carl, 2021) • Impact of computational modelling on theory building (Carl, 2023) • Impact of augmented translation on human behaviour (O'Brien, 2023) • Advances in human-machine communication (Lacruz, 2023) • Impact of artificial intelligence on translation education (Cui, Li, & Zhuang, forthcoming) • Characteristics of mediated interlingual communication (Muñoz & Halverson, 2021) • Interface with language industry studies (Angelone, Ehrensberger-Dow & Massey, 2020) • Interface with bilingualism studies (Ferreira & Schwieter, 2023)

language industry and translation, interpreting, machine translation, editing, terminology management, technology and accessibility. Although the volume does not address explicitly the translation and cognition interface, it does point to the cognitive implications entailed in the relationship between cognitive-oriented studies of translation and language industry studies. Shreve (2020) is particularly relevant in that respect as he discusses professional translator development from an expertise perspective.

Interdisciplinarity in cognitive translation studies

Alves and Jakobsen (2021) have edited a handbook of translation and cognition that provides a comprehensive, state-of-the-art overview of how translation and cognition relate to each other. With a strong focus on interdisciplinarity, the volume addresses epistemological and theoretical aspects of the translation and cognition interdisciplinary interface, venturing into an emergent dialogue with areas such as neuroscience, artificial intelligence, cognitive ergonomics and human-computer interaction and discussing several types of cognitive processing, including cognitive aspect of translation related to effort, attention, emotion, creativity, information theory, risk management, expert performance and situated, embodied, distributed, embedded and extended aspects of the translation and cognition interface.

Carl (2021) presented a collection of interdisciplinary contributions aimed at furthering the development of empirical modelling of the translation process. With a focus on empirical research, the volume attempts to bridge the gap between translation process research and machine translation research and to investigate and quantify the relationship between translation quality and translation effort in from-scratch translation, machine translation post-editing and computer-assisted audio-visual translation. To that extent, it discusses, among other relevant topics, translation technology, quality and effort, translation and entropy, translation segmentation and translation difficulty, translation process research and post-cognitivism paradigms.

Muñoz and Halverson (2021) discussed cognitive approaches to translation in the light of multilingual mediated communication. Relevant issues included the increasing interaction between cognitive-related aspects of translation and interpreting research, the emergence of neuroscientific studies of translation, the role of emotion at the interface with cognitive aspects of translation and the impact of cognitive aptitudes on translation performance. The volume also explores the interface with neighbouring research areas such as bilingualism, reading and cognitive psychology, and presents a variety of theoretical frameworks and constructs to support the further advances in empirical research and theoretical development.

Muñoz, Sun and Li (2021) presented empirical advances in the study of translation and cognition, proposing a new analytical framework for studying keylogged translation processes, a framework that reconciles a sociological and a psychological approach for studying expertise in translation, and a pedagogical model of translation competence. The volume expands the investigation of cognitive processes by considering the role of emotional factors and reviews and develops the effort models of interpreting as a didactic construct. The empirical studies in this book revolve around cognitive load and effort; they explore the influences of text factors (e.g. metaphors, complex lexical items, directionality) while considering translator factors and evaluate the user experience of computer-aided translation tools.

Halverson and Marín García (2022) is a volume that reflects on epistemological challenges and developments that impact the study of translation as a cognitive activity. It encourages the further development of the field by grounding new theories, stances and best practices, and also by pushing against disciplinary boundaries and structures while addressing challenging, converting and pluralist epistemologies. Arguing that after decades of empirical study and methodological innovation, the study of translation and cognition is ready for critique and debate towards convergence and difference, the volume takes stock of how different theories of cognition are used to address concepts and constructs such as expertise and process and questions issues related to methodology in terms of their underlying philosophical assumptions and implications.

Translation and cognition vis-à-vis human-computer interaction

Lacruz (2023) scrutinized the ever-increasing interaction between human and artificial intelligence with respect to the impact it has on translation as a cognitive activity. As translation faces a radical transition with the impact of recent technological developments in the area of artificial intelligence and extraordinary advances in neural machine translation, the volume looks at how aspects of performance, expertise, complexity, productivity, efficiency and sustainability, among other aspects, have changed as the result of technologies that have radically changed the way human translators work.

Translation and bilingualism

Ferreira and Schwieter (2023) edited a handbook at the interface between bilingualism, translation and cognition. They look at translation and interpreting as two special subtypes of bilingual communication to establish a dialogue with the field of bilingualism. It addresses the interface between translation, interpreting and bilingualism from a cognitive perspective and discusses theories and methods that can bridge the gap between them. It then looks into neurocognitive aspects of translation, interpreting and bilingual performance and differences in their architecture, including the role of working memory, interference control and emotions, among other features. From a more applied perspective, it also discusses how to train bilinguals to become translators and interpreters.

Emerging trends

Apart from the collected volumes mentioned above, it is worth singling out individual publications that point to new trends in the evolution of research in cognitive aspects of translation.

O'Brien (2023) addressed the emergence of human-centred augmented translation. She considered various definitions of augmentation from an augmented cognition standpoint and examined definitions focusing on problem-solving, interdisciplinary field theories and cognition supported by recent technological developments in artificial intelligence. O'Brien drew on the notions of antagonistic dualisms and human-centred artificial intelligence (HCAI) and reflected on the likely consequences if envisaged prospects for augmented cognition are materialized. She also considered the mechanisms and technical and ethical challenges of achieving augmented translation to its fullest extent and suggested that HCAI should focus on intelligence amplification rather than on the replacement of human ability, arguing in favour of human empowerment in the development of HCAI.

Carl (2023) proposed an extension of the monitor model to incorporate aspects of relevance theory to adopt the free energy principle as a generative model to elucidate translational behaviour. He mapped these concepts on the translation process and used behavioural data to illustrate his point, based on the notion of translation units that exhibit observable traces of the translator's epistemic and pragmatic engagement with their translation environment that can be measured in terms of translation effort and effects. Sequences of translation units cluster into translation states (steady state, orientation and hesitation). By drawing on active inference, sequences of translation states combine into translation policies that reduce expected free energy, Carl attempted to show how the notion of free energy is compatible with the concept of *relevance*, as developed in relevance theory, and how essential concepts of the monitor model and relevance theory can be formalized as deep temporal generative models that can be interpreted under a representationalist view, but also support a non-representationalist account.

Finally, a forthcoming issue of *Translation and Interpreter Training* (ITT), to be edited by Feng Cui, Defeng Li and Chiyuan Zhuang, will focus on the transformation of translation education through artificial intelligence. The special issue will explore the impact of technological developments in AI on translation education at the university level, attempting to investigate new goals and objectives for translation education, the adaptation of translation trainers/educators and how students can profit from AI-assisted translation technology to help them improve the quality and efficiency of their performances. This special issue of ITT will also address how translation trainers/educators can use AI to design innovative translation teaching methods and improve assessment and testing procedures. It will also discuss ethical and identity issues resulting from the advent of these emerging technological innovations in artificial intelligence.

4.3.6 Challenges ahead

As we have seen throughout Section 4.3, there has been an impressive evolution in research on cognitive-related aspects of translation over the past five decades. From the sole use of think-aloud protocols in the 1980s to emerging trends in artificial intelligence at present, the study of translation as a cognitive activity is now ready to embrace new challenges and take new directions. Chapter 5 will summarize the most relevant aspects addressed in the book and reflect on an outlook for the future.

Notes

1 In what follows, we draw explicitly on Neunzig (2011) and use his own words to describe the criteria for accuracy in empirical research.
2 Neunzig (2011) refers to this concept as internal validity.
3 Neunzig (2011) refers to this concept as reliability.
4 To compile the information presented in Section 4.2, we have drawn extensively on the contents provided by the TREC website in the section related to Resources.
5 *Proxy* was a user monitoring program that allowed the remote control of workstations and users connected to the same network. In 2006, *Proxy* was discontinued.
6 See Jakobsen (2006) for a detailed account of the development of research using a multi-methodological approach.
7 Currently, former PETRA members and new affiliates are grouped together at the MC2 Lab (https://mc2-lab.net/)
8 CRITT has been relocated and is now situated at Kent State University in the United States.
9 In this chapter, we have reviewed studies published until the early 2020s and tried to account for their main results. As research unfolds rapidly, we are aware of the fact that our account may not be as accurate and complete as desired and apologize for any shortcomings that may appear in our account.
10 The Tricklet project (Translation Research in Corpora, Keystroke Logging and Eye-Tracking), based on RWTH-Aachen in Germany, carried out research on the process-product interface in translation from 2014 to 2023.

References

Alves, F. (1995). *Zwischen Schweigen und Sprechen: Wie bildet sich eine transkulturelle Brücke?: Eine psycholinguistisch orientierte Untersuchung von Übersetzungsvorgängen zwischen portugiesischen und brasilianischen* Übersetzern. Hamburg: Dr. Kovac.

Alves, F. (2001). A triangulação como opção metodológica em pesquisas empírico-experimentais em tradução. In A. Pagano (Ed.), *Metodologias de pesquisa em tradução* (pp. 69–93). Belo Horizonte: Faculdade de Letras.

Alves, F. (Ed.). (2003). *Triangulating translation: Perspectives in process oriented research.* Amsterdam: John Benjamins.

Alves, F. (2005). Ritmo cognitivo, metarreflexão e experiência: Parâmetros de análise processual no desempenho de tradutores novatos e experientes. In A. Pagano, C. Magalhães, & F. Alves (Eds.), *Competência em tradução: Cognição e discurso* (pp. 90–122). Belo Horizonte: Editora UFMG.

Alves, F., & Da Silva, I.A.L. (2021). Bridging paradigms to approach expertise in cognitive translation studies. In R. Muñoz Martín, S. San, & D. Li (Eds.), *Advances in cognitive translation studies* (pp. 89–108). Singapore: Springer Nature.

Alves, F., & Da Silva, I.A.L. (2022). Looking back to move forward: Towards a situated, distributed, and extended account of expertise. In S.L. Halverson & A. Marín García (Eds.), *Contesting epistemologies in cognitive translation and interpreting studies* (pp. 153–175). London: Routledge.

Alves, F., & Gonçalves J.L. (2003). A relevance theory approach to the investigation of inferential processes in translation. In F. Alves (Ed.), *Triangulating translation: Perspectives in process oriented research* (pp. 11–34). Amsterdam: John Benjamins.

Alves, F., & Gonçalves, J.L. (2007). Modelling translator's competence: relevance and expertise under scrutiny. In Y. Gambier, M. Shlesinger, & R. Stolze (Eds.), *Translation studies: Doubts and directions. Selected papers from the IV congress of the European society for translation studies* (pp. 41–55).Amsterdam:John Benjamins.

Alves, F., & Gonçalves, J.L. (2013). Investigating the conceptual/procedural distinction in translation: A relevance-theoretic analysis of micro and macro translation units. *Target*, *25*(1), 107–124.

Alves, F., Gonçalves, J.L., & Szpak, K. (2014). Some thoughts about the conceptual-procedural distinction in translation: A key-logging and eye-tracking study of processing effort. *MonTi*, *1*, 151–175.

Alves, F., Hurtado Albir, A., & Lacruz, I. (Eds.). (2015). Translation as a cognitive activity. *Translation Spaces*, *4*(1). Special Issue.

Alves, F., & Jakobsen, A.L. (Eds.). (2021). *The Routledge handbook of translation and cognition.* London: Routledge.

Alves, F., Koglin, A., Mesa-Lao, B., García Martínez, M., Fonseca, N.B.L., Melo Sá, A., Gonçalves, J.L., Szpak, K.S., Sekino, K., & Aquino, M. (2016). Analysing the impact of interactive machine translation on post-editing effort. In M. Carl, S. Bangalore, & M. Schaeffer (Eds.), *New directions in empirical translation process research* (pp. 77–94). Singapore: Springer.

Alves, F., & Liparini Campos, T. (2009). Translation technology in time: Investigating the impact of translation memory systems and time pressure on types of internal and external support. In S. Göpferich, A.L. Jakobsen, & I.M. Mees (Eds.), *Behind the mind.Methods, models and results in translation process research* (pp. 191–218). Copenhagen: Samfundslitteratur.

Alves, F., & Magalhães, C. (2004). Using small corpora to tap and map the process-product interface in translation. *TradTerm*, *10*, 179–211.

Alves, F., Magalhães, C., & Pagano A. (2004). Autonomy in translation: Approaching translators' education through awareness of discourse processing. *Cadernos de Tradução*, *10*(2), 167–192.

Alves, F., Magalhães, C., & Pagano, A. (Eds.). (2005). *Competência em Tradução: Cognição e Discurso*. Belo Horizonte: Editora UFMG,
Alves, F., Pagano, A., & Da Silva, I.A.L. (2009). A new window on translators? cognitive activity: Methodological issues in the combined use of eye tracking, key logging and retrospective protocols. In I. Mees, F. Alves, & S. Göpferich (Eds.), *Methodology, technology and innovation in translation process research: A tribute to Arnt Lykke Jakobsen* (pp. 267–291). Copenhagen: Samfundslitteratur.
Alves, F., Pagano, A., & Da Silva, I.A.L. (2011). Towards an investigation of reading modalities in/for translation: An exploratory study using eye-tracking data. In S. O'Brien (Ed.), *Cognitive explorations of translation* (pp. 175–196). London: Continuum.
Alves, F., Pagano, A., Neumann, S., Steiner, E., & Hansen-Schirra, S. (2010). Units of translation and grammatical shifts: Towards an integration of product- and process-based research in translation. In G. Shreve & E. Angelone (Eds.), *Translation and cognition* (pp. 109–142). Amsterdam: John Benjamins.
Alves, F., Szpak, K.S., & Buchweitz, A. (2019). Translation in the brain: Preliminary thoughts about a brain-imaging study to investigate psychological processes involved in translation. In D. Li, V. Lei, & Y. He (Eds.), *Researching cognitive processes of translation* (pp. 121–138). Singapore: Springer Nature.
Alves, F., & Vale, D.C. (2009). Probing the unit of translation in time: Aspects of the design and development of a web application for storing, annotating, and querying translation process data. *Across Languages and Cultures,10*(2), 251–273.
Alves, F., & Vale, D.C. (2011). On drafting and revision in translation: A corpus linguistics oriented analysis of translation process data. *Translation: Computation, Corpora, Cognition,1*(1), 105–122.
Angelone, E. (2010). Uncertainty, uncertainty management and metacognitive problem solving in the translation task. In G. Shreve & E. Angelone (Eds.), *Translation and cognition* (pp. 17–40). Philadelphia: John Benjamins.
Angelone, E., Ehrensberger-Dow, M., & Massey, G. (Eds.). (2020). *Bloomsbury companion to the language industry studies*. London: Bloomsbury.
Annoni, J., Lee-Jahnke, H., & Sturm, A. (2012). Neurocognitive aspects of translation. *Meta*, *57*(1), 96–107.
Balling, L.W. (2008). A brief introduction to regression designs and mixed-effects modelling by a recent convert. In S. Göpferich, A.L. Jakobsen, & I.M. Mees (Eds.), *Looking at eyes. Eye-tracking studies of reading and translation processing* (pp. 175–192). Copenhagen: Samfundslitteratur.
Balling, L.W., & Hvelplund, K.T.J. (2015). Design and statistics in quantitative translation (process) tesearch. *Translation Spaces*, *4*(1), 170–187.
Bangalore, S., Behrens, B., Carl, M., Ghankot, M., Heilmann, A., Nitzke, J., Schaeffer, M., & Sturm, A. (2016). Syntactic variance and priming effects in translation. In M. Carl, S. Bangalore, & M. Schaeffer (Eds.), *New directions in empirical translation process research* (pp. 211–238). Singapore: Springer.
Barbosa, H., & Neiva, A. (2003). Using think-aloud protocols to investigate the translation process of foreign language learners and experienced translators. In F. Alves (Ed.), *Triangulating translation. Perspectives in process oriented research* (pp. 138–155). Amsterdam: John Benjamins.
Bayer-Hohenwarter, G. (2009). Translational creativity: How to measure the unmeasurable. In S. Göpferich, A.L. Jakobsen, & I.M. Mees (Eds.), *Behind the mind: Methods, models and results in translation process research* (Copenhagen Studies in Language 37, pp. 39–59). Copenhagen: Samfundslitteratur.
Bayer-Hohenwarter, G. (2010). Comparing translational creativity scores of students and professionals: Flexible problem-solving and/or fluent routine

behaviour? In S. Göpferich, F. Alves, & I.M. Mees (Eds.), *New approaches in translation process research* (Copenhagen Studies in Language 39, pp. 83–111). Copenhagen: Samfundslitteratur.

Behrens, B. (2016). The task of structuring information in translation. In M. Carl, S. Bangalore, & M. Schaeffer (Eds.), *New directions in empirical translation process research* (pp. 265–278). Springer: Singapore.

Buchweitz, A. (2006). *Two languages, two input modalities, one brain: An fMRI study of Portuguese-English bilinguals and Portuguese listening and reading comprehension effects on brain activation*. Unpublished PhD Dissertation. Universidade Federal de Santa Catarina.

Bunge, M. (1972). *La investigación científica. Su estructura y su filosofía*. Barcelona: Ariel.

Carl, M. (2009). Triangulating product and process data: Quantifying alignment units with keystroke data. In I. Mees, F. Alves, & S. Göpferich (Eds.), *Methodology, technology and innovation in translation process research: A tribute to Arnt Lykke Jakobsen* (pp. 225–247). Copenhagen: Samfundslitteratur.

Carl, M. (2011). Patterns of shallow text production in translation. *Copenhagen Studies in Language*, *41*, 143–151.

Carl, M. (Ed.). (2021). *Explorations in empirical translation process research*. Singapore: Springer.

Carl, M. (2023). Models of the translation process and the free energy principle. *Entropy*, *25*(6), 928.

Carl, M., & Dragsted, B. (2012). Inside the monitor model: Processes of default and challenged translation production. *Translation: Computation, Corpora, Cognition*,*2*(1), 127–143.

Carl, M., Dragsted, B., Elming, J., Hardt, D., & Jakobsen, A.L. (2011). The process of post-editing. A pilot study. *Copenhagen Studies in Language*, *41*, 131–142.

Carl, M., Gutermuth, S., & Hansen-Schirra, S. (2015). Post-editing machine translation: Efficiency, strategies, and revision processes in professional translation settings. In A. Ferreira & J.W. Schwieter (Eds.),*Psycholinguistic and cognitive inquiries into translation and interpreting* (pp. 145–174). Amsterdam: John Benjamins.

Carl, M., Jakobsen, A.L., & Jensen, K.T.H. (2008). *Studying human translation behavior with user-activity data*. Proceedings of the 5th International Workshop on Natural Language Processing and Cognitive Science. NLPCS, Barcelona.

Carl, M., & Kay, M. (2011), Gazing and typing activities during translation: A comparative study of translation units of professional and student translators. *Meta*, *56*(4), 952–975.

Carl, M., Schaeffer, M., & Bangalore, B. (2016). The CRITT translation process research database. In M. Carl, S. Bangalore, & M. Schaeffer (Eds.), *New directions in empirical translation process research* (pp. 13–54). Singapore: Springer.

Chesterman, A. (1997). *Memes of translation*. Amsterdam: John Benjamins.

Chi, M.T.H. (2006a). Two approaches to the study of experts' characteristics. In K.A. Ericsson, N. Charness, P.J. Feltovich, & R.R. Hoffman (Eds.), *The Cambridge handbook of expertise and expert performance* (pp. 21–30). Cambridge: Cambridge University Press.

Chi, M.T.H. (2006b). Laboratory methods for assessing experts' and novices' knowledge. In K.A. Ericsson, N. Charness, P.J. Feltovich, & R.R. Hoffman (Eds.), *The Cambridge handbook of expertise and expert performance* (pp. 167–184). Cambridge: Cambridge University Press.

Clifton, C. Jr., Staub, A., & Rayner, K. (2007). Eye movements in reading words and sentences. In R.P.G. van Gompel, M.H. Fischer, W.S. Murray, & R.L. Hill (Eds.), *Eye movements: A window on mind and brain* (pp. 341–371). Oxford: Elsevier.

Collins, H., & Evans, R. (2007). *Rethinking expertise*. Chicago and London: University of Chicago Press.
Couto-Vale, D. (2017). What does a translator do when not writing? In S. Hansen-Schirra, O. Czulo, & S. Hofmann (Eds.), *Empirical modelling of translation and interpreting* (pp. 209–237). Berlin: Language Science Press.
Couto-Vale, D., Neumann, S., & Niemietz, P. (2016). *Automatic recognition of linguistic replacements in text series generated from keystroke logs*. Proceedings of the 10th Language Resources and Evaluation Conference, pp. 3617–3623.
Cui, F., Li, D., & Zhuang, C. (forthcoming). Transforming translation education through artificial intelligence. *The Interpreter and Translator Trainer*. Special Issue.
Da Silva, I.A.L. (2015). On a more robust approach to triangulating retrospective protocols. In A. Ferreira & J.W. Schwieter (Eds.),*Psycholinguistic and cognitive inquiries into translation and interpreting* (pp. 175–201). Amsterdam: John Benjamins.
Da Silva, I.A.L. (2021). Translation, expert performance and cognition. In F. Alves & A.L. Jakobsen (Eds.), *The Routledge handbook of translation and cognition*(pp. 461–477). Routledge.
Daems, J., Carl, M., Vandepitte, S., Hartsuiker, R., & Macken, L. (2016). The effectiveness of consulting external resources during translation and post-editing of general text types. In M. Carl, S. Bangalore, & M. Schaeffer (Eds.), *New directions in empirical translation process research* (pp. 111–133). Singapore: Springer.
Denver, L. (2009). Unique items in translations. In S. Göpferich, A.L. Jakobsen, & I.M. Mees (Eds.), *Behind the mind.Methods, models and results in translation process research*(pp. 125–147). Copenhagen: Samfundslitteratur.
Denzin, N. K. (1978). *The research act* (2nd ed.). New York: McGraw-Hill.
Dragsted, B. (2004). *Segmentation in translation and translation memory systems: An empirical investigation of cognitive segmentation and effects of integrating a TM-System into the translation process*. Unpublished PhD Thesis, Copenhagen Business School. Samfundslitteratur, Copenhagen.
Dragsted, B. (2005). Segmentation in translation differences across levels of expertise and difficulty. *Target*,*17*(1), 49–70.
Dragsted, B., Gorm Hansen. I., & Sørensen, H.S. (2009). Experts exposed. In I. Mees, F. Alves, & S. Göpferich (Eds.), *Methodology, technology and innovation in translation process research: A tribute to Arnt Lykke Jakobsen* (pp. 293–317). Copenhagen: Samfundslitteratur.
Dragsted, B., & Hansen, I.G. 2008. Comprehension and production in translation: A pilot study on segmentation and the coordination of reading and writing processes. In S. Göpferich, A.L. Jakobsen, & I.M. Mees (Eds.), *Looking at eyes. Eye-tracking studies of reading and translation processing* (pp. 9–30). Copenhagen: Samfundslitteratur.
Ehrensberger-Dow, M. (2014). Challenges of translation process research at the workplace. *MonTI1*,355–383.
Ehrensberger-Dow, M. (2021). Translation, ergonomics and cognition. In F. Alves & A. L. Jakobsen (Eds.), *The Routledge handbook of translation and cognition* (pp. 147-160). London: Routledge.
Ehrensberger-Dow, M., & Englund-Dimitrova, B. (Eds.). (2016). *Translation Spaces*, *5*(1). Special Issue.
Ehrensberger-Dow, M., Englund Dimitrova, B., Hubscher-Davidson, S., & Norberg, U. (Eds.) (2013). Describing cognitive processes in translation: Acts and events. *Translation and Interpreting Studies*, *8*(2). Special Issue. Republished in *Benjamins Current Topics*, *77*(2015).

Ehrensberger-Dow, M., & Hunziker Heeb, A. (2016). Investigating the ergonomics of a technologized translation workplace. In R. Muñoz (Ed.), *Reembedding translation process research*(pp. 69–88). Amsterdam: John Benjamins.
Ehrensberger-Dow, M., & Künzli, A. (2010). Methods of accessing metalinguistic awareness: A question of quality? In F. Alves, F., I. Mees, & S. Göpferich (Eds.), *New approaches in translation process research* (pp. 113–132). Copenhagen: Samfundslitteratur.
Ehrensberger-Dow, M., & O'Brien, S. (2015). Ergonomics of the translation workplace: Potential for cognitive friction. *Translation Spaces*, *4*(1), 98–118.
Englund Dimitrova, B. (2005). *Expertise and explication in the translation process.* Amsterdam: John Benjamins.
Ericsson, K.A. (2000). Expertise in interpreting: An expert-performance perspective. *Interpreting*,*5*(2), 187–220.
Ericsson, K.A. (2002). Expertise in interpreting: An expert-performance perspective. *Interpreting*, *5*(2), 187–220.
Ericsson, K.A. (2006). An introduction to The Cambridge handbook of expertise and expert performance. In K.A. Ericsson, N. Charness, P.J. Feltovich, & R.R. Hoffman (Eds.), *The Cambridge handbook of expertise and expert performance.* (2nd Rev. ed., 2018). Cambridge: Cambridge University Press.
Ericsson, K.A., Charness, K.AN., Feltovich, P.J., & Hoffman, R.R. (Eds.). (2006). *The Cambridge handbook of expertise and expert performance* (2nd Rev. ed., 2018). Cambridge: Cambridge University Press.
Ericsson, K.A., & Simon, H.A. (1984). *Protocol analysis. Verbal reports as data.* Cambridge, MA: MIT Press.
Evert, S., & Neumann, S. (2017). The impact of translation direction on characteristics of translated texts. A multivariate analysis for English and German. In G. De Sutter, M.-A. Lefer, & I. Delaere (Eds.), *Empirical translation studies* (pp. 47–80). Berlin: De Gruyter.
Faber, D., & Hjort-Pedersen, M. (2009). Translation preferences in legal translation: Lawyers and professional translators compared. In I. Mees, F. Alves, & S. Göpferich (Eds.), *Methodology, technology and innovation in translation process research: A tribute to Arnt Lykke Jakobsen* (pp. 339–357). Copenhagen: Samfundslitteratur.
Ferreira, A., Gottardo, A., & Schwieter, J. (2018). Decision-making processes in direct and inverse translation through retrospective protocols. *Translation, Cognition & Behavior*, *1*(1), 98–118.
Ferreira. A., & Schwieter, J.W. (Eds.). (2015). *Psycholinguistic and cognitive inquiries into translation and interpreting.* Amsterdam: John Benjamins.
Ferreira, A., & Schwieter, J.W. (Eds.). (2023). *The Routledge handbook of translation, interpreting and bilingualism.* London: Routledge.
Ferreira, A., Schwieter, J.W., Gottardo, A., & Jones, J. (2016). Cognitive effort in direct and inverse translation performance: Insight from eye-tracking technology. *Cadernos de Tradução*, *36*(3), 60–80.
Fraser, J. (1993). Public accounts: Using verbal protocols to investigate community translation. *Applied Linguistics*, *14*(4), 325–343.
Fraser, J. (1994). The translator investigated: Learning from translation process analysis. *The Translator*,*2*(1), 65–79.
Fraser, J. (1996). Mapping the process of translation. *Meta*, *41*(1), 84–96.
Freiwald, J., Heilmann, A., Serbina, T., & Neumann, S. (2020). Automatization in translation behavior: Evidence from a translation experiment for the language pair German-English. In L. Vandevoorde, J. Daems, & B. Defrancq (Eds.), *New empirical perspectives on translation and interpreting* (pp. 179–212). London: Routledge.

García, A.M. (2014). The interpreter advantage hypothesis: Preliminary data patterns and empirically motivated questions. *Translation and Interpreting Studies*,*9*(2), 219–238.
García, A.M. (2015a). Translating with an injured brain: Neurolinguistic aspects of translation as revealed by bilinguals with cerebral lesions. *Meta*,*60*(1), 112–134.
García, A.M. (2015b). Psycholinguistic explorations of lexical translation equivalents: Thirty years of research and their implications for cognitive translatology. *Translation Spaces*,*4*(1), 9–28.
García, A.M. (2019). *The Neurocognition of translation and interpreting*. Amsterdam: John Benjamins.
García, A.M., Mikulan, E., & Ibáñez, A. (2016). A neuroscientific toolkit for translation studies. In R. Muñoz Martín (Ed.), *Reembedding translation process research*(pp. 21–46). Amsterdam: John Benjamins.
García, A. M., & Muñoz, E. (2021). Translation, neuroscience and cognition. In F. Alves & A.L. Jakobsen (Eds.), *The Routledge handbook of translation and cognition* (pp. 239–259). London: Routledge.
Gerloff, P. A. (1988). *From French to English: A look at the translation process in students,bilinguals, and professional translators*. Unpublished PhD Dissertation. Harvard University
Giegler, H. (1994). Test und Testtheorie. In R. Asanger & G. Wenninger (Eds.), *Wörterbuch der Psychologie* (pp. 782–789). Weinheim: Psychologie Verlags Union.
Gile, D. (1998). Observational studies and experimental studies in the investigation of conference interpreting. *Target*, *10*(1), 69–93.
Goldman-Eisler, F. (1972). Pauses, clauses, sentences. *Language and Speech*, *15*, 103–113.
Gonçalves, J.L. (2003). *O desenvolvimento da competência do tradutor: Investigando o processo através de um estudo exploratório-experim*ental. Unpublished PhD Dissertation. Belo Horizonte: Universidade Federal de Minas Gerais.
Göpferich, S. (2009). Towards a model of translation competence and its acquisition: The longitudinal study TransComp. In S. Göpferich, A.L. Jakobsen, & I.M. Mees (Eds.), *Behind the mind: Methods, models and results in translation process research* (pp. 12–38). Copenhagen: Samfundslitteratur.
Göpferich, S., Jakobsen, A.L., & Mees, I.M. (Eds.). (2008). *Behind the mind.Methods, models and results in translation process research*. Copenhagen: Samfundslitteratur.
Halverson, S., & Marín García, A. (Eds.). (2022). *Contesting epistemologies in cognitive translation and interpreting studies*. London: Routledge.
Hansen, G. (2002) Selbstaufmerksamkeit im Übersetzungsprozess. In G. Hansen (Ed.), *Empirical translation studies: Process and product* (pp. 9–27). Copenhagen: Samfundslitteratur.
Hansen-Schirra, S., Czulo, O., & Hofmann, S. (Eds.). (2017). *Empirical modelling of translation and interpreting*. Berlin: Language Science Press.
Heilmann, A. (2021). *Profiling effects of syntactic complexity in translation: A multi-method approach*. Unpublished PhD Dissertation. RWTH Aachen University.
Heilmann, A., Freiwald, J., Neumann, S., & Miljanović, Z. (2022). Analyzing the effects of entrenched grammatical constructions on translation. *Translation, Cognition & Behavior*, *5*(1), 110–143.
Heilmann, A., & Neumann, S. (2016). *Dynamic pause assessment of keystroke logged data for the detection of complexity in translation and monolingual text*

production. Coling 2016 Workshop on Computational Linguistics for Linguistic Complexity, 98–103.
Heilmann, A., Serbina, T., Couto Vale, D., & Neumann, S. (2019). Shorter than a text, longer than a sentence: Source text length for ecologically valid translation experiments. *Target*, *31*(1), 98–124.
Heilmann, A., Serbina, T., Freiwald, J., & Neumann, S. (2021). Animacy and agentivity of subject themes in English-German translation. *Lingua*, *261*, 102813.
Heilmann, A., Serbina, T., & Neumann, S. (2018). Processing of grammatical metaphor: Insights from controlled translation and reading experiments. *Translation, Cognition & Behavior*, *1*(2), 195–220.
Hvelplund, K.T. (2011). *Allocation of cognitive resources in translation: An eye-tracking and keylogging study*. Unpublished PhD Dissertation. Copenhagen: Samfundslitteratur.
Hvelplund, K.T. (2014). Eye tracking and the translation process: Reflections on the analysis and interpretation of eye-tracking data. In R. Muñoz Martín (Ed.), *MonTI. Special Issue* (pp. 201–223). Alicante: University of Alicante Press.
Hvelplund, K.T. (2016). Cognitive efficiency in translation. In R. Muñoz Martín (Ed.), *Reembedding translation process research* (pp. 149–170). Amsterdam: John Benjamins.
Hvelplund, K.T. (2017). Eye tracking in translation process research. In J.W. Schwieter & A. Ferreira (Eds.), *The handbook of translation and cognition* (pp. 248–264). Hoboken, NJ: Wiley-Blackwell.
Hurtado Albir, A. (1999). La competencia traductora y su adquisición. *Perspectives, Studies in Translatology*, *7*(2), 177–188.
Hurtado Albir, A. (2001). *Traducción y traductología. Introducción a la traductología* (5th Rev. ed., 2011). Madrid: Cátedra.
Hurtado Albir, A. (2005). A aquisição da competência tradutória: aspectos teóricos e didáticos. In F. Alves, C. Magalhães, & A. Pagano (Eds.), *Competência em tradução: cognição e discurso* (pp. 19–57). Belo Horizonte: Editora UFMG.
Hurtado Albir, A. (Ed.). (2017). *Researching translation competence by PACTE group*. Amsterdam: John Benjamins.
Hurtado Albir, A., & Rodriguez-Inés, P. (2022a). Perspectivas de la investigación. In A. Hurtado Albir & P. Rodríguez-Inés (Eds.), Hacia un marco europeo de niveles de competencias en traducción. El Proyecto NACT del Grupo PACTE /Towards a European framework of competence levels in translation. The PACTE Group's NACT project. *MonTI*, *7*, Special Issue, 204–209.
Hurtado Albir, A., & Rodríguez-Inés, P. (2022b). Segunda propuesta de descriptores de nivel. In A. Hurtado Albir & P. Rodríguez-Inés (Eds.), Hacia un marco europeo de niveles de competencias en traducción. El Proyecto NACT del Grupo PACTE / Towards a European framework of competence levels in translation. The PACTE Group's NACT project. *MonTI*, *7*, Special Issue, 119–203.
Jakobsen, A.L. (1999). Logging time delay in translation. In G. Hansen (Ed.), *LSP texts and the process of translation* (Copenhagen Working Papers 1, pp. 71–101). Copenhagen: Copenhagen Business School.
Jakobsen, A.L. (2002). Translation drafting by professional translators and by translation students. In G. Hansen (Ed.), *Empirical translation studies: Process and product* (pp. 191–204). Copenhagen: Samfundslitteratur.
Jakobsen, A.L. (2003). Effects of think aloud on translation speed, revision and segmentation. In F. Alves (Ed.), *Triangulating translation. Perspectives in process oriented research*(pp. 69–95). Amsterdam: John Benjamins.
Jakobsen, A.L. (2005). Investigating expert translators' processing knowledge. In H.V. Dam, J. Engberg, & H. Gerzymisch-Arbogast (Eds.), *Knowledge systems and translation* (pp. 173–189). Berlin and New York: Mouton de Gruyter.

Jakobsen, A.L. (2006). Research methods in translation: Translog. In E. Lindgren & K.P.H. Sullivan (Eds.), *Computer keystroke logging and writing: Methods and applications* (Studies in Writing, Vol. 18 pp. 95–105). Oxford: Pergamon Press.
Jakobsen, A.L. (2011). Tracking translators' keystrokes and eye movements with Translog. In C. Alvstad, A. Hild, & E. Tiselius (Eds.), *Methods and strategies of process research: Integrative approaches in translation studies*(pp.37–55). Amsterdam: John Benjamins.
Jakobsen, A.L., & Jensen K.T.H. (2008). Eye movement behaviour across four different types of reading task. In S. Göpferich, A.L. Jakobsen, & I.M. Mees (Eds.), *Looking at eyes: Eye-tracking studies of reading and translation processing*. (Copenhagen Studies in Language 36, pp. 103–124). Copenhagen: Samfundslitteratur.
Jakobsen, A.L., & Mesa-Lao, B. (Eds.). (2017). *Translation in transition.Between cognition, computing and technology* (Benjamins Translation Library 133). Amsterdam: John Benjamins.
Jakobsen, A.L., & Schou, L. (1999). Translog documentation. In G. Hansen (Ed.), *Probing the process in translation: Methods and results* (pp. 1–36). Frederiksberg: Samfundslitteratur.
Jääskeläinen, R. (1987). *What happens in a translation process: Think-aloud protocols of translation*. Unpublished MA Thesis, Savonlinna School of Translation Studies, University of Joensuu.
Jensen, K.T.H. (2009). Indicators of text complexity. In S. Göpferich, A.L. Jakobsen, & I.M. Mees (Eds.), *Behind the mind.Methods, models and results in translation process research*(pp. 61–60). Copenhagen: Samfundslitteratur.
Jensen, K.T.H., Sjørup, A.C., & Balling, L.W. (2009). Effects of L1 syntax in L2 translation. In I.M. Mees, F. Alves, & S. Göpferich (Eds.), *Methodology, technology and innovation in translation process research: A tribute to Arnt Lykke Jakobsen* (pp. 319–336). Copenhagen: Samfundslitteratur.
Jick, T.D. (1979). Mixing qualitative and quantitative methods: Triangulation in action. *Administrative Science Quarterly*, *24*, 602–611.
Just, M.A., & Carpenter, P.A. (1980). A theory of reading: From eye fixations to comprehension. *Psychological Review*,*87*(4), 329–354.
Kiraly, D. (1995). *Pathways to translation.Pedagogy and process*. Kent, OH: The Kent State University Press.
Kiraly, D. (2000). *A social constructivist approach to translator education*. Manchester: St Jerome
Koglin, A. (2016). Processos de pós-edição em inglês-português. Unpublished PhD Dissertation. Universidade Federal de Minas Gerais.
Königs, F.G. (1987). Was beim Übersetzen passiert. Theoretische Aspekte, empirische Befunde und praktische Konsequenzen. *Die Neueren Sprachen*,*86*(2), 162–185.
Krings, H.P. (1986). *Was in den Köpfen von Übersetzern vorgeht*. Tübingen: Gunter Narr.
Kruger, J.L., Doherty, S., Fox, W., & de Lissa, P. (2017). Multimodal measurement of cognitive load during subtitle processing: Same-language subtitles for foreign-language viewers. In I. Lacruz & R. Jääskeläinen (Eds.), *Innovation and expansion in translation process research*(pp. 267–294). Amsterdam: John Benjamins.
Künzli, A., & Ehrensberger-Dow, M. (2011). Innovative subtitling: A reception study. In C. Alvstad, A. Hild, & E. Tiselius (Eds.), *Methods and strategies of process research* (pp. 187–200). Amsterdam: John Benjamins.
Kuznik, A., & Olalla-Soler, C. (2018). Results of PACTE group's experimental research on translation competence acquisition. The acquisition of the instrumental sub-competence. *Across Languages and Cultures*, *19*(1), 19–51.

Lacruz, I. (Ed.). (2023). *Translation in Transition. Human and machine intelligence* (American Translators Association Scholarly Monograph Series, XX). Philadelphia, PA: John Benjamins.
Lacruz, I., & Jääskeläinen, R. (Eds.). (2018). *Innovation and expansion in translation process research* (American Translators Association Scholarly Monograph Series, XVIII). Philadelphia: John Benjamins.
Lakoff, G., & Johnson, M. (1980). *Metaphors we live by.* Chicago: University of Chicago Press.
Lakoff, G., & Johnson, M. (1999). *Philosophy in the flesh.* New York: Basic Books.
Lehr, C. (2014). *The influence of emotion on language performance.* Unpublished PhD Dissertation, University of Geneva.
Li, D., Lei, V., & He, Y. (Eds.). (2019). *Researching cognitive processes of translation* (New Frontiers in Translation Studies Series). Singapore: Springer.
Livbjerg, I., & Mees, I. (2003). Patterns of dictionary use in non-domain-specific translation (pp. 123–136). Amsterdam: John Benjamins.
Lörscher, W. (1991). *Translation performance, translation process, and translation strategies. A psycholinguistic investigation.* Tübingen: Narr.
Lörscher, W. (1992). Investigating the translation process. *Meta*, *37*(3), 426–439.
Lörscher, W. (1993). Translation process analysis. In Y. Gambier & J. Tommola (Eds.), *Translation and knowledge* (pp. 195–212). Turku: University of Turku.
Lorenzo, M.P. (2002). ¿Es possible la traducción inversa? Resultados de un experimento sobre traducción profesional a una lengua extranjera. In G. Hansen (Ed.) *Empirical translation studies: Process and product* (pp. 85–124.). Copenhagen: Samfundslitteratur.
Marín García, A. (2017). *Theoretical hedging: The scope of knowledge in translation process research.* Unpublished PhD Dissertation. Kent State University, Kent.
Marín García, A. (2019). The opportunities of epistemic pluralism for cognitive translation studies. *Translation, Cognition & Behavior*, *2*(2), 147–168.
Massana-Roselló, G. (2016). *La adquisición de la competencia traductora portugués-español: Un estudio en torno a los falsos amigos.* PhD dissertation. Barcelona: Universitat Autònoma de Barcelona.
Matthews, B., & Ross, L. (2010). *Research methods. A practical guide for the social sciences.* London: Pearson Longman.
Mees, I.M., Dragsted, B., Hansen, G.H., & Jakobsen, A.L. (2013). Sound effects in translation. *Target*, *25(*1), 140–154.
Mellinger, C., & Hanson, D. (2017). *Quantitative research methods in translation and interpreting studies.* New York: Routledge.
Mellinger, C., & Shreve, G.M. (2016). Match evaluation and over-editing in a translation memory environment. In R. Muñoz Martín (Eds.), *Reembedding traanslation process research* (pp. 131-148). Amsterdam: John Benjamins.
Muñoz Martín, R. (2009a). The way they were: Subject profiling in translation process research. In I.M. Mees, F. Alves, & S. Göpferich (Eds.), *Methodology, technology and innovation in translation process research: A tribute to Arnt Lykke Jakobsen* (pp. 87–108). Copenhagen: Samfundslitteratur.
Muñoz Martín, R. (2009b). Typos & Co. In S. Göpferich, A.L. Jakobsen, & I.M. Mees (Eds.), *Behind the mind: Methods, models and results in translation process research* (*Copenhagen Studies in Language*, 37, pp. 167–189). Copenhagen: Samfundslitteratur.
Muñoz Martín, R. (2012). Just a matter of scope. Mental load in translation process research. *Translation Spaces*, *1*, 169–178.
Muñoz, Martín, R. (2014). A blurred snapshot of advances in translation process research. *MonTI*, *1*, 49–84.

Muñoz, Martín, R. (Ed.). (2016). *Reembbeding translation process research* (Benjamins Translation Library 128). Amsterdam: John Benjamins.
Muñoz Martín, R. (2017). Looking toward the future of cognitive translation studies. In J.W. Schwieter & A. Ferreira (Eds.), *The handbook of translation and cognition* (pp. 555–572). Hoboken, NJ: John Wiley & Sons, Inc.
Muñoz Martín, R., & Halverson, S.L. (Eds.). (2021). *Multilingual mediated communication and cognition*. London: Routledge.
Muñoz Martín, R., Sun, S., & Li, D. (Eds.). (2021). *Advances in cognitive translation studies* (New Frontiers in Translation Studies Series). Singapore: Springer.
Neumann, S. (2020). Translation: Enriching our understanding of language use. [Invited Youtube talk]. Abralin Ao Vivo – Linguists Online. Accessible via https://ao-vivo.abralin.org/en/lives/stella-neumann-2/
Neumann, S., & Hansen-Schirra, S. (2012). Corpus methodology and design. In S. Hansen-Schirra, S. Neumann, & E. Steiner (Eds.), *Cross-linguistic corpora for the study of translations: Insights from the language pair English-German* (pp. 21–34).
Neumann, S., & Serbina, T. (2021). Translation, corpus linguistics and cognition. In F. Alves & A.L. Jakobsen (Eds.), *The Routledge handbook of translation and cognition* (pp. 188–203). London: Routledge.
Neunzig, W. (1999). *Sobre la investigación empírica en traductología. Cuestiones epistémicas y metodológicas*. Unpublished MPhil Thesis. Universitat Autonoma de Barcelona.
Neunzig, W. (2001). *La intervención pedagógica en la enseñanza de la traducción on-line. Cuestiones de método y estudio empírico*. Unpublished PhD Dissertation, Universitat Autònoma de Barcelona.
Neunzig, W. (2002). Estudios empíricos en traducción: Apuntes metodológicos. *Cadernos deTradução,10*, 75–96.
Neunzig, W. (2011). Empirical studies in translation: Methodological and epistemological questions. *Traduction, Terminologie, Rédaction*, *24*(2), 15–40.
Neunzig, W. (2017). Methodological background. In A. Hurtado Albir (Ed.), *Researching translation competence by PACTE group* (pp. 43–59). Amsterdam: John Benjamins.
Neunzig, W., & Tanqueiro, T. (2007). *Estudios empíricos en traducción: Enfoques y métodos*. Girona: Documenta Universitaria.
Nitzke, J., & Oster, K. (2016). Comparing translation and post-editing: An annotation schema for activity units. In M. Carl, S. Bangalore, & M. Schaeffer (Eds.), *New directions in empirical translation process research* (pp. 293–308). Singapore: Springer.
O'Brien, S. (2006). Eye-tracking and translation memory matches. *Perspectives: Studies in Translatology*, *14*, 185–203.
O'Brien, S. (2013a). The borrowers: Researching the cognitive aspects of translation. *Target*,*25*(1), 5–17.
O'Brien, S. (2013b). Translation as human–computer interaction. *Translation Spaces*, *1*(1), 101–122.
O'Brien, S. (2021). Translation, human-computer interaction and cognition. In F. Alves & A.L. Jakobsen (Eds.), *The Routledge handbook of translation and cognition* (pp. 376–388). London: Routledge.
O'Brien, S. (2023). *Human-Centered augmented translation: Against antagonistic dualisms*. Perspectives (published online). ttps://doi.org/10.1080/0907676X.2023.2247423
Orozco, M. (2000). *Instrumentos de medida de la adquisicón de la competencia traductora:Construcción y validación*. Unpublished PhD Dissertation, Universitat Autònoma de Barcelona.

PACTE. (1998). *La competencia traductora y su aprendizaje: Objetivos, hipótesis y metodología de un proyecto de investigación*. Poster, IV Congrés Internacional sobre Traducció, Universitat Autònoma de Barcelona.
PACTE. (2000). Acquiring translation competence: Hypotheses and methodological problems in a research project. In A. Beeby, D. Ensinger, & M. Presas (Eds.), *Investigating translation* (pp. 99–106). Amsterdam: John Benjamins.
PACTE. (2001). La competencia traductora y su adquisición. *Quaderns. Revista de Traducció*, 6, 39–45.
PACTE. (2002). Exploratory tests in a study of translation competence. *Conference Interpretation and Translation*, *4*(2), 41–69.
PACTE. (2003). Building a translation competence model. InF. Alves (Ed.), *Triangulating translation: Perspectives in process oriented research* (pp. 43–66). Amsterdam: John Benjamins.
PACTE. (2005). Investigating translation competence: Conceptual and methodological issues. *Meta*, *50*(2),609–619.
PACTE. (2008). First results of a translation competence experiment: 'Knowledge of translation' and 'efficacy of the translation process'. In J. Kearns (Ed.), *Translator and interpreter training. Issues, methods and debates* (pp. 104–126). London: Continuum.
PACTE. (2009). Results of the validation of the PACTE translation competence model: Acceptability and decision-making. *Across Language and Cultures*, *10*(2), 207–230.
PACTE (2011a). Results of the validation of the PACTE translation competence model: Translation problems and translation competence. In C. Alvstad, A. Hild, & E. Tiselius (Eds.), *Methods and strategies of process research: Integrative approaches in translation studies* (pp. 317–343). Amsterdam: John Benjamins.
PACTE (2011b). Results of the validation of the PACTE translation competence model: Translation project and dynamic translation index. In S. O'Brien (Ed.), *Cognitive explorations of translation* (pp. 30–53). London: Continuum.
PACTE. (2014). First results of PACTE group's experimental research on translation competence acquisition: The acquisition of declarative knowledge of translation. *MonTI. Special issue*,*1*,85–115.
PACTE. (2015). Results of PACTE's experimental research on the acquisition of translation competence: The acquisition of declarative and procedural knowledge in translation. The dynamic translation index. *Translation Spaces*,*4*(1), 29–35.
PACTE. (2017). The performance of the top-ranking translators. In A. Hurtado Albir (Ed.), *Researching translation competence by PACTE group* (pp. 269–280). Amsterdam: John Benjamins.
PACTE. (2018). Competence levels in translation: Working towards a European framework. *The Interpreter and Translator Trainer*, *12*(2), 111–131.
PACTE. (2019a). Evolution of the efficacy of the translation process in translation competence acquisition. Results of the PACTE. Group's experimental research. *Meta*, *64*(1), 242–265.
PACTE. (2019b). Establecimiento de niveles de competencia en traducción. Primeros resultados del proyecto NACT. *Onomazein*, *43*, 1–25.
PACTE. (2020) Translation competence acquisition. Design and results of the PACTE Group's experimental research. *The Interpreter and Translator Trainer*, *14*(2), 95–233.
Pavlović, N. (2009). More ways to explore the translating mind: Collaborative translation protocols. In S. Göpferich, A.L. Jakobsen, & I.M. Mees (Eds.), *Behind the mind: Methods, models and results in translation process research*. (*Copenhagen Studies in Language*, 37, pp. 81–106). Copenhagen: Samfundslitteratur.

Pavlović, N., & Jensen, K.T.H. (2009). Eye tracking translation directionality. In A. Pym & A. Perekrestenko(Eds.), *Translation research projects* (pp. 101–119). Tarragona: Universitat Rovira i Virgili.
Popper, K. (1963). *Vermutungen und Widerlegungen*. Mohr Siebeck: Tübingen.
Premack, D., & Woodruff, G. (1978). Does the chimpanzee have a theory of mind? *Behavioral and Brain Sciences*, *1*(4), 515–526.
Rayner, K. (1998). Eye movements in reading and information processing: 20 years of research. *Psychological Bulletin*, *124*(3), 372.
Rayner, K., & Duffy, S.A. (1986). Lexical complexity and fixation times in reading: Effects of word frequency, verb complexity, and lexical ambiguity. *Memory & Cognition*, *14*(3), 191–201.
Rodríguez-Gómez, G., Gil Flores, J., & García Jiménez, E. (1996). *Metodología de la investigación cualitativa*. Málaga: Aljibe.
Rojo López, A.M. (2013). *Diseños y métodos de investigación en traducción*. Madrid: Síntesis.
Rojo López, A.M., & Ramos Caro, M. (2014). The impact of translators' ideology on the translation process: A reaction time experiment. *MonTi*, *1*, 247–271.
Rojo López, A.M., & Ramos Caro, M. (2016). Can emotion stir translation skill? In R. Munoz Martín (Ed.), *Reembedding translation process research* (pp. 107–130). Amsterdam: John Benjamins.
Rydning, A.F., & Lachaud, C. (2011). Are primary conceptual metaphors easier to understand than complex conceptual metaphors? In C. Alvstad, A. Hild, & E. Tiselius (Eds.), *Methods and strategies of process research* (pp. 169–186). Amsterdam: John Benjamins.
Saldanha, G., & O'Brien, S. (2013). *Research methodologies in translation studies*. Manchester: St Jerome.
Sandrock, U. (1982). *Thinking aloud protocols (TAPs) – Ein Instrument zur Dekomposition des komplexen Prozesses 'Übersetzen'*. Unpublished PhD Dissertation. Universität Kassel.
Schäffner, C., & Adab, B. (Eds.). (2000). *Developing translation competence*. Amsterdam: John Benjamins.
Schaeffer, M., Dragsted, B., Hvelplund, K., Balling, L., & Carl, M. (2016). Word translation entropy: Evidence of early target language activation during reading for translation. In M. Carl, S. Bangalore, & M. Schaeffer (Eds.), *New directions in empirical translation process research* (pp. 183–210). Singapore: Springer.
Schaeffer, M., Huepe, D., Hansen-Schirra, S., Hofmann, S., Muñoz, E., Kogan, B., Herrera, E., Ibáñez, A., & García, A.M. (2020). The translation and interpreting competence questionnaire: An online tool for research on translators and interpreters. *Perspectives*, *28*(1), 90–108.
Schäffner, C., & Shuttleworth, M. (2013). Metaphor in translation: Possibilities for process research. *Target*, *25*(1), 93–106.
Schilperoord, J. (1996). *It's about time. Temporal aspects of cognitive processes in text production*. Utrecht: Rodopi.
Schmaltz, M., Leal, A., Wong, D. Chao, L., Silva, A.L., Alves, F., Pagano, A., & Quaresma, P. (2016). Cohesive relations in text comprehension and production: An exploratory study comparing translation and post-editing. In M. Carl, S. Bangalore, & M. Schaeffer (Eds.), *New directions in empirical translation process research* (pp. 239–263). Singapore: Springer.
Schwieter, J., & Ferreira, A. (Eds.). (2017). *The handbook of translation and cognition*. Hoboken, NJ: Wiley-Blackwell.
Séguinot, C. (Ed.). (1989). *The translation process*. Toronto: York University Press.
Séguinot, C. (1991). A study of student translation strategies. In S. Tirkkonen-Condit (Ed.), *Empirical research in translation and intercultural studies* (pp. 79–88). Tübingen: Gunter Narr.

Sekino, K. (2016). *Investigando processos de pós-edição e de tradução: uma análise cognitivo-pragmática da relação esforço/efeito no par linguístico japonês/português*. Unpublished PhD Dissertation. Universidade Federal de Minas Gerais.
Serbina, T. (2015). *A construction grammar approach to the analysis of translation shifts: A corpus-based study*. Unpublished PhD Dissertation. RWTH Aachen University.
Serbina, T., Hintzen, S., Niemietz, P., & Neumann, S.M. (2017). Changes of word class during translation. Insights from a combined analysis of corpus, keystroke logging and eye-tracking data. In S. Hansen-Schirra, O. Czulo, & S. Hofmann (Eds.), *Empirical modelling of translation and interpreting* (pp. 177–208). Berlin: Language Science Press.
Serbina, T., Niemietz, P., Fricke, M., Meisen, P., & Neumann, S. (2015). *Part of speech annotation of intermediate versions in the keystroke logged translation corpus*. Proceedings of the 9th Linguistic Annotation Workshop (held in conjunction with NAACL 2015), pp. 102–111.
Sharmin, S., Špakov, O, Räihä, K., & Jakobsen, A.L. (2008). Where on the screen do translation students look while translating, and for how long? In S. Göpferich, A.L. Jakobsen & I.M. Mees (Eds.), *Looking at eyes: Eye-tracking studies of reading and translation Processing* (Copenhagen Studies in Language 36, pp. 31–51). Copenhagen: Samfundslitteratur.
Shreve, G.M. (2002). Knowing translation: Cognitive and experiential aspects of translation expertise from the perspective of expertise studies. In A. Riccardi (Ed.), *Translation studies: Perspectives on an emerging discipline*(pp. 150–171). Cambridge: Cambridge University Press.
Shreve, G.M. (2006). The deliberate practice: translation and expertise. *Journal of Translation Studies*,*9*(1), 27–42.
Shreve, G.M. (2020). Professional translator development from an expertise perspective. In E. Angelone, M. Ehrensberger-Dow, & G. Massey (Eds.), *The Bloomsbury companion to language industry studies*. (pp. 153–178). London: Bloomsbury Academic.
Shreve, G., Angelone, E., & Lacruz, I. (2011). Sight translation and speech disfluency: Performance analysis as a window to cognitive translation processes. In C. Alvstad, A. Hild, & E. Tiselius (Eds.), *Methods and strategies of process research* (pp. 121–146). Amsterdam: John Benjamins.
Shreve, G., Angelone, E., & Lacruz, I. (2014). Efficacy of screen recording in the other-revision of translations: episodic memory and event models. *MonTi*, *1*, 225–245.
Shreve, G.M., Angelone, E., & Lacruz, I. (2018). Are expertise and translation competence the same? Psychological reality and the theoretical status of competence. In I. Lacruz & R Jääskeläinen (Eds.), *Innovation and expansion in translation process research* (pp. 37–54). Amsterdam: John Benjamins.
Smith, H.W. (1975). *Strategies of social research: The methodological imagination*. Englewood Cliffs, NJ: Prentice Hall.
Sperber, D., & Wilson, D. (1986). *Relevance. Communication and cognition*. Oxford: Basil Blackwell. 2nd ed. published in 1995.
Sturm, A. (2016). On the role of metacognitive proficiency in translation. Investigating the role of Theory of Mind in translation in terms of neural substrates, process and product data. Unpublished PhD Dissertation. University of Geneva.
Szpak, K.S. (2017). *A atribuição de estados mentais em atividades de tradução: Um estudo conduzido com rastreamento ocular e ressonância magnética functional* Unpublished PhD Dissertation). Universidade Federal de Minas Gerais, Belo Horizonte, Brazil.

Szpak, K.S., Alves, F., & Buchweitz, A. (2021). Perspective taking in translation. In search of neural correlates of representing and attributing mental states to others. In R. Muñoz & S. Halverson (Eds.), *Multilingual mediated communication and cognition* (pp. 133–154). London: Routledge.

Tausch, R., & Tausch, A.-M. (1991). *Erziehungspsychologie. Begegnung von Person zu Person.* Hogrefe: Göttingen.

Teich, E. (2003). *Cross-Linguistic variation in system and text: A methodology for the investigation of translations and comparable texts.* Berlin: De Gruyter.

Tirkkonen-Condit, S. (1989). Professional vs. non-professional translation. A think-aloud protocol study. In C. Séguinot (Ed.), *The translation process* (pp. 73–86). Toronto: H.G. Publications.

Tirkkonen-Condit, S. (Ed.). (1991). *Empirical research in translation and intercultural studies. Selected papers of the TRANSIF seminar, Savonlinna 1988.* Tübingen: Narr.

Tirkkonen-Condit, S. (2005). The monitor model revisited: Evidence from process research. *Meta*, *50*(2), 405–414.

Toury, G. (1995). *Descriptive translation studies and beyond* (2nd ed., 2012). Amsterdam: John Benjamins.

Tymoczko, M. (2012). The neuroscience of translation. *Target*,*24*(1), 83–102.

Vandepitte, S., & Hartsuiker, R. J. (2011). Metonymic language use as a student translation problem: towards a controlled psycholinguistic investigation. In C. Alvstad, A. Hild, & E. Tiselius (Eds.), *Methods and strategies of process research: Integrative approaches in translation studies* (pp. 67–92). Amsterdam: John Benjamins.

Vandepitte, S., Hartsuiker, R.J., & van Assche, E. (2015). Process and text studies of a translation problem. In A. Ferreira, & J.W. Schwieter (Eds.),*Psycholinguistic and cognitive inquiries into translation and interpreting* (pp. 127–144). Amsterdam: John Benjamins.

Von der Malsburg, T., & Vasishth, S. (2011). What is the scanpath signature of syntactic reanalysis? *Journal of Memory and Language*, *65*(2), 109–127.

Whyatt, B. (2019). In search of directionality effects in the translation process and in the end product. *Translation, Cognition & Behavior*, *2*(1), 79–100.

Whyatt, B., Kajzer-Wietrzny, M., & Stachowiak, K. (2016). Similar and different: Cognitive rhythm and effort in translation and paraphrasing. *Poznan Studies in Contemporary Linguistics*, *52*(2), 175–208.

Williams, J., & Chesterman, A. (2002). *The map. A beginner's guide to doing research in translation studies.* London: Routledge.

Wollin, L., & Lindqvist, W. (Eds.). (1986). *Translation studies in Scandinavia: Proceedings from the Scandinavian symposium on translation theory (SSOTT) II.* Lund: CWK Gleerup.

5

CONCLUDING REMARKS

Relevant issues concerning the study of translation as a cognitive activity

5.1 The cognitive turn

We started this book with a bold claim in Chapter 1, defining translation as a complex human activity which entails a set of knowledge and specific abilities, requiring much more than simply handling the transfer of linguistic structures between two texts. For us, translation is, thus, an inter-textual activity, a complex act of intercultural communication as well as a particular type of behaviour resulting from cognitive activity on the part of a subject, the translator, who engages in a complex mental process to which specific knowledge and abilities (translation competence) must be applied so that the task is performed satisfactorily. In doing so, we have also pointed out that, in addition to this inherent complex difficulty of translation, the study of any cognitive activity involves phenomena which are not directly observable.

Our position takes into consideration the inherent complexity of the object of study, namely translation as a cognitive activity, and assumes that both quantitative and qualitative methodologies should be integrated in order to develop a paradigm which can accommodate the multitude of factors at play when one approaches the study of translation as a cognitive activity.

As such, investigating the cognitive aspects of translation offers a major challenge for the discipline of translation studies. Growing exponentially from the mid-1980s onwards, the discipline of translation studies has seen a great interest in the study of cognitive aspects of translation over the last decades. This interest signals the beginning of what some scholars have named the *cognitive turn* (Tymoczko, 2005; Snell-Hornby, 2006) in translation studies or, perhaps more appropriately, cognitive translation studies (Halverson, 2010).

DOI: 10.4324/9781003006978-6

In this final chapter, we review the major points raised in this book and present some concluding remarks and our thoughts about relevant issues concerning the study of translation as a cognitive activity.[1]

5.1.1 Epistemological and paradigmatic stances

As we have shown throughout this book, the study of translation as a cognitive activity has been carried out from disparate theoretical and methodological perspectives. We have seen that a myriad of different models have been proposed to explain the translation process and the underlying capabilities inherent to that type of process (translation competence and its acquisition) and the traits and specificities of translation expertise. We have also shown that borrowing has occurred, sometimes implicitly and mostly explicitly, from studies that have been carried out in other disciplines that also focus on human cognitive activities and investigate general and particular characteristics of human cognition.

In Chapter 1, we presented a series of disciplines which, in our view, have most directly influenced research on translation as a cognitive activity: neuroscience, cognitive science, psycholinguistics, reading and writing studies and expertise studies. We have argued that some of these disciplines, such as psycholinguistics and cognitive science, including the recent discussion about 4EA cognition (embodied, embedded, enacted, extended and affective), provide the epistemological, paradigmatic and methodological basis for the study of translation as a cognitive activity, while others, such as reading and writing studies and expertise studies, focus on more specific objects of study and provide a conceptual paradigm for the study of certain aspects of translators' cognitive activity.

We have also emphasized the importance of what we consider to be disciplines which have had an indirect impact on the study of translation as a cognitive activity. Indirect disciplines would include, among others, anthropology, contact linguistics, corpus linguistics, ergonomics, human-computer interaction and linguistics – with a special emphasis on pragmatics, pedagogy and psychology of work.

In recent years, the discussion about the interdisciplinary aspects related to the study of translation as a cognitive activity has grown exponentially and scholars such as Muñoz (2010), Jääskeläinen (2011), , O'Brien (2013) and Alves (2015), among others, have dwelt on the basis for such an interdisciplinary dialogue. These authors insist on the need to ground research on firm epistemological and paradigmatic bases upon which the study of translation as a cognitive activity can grow and prosper. Following O'Brien (2013), we believe that borrowing from neighbouring disciplines has contributed to this exponential growth. We also believe that having reached a stage of consolidation, cognitive translation studies is now in a position to start lending and this contributing to the growth of these neighbouring disciplines.

Throughout the book, we have emphasized the inherent need for an interdisciplinary framework for the study of translation as a cognitive activity. We believe that such an interdisciplinary framework is necessary due to the complexity and diversity related to the disparate aspects that entail the study of translation as a cognitive activity. As we have consistently pointed out, our current standpoint is that a focus on complementarity and reciprocity should be pursued to ensure that developments in this field of study are consistent and relevant. With the current advances in research on translation as a cognitive activity, these related areas have much to gain with closer affiliation links and probably nothing to lose in the process.

5.1.2 Research carried out over the past 40 years: Conceptual and methodological aspects

In the course of this book, looking back at the evolution of research on cognitive aspects of translation, we have highlighted the main characteristics of models of the translation process (see Table 2.3), the evolution of research on translation competence (see Table 3.4) and translation competence acquisition (see Table 3.5) as well as considerations about the phases of research on cognitive aspects of translation (see Tables , 4.2, 4.3, 4.4, 4.5 and 4.6). We would like to refer the interested reader to these tables for an overview of the main topics developed in this section.

5.1.2.1 Fields of research

As we hope to have shown, research on cognitive aspects of translation has focused on the following related fields, namely, the translation process, translation competence and its acquisition and translation expertise. More recently, studies about translation competence levels have also gained prominence in the study of translation as a cognitive activity.

Translation process research

In Chapter 2, we presented the evolution of research concerning the translation process as well as the different models proposed. The evolution of research can be mapped into three distinct yet interrelated stages.

In the first stage, from the late 1960s to the late 1980s, there was a major approach developed around the Interpretive theory of translation (Seleskovitch, 1968; Seleskovitch & Lederer, 1984, etc.). Although the reflections build on a phenomenological perspective, this pioneering research introduced relevant topics of discussion concerning the functioning of the translation process, such as the identification of phases in the process, the role of the units of sense, the notion of deverbalization, the importance of memory and the combination of linguistic and extra-linguistic knowledge, which would become objects of experimental scrutiny in ensuing stages of research.

From the late 1980s to the mid-1990s, a second stage in the investigation of the translation process gave rise to a series of cognitive models of the translation process: Krings (1986) builds on the concept of strategy to usher the development of a new phase, modelling the translation process from an empirical perspective. Königs (1987) presents the dual notion of ad-hoc (automatic) and rest (metacognitive) blocks; Wilss (1988, 1996) draws on input from cognitive psychology; Hönig (1991) suggests non-linearity characteristics for the translation process; Bell (1991) draws on cognitive science, artificial intelligence and text linguistics (systemic functional linguistics); Gutt (1991) uses relevance theory; Alves (1995) blends in Königs's (1987) core concepts with a relevance-theoretic approach and puts Gutt's conceptualization to the empirical test; and Kiraly (1995) presents a psycholinguistic and sociolinguistic model. In general, these models portray the translation process as a special type of information processing model from disparate perspectives. Overall, the different models of the translation process differ both in terms of their theoretical framework and the terminology they use. They also differ in terms of the conceptual frameworks they adopted and the disparate methodological approaches used to design each model.

Altogether, we consider these two first stages to provide a conceptual development of translation process research which are still valid today. As from 2000 onwards, few additional models of the translation process have appeared. Halverson (2003) introduces the gravitational pull hypothesis, postulating that some patterns of activation within schematic networks would be more prominent than others due to their higher frequency of use over time. Tirkkonen-Condit (2005) revisits the notion of the monitor model in the translation process, suggesting a tendency for literal translations to appear as a default procedure in products and processes among novice and expert translators. Jakobsen (2011) outlines the basis for the computational modelling of the translation process. Schaeffer and Carl (2013/2015) propose a recursive model of the translation process, which includes recursive vertical and horizontal translation processes. Later on, Carl and Schaeffer (2017, 2019) refined the model by considering the role of machine translation and post-editing in the unfolding of the translation process.

In parallel to modelling, a series of empirical-experimental studies have been carried out, focusing on the investigation of particular traits of the translation process: translation unit, segmentation patterns, cognitive rhythm and phases of the translation process, among many others. These studies grew stronger during the third stage in the evolution of the investigation and we shall refer to them in Section 5.2 when we discuss relevant aspects of the translation process stemming from the results of empirical research.

Translation competence research

In Chapter 3, we described the underlying system of knowledge and skills that distinguish the translator from other multi-lingual language users, namely translation competence (TC). With the exception of some pioneering studies addressing this issue within translation studies (Wills, 1976; Koller, 1979), the notion of TC only began to be studied much later and the first empirical results only appear in the early 2000s (PACTE, 2002, 2003).

We identified two stages related to the research on TC. The first stage starts in the late 1970s and goes up to 2000. In the 1980s and early 1990s, several proposals of TC models were presented: Wilss (1976), Roberts (1984), Hewson and Martin (1991), Nord (1988/1991, 1992), Neubert (1994), Kiraly (1995), Hurtado Albir (1996), Hansen (1997) and Risku (1998), among others. Most of them are componential models that focus on describing the components that comprise TC.

Although most of these initial proposals on TC are isolated contributions that deal only tangentially with the topic, they all agree that TC requires additional components beyond linguistic components and that it consists of various components: linguistic knowledge, extra-linguistic knowledge, documentation skills and skills in the use of tools, transfer competence and so on. The authors mentioned above also agree that these components are of various kinds (knowledge, abilities, skills, attitudes) and that there are certain differences between the competences for direct translation and inverse translation.

Characteristically, early models of TC also postulate a so-called transfer competence as a component of TC. However, it should be noted that only a few authors associated TC with studies of expertise and expert performance, as expanded later in Shreeve (2006), and fewer authors stressed the importance of the strategic component in TC (see Hurtado Albir, 1996; Cao, 1996; Beeby, 1996; Hatim & Mason, 1997; PACTE, 2000). This first stage is also characterized by a lack of empirical studies.

As we enter the 21st century, we identified a second stage in the study of TC. Research on TC increases significantly and occupies an area of major importance in translation studies. A more interdisciplinary framework emerges since many TC proposals are based on research carried out in other disciplines, and one also sees attempts towards the empirical validation of proposals (PACTE, 2005, 2007a, 2007b, 2008, 2011a, 2011b, etc; Alves and Gonçalves, 2007; Hurtado Albir, 2017, 2021). The study of translation competence expands to embrace different and yet complementary perspectives including a relevance-theoretic approach (Alves & Gonçalves, 2007), an expertise studies approach (Shreve, 2006; Göpferich, 2008, 2009) and a knowledge management approach (Risku, Dickinson, & Pircher, 2010) as well as a didactic approach (Kelly, 2005; PACTE, 2003, etc.), and a professional and a behavioural perspective (Gouadec, 2005; Rothe-Neves, 2005, etc.).

However, most TC models have not been validated empirically and only a few authors have drawn on empirical-experimental research in order to validate their models (see PACTE, 2005a, 2005b, 2008, 2009, 2011a, 2011b, etc; Hurtado Albir, 2017; Alves & Gonçalves, 2007). We assume that this lack of empirical validation is due to the inherent complexity of translation competence. As we have seen, TC is the set of several knowledge and skills and their study requires complex research designs, with overlapping variables and indicators, and cross-variable studies of a broader scope.

Translation expertise research

When one discusses the relationship between translation competence and translation expertise (see Shreve, Angelone & Lacruz, 2018), it is important to establish a relation of degree and kind between levels of TC and those of expertise in translation. Along these lines, PACTE's (2017) analyses of the performance of the nine best translators in their experiment on translation competence, as shown in Chapter 3 of this book, provide empirical evidence of the characteristics that distinguish top performers from the rest of the sample.

Translation competence acquisition research

Unlike the multi-model approach used for TC, we have seen that there are fewer proposals of models for translation competence acquisition (TCA). Such models have been proposed since the 1970s and include Harris's (1973, 1977, 1980) *natural translation*; Toury's (1995) *socialization of translation*; Shreve's (1997, 2006) from natural to *constructed translation* – and the notion of expertise trajectory; Chesterman's (1997) five stages of translation expertise (novice, advanced beginner, competence, proficiency, and expertise); PACTE's (2000, 2003, 2014, 2015, 2019, 2020) dynamic and non-linear model; Alves and Gonçalves's (2007) relevance-theoretic model; and Kiraly's (2013) four-dimensional model of the *emergence* of translator competence. Most existing models of TCA are based on observation and experience and studies in other disciplines and, with the exception of Alves and Gonçalves (2007), PACTE (2014, 2015, 2019, 2020), not many authors have attempted an empirical validation of their models.

As of the 1980s, there has been a wide range of empirical studies on particular issues related to TCA . These studies focus on the performance of students in translation or compare the performance of professional translators and translation students or translation students at different levels of their training, addressing issues such as creativity, process automatization, the use of translation strategies, the process of understanding, the use of sources of documentation, processes of decision-making and so on. However, few studies have engaged in monitoring the process of TCA as a whole and with large and representative samples. As we have observed with respect to TC research, the lack of empirical validation for research on TCA may be due to the inherent complexity of the object of study. Göpferich (2009), with the TransComp project at the University of Graz; Massey and Ehrensberger-Dow (2011) as well as Ehrensberger-Dow and Massey (2013), with the CTP (Capturing the Translation Process) project at the Zurich University of Applied Sciences; and PACTE's (2014, 2015, 2019, 2020) at Universitat Autònoma de Barcelona are exceptions to the norm with attempts to monitor the process of translation competence acquisition.

Translation competence levelling research

The establishment and description of translation competence levels are directly related to research on TC and its acquisition and on studies of translation expertise. Unlike in other disciplines, few attempts have been made to establish performance levels for TC. Although proposals from the professional and academic areas exist, they are poorly described and there are no empirical studies to validate them. As we have shown, recent projects (NACT and EFFORT) have developed scales of level descriptors for the various categories of competences that make up TC.

Moreover, in the case of translation, unlike in other disciplines, there are no level tests that measure the performance level of TC individually (for translation students or professional translators). To bridge this gap, the EACT project aimed at designing translation-level tests for most of the competence levels proposed in the NACT project.

5.1.2.2 Contributions from empirical studies

From the mid-1980s, in parallel to the conceptual development of the study of the translation process and translation competence and its acquisition, empirical research begins to develop strongly, and even more research output is produced as from the mid-1990s onwards. We have divided these empirical studies into five phases, highlighting the methodological approaches and the instruments used to collect data in each phase as well as providing information about distinct or complementary results in the five phases.[2]

The first phase encompasses the period spanning from the mid-1980s to the mid-1990s and consists mostly of works which draw primarily on input from think-aloud protocols. The translation process, on the whole, seems to be the primordial object of study and a myriad of factors (translation unit, text types, subject profiles, etc.) are intertwined in research designs; this poses difficulties for the isolation of factors, thus preventing the formulation of specific research questions and hindering the quality of the results.

The second phase ranges from the late-1990s to the mid-2000s. It begins with the use of keylogging and screen-recording software as an attempt to track writing processes in real time through pauses, regressions and editing procedures. Building on the paradigmatic approach known as *triangulation* (Alves, 2003), studies carried out in this second phase also draw on questionnaires, interviews and analyses of verbal protocols to foster the paradigm of data triangulation. Additionally, some researchers also include a corpus-oriented analysis of the translation product to triangulate it with translation process data.

The third phase encompasses the period from 2005 to 2010 and is defined by the consolidation of the multi-methodological paradigm (*triangulation*) through the introduction of new technological tools for data collection. This new trend is spearheaded by the use of eye-tracking technology, the emergence of more robust designs and the use of statistics to assess the significance of results.

From the early 2010s to the present date, a fourth phase in empirical research on cognitive aspects of translation emerged. This fourth phase is marked by a stronger interface with translation technology and the development of interactive translation tools as well as by enhancing dialogue with computational linguistics, computer science, studies of human-computer interaction (HCI), machine translation (MT) and (interactive) post-editing. This phase is also marked by the further integration of data collected by means of keylogging and eye-tracking software using the same timestamp and creating what Carl (2010) calls *user activity data* (UAD).

In our view, topics emerging from results of empirical investigation can point to: (1) aspects which are directly related to the cognitive study of translation; (2) the impact of different factors in the translation process; (3) the training of translators; and (4) different methodological approaches to empirical research. These four topics are detailed below.

Topics concerning the cognitive study of translation which are most often investigated focus on:

- Segmentation patterns, including the study of phases of the translation process (orientation, drafting and revision; comprehension and re-expression) and cognitive rhythm.
- Translation units, including the study of attention units, production units, alignment units, translation units and UAD.

- Problem-solving, decision-making processes and translation strategies, including strategies of internal support (cognitive strategies) and external support (sources of documentation and translation technology).
- Aspects related to metalinguistic awareness and metacognitive activity in translation.
- The role of creativity in translation.
- The role of directionality in the translation process.
- Differences related to particular aspects such as domain specificity, text genres and so on.
- Traits of translation competence and translation expertise.
- Characteristics of translation competence acquisition.
- Description of translation competence levels and establishment of descriptors for each level.
- The specificities of translation modalities, such as audio-visual translation (subtitling, dubbing, etc.) and sight translation, on cognitive processing.
- Neurophysiological aspects of translation, including comparative studies of behavioural data (mostly with eye tracking) and neuroimaging data (mostly with fMRI).

Results of empirical studies looking at the influence of different factors in the unfolding of the translation process point to the impact of:

- Time pressure on results of translation task execution, including cognitive effort and monitoring processes.
- Translation technologies on processing effort, including the study of translation memory systems, post-editing and interactive machine translation.
- Human-computer interaction, particularly post-editing tasks, on processing effort.
- Task modality on the translation process, including tasks such as copying, reading for different purposes, paraphrasing and so on.
- Ergonomic factors (cognitive ergonomics) and the technologized knowledge work on translation task execution.
- Textual complexity and textual features, including cases of word frequency; word order; idioms, metonymy, metaphor, (de)metaphorization, subjectivity markers, syntactic variance, reference assignment; logical semantic relations, language variation and entropy.
- Ideology and emotions on cognitive processing.

As far as the training of translators is concerned, differences observed in empirical studies concerning characteristics of cognitive processing among beginners, novice, advanced and expert translators can lead to the establishment and description of translation competence levels, and considerations to the development of training programmes.

Finally, in terms of methodology, topics on empirical studies quite often point to the impact of:

- Experimental conditions on results, including the impact of concurrent verbalization on processing effort and the impact of eye-tracking data on measurements of processing effort.
- Ecological validity on experimental designs and, consequently, on experimental results.
- Issues related to the process/product interface on data analyses and results.
- Tools and techniques such as fMRI, FNIRS, EEG and galvanic skin response, which are used to establish a link between behavioural and neurophysiological aspects of translation located in the brain.

5.2 Relevant aspects of research on translation as a cognitive activity

In the next subsections, we highlight the most relevant aspects of the translation process, translation competence (including translation expertise), translation competence acquisition and translation competence levels.

5.2.1 Relevant aspects of the translation process

In Chapter 2, we have seen that all models of the translation process seem to agree, one way or another, that translation is a special case of cognitive behaviour and an integral part of the more general phenomenon of human information processing. In this sense, the translation process is related to processes involved in information processing (comprehension, expression) and their characteristics (inferential nature, interactivity of elements, the role of memory, etc.). Nevertheless, although the translation process is intrinsically related to general processes of human information processing, it also has its own characteristics. The basic processes of understanding and re-expression which occur in monolingual communication have their own peculiarities in translation because the translator is a special kind of receiver and sender.

On the one hand, as receivers of the source text, translators are placed in a different situation than of receivers of the source text. Generally, translators are not embedded in the linguistic-cultural community of the source text. To compensate for lacking that embeddedness, translators have to apply strategies using internal support (i.e. linguistic and extra-linguistic knowledge, inference mechanisms) and also make use of external support (i.e. sources of documentation and translation technologies) to help throw light into aspects of the source text and convey them in the target text. Translators, unlike monolingual receivers, do not read only to understand; first and foremost, they read to translate. Therefore, their understanding is quite different from that of a normal receiver: translators' understanding is deliberate and more analytical, requiring a higher degree of comprehension so that the source text can be fully re-instantiated as a target text counterpart.

On the other hand, translators are special senders of the translation in the target language. In other words, translators are not natural senders since they must produce a text that they have not drafted themselves with a particular brief that cannot be the same as the original source text. Moreover, they have to produce texts in domains in which they are not necessarily domain specialists and this may pose specific constraints to translators' behaviour.

Finally, some authors agree that understanding does not occur at once. It is possible to return several times to the source text, creating, through successive readings, different mental representations of the target text. The processing of translation units can be successive or recursive, returning to previously translated units. In this sense, it is important to consider that one should not expect a strictly linear order in the unfolding of the translation process with understanding occurring first and then re-expression following it. However, when constant regressions occur, they force re-expression to go back into understanding or vice-versa. Moreover, particularly for written translation, extra processing usually has an impact on previously translated units, with regressions creating modifications in already translated units.

As described earlier, the translation process entails a complex cognitive process of a recursive, cyclical nature in which elements of different kinds play a fundamental role. To this intrinsic complexity of the translation process, one must add the fact that different embodied and situated factors may have an impact on its unfolding, depending on the personality of the translator, the purpose of the translation and method chosen and the type of translation (legal, literary, technical, etc.) and modality (written translation, sight translation, audio-visual translation, etc.). To that extent, rigorous empirical studies about the unfolding of the translation process in different modalities of translation should provide reliable information about the specificities of each cognitive operation, their commonalities and their differences. This is one of the major challenges related to research on the nature of the translation process.

Better knowledge about it will help us to understand the characteristics of the translation process as a whole, not only in their specificity as a special type of information processing but also in relation to the neurophysiological activities underlying it.

As we have stated repeatedly in Hurtado Albir (2001, pp. 367–375), Hurtado Albir and Alves (2009), Alves and Hurtado Albir (2010) and Alves and Hurtado Albir (2017), the following traits account for the complexity of the translation process:

- The existence of basic processes with two main phases (comprehension and re-expression) is valid for all types and modalities of translation; besides, some authors include an intermediate phase of a non-verbal nature.
- The potential division of the process into three phases: orientation, drafting and revision, particularly for written translation tasks or for methodological purposes in translation process research.
- The role of short- and long-term memory.
- The need to integrate internal (cognitive) and external resources (documentation).
- The role of processing units and segmentation patterns.
- The multi-directional and non-linear nature of the process, particularly with respect to the overlapping, recursive nature of the phases which unfold in a non-linear process.
- The dynamic and interactive nature of the several elements that make up the translation process, including linguistic and extra-linguistic knowledge, deductive and inductive processes and so on.
- The existence of automatized (uncontrolled) and non-automatized (controlled) processes that tend to operate in parallel.
- The occurrence of processes of problem-solving, use of strategies and decision-making.
- The existence of specific traits according to the type of translation (legal, literary, technical, etc.) and modality (written translation, sight translation, audio-visual translation, etc.).

Obviously, these characteristics have a direct impact on all cognitive aspects of translation, including the functioning of TC and TCA as well as in identifying traits of translation expertise and the establishment of TC levels.

5.2.2 Relevant aspects of translation competence and translation expertise

As we have seen in Chapter 3, TC models have been developed for various purposes: in some cases, they are designed with a view to their use in curriculum design; in other cases, models are developed to enhance professional performance; other models have theoretical goals and aim at identifying and describing the operation of the competences required of the translator. Most authors propose componential models, Pym's (2003) minimalist model being a well-known exception. These models include the following main components: linguistic, extra-linguistic, instrumental and strategic; some models also include an attitudinal component. TC models differ in their approaches, in the terminology used and in the distribution and importance given to each one of their components.

Generally, most of the proposed models are cognitive in nature. However, we have also seen proposals based on behavioural approaches. These two approaches (what is needed to know to be a translator and what translators do) are, in our view, complementary when describing the nature of operations which are intrinsic to TC.

As we have also pointed out in Chapter 3 (see Section 3.4.1), apart from the lack of empirically validated models, the major difficulty in the investigation of TC stems from the complexity, heterogeneity and diversity of TC itself. Research on TC is hampered by its complex nature, given the variety of cognitive domains and activities involved and the complexity of their relationships. Its heterogeneity is another aspect that makes the investigation difficult because it involves very different abilities and varies according to the subjects. A final factor is the diversification of the TC as it varies according to the professional profiles and directionality (L1/L2 or L2/L1 translation).

Thus, there is great difficulty in observing the cognitive operations of the TC and the relationships between its components given its complexity and the differences depending on the subjects and directionality; besides, each specialized professional profile has its specific characteristics, which entails an additional difficulty.

In Chapter 3, we discussed particular cognitive traits linked to TC and translation expertise. In our view, the most representative issues are as follows:

- Consideration of TC as basically comprising procedural knowledge.
- Importance of the strategic component.
- Establishment of differences between TC and expertise.
- Reinforcement of the need for empirical validation.

Additionally, authors have also dwelt on translation expertise and aspects of expert performance in translation. As we have seen in Chapter 3, the relationship between TC and translation expertise, as discussed in Shreve, Angelone and Lacruz (2018), can be considered as the relation of degree and kind between levels of translation competence and those of expertise in translation. For us, there is a difference between TC and translation expertise with expert translators showing signs of consistently superior performance at the very end of the cline.

5.2.3 Relevant aspects of translation competence acquisition

Practically all authors agree that TC is not innate but rather acquired. Chesterman (1997), PACTE (2003, 2014, 2015, 2019, 2020), Shreve (2006),

Alves and Gonçalves (2007), among others, describe this acquisition process as similar to any process of acquisition of knowledge, a cyclical process from an initial kind of novice behaviour to a stage of consolidation of competences, geared by a process of gradual automatization as proceduralization occurs.

Being a cyclical process, various phases are indicated in the process of TCA, which vary according to different authors. However, there is a lack of more robust empirical knowledge of these different phases of TCA. Detailed knowledge of these phases could provide input to establishing levels of competences in translation.

In Chapter 3, we discussed aspects of TCA. We referred to basic concepts of natural translation, i.e. an innate ability in bilinguals (Harris, 1973, 1977, 1980, Harris and Sherwood (1978). We also looked at the concepts of native translators, i.e. bilinguals who acquired translation ability progressively without formal instruction as well as the socialization of translation, including the importance of feedback, essentially normative, of the social environment in acquiring translation competence (Toury, 1980, 1995).

Additionally, we offered a description of the TCA process, including internal mechanisms of gradual control, the description of the five steps of novice, advanced beginner, competent, proficiency and expert translators (Dreyfus & Dreyfus, 1986; Chesterman, 1997), highlighting that TC is developed deliberately in a continuum from natural translation to constructed translation (professional translator) as postulated by Shreve (2006).

In Chapter 4, we presented results based on the model of TCA developed by PACTE (2003) and described in more detail the characteristics of the acquisition process as shown in PACTE (2020). We dealt with the existence of a pre-translation competence, the characteristics of novice knowledge, the components of TC (bilingual, extra-linguistic, knowledge-of-translation, instrumental, strategic subcompetences and psychophysiological components) and a description of the TCA process as a dynamic, cyclic and spiral-shaped process that entails restructuring and developing from a novice knowledge (pre-translation competence) to stages of competence usually found in professional translators to the end-stage of an expert translator.

5.2.4 Relevant aspects of translation competence levelling

As mentioned in Chapter 3, there have been few attempts to elaborate scales of translation competence level descriptors. However, there are several reasons why it is essential to have a consensus on the level scales for translation in the educational and professional translation sectors.

From the academic point of view, there is a wide disparity in the criteria for the levels of training required, as the same degree (bachelor's, master's) can lead to very different levels of training depending on the institution (or even within the same institution, depending on the language combination) and the country. Thus, for example, there are master's degrees that offer a generalist (or theoretical) training in translation, achieving a lower level of training in translation than certain bachelor's degrees. However, the qualification obtained in a master's degree is higher than that of a bachelor's degree. This situation is unfair to students and it is not good for the profession.

From the professional point of view, there are different levels of performance and different specializations (professional and non-professional translators of different types and with different levels of performance) in the labour market. The lack of agreed performance levels is a negative element for translators, employers and users of translation, as there is no transparency and concreteness (as in the case of language proficiency, for example) of the performance level that a given translator can guarantee.

In addition, increasing academic and professional mobility and the globalization of the translation market also require transparency and clarification of performance levels.

Therefore, agreed scales of performance levels are indispensable for the academic and professional fields of translation. In the educational sector, it would facilitate the recognition and validation of certifications. It would also serve as a reference for the design of training programmes in translation and it would guide the progression of levels of difficulty and assessment. In the professional sector, it would be useful for translators and employers, as it would provide clear definitions of translator performance levels, facilitating recruitment processes. It could also serve as a guide for the establishment of professional quality standards, which would also benefit translation users.

Finally, a relevant aspect of establishing and describing levels of translation competence is that, as is typical of the development of scales of level descriptors, the descriptors of each level of competence must be established in terms of observable behaviours (*can do*) that can be evaluated. Only in this way can the level of acquired competence be measuredso the appropriate assessment procedures can be designed for each level.

5.3 Challenges and perspectives

As we have already stated in Alves and Hurtado Albir (2017), the road to consolidation in cognitive translation studies opens before us, posing some challenges and offering perspectives for the discipline. In closing this book, we would like to refer to these challenges and perspectives and collect our thoughts respectively.

5.3.1 Challenges ahead

We hope to have shown that the results achieved so far have helped scholars build a multi-faceted conceptual framework for research on cognitive aspects of translation. We have also highlighted that, from a methodological point of view, the field is now in a position to use different data elicitation techniques and instruments as a way of capturing the process-product interface in translation, strengthening its potential to provide more robust evidence concerning what actually takes place in the cognitive operations involved in translation. These conceptual and methodological developments notwithstanding, we have pointed out that there are still some problems that hinder the evolution of this field of study.

1) The inherent difficulties of the object of the study. One has to take into consideration the inherent difficulties stemming from the great complexity of the object of study. As we have stated in the book, translation is an extremely complex cognitive activity entailing several mechanisms and processes that are not directly observable and, thus, not likely to be amenable to scientific investigation. Besides, several extraneous variables, such as personality traits, levels of experience and familiarity with tasks and technological tools, can affect research due to differences in subject profiling; furthermore, the inevitability of factors such as fatigue, stress and emotions, among others, can intervene in the unfolding of data collection.
2) The lack of a consistent tradition of empirical-experimental investigation. As we have also pointed out, differently from what has already happened in neighbouring disciplines, translation studies on the whole still lacks a consistent tradition of empirical investigation. Other disciplines, such as cognitive psychology, have a long-standing tradition of empirical-experimental investigation and this has enabled them to obtain validated instruments capable of collecting reliable data (tests, questionnaires, etc.). The lack of a previous descriptive basis hinders the application of the empirical method and it leads to reinforcing the tendency to borrow conceptual frameworks as well as techniques, instruments and technological tools from other disciplines.
3) The challenges of research design. It is worth noting that there are still difficulties related to the intricacies and complexities of research designs. Among them, we would list the following:

- Challenges to ensure the ecological validity of experiments that allow the reproduction of the translators' workplaces in controlled laboratory settings without incurring the artificial simulation common to experimental situations.
- Lack of validation of field-specific instruments of data collection.
- Difficulties in creating large samples of data with several groups of subjects, including different profiles, language combinations and contexts.
- Lack of a pool of more unified conceptual and methodological resources upon which hypotheses can be empirically tested.

5.3.2 Perspectives

As far as perspectives are concerned, as we look into the future of cognitive translation studies, we can envisage several research avenues that are worth pursuing further. We can classify these perspectives under three types of developments: conceptual, methodological and appliable.

1) Conceptual developments. As far as conceptual developments are concerned, we would list the following perspectives:

- Development of fine-grained conceptualizations about behavioural processes observed in empirical research.
- Incorporation of new assumptions necessary to guide eye-tracking-oriented research with eye movements seen as cognitively embodied action.
- Developments of cognitive ergonomics for translation purposes, leading to designs of translators' workplaces best suited to the specificities of translators' needs.
- Progress in the investigation of neurophysiological processes related to the functioning of the bilingual brain with special attention to how it relates to the process of translation, thus shedding light on and confirming results obtained by means of behavioural studies.
- Implications of the increasingly frequent use of artificial intelligence in translation on cognitive translation processes, as well as on the characteristics of translation competence, its acquisition and levelling. Consequently, one needs to develop:
    - Research on whether the use of artificial intelligence changes the translation process and whether it facilitates the process or generates some type of cognitive overload.
    - Research on the implications of using artificial intelligence for translation purposes on the relevance and distribution of the competences that make up TC, as well as on its acquisition and levelling.

2) Methodological developments. With respect to improvements in methodology, we would list the following needs in research designs:

- Rigorous selection of relevant and precise objects of study geared to foster the production of knowledge about cognitive aspects of translation so that the results of the investigation are meaningful for the field.
- Selection of adequate techniques and instruments oriented towards the concrete object of study and the type of research.
- Development of new experimental designs aiming at a stronger power of generalization by using larger and more representative samples.
- Use of a common set of techniques and instruments of data collection, thus strengthening the triangulation paradigm and allowing data to be

cross-analysed. Such a joint action will create the necessary conditions to provide better access to the diversity and complexity of mechanisms and processes inherent to the study of cognitive aspects of translation.

- Validation of field-specific instruments of data collection. Researchers need to design specific instruments for data collection (questionnaires, texts with prototypical translation problems, etc.) and put them to the test in exploratory and pilot studies in order to guarantee the reliability of the data to be collected.
- Wider use of statistical analyses in large population samples to arrive at more robust evidence.
- Encouragement to progress steadily with replication practices, thus allowing the validation or falsification of previously found evidence.
- Research on the impact of using artificial intelligence for translation purposes on the unfolding of the translation process and on translation competence and its acquisition, comparing it with similar studies carried out earlier.

3) Applicable developments. As far as the development of applications (for translation and translation research) is concerned, we would list the following perspectives:

- Enhancement of the interactive channels of communication between humans and machines in the scope of human-machine interaction in translation, thus improving interactive platforms for post-editing and sight translation tasks.
- Development of new applications for translation, including not only writing components but also adding visual, auditory and sensory components as complementary sources of input for written translation.
- Creation and development of databases to store metadata, resources, publications and research projects, specially designed to cater for the needs of the research community. There are attempts, such as the CRITT database, that bring together data from experimental studies involving different language pairs, including direct and inverse translation tasks and the use of technological tools, and the TREC Network database.
- Establishment and description of TC levels validated by means of empirical studies and overall consensus.

We would like to highlight promising perspectives for refined conceptual frameworks and clearer objects of study as well as the increasing development of resources and applications available to the public. Taking into consideration the body of knowledge produced in recent years and the progress achieved, we believe the field is now ready to contribute to the development of neighbouring disciplines by lending insights and evidence in a bidirectional exchange, changing current patterns that still dwell on exclusively borrowing from these neighbouring disciplines.

5.4 Final remarks

As we close this book, we hope to have shown the relevance of research on cognitive aspects of translation not only for those interested in the specificities of our object of study but also with respect to the implications this type of research may have for the discipline of translation studies at large.

Throughout the book, we have covered research carried out over the last decades, and in particular of research developed since the 1980s, referring extensively to the work carried out by research groups worldwide, including references to PhD theses and a multitude of publications in journals and books. This, we believe, highlights the breadth and scope of empirical-experimental research in translation as a cognitive activity as well as the progress and innovation made in this fledgling field. We feel confident to state that research on translation as a cognitive activity has come of age, evolving from the first phenomenological considerations postulated in the 1960s to current experimental designs that can build sound hypotheses, put them to the empirical test and provide robust evidence to corroborate previously made claims with a much stronger power of generalization.

If we go back to Seleskovitch (1968, p. 36), when she writes that "our aim in this work is [...] to shed light on the mental process that make possible the virtually instantaneous transmission of an oral message into another language",[3] we are now in a position not only to empirically consubstantiate her claims but also to open up new fronts of research, including studies at the interface between behavioural and neurophysiological aspects of translation as well as analysing the impact of emerging technologies on the unfolding of the translation process and on translation competence and its acquisition. The study of translation as a cognitive activity has certainly come of age.

Notes

1 A preliminary version of these concluding remarks was published in Alves and Hurtado Albir (2017) containing the authors' views on the evolution, challenges and perspectives for research on cognitive aspects of translation.
2 As mentioned in Chapter 4, the interested reader will find further information about empirical methods used in cognitive approaches to translation in Saldanha and O'Brien (2013) and Mellinger and Hanson (2017).
3 Original citation: "Notre but dans cet ouvrage [...] est d'essayer de mettre en lumière le processus mental qui rend possible la transmission quasi instantanée d'un message oral dans une autre langue".

References

Alves, F. (1995). *Zwischen Schweigen und Sprechen: Wie bildet sich eine transkulturelle Brücke? Eine psycholinguistisch orientierte Untersuchung von Übersetzungsvorgängen zwischen portugiesischen und brasilianischen Übersetzern*. Hamburg: Dr. Kovac.

Alves, F. (Ed.). (2003). *Triangulating translation. Perspectives in process oriented research*. Amsterdam: John Benjamins.

Alves, F. (2015). Translation process research at the interface. Paradigmatic, theoretical, and methodological issues in dialogue with cognitive science, expertise studies, and psycholinguistics. In A. Ferreira & J. W. Schwieter (Eds.), *Psycholinguistic and cognitive inquiries into translation and interpreting* (pp. 17–40). Amsterdam: John Benjamins.

Alves, F., & Gonçalves, J.L. (2007). Modelling translator's competence: Relevance and expertise under scrutiny. In Y. Gambier, M. Shlesinger, & R. Stolze (Eds.), *Translation studies: Doubts and directions* (pp. 41–55). Amsterdam: John Benjamins.

Alves, F., & Hurtado Albir, A. (2010). Cognitive approaches to translation. In Y. Gambier & L. van Doorslaer (Eds.), *The John Benjamins handbook of translation studies* (pp. 28–35). Amsterdam: John Benjamins.

Alves, F., & Hurtado Albir, A. (2017). Evolution, challenges, and perspectives for research on cognitive aspects of translation. In J.W. Schwieter & A. Ferreira (Eds.), *The handbook of translation and cognition* (pp. 535–554). Hoboken, NJ: John Wiley & Sons, Inc.

Beeby, A. (1996). *Teaching translation from Spanish to English* (Didactics of Translation Series 2). Ottawa: University of Ottawa Press.

Bell, R.T. (1991). *Translation and translating*. London: Longman.

Cao, D. (1996). Towards a model of translation proficiency. *Target*, *8*(2), 325–340.

Carl, M. (2010). A *computational framework for a cognitive model of human translation processes*. Paper presented at the translating and the computer 32, London.Retrieved from http://www.mt-archive.info/10/Aslib-2010-Carl.pdf

Carl, M., & Schaeffer, M.J. (2017). Sketch of a noisy channel model for the translation process. In S. Hansen-Schirra, O. Czulo, & S. Hofmann (Eds.), *Empirical modelling of translation and interpreting* (pp. 71–116). Berlin: Language Science Press.

Carl, M., & Schaeffer, M.J. (2019). Outline for a relevance theoretical model of machine translation post-editing. In D. Li, V. Lei, & Y. He (Eds.), *Researching cognitive processes of translation*(pp. 49–67.). Singapore: Springer.

Chesterman, A. (1997). *Memes of translation*. Amsterdam: John Benjamins.

Dreyfus, H.L., & Dreyfus, S.E. (1986). *Mind over machine*. Oxford: Blackwell.

Ehrensberger-Dow, M., & Massey, G. (2013). Indicators of translation competence: Translators' self-concepts and the translation of titles. *Journal of Writing Research*, *5*(1), 103–131.

Göpferich, S. (2008). *Translationsprozessforschung: Stand- Methoden- Perspektiven*. Translationswissenschaft 4. Tübingen: Narr.

Göpferich, S. (2009). Towards a model of translation competence and its acquisition: The longitudinal study 'TransComp. In S. Göpferich, A. L. Jakobsen & I.M. Mees (Eds.), *Behind the mind: Methods, models and results in translation process research* (pp. 11–37). Copenhagen: Samfundslitteratur.

Gouadec, D. (2005). Modélisation du processus d'exécution des traductions. *Meta*,*50*(2), 643–655.

Gutt, E.-A. (1991). *Translation and relevance: Cognition and context*. Oxford: Basil Blackwell. (2nd Rev. ed., 2010). Manchester: St Jerome.

Halverson, S.L. (2003). The cognitive basis of translation universals. *Target, 15*(2), 197–241.
Halverson, S.L. (2010). Cognitive translation studies: Developments in theory and methods. In G. Shreve & E. Angelone (Eds.), *Translation and cognition* (pp. 349–370). Amsterdam: John Benjamins.
Hansen, G. (1997). Success in translation. *Perspectives: Studies in Translatology, 5*(2), 201–210.
Harris, B. (1973). La traductologie, la traduction naturelle, la traduction automatique et la sémantique. *Cahiers de Linguistique, 10*, 11–34.
Harris, B. (1977). The importance of natural translation. *Working Papers on Bilingualism, 12*, 96–114.
Harris, B. (1980). How a three-year-old translates. In A. Evangelos & A. Afrendas (Eds.), *Patterns of bilingualism* (pp. 370–393). Singapore: National University of Singapore Press.
Harris, B., & Sherwood, B. (1978). Translating as an innate skill. In D. Gerver & H.W. Sinaiko (Eds.), *Language, interpretation and communication* (pp. 155–170). Oxford: Plenum Press.
Hatim, B., & Mason, I. (1997). *The translator as communicator*. London: Routledge.
Hewson, L., & Martin, J. (1991). *Redefining translation. The variational approach*. London: Routledge.
Hönig, H.G. (1991). Holmes' 'mapping theory' and the landscape of mental translation processes. In K. van Leuven-Zwart & T. Naajkens (Eds.), *Translation studies: The state of the art. Proceedings from the First James S. Holmes Symposium on Translation Studies* (pp. 77–89). Amsterdam: Rodopi.
Hurtado Albir, A. (1996). La cuestión del método traductor. Método, estrategia y técnica de traducción. *Sendebar, 7*, 39–57.
Hurtado Albir, A. (2001). *Traducción y traductología. Introducción a la traductología* . Madrid: Cátedra. 5th Revised edition, 2011.
Hurtado Albir, A. (2017). Translation and translation competence. In A. Hurtado Albir (Ed.), *Researching translation competence by PACTE Group* (pp. 3–33). Amsterdam: John Benjamins.
Hurtado Albir, A. (2021). Translation competence and its acquisition. In F. Alves & A.L. Jakobsen (Eds.), *The Routledge handbook of translation and cognition* (pp. 389–414). London: Routledge.
Hurtado Albir, A., & Alves, F. (2009). Translation as a cognitive activity. In J. Munday (Ed.), *The Routledge companion to translation studies* (pp. 210–234). London: Routledge.
Jääskeläinen, R. (2011). Studying the translation process. In K. Malmkjaer & K. Windle (Eds.), *The Oxford handbook of translation studies*(pp. 123–135). Oxford: Oxford University Press.
Jakobsen, A.L. (2011). Tracking translators' keystrokes and eye movements with Translog. In C. Alvstad, A. Hild, & E. Tiselius (Eds.), *Methods and strategies of process research* (pp. 37–55). Amsterdam: John Benjamins.
Kelly, D. (2005). *A handbook for translator trainers*. Manchester: St. Jerome.
Kiraly, D. (1995). *Pathways to translation.Pedagogy and process*. Kent: The Kent State University Press.
Kiraly, D. (2013). Towards a view of translator competence as an emergent phenomenon: Thinking outside the box(es) in translator education. In D. Kiraly, S. Hansen-Schirra, & K. Maksymski (Eds.), *New prospects and perspectives for educating language mediators* (pp. 197–224). Tubingen: Günther Narr Verlag.
Koller, W. (1979). *Einführung in die Übersetzungswissenschaft*. Heidelberg: Quelle und Meyer.
Königs, F.G. (1987). Was beim Übersetzen passiert. Theoretische Aspekte, empirische Befunde und praktische Konsequenzen. *Die Neueren Sprachen, 86*, 162–185.

Krings, H.P. (1986). *Was in den Köpfen von Übersetzern vorgeht. Eine empirische Untersuchung der Struktur des Übersetzungsprozesses an fortgeschrittener französischer Lernenden*. Tübingen: Gunter Narr.
Massey, G., & Ehrensberger-Dow, M. (2011). Investigating information literacy: A growing priority in translation studies. *Across Languages and Cultures*, *12*(2), 193–211.
Mellinger, C., & Hanson, T. (2017). *Quantitative research methods in translation and interpreting studies*. London: Routledge.
Muñoz Martín, R. (2010). On paradigms and cognitive translatology. In G. Shreve & E. Angelone (Eds.), *Translation and cognition*(pp. 169–187). Amsterdam: John Benjamins.
Neubert, A. (1994). Competence in translation: A complex skill, how to study and how to teach it. In M. Snell-Hornby, F. Pöchhacker, & K. Kaindl (Eds.), *Translation studies. An interdiscipline* (pp. 411–420). Amsterdam: John Benjamins.
Nord, C. (1988). *Textanalyse und Übersetzen*. Heidelberg: J. Groos Verlag. [English edition. Nord, C. (1991). *Text analysis in translation*. Amsterdam: Rodopi].
Nord, C. (1992). Text analysis in translator training. In C. Dollerup & A. Loddegaard (Eds.), *Teaching translation and interpreting* (pp. 39–48). Amsterdam: John Benjamins.
O'Brien, S. (2013). The borrowers: researching the cognitive aspects of translation. *Target*, *25*(1), 5–17.
PACTE. (2000). Acquiring translation competence: Hypotheses and methodological problems in a research project. In A. Beeby, D. Ensinger, & M. Presas (Eds.), *Investigating translation* (pp. 99–106). Amsterdam: John Benjamins.
PACTE. (2002). Exploratory tests in a study of translation competence. *Conference Interpretation and Translation*, *4*(2), 41–69.
PACTE. (2003). Building a translation competence model. In F. Alves (Ed.), *Triangulating translation: Perspectives in process oriented research* (pp. 43–66). Amsterdam: John Benjamins.
PACTE. (2005a). Investigating translation competence: Conceptual and methodological issues. *Meta*, , *50*(2), 609–619.
PACTE. (2005b). Primeros resultados de un experimento sobre la Competencia Traductora. In *Actas del II Congreso Internacional de la AIETI (Asociación Ibérica de Estudios de Traducción e Interpretación)* (pp. 573–587). Madrid: Publicaciones de la Universidad Pontificia Comillas.
PACTE. (2007a). Une recherche empirique expérimentale sur la compétence de traduction. In D. Gouadec (Ed.), *Quelle qualification pour les traducteurs?* (pp. 95–116). Paris: La Maison du Dictionnaire.
PACTE. (2007b). Zum Wesen der Übersetzungskompetenz – Grundlagen für die experimentelle Validierung eines ÜK-Modells. In G. Wotjak (Ed.) *Quo vadis Translatologie? Ein halbes Jahrhundert universitäre Ausbildung von Dolmetschern und Übersetzern in Leipzig* (pp. 327–342). Berlin: Frank & Timme.
PACTE. (2008). First results of a translation competence experiment: 'Knowledge of translation' and 'efficacy of the translation process'. In J. Kearns (Ed.), *Translator and interpreter training. Issues, methods and debates* (pp. 104–126). London: Continuum.
PACTE. (2009). Results of the validation of the PACTE translation competence model: Acceptability and decision making. *Across Languages and Cultures*, *10*(2), 207–230.
PACTE. (2011a). Results of the validation of the PACTE translation competence model: Translation problems and translation competence. In C. Alvstad, A. Hild,

& E. Tiselius (Eds.), *Methods and strategies of process research: Integrative approaches in translation studies* (pp. 317–343). Amsterdam: John Benjamins.
PACTE. (2011b). Results of the validation of the PACTE translation competence model: Translation project and dynamic translation index. In S. O'Brien (Ed.), *Cognitive explorations of translation* (pp. 30–53). London: Continuum.
PACTE. (2014). First results of PACTE group's experimental research on translation competence acquisition: The acquisition of declarative knowledge of translation. *MonTI. .Special issue,1*, 85–115.
PACTE. (2015). Results of PACTE's experimental research on the acquisition of translation competence: the acquisition of declarative and procedural knowledge in translation. The dynamic translation index. *Translation Spaces*, *4*(1), 29–35.
PACTE. (2017). Defining features of translation competence. In A. Hurtado Albir (Ed.), *Researching translation competence by PACTE Group*(pp. 281–302). Amsterdam: John Benjamins.
PACTE. (2019). Evolution of the efficacy of the translation process in translation competence acquisition. Results of the PACTE Group's experimental research. *Meta, s*, *64*(1), 242–265.
PACTE. (2020). Translation competence acquisition. Design and results of the PACTE group's experimental research. *The Interpreter and Translator Trainer*, *14*(2), 95–233.
Pym, A. (2003). Redefining translation competence in an electronic age: In defence of a minimalist approach. *Meta*, *48*(4), 481–497.
Risku, H. (1998). *Translatorische Kompetenz. Kognitive Grundlagen des Übersetzens als Expertentätigkeit.* Tübingen: Stauffenburg.
Risku, H., Dickinson, A., & Pircher, R. (2010). Knowledge in translation practice and translation studies: Intellectual capital in modern society. In D. Gile, G. Hansen, & N.K. Pokorn (Eds.), *Why translation studies matters* (pp. 83–96). Amsterdam: John Benjamins.
Roberts, R.P. (1984). Compétence du nouveau diplômé en traduction. In G.-M. Boivin (Ed.), *Traduction et qualité de langue. Actes du colloque société des traducteurs du Québec/Conseil de la langue française* (pp. 172–184). Québec: Éditeur Official du Québec.
Rothe-Neves, R. (2005). A abordagem comportamental das competências. Aplicabilidade aos estudos da tradução. In F. Alves, C. Magalhães, & A. Pagano (Eds.), *Competência em tradução: cognição e discurso* (pp. 91–107). Belo Horizonte: Editora UFMG.
Saldanha, G., & O'Brien, S. (2013). *Research methodologies in translation studies.* Manchester: St Jerome.
Schaeffer, M., & Carl, M. (2013). Shared representations and the translation process: A recursive model. *Translation and Interpreting Studies*, *8*(2), 169–190. Reprinted in M. Ehrensberger-Dow, B. Englund Dimitrova, S. Hubscher-Davidson, & U. Norberg (Eds.). (2015). *Describing cognitive processes in translation: Acts and events* (pp. 21–42). Amsterdam: John Benjamins.
Seleskovitch, D. (1968). *L'interprète dans les conférences internationales. Problèmes de langage et de communication.* Paris: Minard. [Translation into English. Seleskovitch, D. (1978). *Interpreting for international conferences: problems of language and communication.* Washington: Pen and Booth.]
Seleskovitch, D., & Lederer, M. (1984/2001). *Interpréter pour traduire*, Col Traductologie 1. Paris: Didier Érudition.
Shreve, G.M. (1997). Cognition and the evolution of translation competence. In J. Danks, G.M. Shreve, S. Fountain, & M. McBeath (Eds.), *Cognitive processes in translation and interpreting* (pp. 120–136). Thousand Oaks, CA: Sage.
Shreve, G.M. (2006). The deliberate practice: Translation and expertise. *Journal of Translation Studies*, *9*(1), 27–42.

Shreve, G., Angelone, E., & Lacruz, I. (2018). Are expertise and translation competence the same? Psychological reality and the theoretical status of competence. In I. Lacruz & R Jääskeläinen (Eds.), *Innovation and expansion in translation process research* (pp. 37–54). Amsterdam: John Benjamins.
Snell-Hornby, M. (2006). *The turns of translation studies: New paradigm or shifting viewpoints*. Amsterdam: John Benjamins.
Tirkkonen-Condit, S. (2005). The monitor model revisited: Evidence from process research. *Meta*, *50*(2), 405–414.
Toury, G. (1980). *In search of a theory of translation,The Porter Institute for Poetics and Semiotics*. Tel Aviv: Tel Aviv University.
Toury, G. (1995). *Descriptive translation studies and beyond* (2nd ed., 2012). Amsterdam: John Benjamins.
Tymoczko, M. (2005). Trajectories of research in Translation Studies. *Meta*, *50*(4), 1082–1097.
Wilss, W. (1976). Perspectives and limitations of a didactic framework for the teaching of translation. In R. W. Brislin (Ed.), *Translation: Applications and research* (pp. 117–137). New York: Gardner.
Wilss, W. (1988). *Kognition und Übersetzen: Zu Theorie und Praxis der menschlichen und der maschinellen Übersetzung*. Tübingen: Niemeyer.
Wilss, W. (1996). *Knowledge and skills in translator behavior*. Amsterdam: John Benjamins.

INDEX

Note: Page numbers in **bold** reference tables. Page numbers in *italics* reference figures.